Table of Contents

Foreword..1

Introduction...2

    Tom Awad and Iain Fyffe..4

    What to Expect...5

    Onwards, Ho!...7

What are the Hall of Fame's Standards?...8

    Hall of Fame Standards for Post-Expansion Goaltenders.........................9

    Hall of Fame Standards for Pre-Expansion Goaltenders.........................11

    Hall of Fame Standards for Pre-War Goaltenders...................................13

    Hall of Fame Standards for Post-Expansion Defencemen.......................14

    Hall of Fame Standards for Pre-Expansion Defencemen........................16

    Hall of Fame Standards for Pre-War Defencemen...................................18

    Hall of Fame Standards for Post-Expansion Forwards............................20

    Hall of Fame Standards for Pre-Expansion Forwards.............................24

    Hall of Fame Standards for Pre-War Forwards.......................................26

    Predicting Future Players Inductions...29

    Closing Thoughts...32

Shot Quality...33

    The Components of Shot Quality...33

        Shot Location...33

        Rebounds..35

        Power Plays...37

    Game Score..38

        Other Minor Factors..39

        The Bottom Line..39

    Shot Quality for Players...39

        Power Play Positions...40

    Shot Quality for Teams..41

    Closing Thoughts...44

What Are Score Effects?...45

    The Big Picture..45

    Results by Period...48

    Penalties..50

    Effect on Player Statistics..51

    Closing Thoughts...52

What Makes Good Players Good? Part 1: Forwards...53

    2013–14 Season Results...54

    2012–13 Season Results...55

    Three-Season Results...56

    Factors Affecting Player Results...57

    Goals, Assists, and Points...58

    Penalties..60

    Power Play...61

    Penalty Killing..64

    Closing Thoughts...65

What Makes Good Players Good? Part 2: Defencemen......................................67

2013–14 Season Results..67
2012–13 Season Results..68
Factors Affecting Player Results..68
Goals, Assists, and Points...69
Power Play...70
Penalty Killing..71
Penalties..73
Closing Thoughts...74
What Makes Good Players Good? Part 3: Goaltenders............................76
2013–14 Season Results..76
2012–13 Season Results..77
2011–12 Season Results..77
Factors Affecting Player Results..78
Penalty Killing..79
Penalties..81
Closing Thoughts...81
Goaltending Analytics Revisited...83
Quality Starts...83
Shot Quality...86
Shootout Specialists..95
Other Skills..99
Goaltending Q & A...101
Closing Thoughts...111
Team Essays..112
Player Usage Charts..112
The Hockey Abstract Checklist...116
Closing Thoughts...126
Anaheim Ducks..128
Arizona Coyotes...130
Boston Bruins...132
Buffalo Sabres..134
Calgary Flames..136
Carolina Hurricanes...138
Chicago Blackhawks..140
Colorado Avalanche...142
Columbus Blue Jackets..144
Dallas Stars..146
Detroit Red Wings..148
Edmonton Oilers...150
Florida Panthers...152
Los Angeles Kings...154
Minnesota Wild...156
Montreal Canadiens...158
Nashville Predators..160
New Jersey Devils...162
New York Islanders...164
New York Rangers..166
Ottawa Senators...168
Philadelphia Flyers...170

Pittsburgh Penguins..172
San Jose Sharks...174
St. Louis Blues..176
Tampa Bay Lightning...178
Toronto Maple Leafs...180
Vancouver Canucks..182
Washington Capitals...184
Winnipeg Jets...186
Who is the Best Goal Scorer?..188
   Accounting for Manpower Situation...189
   Accounting for Opportunity..192
   Accounting for Linemates..196
   Digression: Can Goal-Scoring Linemates Boost Assist Totals?..198
   Other Considerations...200
   Closing Thoughts...202
Who is the Best at Drawing Penalties?...204
   Penalty Drawing Leaders..204
   Where are the Defencemen?..205
   The Effect of Manpower Situation..206
   What About Score Effects?..207
   How Great is the Home Team Advantage?...208
   Net Penalty Differential...209
   Anatomy of a Penalty Drawer...211
   Can a Team be Built Around Drawing Penalties?...213
   Closing Thoughts...214
Who is the Best Penalty Killer?..216
   The Subjective Opinion..216
   Penalty-Killing Defencemen 218
      Frequency of Usage 221
      Individual Goals Against Average..222
      Attempted Shots Allowed..224
      Defensive Zone Starts...226
      Quality of Competition...228
      Putting it All Together..231
   Penalty-Killing Forwards 232
      Attempted Shots Allowed..235
      Penalty-Killing Extras (PKE)..237
      PKE for Defencemen..240
   Closing Thoughts...241
Who is the Best Power Play Specialist?..243
   Forwards...243
      The Leader Board...249
      Individual Point Percentage (IPP%)..251
      Zone Start Percentage (ZS%)...253
      Goals For Average (GFA)...255
      Attempted Shots per 60 Minutes (AS/60)...256
      Shots and Passes per 60 Minutes (Sh/60 and Pa/60)...257
      Modified Points per 60 Minutes (MP/60)...258
      Defensive Considerations...258

The Top Candidates...259
 The Case for Claude Giroux..259
 The Case for Sidney Crosby or Evgeni Malkin..260
 The Case for Alexander Ovechkin or Nicklas Backstrom......................................261
 The Case for Someone Else...262
Defencemen...263
 The Case for Erik Karlsson..266
 The Case for P.K. Subban...267
 The Case for Shea Weber..268
 The Case for Someone Else...269
Closing Thoughts...270
What Value do Enforcers Have in Today's NHL?...272
 Who Are the Most Dangerous Players in the NHL?...272
 Who Can Save Us From Those Dirty Rats?..277
 If Enforcers Don't Control the Rats, What Good Do They Do?.............................282
 Closing Thoughts...286
Questions and Answers..287
 How Important are Controlled Zone Exits and Entries?.......................................287
 How Accurate are the Passing Estimates?...291
 What is Delta?...298
 Why Didn't Ottawa Finish First in 2013–14?..299
Conclusion...308
Glossary of Terms...309
About the Authors...314
 Rob Vollman..314
 Iain Fyffe..314
 Tom Awad..315
 Josh Smith, Illustrator...316
Alphabetical Index...317

Foreword

There are two kinds of fans in the world: those who observe the game for the pure joy and beauty of it, and those who see the joy and beauty and would like to know the "why" of it. For hockey fans, the "why" is a monster, and at some level the idea of hockey analytics is pure madness.

There are so many events in a one-minute span of NHL action the mind is unable to keep track of it. Even simple strategies being changed can be passed over by knowledgeable fans because it's happening so damn fast!

I come from a world that did not contain analytics. The numbers made available to the generation of my youth were interesting and had value at the time, but have been exposed as miserably misleading as we grind the game into sequence and segment.

It was my good fortune to discover advanced stats early in the process, around the turn of the century. My usage of hockey's analytics department has consisted of 15 straight years of saying "dumb it down for me" and the math men have obliged and helped me understand.

If you're like me, Rob Vollman and his unique way of presenting analytics is important to your understanding of the new math of the game. The group of people who collect and analyze advanced stats are a small portion of the actual hockey population. Their ability to ask the "why" of hockey and express it in layman's terms adds to my enjoyment of the game.

If you're reading this, and the "why" is something you'd like to solve, I recommend you start with Rob Vollman's *Hockey Abstract*. I've read his book cover to cover and back again, from the warmth of the sun on the coast to the warmth of the fireplace in my living room. I've been able to ask Rob questions, and as with most analytics experts he delivers the best answers available. I have come away with a better understanding of what works and why, and more important what doesn't work and the reasons behind those things, too.

There's so much about the game we do not see, we cannot measure with the naked eye. An informed opinion enhances my enjoyment of hockey, and all I've ever had to do is knock on the door and keep an open mind.

Rob Vollman's *Hockey Abstract* serves as a great thought starter, answer book and referral guide. It's a splendid read.

Allan Mitchell
Host, The Lowdown with Lowetide
TSN 1260 Edmonton

Introduction

Last year I wrote that "statistical analysis is coming to hockey in a wave very similar to the one that hit baseball years ago," and guess what? The wave is here.

With every passing season, there's another explosion of new analysts, new websites, new perspectives, and new developments. More non-traditional statistics are being used in TV and radio broadcasts, front offices are hiring statistical analysts, and newspapers and magazines are including whole new sets of data. It used to be that front offices, agencies, and media outlets would use analytics to get an edge, but now it's being used to avoid falling behind. Soon, venturing forward without an analytics team will be like venturing forward without trainers, or equipment managers.

While we fans can certainly continue to enjoy the sport without analytics (and equipment managers), the underlying numbers can help stretch that enjoyment, especially when it's testing the validity of the conventional wisdom. And now, we can also use this type of analysis to gain insight into what teams are doing behind the scenes, and maybe what they should be doing.

You hold in your hands the second edition of *Hockey Abstract*, a book that's not about what we know about hockey, but what we don't know. Most topics begin with a question, which is then explored without any preconception of what the answer should be. Virtually everything I have ever done in this field began with the words "I don't know."

This book is also not a textbook, full of heavy statistics, math, and unapplied theories. It is not an annual yearbook, nor a guide for fantasy pools, either. And it definitely isn't meant as a substitute for watching the game. The work within is intended as a complement to traditional analysis, not a replacement.

So what is this book, then? Inspired by the work of Bill James and his annual *Baseball Abstract* of the 1970s and 80s, it's all about how analytics can be used to examine our sport in a different way. What makes a good player good? How do you get into the Hall of Fame? Who is the best penalty killer? These are the types of topics of which we can develop a greater understanding by adding this new perspective.

This year's volume is bigger and better than the first, an effort that was made easier with the tremendous support I received. Not only was it a huge boost to me personally, and one for which I'll be eternally thankful, but it helped me understand how to improve upon it, and what could be achieved with this second edition.

Last year's book was a basic primer, for example, which covered the fundamentals of the mainstream applications (and limitations) of hockey analytics. This book can take the next step, building on that solid foundation with a deeper look into today's leading edge topics. It can break new ground, and include more of the underlying math, and yet remain enjoyable to all fans, regardless of their current experience with these statistics.

It was also no accident that last year's book had so many footnote references. It was a very intentional choice to use *Hockey Abstract* as a platform to be shared with the countless brilliant analysts in our quickly growing field. This year, that mission can continue in a more direct fashion, by welcoming my two co-authors, Tom Awad and Iain Fyffe, without whom I couldn't have embarked upon this more ambitious venture.

And, of course, this second book affords the opportunity to provide updates on some of the important yet hard-to-find data that was introduced last year.

One thing that won't change in this second book is my approach. I love stats! I've been playing with numbers since childhood and I've always loved learning what they can do, and watching games with the new perspectives they bring me. I truly love this stuff and it's a joy to have an audience with whom to share it all. I may have been a little shy with my personal views and sense of humour last year, but what I did share was well-received, and those that know me best advise me to inject even more of that passion into my work. I'll do my best, but thankfully Josh Smith has returned with his illustrations to handle some of the humour.

- NHL OUTDOOR GAME IN FLORIDA -

But hey, I know that analytics can sometimes leave a bad taste in people's mouths. If it's not presented properly, a statistical analysis can be tedious and useless at best, negative or arrogant at worst, and ultimately suck the fun right out of our favourite sport.

That's a big reason why I spent this last season writing for *Bleacher Report* further refining my voice. It's a great website with great fans who really understand and love our great game. The key challenge is to share analytics with them in a way that's both interesting and relevant, and to avoid some of the unfortunate wording choices that can distract a passionate fan from enjoying its full value.

And let me tell you, it isn't always easy to write about hockey analytics. It's a relatively new field and we're still figuring out how these ideas can be best expressed. My basic philosophy is usually well-received, specifically that the analysis isn't being presented as something definitive, but rather as a new perspective that can supplement traditional analysis. I feel that I'm still learning how to hit that target, and I have been known to stumble, which is one reason why I'm pleased to have some extra help this year.

Tom Awad and Iain Fyffe

I'm thrilled that the two brilliant analysts who are most responsible for helping me develop my craft agreed to join me as co-authors in this second edition, Tom Awad and Iain Fyffe. I've been working with hockey statistics since childhood, and learned the fundamentals in University, but it was these two friends, more than anyone else, who really helped me hone my craft. When I wrote last year about how I was patiently waiting for someone to write a hockey version of *Baseball Abstract* before finally writing it myself, these were two of the gentlemen that I had foremost in mind.

I met Iain Fyffe first, some time in the late 1990s. As far as I could tell, he was the only hockey statistical analyst on the Internet at the time, with a website called *Puckerings*. My first publication in this field was actually back in 2001, when he gave me a co-author credit on a paper about adjusted plus/minus in the *Society for International Hockey Research*'s (SIHR) Hockey Research Journal. As I recall, I helped make the proper adjustment for special teams play.

Iain's involvement will be a special treat for those who enjoy historical content. In a fascinating application of analytics, Iain has developed a system called the Inductinator, which has captured the intrinsic standards for the Hall of Fame. The Inductinator can actually determine what contributions got players voted in and predict who will receive this honour in the future. He also refused to shy away from a controversial topic and shared his latest stat-based research on the value of enforcers.

I'm also thrilled to have Tom Awad as a co-author. I met him through the Hockey Analysis Group that Iain organized on Yahoo back in April, 2004. Now I'm pretty good with numbers, but Tom is a flat-out genius. Like most geniuses, he's also a man of great patience and precision, and over the past decade I'm one of many people to whom he's been invaluable for flushing out rough ideas.

Tom is perhaps best known as the creator of Goals Versus Threshold (GVT) and the VUKOTA projection system. In this book, he'll be presenting his work on what makes good players good. While written in a way that will be accessible to all, this series is a great reward for those who picked up the fundamentals of the field from last year's book (or elsewhere).

Tom's contributions don't end there, incidentally. It's also a tremendous thrill to have the pioneer of the entire shot quality debate bring us all up to speed on the subject. He also covered one notable topic I neglected in last year's primer, score effects, and spent many an evening reviewing my own chapters. Great stuff!

It's always been important to me to use my platform to promote the work of others. I've always wanted to help dispel this notion that there are only a few of us, and that we all share a single perspective. Quoting over a hundred studies from about 50 different analysts last year was intended not just to establish a strong basis for my own work, but to demonstrate just how many analysts are out there, making contributions across the entire spectrum. It's not just five guys counting Corsi numbers anymore!

Outside of a half-dozen of the most prominent, most analysts never get enough credit for their work, and appreciate having the exposure. They don't do it for money, respect or recognition, but out of a real passion for the sport. They're an amazing and largely untapped resource for radio programs and television coverage that sometimes struggle for good content.

For readers, all those footnotes were a handy resource to find the most recent research, and worth the price of the book all by itself, according to some. As such, we've invested a great deal of time finding even more studies, over an even wider array of topics.

What to Expect

Taking on this second edition was quite a challenge. Last year's *Hockey Abstract* was almost a decade in the making, while this year's book was written in under a year. Last year's book may have received a bit of a pass for being the first of its kind, but the expectations are higher now. I've won your attention, covered the basics, and now I need to take it to a new level.

Fortunately, I received a lot of great feedback on which direction to head next. I've been clearly instructed on what to keep, and where to move on. These suggestions included:

- Player usage charts! I suppose these are my calling card and will indeed be included again this year. In fact, there will be updates to all the otherwise hard-to-find data introduced last year, like setup passes and quality starts, for example.
- A chapter on shot quality, a controversial topic which will be covered by Tom Awad, the foremost expert in this field. He also took a more detailed look at score effects.
- Team essays, much like those featured in Bill James' annual *Baseball Abstract* books. While my intention is to make a timeless book that won't expire after a single season, I did include a page or two of team analysis with the player usage charts, though mostly as an exercise on *how* to interpret team-based data.
- More historical content, for which I'm pleased that famed historical analytics guru Iain Fyffe has contributed chapters on the Hall of Fame.
- More analytics about coaching, which I was happy to oblige, but unfortunately could not secure the necessary data in time. However, I did update last year's study, for

active coaches.

- A deeper look at goaltending. Not only did I dedicate a chapter that revisits all the cutting edge developments in this field, but Tom Awad took a swing at it as well. Joshua Smith, our illustrator, even put a goalie instead of a skater on the cover!
- A look at zone exits and entries, an advance that is on the leading edge of analytics. While I have no work of my own in this area, Corey Sznajder gave me a teaser for a book of his own that is coming out shortly, and I do have some opinions to share. That's why I created a Q&A chapter, to include topics that had some important ground to cover, but didn't warrant an entire, dedicated chapter.
- A look back at how my standings predictions were so spectacularly blown, which is a topic I feel no need to shy away from. It's in that Q&A chapter.
- An e-Book version, for the Kindle. I tried! That format is just not friendly to books with a lot of charts and/or tables.
- Use the same time range for tables and charts throughout the book. Sample sizes and availability of data guided my decisions last year, but I can definitely accommodate this request. This time, all tables and charts will be kept to exactly three seasons.

The first half of last year's book was especially well-received, so I found four more questions to tackle with hockey analytics, and plunged my analysis even deeper. I'm glad readers found these enjoyable, because they're just as much fun to create. Who is the best at scoring goals, drawing penalties, killing penalties, and working the power play? Find out how analytics can be used to answer these types of questions!

There was a call for me to weigh in on some of the more controversial aspects of our field, like how to confront our critics, and/or those that are doing analytics "wrong." Quite frankly, most skeptics who are open-minded, and most statisticians set positive examples (many of whom started off by making mistakes), so it seems like a waste of time to touch on either of those topics. Besides, who am I to tell anyone that what they're doing is wrong? Pass!

There were those who felt that last year's book featured too wide a variety of analysts and statistics, and not enough on Corsi and its pioneers. That was a philosophical choice on my part, I agree. I do believe in shot-based analysis but, at the risk of appearing defensive, I also believe in attacking problems from as many different angles as possible, especially in an introductory book. That includes quoting authors and using statistics that are perhaps not as well established. In fact, Corsi analysis itself would have fallen into that bucket not long ago, and may yet again a few years from now.

At times, the second half of last year's book, which introduced and explained many of today's key concepts and statistics, came across as a little more clinical, and a little less fun. Some parts struck readers as being overly complicated and/or of limited practical value, even when taken from the perspective of how statistics are developed, rather than being the details of any particular one. I regret missing the mark but, fortunately, there's far less need for explanatory chapters like those in this second book.

I was quite fortunate that readers were comfortable with my title choice, despite the audacity of a comparison to Bill James and his *Baseball Abstract*. As for James himself, he has yet to respond to my emails, unfortunately. With the thrill of co-authoring a book with Tom Awad and Iain Fyffe, meeting James remains one of the few items left on my analytics bucket list.

In the end, with your guidance, and the assistance of my two celebrated co-authors, I ventured out to make a second *Hockey Abstract* worthy of the title.

Onwards, Ho!

If I can emphasize any single point, it's how much your deeply appreciated support means to me. This book would not exist without it, nor those like it by the many brilliant authors that are doubtlessly to follow.

In the world of sports writing, where we're regularly accused of having lost all credibility, and/or being in urgent need of mental health care, we're always braced for the worst. Instead, *Hockey Abstract* was received with great interest, support and understanding, even in cases where I flat-out blew it (*cough* Ottawa Senators for the President's trophy *cough*).

There is a great thirst for hockey analytics right now and, on behalf of my co-authors, we are honoured to be allowed to continue to serve as three of its voices. It is with great gratitude that we thank you for supporting us once again, and with great pleasure that we present our latest work.

Let the conversations continue! Please enjoy.

What are the Hall of Fame's Standards?

By Iain Fyffe

The Hockey Hall of Fame was established in 1943, with the goal of recognizing the foremost players in the history of the great winter game. The Hall's selection committee is tasked with choosing players for the honour based on the criteria of playing ability, sportsmanship, character and contribution to their teams, and to the sport in general. The first players recognized in 1945 were Hobey Baker, Charlie Gardiner, Eddie Gerard, Frank McGee, Howie Morenz, Tommy Phillips, Harvey Pulford, Hod Stuart and Georges Vezina, after it was decided that the first class should be entirely posthumous in nature. Selections then proceeded on an irregular basis until eventually the current practice was adopted of holding a vote every year, with a maximum placed on the number of players that can be inducted annually. Through 2013, a total of 256 men have been inducted into the Hall of Fame to honour their playing careers.

Any longtime fan of the game knows that the identity of the players in the Hockey Hall of Fame, and of the players who have not been inducted, can be a source of great debate among the faithful. Almost everyone has a favoured player they really feel deserve the honour, and can name several players already in the Hall that probably shouldn't be there, especially not ahead of their preferred hockeyist. These disagreements arise not only because of the selection committee's opaqueness when it comes to the selection process, but also because there are obviously no objective standards as to who should be a Hall-of-Famer and who should not. You cannot look at a player's career, add up all his awards and accomplishments, compare the total to a chart, and arrive at a "yes" or "no" answer. It's just not that simple.

However, even though there are no objective standards, we can try to figure out whether the Hall of Fame selection committee has any *implicit* standards; that is, standards that can be determined based on who has been inducted into the Hall of Fame and, just as importantly, who has not, in a sort of reverse engineering of the selection standards. Such a system could be used to discuss past selections, but perhaps more interestingly, it could also be used to predict future inductees based on the career records of active or recently-retired players. So, can we examine the career statistical records of Hall-of-Famers and non-Hall-of-Famers, and come up with a formula that represents the basis the selection committee apparently used to select the players for the honour?

As it turns out, we *can* derive these standards and we call the resulting system the Inductinator. The Inductinator calculates a score for every hockey player and any player who achieves a score of **100 or more** meets the implicit standards of the Hall of Fame selection committee. It's important to remember that this system is not concerned with who *should* or *should not* be in the Hockey Hall of Fame, but rather who can be expected to be, based on the selection committee's apparent standards. It is descriptive rather than prescriptive; it does not deal with what should be, but what is. You might not agree with the standards that the committee uses and, indeed, some of them probably don't make a great deal of sense. However, the Inductinator is designed to deal with the reality of the situation rather than some idealized, alternative, and entirely fictional situation.

The inspiration for the Inductinator is really twofold. First is, of course, the Hall of Fame Monitor system devised by Bill James in the mid-1990s, for use in predicting future members of the Baseball Hall of Fame. Like the Inductinator, it was designed to predict who would be selected, without commenting on who should be selected. The second inspiration was my own Projectinator system, which was developed to predict a player's professional career based on his major junior or college statistics. The development of this system over a number of years provided useful experience and insight into manipulating this type of data in interesting and useful ways.

The Inductinator categorizes players into one of three eras, being the post-expansion era, the pre-expansion era, and the pre-war era. Presently the system only considers players from the 1929–30 season onward, when the modern offside rules were introduced. Also, due to disparities in statistical information[1] (and the fact that the selection committee's standards for selecting international players could *never* be rationalized), only NHL players are considered. We will examine the results of the Inductinator position-by-position (goaltender, defenceman, and forward) and era-by-era, beginning with the netminders.

Hall of Fame Standards for Post-Expansion Goaltenders

We'll start with post-expansion goaltenders, specifically goaltenders who played the majority of their careers after the Great Expansion in 1967. There have been 10 such goaltenders inducted into the Hockey Hall of Fame. These players, their years of eligibility and induction, and their Inductinator scores are listed below. Remember that any player with an Inductinator score of 100 or more meets the Hall of Fame's implicit standards for induction. The 1990s were a remarkably poor time for goaltenders seeking entrance to the Hall of Fame. From 1988, when Tony Esposito was honoured, to 2003, when Grant Fuhr was inducted, only one NHL goaltender was selected for the Hall of Fame.

Post-Expansion Hall-of-Fame Goaltenders

Goaltender	Eligible	Inducted	Score
Dominik Hasek	2014	2014	545
Patrick Roy	2006	2006	536
Grant Fuhr	2003	2003	212
Ed Belfour	2010	2011	185
Billy Smith	1992	1993	183
Ken Dryden	1982	1983	167
Tony Esposito	1987	1988	157
Bernie Parent	1982	1984	144
Ed Giacomin	1981	1987	111
Gerry Cheevers	1983	1985	104

1 Acknowledgement: All statistical data in this chapter sourced from SIHR, http://www.sihrhockey.org and Hockey Reference http://www.hockey-reference.com.

For post-expansion goaltenders, the Inductinator score is calculated based on a variety of factors, each of which is weighted to arrive at the appropriate results. It should be noted that a player's World Hockey Association (WHA) totals, if any, are included in his career totals. If this were not the case, there is no way that Gerry Cheevers would meet any sort of implicit standard that would not also be met by several other non-Hall-of-Fame goalies.

Let's work through an example, so you can see what sort of calculations the Inductinator uses. We'll take Eddie Giacomin as our example. He has a total score of 111, made up of the following factors: 75 points for his All-Star Team selections, 12 for his Vezina Trophy, another 12 for his win-loss differential, 10 points for his Goals Against Average (GAA) relative to league average, and 2 points for his wins.

All-Star Team selections begin at five points for the first, and increase by five for each subsequent one (10 for the second, 15 for the third) up to a maximum of 25 for the fifth and subsequent selections. Giacomin made five All-Star Teams, giving him 75 points. Vezina trophies are worth 12 points for the first one, and 40 points for the second and each subsequent award.

For the won-loss differential, a goaltender gains a point for each 1.7 differential above 60. Giacomin had 289 wins versus 209 losses, resulting in 12 points. Giacomin's career GAA of 2.82 was 0.33 lower than the approximate league GAA over his career of 3.15, and he receives points equal to 30 times this difference. Goaltenders of this era receive a point for every 20 career wins they have above 250, and so Giacomin's 289 wins earn him two points here, to bring his total to 111.

There are a number of other things that Giacomin could have earned points for, if he had achieved them. Playing over 800 games provides one point for each 18 games over 800. Every 10 playoff games over 90 also provides one point. Every three games played for one's country in a major senior-level international tournament also scores a point.

Stanley Cup championships are worth eight points for each of the first two and 40 points for each one beyond that, up to a maximum total of 200 points. Each Hart Trophy is worth 40 points, while a Smythe is worth 15 for the first and 50 for each subsequent one.

Finally, any goaltender from this era who played fewer than 600 career games has his total score reduced proportionately. Since Giacomin played 609 games, he gets full value for his score. This illustration is intended to demonstrate the type of calculations used in the Inductinator; we will not be doing a point-by-point illustration for each position and each era.

Overall, the factors making up the score and the percentage of the total score they contribute to the Hall-of-Famers are as follows:

Post-Expansion Goaltender Inductinator Factors

Factor	Percentage
Stanley Cup won as a starter	20.8
Post-season All-Star Teams	19.8
Regular season wins minus losses	18.2

Vezina Trophy wins	12.9
Conn Smythe Trophy wins	8.3
Regular season GAA versus league average	6.4
Games in major international tournaments	5.7
Regular season games played	3.8
Regular season wins	3.1

With these factors in place, we can look at goaltenders who have not been inducted to determine where they fall short of the players who have received the honour. As of 2013, there were only three post-expansion goaltenders who scored higher than 80, but less than 100 on the Inductinator scale:

Post-Expansion Goaltenders Outside the Hall

Goaltender	Eligible	Inducted	Score
Tom Barrasso	2006	-	90
Mike Vernon	2005	-	87
Andy Moog	2001	-	82

Tom Barrasso is the closest to reaching the standard. He played and won more games than Billy Smith, Bernie Parent, Ed Giacomin, Gerry Cheevers, and Ken Dryden. He was named to three All-Star Teams, as many as Ed Belfour, and more than Smith, Cheevers, Parent and Grant Fuhr. He also won a Vezina Trophy. He even had a better won-loss differential than Smith, Parent and Giacomin, though not by much, and other goaltenders beat Barrasso here as well, such as Mike Vernon, Andy Moog, and Curtis Joseph. So Barrasso could have been in the lower tier of Hall-of-Fame netminders, if he didn't allow quite so many goals. His career GAA is barely better than the league average for when he played. Eight of the 10 Hall-of-Famers are miles ahead of Barrasso in this regard and the only one who isn't far ahead, Grant Fuhr, beats Barrasso handily in most other categories. This seems to be the reason that the Hall of Fame has not found that Barrasso is worthy of induction. At least not yet. No post-expansion goaltender has had to wait longer than six years for induction, but we cannot be sure that Barrasso will remain on the outside forever. The Hockey Hall of Fame selection process and voting results are not discussed publicly and the only information that is ever disclosed are the names of the players that are given the honour.

Hall of Fame Standards for Pre-Expansion Goaltenders

The pre-expansion era essentially coincides with the "Original Six." However, while the latter begins in 1942 when the Brooklyn Americans folded, the former begins in 1945 when players fighting in WWII returned to the NHL, restoring the quality to a league that had suffered great losses of talent for several years. The following season, the NHL increased its schedule from 50 games to 60, and a few years later increased it again to 70. The NHL season was beginning to take on a more modern shape, notwithstanding the fact that only six teams competed in it.

Pre-Expansion Hall-of-Fame Goaltenders

Goaltender	Eligible	Inducted	Score
Jacques Plante	1978	1978	485
Terry Sawchuk	1971	1971	405
Glenn Hall	1974	1975	403
Gump Worsley	1977	1980	225
Johnny Bower	1973	1976	190
Bill Durnan	1953	1964	168
Harry Lumley	1963	1980	124
Chuck Rayner	1956	1973	100

Team playoff performance, in terms of winning the Stanley Cup, is somewhat more important in this era than in the post-expansion era, but team regular season performance, in the form of wins minus losses, is much less important. And the goaltender's individual awards, which are really only the All-Star Team selections since the Vezina was a team award in this era, are also more important to the standards. As such All-Star Teams and Stanley Cup wins represent over three-quarters of the Inductinator values for goalies from this time period.

Pre-Expansion Goaltender Inductinator Factors

Factor	Percentage
Post-season All-Star Teams	50.1
Stanley Cup won as a starter	27.1
Regular season games played	5.7
Regular season GAA versus league average	5.2
Regular season wins minus losses	3.7
Regular season wins	2.8
Other	5.4

Now that we know what makes up the standards for this era, are there any goaltenders who came close to the standards? The Hall-of-Famers do not represent all of the All-Star Team selections of this era, for instance, nor all of the Cup-winning netminders. But there's only one within sniffing distance, and even he's really not that close:

Pre-Expansion Goaltenders Outside the Hall

Goaltender	Eligible	Inducted	Score
Jim Henry	1958	-	73

"Sugar" Jim Henry played more games than Bill Durnan and recorded more wins than Chuck Rayner. But he made only one All-Star Team, which matches only Johnny Bower among the Hall-of-Famers, and Bower rates far ahead of Henry in everything else. There really isn't anyone else close to the Hall in the pre-expansion era.

Hall of Fame Standards for Pre-War Goaltenders

The pre-war era, for Inductinator purposes, covers the seasons from 1929–30, when the forward passing rules were revised to something resembling the modern version of the rule, to 1944–45, when many players were still away fighting in WWII. Before this time, the nature of the sport was quite different, from the length of schedule to the number of leagues over which the best players were spread, to the differences in scoring levels from season to season. So this is as far back as we can reasonably go in developing these standards using this methodology. The conditions under which players played from 1875 (when the first organized hockey match was played) to 1928–29 varied too much to make such comparisons possible using this particular sort of analysis.

Pre-War Hall-of-Fame Goaltenders

Goaltender	Eligible	Inducted	Score
Frank Brimsek	1953	1966	247
Turk Broda	1955	1967	239
Tiny Thompson	1947	1959	183
Chuck Gardiner	1945	1945	159
George Hainsworth	1947	1961	119
Roy Worters	1947	1969	118

Unlike later eras, the number of years a pre-war player waited between eligibility and induction really says very little about his calibre in the eyes of the selection committee. When these players were being voted on, the committee was still in the process of catching up to history, so they had to consider all players up to that point in their deliberations. We can't read anything into Frank Brimsek not being inducted until 1966, 13 years after he was eligible. In 1965, the committee was selecting players such as Jack Marshall, who retired in 1917 and Art Farrell, who retired in 1901. Often, more recent players simply had to wait their turns.

Pre-War Goaltender Inductinator Factors

Factor	Percentage
Post-season All-Star Teams	54.5
Stanley Cup won as a starter	15.6
Regular season wins	7.3
Regular season GAA versus league average	6.3
Regular season games played	4.9
Regular season wins minus losses	4.6
Other	6.8

Like the pre-expansion netminders, the pre-war standards are almost entirely about being named to All-Star Teams and being the starting goaltender on Cup-winning teams. Only George Hainsworth made the Hall without an All-Star selection, but he did have a significant career before the first All-Star Teams were selected in 1931, and the Inductinator considers the entirety of a player's career rather than just the part that falls within the era in question, so that's understandable.

Let's see who fell just short among pre-war goaltenders:

Pre-War Goaltenders Outside the Hall

Goaltender	Eligible	Inducted	Score
Dave Kerr	1947	-	96
Lorne Chabot	1947	-	86

Lorne Chabot is a player about whom the question "why isn't he in the Hall of Fame?" is often asked. The Inductinator analysis provides a reasonable answer to this question. His 2.03 career GAA is the fourth lowest in NHL history, which would seem to be a large point in his favour. But the three players ahead of Chabot were all contemporaries of his: Alec Connell (1.91), George Hainsworth (1.93), and Chuck Gardiner (2.02). This suggests the era had a very strong effect on these players' career GAA. On the other hand, all three of these other netminders are Hall-of-Famers (Connell is not discussed here because the bulk of his career was before 1930), as is the #5 man on the career GAA list, Tiny Thompson. So these players must have something Chabot does not.

And it's actually quite simple: Chabot's career was not long enough to earn a Hall-of-Fame berth. He played 412 major-league regular season games, which is 72 fewer than Roy Worters, and over a 100 fewer than every other Hall-of-Famer from this era, other than Gardiner who died mid-career at the age of 29. If Chabot had managed one more full season as an NHL goaltender, even if he hurt his career GAA by doing so, the Inductinator suggests he would have been a Hall-of-Famer. Chabot injured his knee in training camp in 1935, after which he played only 22 NHL games. It's therefore clear that had this injury not occurred, Chabot would likely be in the Hall of Fame based on the selection committee's implicit standards for goaltenders of his era.

Dave Kerr (#6 on the career GAA list at 2.15) is in the same boat as Chabot. Another half-season's worth of play in the NHL and he'd meet the implicit standards for the Hall of Fame. Kerr retired from the game fairly young, at age 32. If he'd stayed in the game for just a bit longer, chances are good that he'd be an honoured member of the sacred hall.

Hall of Fame Standards for Post-Expansion Defencemen

We now turn our attention to defencemen, who are also quite simple to derive implicit standards for, as it turns out. There are 18 Hall-of-Fame blueliners from the post-expansion era, with Rob Blake being the most recent honouree in 2014, following Chris Chelios and Scott Niedermayer in 2013. None of these players were surprises; the Inductinator predicted that both of the 2013 inductees would be inducted in their first year of eligibility, and they were. The most remarkable part about this is that Chelios is over 11 years older than Niedermayer, but they were both first eligible in the same year. Blake was given his ticket to the Hall perhaps a bit earlier than the system would have suggested, but his honour was also predicted by the Inductinator.

Post-Expansion Hall-of-Fame Defencemen

Defenceman	Eligible	Inducted	Score
Ray Bourque	2004	2004	744
Bobby Orr	1979	1979	622
Paul Coffey	2004	2004	387
Chris Chelios	2013	2013	367
Larry Robinson	1995	1995	341
Denis Potvin	1991	1991	329
Al MacInnis	2007	2007	286
Scott Stevens	2007	2007	257
Brian Leetch	2009	2009	250
Scott Niedermayer	2013	2013	211
Brad Park	1988	1988	182
Borje Salming	1993	1996	149
Serge Savard	1986	1986	131
Larry Murphy	2004	2004	126
Rob Blake	2013	2014	123
Guy Lapointe	1987	1993	122
Rod Langway	1996	2002	109
Mark Howe	1998	2011	103

Ray Bourque rates ahead of Bobby Orr, despite the latter's three Hart trophies, which no other blueliner can come close to matching, because #77's career was so much longer than #4's. It's possible that Orr "should" have a higher Inductinator score. He receives no credit for his two scoring titles; since he's the only defenceman to win one (much less two), any points awarded for that would be completely arbitrary, with nothing to base them on. A forward would receive 25 points for two scoring titles, so a blueliner would surely deserve more, but it seems unlikely that it would be enough to overcome Bourque's 120-point lead. Borje Salming was the first European Hall-of-Famer based on a career in North America (Vladislav Tretiak was inducted in 1989, and although he was drafted by Montreal, he never played a game in the NHL). Paul Coffey shows up as the third highest rated defenceman by this analysis, which illustrates how important the Hall of Fame apparently considers scoring to be in evaluating these defenders.

Post-Expansion Defencemen Inductinator Factors

Factor	Percentage
Post-season All-Star Teams	43.8
Norris Trophies won	20.2
Regular season points scored	11.9
Conn Smythe Trophies won	8.1
Stanley Cups won	8.0
Regular season games played	3.4
Hart Trophies won	2.1
Other	2.5

The Hall of Fame selection committee doesn't really care for defensive defencemen in the current era. It seems that no hockey insider with the ability to bestow hockey honours really cares for them. Defensive defencemen have a hard time winning berths on All-Star Teams, they almost never win the Norris Trophy, and don't get a sniff at the Conn Smythe. The Hall of Fame sees no reason to disagree with this consensus, apparently. Scoring points is more of a factor for defencemen than winning the Hart Trophy, essentially because the latter is so rare for any blueliner, much less a purely defensive one.

Post-Expansion Defencemen Outside the Hall

Defenceman	Eligible	Inducted	Score
Doug Wilson	1996	-	94
J-C Tremblay	1982	-	88
Phil Housley	2006	-	75
Kevin Lowe	2001	-	74

We see here that the three post-expansion defencemen closest to meeting the implicit Hall of Fame standards (an Inductinator score of 100) are offensively-focused, especially Phil Housley. You might be surprised at how low J-C Tremblay is rated, although he had a good long career, won five Stanley Cups and piled up the points in the WHA, he never won a single NHL award and made only two All-Star Teams. WHA totals are included in a modern player's stats when calculating his score, but Tremblay did not begin to record really impressive point totals until the 1970–71 season when he was 32 years old, which limited his career totals. Doug Wilson is closer, even though he played barely over 1,000 NHL games, which is a low figure for a Hall-of-Famer from this era. Wilson's 39 goals in 1981–82 won him the Norris Trophy (another fine selection, hockey insiders!), and he made three All-Star Teams to Tremblay's two.

Hall of Fame Standards for Pre-Expansion Defencemen

Even though the post-expansion era now covers a much longer time period than the pre-expansion era, and although there is a much larger pool of players in the post-expansion era due to the influx of European talent, it wasn't until 2013 that there were more post-expansion defencemen than pre-expansion defencemen in the Hall of Fame. There are 15 pre-expansion blueliner inductees, detailed below. Red Kelly is considered a defenceman here, since he spent the larger part of his career on the blue line, and moreover earned most of his accolades at that position. His years at centre for Toronto certainly padded his scoring totals. However, when calculating the Inductinator score, his raw point totals are not used; they are adjusted based on the fact that he played about 36% of his NHL career as a forward. This ensures that his higher point totals in his later years do not unduly influence his rating as a defenceman.

Pre-Expansion Hall of Fame Defencemen

Defenceman	Eligible	Inducted	Score
Doug Harvey	1972	1973	655
Red Kelly	1969	1969	542
Pierre Pilote	1972	1975	396
Tim Horton	1970	1970	317

Bill Gadsby	1969	1970	259
Harry Howell	1979	1979	227
Marcel Pronovost	1973	1978	205
Butch Bouchard	1959	1966	204
Allan Stanley	1972	1981	199
Tom Johnson	1968	1970	148
Bill Quackenbush	1959	1976	146
Jack Stewart	1955	1964	131
Fern Flaman	1964	1990	128
Ken Reardon	1953	1966	109
Leo Boivin	1973	1986	100

Defensive defencemen do much better in this era than in the post-expansion era. Indeed, most of these honoured players were what would be called defensive defencemen by today's standards. However, a large part of this is due to the fact that defencemen from this era simply did not participate as much on offence, so (before Bobby Orr came along) a blueliner recording 40 points would be among the leaders at his position. Even so, players like Jack Stewart, Butch Bouchard, and to a lesser extent Bill Quackenbush, probably wouldn't be considered for All-Star Teams or Norris Trophies today, unlike in their own era, due to their limited offensive contributions.

Let's work through an example to illustrate the sort of factors that go into the calculation for pre-expansion defencemen. Harry Howell has a score of 219. His 1,581 regular season games played are actually enough by themselves to meet the standards; he earns one point for every eight games above 970, and a 30-point bonus for playing 1,400 of more games, for a total of 106 points. He would have received one point for every five playoff games above 100, but he had only 45 in his career. He gets one point for every 20 regular season points in excess of 300, for a total of eight. Howell received 10 points for reaching the 50-goal plateau, another 10 for the 100-goal plateau, and another 15 for the 300-point plateau. His one First All-Star Team selection earns him 18 points; if he had had any more they would have been worth 35 apiece. Howell spent two seasons as team captain, and these are worth five points apiece. Finally, his 1967 Norris Trophy earns him 50 points for a total of 227. Howell never won a Stanley Cup, but if he had, he would have received five points for the first, and 10 for additional wins.

Pre-Expansion Defencemen Inductinator Factors

Factor	Percentage
Post-season All-Star Teams	49.1
Norris Trophies won	11.0
Regular season games played	10.8
Regular season points scored	9.7
Stanley Cups won	9.2
Years as team captain	6.5
Other	3.7

Like goaltenders of this era, All-Star Team berths are by the far the most important determining factor in a defenceman's apparent Hall of Fame credentials and since they have a relevant individual award in the Norris Trophy, there's less emphasis on team accomplishments such as Stanley Cup championships. Leadership seems to have been greatly valued for these defencemen, as the number of years a player spent as team captain is a decisive factor for some players. It would be very difficult to explain the presence of Fern Flaman, and especially Leo Boivin, in the Hall of Fame without considering this factor. In terms of earning a spot in the Hall of Fame, this was easily the best era to be a tough, low-scoring team leader.

Pre-Expansion Defencemen Outside the Hall

Defenceman	Eligible	Inducted	Score
Carl Brewer	1983	-	99
Jean-Guy Talbot	1974	-	94
Jimmy Thomson	1961	-	94
Gus Mortson	1962	-	76

Carl Brewer could not be closer to meeting Hall of Fame standards without achieving the honour, thanks largely to his one First All-Star and three Second All-Star Team selections, and three consecutive Stanley Cup championships. But Brewer had something of a habit of retiring during his career, for a variety of reasons. He first retired in 1965, and missed four NHL seasons, even being reinstated as an amateur to play in the 1967 World Championships. He retired from the NHL for a second time in 1972, but was back a year later in the WHA before retiring again, this time for five full seasons before playing another 20 NHL games in 1979–80. If he had a more typical career trajectory, it's clear that Brewer would meet the implicit Hall of Fame standards.

Jean-Guy Talbot had quite a long career for the era, won seven Stanley Cups, and made the First All-Star Team once. He tended not to be at the top of the Canadiens' pecking order however, which prevented him from additional individual awards and ultimately kept him out of the Hall. Gus Mortson is the only blueliner who was captain of his team for at least three seasons that is not in the Hall. His career was ultimately too short and his single All-Star Team selection is not enough to put him over the top.

Hall of Fame Standards for Pre-War Defencemen

The pre-war era (1929–30 to 1944–45, which incidentally is the year the first class of Hall of Fame inductees were named) contributes 14 defencemen to the Hall of Fame. Three of these men (Dit Clapper, Albert Siebert, and Ebbie Goodfellow) started their NHL careers as forwards, and Clapper even made two Second All-Star Teams at right wing before later making four All-Star Teams as a blueliner. Siebert and Goodfellow only made All-Star Teams after switching to the defence. All three of these players made greater contributions to their teams and the game after switching positions.

Pre-War Hall of Fame Defencemen

Defenceman	Eligible	Inducted	Score
Eddie Shore	1947	1947	456
Dit Clapper	1947	1947	374
Earl Seibert	1949	1963	299
Albert Siebert	1947	1964	234
King Clancy	1947	1958	180
Ebbie Goodfellow	1947	1963	163
Sylvio Mantha	1947	1960	162
Hap Day	1947	1961	149
Red Dutton	1947	1958	146
Art Coulter	1947	1974	144
Babe Pratt	1955	1966	104
Lionel Conacher	1947	1994	101
Ching Johnson	1947	1958	100
Red Horner	1947	1965	100

The gap between eligibility for the Hall and induction in this era cannot really be taken as a sign of how worthy a player was seen of the honour. Since the first non-posthumous inductions were in 1947, there was an incredible backlog of worthy players, and the selection committee met irregularly in the early years of the Hall of Fame, so it took many years before the backlog was cleared. As late as 1965, the Hall of Fame was inducting a large class of older players, players who presumably would have already been in had the inductions begun before 1945.

Pre-War Defencemen Inductinator Factors

Factor	Percentage
Post-season All-Star Teams	31.5
Years as team captain	21.8
Regular season penalty minutes	14.5
Hart Trophies won	10.3
Regular season points scored	8.4
Stanley Cups won	6.6
Regular season games played	4.9
Other	2.0

Defencemen from the pre-war era get a lot of credit for leadership and toughness. Of Red Dutton's 146 Inductinator "points", 129 of them come from his years as team captain and his penalty minutes. Without considering career penalty minutes, we would not be able to explain the inductions of Dutton, Lionel Conacher, Ivan Johnson, or Red Horner. Clearly, physical play (even that which resulted in one's team being a man short for two minutes or more) was highly valued among defencemen, retroactively. Or perhaps, since these selections were being made long after the fact, the committee simply used any numbers they had available to them, even if those numbers ultimately represent something negative. All-Star Teams are still the most important factor, which is good because these reflect who was seen as the best blueliners at the time they were playing.

Defenceman	Eligible	Inducted	Score
Flash Hollett	1949	-	99
Ott Heller	1949	-	87

Bill Hollett was likely the best offensive defenceman from this era. He made two All-Star Teams (one first, one second) and even served as team captain for two seasons, so he presumably wasn't seen as being a completely one-note player by his peers. He also won two Stanley Cups. Given the above, it seems the one thing Hollett did not do sufficiently to earn a berth in the Hall of Fame was take penalties. He averaged only 0.64 PIM per career game, and the only contemporary Hall-of-Fame defencemen with such a low number is Dit Clapper, who spent about half of his career as a forward and is otherwise much more qualified for the honour than Hollett. All the other Hall-of-Famers have a much higher rate of penalties per game. The willingness to flaunt the rules was apparently seen as a virtue in this era by the selection committee, possible due to the misguided belief that players who do not take penalties are too soft.

Hall of Fame Standards for Post-Expansion Forwards

We now come to probably the most over-represented class of players in the Hall of Fame: post-expansion forwards. There are 48 post-expansion forwards in the Hall of Fame out of a total of 76 honourees from this era, meaning that 63% of the inducted players are forwards. You might think this is an appropriate percentage, since a current NHL hockey team has 12 forwards out of 20 players, or 60%. But that's not really the right approach. The Hall of Fame is reserved for the very best players; at a minimum, these players would be first-line forwards, first-pairing defencemen, and starting goaltenders. This suggests that only half of honoured players should be forwards, and this is more or less borne out in earlier eras:

Hall-of-Fame Players by Era and Position

	Pre-War	Pre-Expansion	Post-Expansion
Goaltenders	6	8	10
Defencemen	14	15	18
Forwards	24	26	48

In the pre-war era, 55% of honourees are forwards, and in the pre-expansion era this figure is 53%, both of which are much closer to the presumed 50% figure than 63%. In both the pre-war and pre-expansion eras, there are 1.7 forwards in the Hall for each defenceman. In the post-expansion era, this figure jumps to 2.7. The greater number of players in the Hall of Fame from the post-expansion era is fine because this era covers a greater number of seasons. But the shift toward more forwards being given the honour is distinct and undeniable. Some of the likely reasons are discussed below, when examining the Inductinator factors for these forwards.

Post-Expansion Hall-of-Fame Forwards

Forward	Eligible	Inducted	Score
Wayne Gretzky	1999	1999	2036
Mario Lemieux	1997	1997	1092
Phil Esposito	1984	1984	896
Bobby Hull	1983	1983	886
Guy Lafleur	1988	1988	877
Marcel Dionne	1992	1992	694
Mark Messier	2007	2007	648
Mike Bossy	1990	1991	588
Stan Mikita	1983	1983	583
Joe Sakic	2012	2012	530
Jari Kurri	2001	2001	520
Bryan Trottier	1997	1997	516
Luc Robitaille	2009	2009	512
Brett Hull	2009	2009	479
Steve Yzerman	2009	2009	409
Michel Goulet	1997	1998	383
Bobby Clarke	1987	1987	344
Yvan Cournoyer	1982	1982	342
Bob Gainey	1992	1992	281
Dave Keon	1985	1986	252
Brendan Shanahan	2012	2013	247
Dale Hawerchuk	2000	2001	246
Ron Francis	2007	2007	243
Lanny McDonald	1992	1992	225
Joe Mullen	2000	2000	220

Johnny Bucyk	1981	1981	217
Peter Stastny	1998	1998	211
Mike Gartner	2001	2001	209
Denis Savard	2000	2000	200
Darryl Sittler	1988	1989	192
Jean Ratelle	1984	1985	184
Gilbert Perreault	1987	1990	178
Steve Shutt	1988	1993	166
Mats Sundin	2012	2012	166
Jacques Lemaire	1982	1984	156
Peter Forsberg	2014	2014	148
Joe Nieuwendyk	2010	2011	143
Mike Modano	2014	2014	142
Glenn Anderson	1999	2008	141
Bernie Federko	1993	2002	119
Pat LaFontaine	2001	2003	115
Bill Barber	1987	1990	114
Dino Ciccarelli	2002	2010	111
Clark Gillies	1991	2002	109
Adam Oates	2007	2012	109
Cam Neely	1999	2005	108
Doug Gilmour	2006	2011	102
Pavel Bure	2006	2012	102

With the expansion era featuring many more teams than before, and a lower average level of competition, players have been able to compile career games played and scoring totals that players from earlier eras simply could not match. As of the end of the 2013–14 season, 79 NHL players have scored 1,000 or more regular season points, and only six of these players are classified as pre-expansion players (Gordie Howe, Alex Delvecchio, Norm Ullman, Jean Beliveau, Frank Mahovlich, and Henri Richard). This number is seen as a very important milestone for offensive players, and players in the expansion era have a huge advantage over earlier players in reaching this number, resulting in some one-dimensional players earning the Hall-of-Fame honour simply by their offensive statistics.

Post-Expansion Forwards Inductinator Factors

Factor	Percentage
Post-season All-Star Teams	26.6
Regular season goals scored	17.1
High points-scoring seasons	12.9
Regular season points scored	9.3
Stanley Cups won	5.7
Hart Trophies won	4.4
Leading league in goals or points	3.7
Lindsay/Pearson Awards won	3.5
Lady Byng Trophies won	3.2
Conn Smythe Trophies won	3.1
High goal-scoring seasons	3.1

Selke Awards won	2.1
Other	5.3

All-Star Team selections are the most important factor here, as they are for nearly every era and type of player. But if we combine all the factors made up of purely scoring totals (goals and points, both career and single-season), we see that 46% of the Inductinator values come from these factors. This is a bit odd, because the selection committee is made up of hockey "insiders", who are the type of expert who will emphasize that scoring totals are nice, but "they don't win hockey games dontcha know". They're the type that says "defence wins championships" and derides "soft" players who don't back-check. And yet, when it comes to selecting players for the Hall of Fame, it seems that these knowledgeable insiders are as easily swayed by scoring totals as casual fans are; it must be very hard to ignore a career record with "1,000 points" at the bottom. As of 2014, the selection committee includes names such as Scotty Bowman, Brian Burke, Colin Campbell, Bobby Clarke, John Davidson, Mike Gartner, Jim Gregory, Anders Hedberg, Igor Larionov, Lanny McDonald, David Poile, Luc Robitaille, Peter Stastny, and Bill Torrey. Surely the level of insider knowledge these men have should enable the committee to move beyond such simplistic thinking as "1,000 points = Hall-of-Famer".

If the members of the selection committee truly valued defence, or all-round play at least, as much as you would expect them to, you should see a player like Guy Carbonneau in the Hall of Fame. Bob Gainey is there, but he's really the only defensive forward from this era in the Hall. His five Selke awards and five Stanley Cups were just too much to ignore. Dave Keon was a dominant defensive player, but his scoring also far outstrips Gainey and Carbonneau, so it would be difficult to say that he's representative of a defensive forward. Carbo won three Selke awards and three Stanley Cups, and played over 1,300 NHL games. He was team captain for five seasons. If you needed evidence that forwards generally earn a Hall-of-Fame berth by scoring goals, you don't have to look much further than this.

Since the Inductinator is built to reflect who *is expected to be* inducted into the Hall of Fame, rather than who *should be* inducted, it relies most heavily on scoring totals for these players. It may not be fair, just, or sensible, but it is what the Hall of Fame does, and that's what we're dealing with here.

Post-Expansion Forwards Outside the Hall

Forward	Eligible	Inducted	Score
Bernie Nicholls	2002	-	98
John Tonelli	1995	-	98
Reggie Leach	1986	-	95
Ken Hodge	1981	-	93
Theoren Fleury	2006	-	91
Pat Verbeek	2005	-	88
Butch Goring	1988	-	86
Kevin Stevens	2005	-	84
Rick Martin	1985	-	83
Brian Bellows	2002	-	76

Despite being one of only five NHL players to score 150 or more points in a season, Bernie Nicholls finds himself outside of the Hall, and since he's been eligible for 13 years it's unlikely he'll ever make it, especially with the glut of forwards that will soon become eligible for the honour who will jump the queue in front of him. So the selection committee is not completely without thought in their induction of high-scoring players. Nicholls may have been only the fifth player to score 150 points, but he still finished only fourth in the NHL scoring race in 1988–89, and he didn't even lead his own team in scoring. Three other players (Mario Lemieux, Wayne Gretzky, and Steve Yzerman) all scored at least 155 points that season, revealing that the feat was not as impressive as it might seem at first glance. For most of his career, without Gretzky on his team, Nicholls was a good but not great scorer.

Hall of Fame Standards for Pre-Expansion Forwards

Forwards from the pre-expansion era of 1945–46 to 1966–67 have contributed 26 players to the Hall of Fame. Many of the top-rated forwards from this era had their careers extend into to post-expansion era, which offered them the opportunity for longer careers than they would otherwise have had, giving them an advantage over players who retired before 1966.

Pre-Expansion Hall of Fame Forwards

Forward	Eligible	Inducted	Score
Gordie Howe	1972	1972	1289
Jean Beliveau	1972	1972	772
Maurice Richard	1961	1961	699
Frank Mahovlich	1981	1981	525
Ted Lindsay	1966	1966	484
Alex Delvecchio	1977	1977	459
Bernie Geoffrion	1971	1972	336
Henri Richard	1978	1979	299
George Armstrong	1974	1975	298
Andy Bathgate	1975	1978	287
Norm Ullman	1980	1982	275
Max Bentley	1957	1966	214
Dickie Moore	1971	1974	207
Ted Kennedy	1960	1966	204
Milt Schmidt	1958	1961	201
Doug Bentley	1957	1964	190
Sid Abel	1957	1969	179
Elmer Lach	1957	1966	171
Bill Mosienko	1958	1965	131
Dick Duff	1975	2006	126
Roy Conacher	1955	1998	118
Buddy O'Connor	1954	1988	114
Bob Pulford	1975	1991	103
Edgar Laprade	1958	1993	102
Bert Olmstead	1965	1985	101

Woody Dumart	1957	1992	100

When preparing the work for this era, the player I thought was going to most resist reaching a score of 100 was Edgar Laprade. He played only 500 NHL games, with thoroughly unremarkable scoring totals of 108 goals and 280 points. It took 38 years for him to be inducted into the Hall of Fame after his playing career ended, suggesting that he was not seen as deserving the honour for many years. Although Laprade is noted as one of the top defensive forwards of his era, we've already noted that the Hall of Fame does not typically recognize defensive specialists, so that doesn't help his case much. He did win a Calder Trophy and a Byng, but those are not nearly enough by themselves, the Calder in particular not being valued by the selection committee.

It was in looking at Buddy O'Connor that I finally realized what could be giving Laprade the cachet required for the Hall of Fame to notice him: the Allan Cup. The early 1940s were the last hurrah of this trophy as a major hockey championship in Canada. Today's amateur teams that compete for the cup often have ex-professional players on them. But as late as the 1940s, senior amateur hockey was still a very important source of players for the NHL. Buddy O'Connor starred in the Allan Cup playdowns in 1939, 1940 and 1941 before joining the Montreal Canadiens for the 1941–42 season. All told, he had 23 goals and 52 points in 37 Allan Cup matches. And yet he's got nothing on Laprade.

Edgar Laprade's Port Arthur Bearcats were fixtures in the Allan Cup matches every season from 1939 to 1943, before "Beaver" joined the war effort, and finally the New York Rangers. The Bearcats won the championship in 1939 and lost in the 1942 finals. But Laprade's individual efforts in these playoffs were remarkable. He played 58 Allan Cup matches in these five seasons, tallying 63 goals and 54 assists for 117 points. He was the top Allan Cup scorer in both 1939 (when he won the championship) and 1942 (when his team lost to the Ottawa RCAF Flyers, featuring players such as Milt Schmidt, Bobby Bauer, and Woody Dumart).

As such, if we accept that the Hall of Fame selection committee knew that it was the Hockey Hall of Fame, and not the NHL Hall of Fame, and therefore recognized amateur hockey excellence at a time when that level of the game still held a good deal of importance, Laprade's inclusion as an inductee makes sense. Now they'll just have to explain why they ignore nearly all international players...

Pre-Expansion Forwards Inductinator Factors

Factor	Percentage
Post-season All-Star Teams	21.3
Regular season goals scored	17.7
Stanley Cups won	9.1
Playoff points scored	9.0
Regular season points scored	8.5
Years as team captain	7.6
Hart Trophies won	6.3
High points-scoring seasons	5.9
Regular season and playoff games played	4.6
High goal-scoring seasons	2.8

Leading league in goals or points	2.6
Lady Byng Trophies won	2.5
Other	2.1

Goals and points play just as much a role in the Inductinator score for pre-expansion forwards as they do for post-expansion forwards, making up about 46% of the scores in both cases. However, in the pre-expansion era, individual honours and awards play less of a role (at least in part because there were fewer individual awards to be won), while Stanley Cup championships are somewhat more important. The number of years a forward spent as team captain is a very important factor for some players in this era, George Armstrong in particular. Armstrong's score of 298 justifies the fact he had to wait only one season before being inducted, and his 11 years as team captain contributes 145 of those points, nearly half of his total. Every forward from the pre-expansion era who was captain of his team for at least four seasons is in the Hall of Fame.

Pre-Expansion Forwards Outside the Hall

Forward	Eligible	Inducted	Score
Doug Mohns	1978	-	99
Claude Provost	1973	-	97
Sid Smith	1958	-	95
Dean Prentice	1977	-	93
Camille Henry	1973	-	76
Harry Watson	1960	-	76

Almost all of Doug Mohns' Inductinator score results from longevity. He was a very good player for a very long time, but the Hall voters clearly did not believe he was outstanding enough to earn a selection. The exclusion of Claude Provost is another indictment of the selection committee's attitude toward defensive standouts at forward. He had a career of over 1,000 NHL games and won nine Stanley Cup championships with the Habs. All other forwards of this era who won at least six Cups are in the Hall of Fame, including many of Provost's teammates. It would be understandable if Provost was just lucky, a hanger-on who benefited from having great teammates for his whole career. But there were no hangers-on who lasted that long in the Original Six era, especially on a good team. And besides that, Provost was renowned as a tenacious checker and was one of the best defensive forwards of his era. In combination with centre Henri Richard, Provost was part of a dominant checking pair, and while Richard likely deserves the lion's share of the credit, "not as good as Henri Richard" is hardly a damning statement. Provost comes extremely close to meeting the Hall of Fame's implicit standards based solely on his offensive numbers and career (team) accomplishments; surely if the selection committee actually valued defensive play that would be sufficient to nudge him over the line.

Hall of Fame Standards for Pre-War Forwards

From the pre-war era of 1929–30 to 1944–45, there are 24 forwards who have been inducted into the Hall of Fame. These were the first great forwards to play with the modern offside rules. They range from absolute legends of the game such as Howie Morenz, to players largely forgotten today such as Marty Barry and Syd Howe, who suffer from the terrible fate of having predated the Original Six era and all its concomitant media attention. Upon his retirement after the 1945–46 season, Syd Howe (no relation to Gordie) was the NHL's leading career scorer. He's almost unknown today.

Pre-War Hall of Fame Forwards			
Forward	Eligible	Inducted	Score
Howie Morenz	1945	1945	452
Bill Cook	1947	1952	432
Frank Boucher	1947	1958	419
Syl Apps	1951	1961	382
Toe Blake	1951	1966	374
Charlie Conacher	1947	1961	361
Nels Stewart	1947	1952	357
Aurel Joliat	1947	1947	347
Bill Cowley	1950	1968	346
Busher Jackson	1947	1971	306
Gordie Drillon	1947	1975	281
Bryan Hextall	1951	1969	210
Hooley Smith	1947	1972	194
Sweeney Schriner	1949	1962	180
Cooney Weiland	1947	1974	155
Syd Howe	1949	1965	150
Marty Barry	1947	1965	149
Ace Bailey	1947	1975	131
Neil Colville	1952	1967	131
Joe Primeau	1947	1963	122
Bobby Bauer	1955	1996	120
Bun Cook	1947	1995	112
Lynn Patrick	1949	1980	105
Herbie Lewis	1947	1989	100

Among this group of forwards, it was most difficult to see why Herbie Lewis would be in the Hall of Fame, while contemporaries with seemingly equal claims were not. Lewis was a very good player, known for his blistering speed and tenacious checking (not that the selection committee cares about checking forwards). But his statistics are largely unremarkable for his era, though he did win two consecutive Stanley Cup championships. But it seemed impossible to get him to a rating of 100 or more without also elevating a host of non-Hall-of-Famers to that level as well.

However, there was one notable fact that was not yet being considered. In the pre-war and pre-expansion eras, there were only seven players who led the NHL in playoff goals more than once: Maurice Richard did it five times, Gordie Howe and Bobby Hull did it three times each, and four players did it twice: Gordie Drillon, Ted Kennedy, Bernie Geoffrion, and Herbie Lewis (in 1934 and 1937). So it seems Lewis has been recognized for his outstanding playoff performance. Leading the NHL playoffs in goals scored is no mean feat, and Lewis was ultimately rewarded for it.

Pre-War Forwards Inductinator Factors

Factor	Percentage
Post-season All-Star Teams	24.5
High points-scoring seasons	14.7
Regular season goals scored	12.6
Leading team in points scored	6.8
High goal-scoring seasons	5.9
Regular season and playoff points	5.0
Stanley Cups won	4.6
Hart Trophies won	4.6
Leading league in playoff goals	4.2
Leading league in goals, assists or points	3.8
Lady Byng Trophies won	3.5
Regular season and playoff games played	3.1
Years as team captain	2.3
Other	4.4

Overall, the factors contributing to a pre-war forward's Inductinator score are very similar to the pre-expansion era. Scoring results are somewhat more important, making up 53% of the score. Individual honours contribute 32%, while both Stanley Cup championships and years as team captain are relevant, but less important than in the Original Six era.

Pre-War Forwards Outside the Hall

Forward	Eligible	Inducted	Score
Lorne Carr	1949	-	98
Johnny Gottselig	1948	-	96
Cecil Dillon	1947	-	79
Bill Thoms	1948	-	76

How does Lorne Carr not meet the Inductinator Hall-of-Fame standard of 100 points when, say, Lynn Patrick does? Carr and Patrick were exact contemporaries and, superficially, Carr seems to have the better numbers. Carr played 580 career games, scoring 204 goals and 426 points. Patrick (who has an Inductinator score of 105) played only 455 games, recording 145 goals and 335 points. Both made two All-Star Teams at a wing position, and Carr won two championships to Patrick's one. So how can Patrick's induction make sense in this light, working of course on the assumption that his family name had nothing to do with it?

There are two reasons, according to this analysis. Patrick missed two seasons to WW II. Carr remained in the NHL during the war and had by far his best offensive seasons when the league was at its weakest. Before the war, Carr never managed even 20 goals or 40 points in a single season; he then put up seasons of 27 and 36 goals, and 60 and 74 points against a depleted talent pool. The Inductinator considers Patrick's missing seasons in arriving at its ratings. But more importantly, Patrick had a huge goal-scoring year that Carr cannot match, even in a war-weakened league. Patrick scored 32 goals in 47 games in 1941–42, one third more tallies than anyone else in the circuit. This league-leading performance represented the first time an NHL player had scored 30 goals since the 1935–36 season, so it was a truly impressive performance. And it's just enough to edge him into Hall of Fame territory, leaving Carr behind.

Predicting Future Players Inductions

While the historical analysis enabled by the Inductinator is fascinating, another strength of the system is that it allows for predictions of future Hall of Fame inductions, using the post-expansion standards.

So here we will first do a position-by-position reckoning, and then make some predictions for the future. First, the goaltenders:

Future Hall of Fame Goalies

Goaltender	Eligible	Inducted	Score
Martin Brodeur	TBD	-	560
Chris Osgood	2014	-	98
Curtis Joseph	2012	-	71
Henrik Lundqvist	TBD	-	70

Among netminders, there is one absolute, no-doubt, first-ballot Hall-of-Famer in Martin Brodeur, and then no one else. Chris Osgood piled up the wins, but he has fewer career wins than Curtis Joseph, and a worse won-loss differential than Andy Moog, so there's no particular reason to suspect that he'll be honoured. There are no other active goaltenders who are close to meeting the 100-point standard. Henrik Lundqvist is the best with a score of 70 at the end of the 2013–14 NHL season, Evgeni Nabokov sits at 60, and Roberto Luongo at 57. The latter two are both in the late stages of their careers, so there's approximately a 0% chance of either of them reaching 100 before they retire. But Lundqvist has a chance. He scores only a 70 now, but if he continues to play for several more seasons, he will move up the list quite quickly.

What does Lundqvist have to do to reach an Inductinator score of 100? If we assume that his 2014–15 season will be similar to 2013–14 and he plays 60 games, wins 30 while recording 3 shutouts with a 2.40 GAA, and then plays 12 playoff games and wins half of them, his Inductinator score would jump to 95 at the end of the season. This leap represents the fact that he will reach one extremely important milestone in the calculation, when he plays his 600th NHL game. This number seems to be when a modern goaltender is considered to have a significant-enough NHL career to merit real consideration for the Hall of Fame. If we then assume that Lundqvist has a 2015–16 season identical to his hypothetical 2014–15, his score will only increase to 98, since there aren't any more milestones to meet. It would take a third season of that quality to finally nudge his Inductinator score to 100 where he will meet the Hall's implicit standards for modern goaltenders. Lundqvist is 32 years of age, so it's certainly not impossible for him to have three more solid seasons such as these, and if he managed to win a Stanley Cup or secure a All-Star Team berth in the next two seasons, that would put him over the top as well. As such, he has a pretty good chance of meeting the standards before his NHL career is up.

Now, for the defencemen:

Future Hall of Fame Defencemen

Defenceman	Eligible	Inducted	Score
Niklas Lidstrom	2015	-	621
Zdeno Chara	TBD	-	185
Chris Pronger	2015	-	164
Duncan Keith	TBD	-	82

After these three future Hall-of-Fame blueliners, and then Duncan Keith, the dropoff is steep. Sergei Zubov has the next-best score, checking in at 51. Keith has an excellent chance to climb the ladder to 100 in the next few seasons, thanks to his second Norris Trophy in 2014. If he plays five more full NHL seasons, even without any further individual awards, his career will be long enough that the honours he has already received would be enough for him to meet the Hall's implicit standards.

The meat of the Hall of Fame inductees in the foreseeable future will be the forwards:

Future Hall of Fame Forwards

Forward	Eligible	Inducted	Score
Jaromir Jagr	TBD	-	883
Alex Ovechkin	TBD	-	416
Teemu Selanne	TBD	-	383
Paul Kariya	2013	-	309
Jarome Iginla	TBD	-	307
Martin St. Louis	TBD	-	258
John LeClair	2010	-	254
Sidney Crosby	TBD	-	215
Sergei Fedorov	2015	-	207
Mark Recchi	2014	-	168
Alexander Mogilny	2009	-	164
Joe Thornton	TBD	-	143
Keith Tkachuk	2013	-	140
Dave Andreychuk	2009	-	139
Markus Naslund	2013	-	136
Pavel Datsyuk	TBD	-	123
Evgeni Malkin	TBD	-	120
Pierre Turgeon	2010	-	115
Jeremy Roenick	2012	-	107
Peter Bondra	2010	-	107
Eric Lindros	2010	-	103
Rod Brind'Amour	2013	-	83

Based on Hall of Fame standards, it seems there will only be more and more post-expansion forwards in the Hall of Fame, most of whom will earn their spot almost entirely through offence. As of the end 2013–14, the standards predict that there are two goalies, four defencemen, and 21 forwards who will eventually be honoured. Although, with so many candidates available at the same time, it's entirely possible that some forwards near the bottom of the list will ultimately be squeezed out by the numbers game.

The Inductinator does not simply spit out a list of future inductees by year, because while it does predict exactly who should be expected to make the Hall of Fame, it does not predict precisely when each player will be honoured. The lower the score, the longer the wait, but the relationship is not perfect. The Hall of Fame also seems to favour centres over wingers; a centre with a score of 140 will not wait as long as a wing with a score of 140. So with this in mind, we can make the following predictions for the next several years. These are the NHL players we can expect to see inducted into the Hockey Hall of Fame in the next three years:

2015: **Niklas Lidstrom, Chris Pronger, and Paul Kariya**.

Lidstrom and Pronger are obvious, but you might be surprised at how qualified Paul Kariya is for the honour. His scoring totals are suppressed because his prime years were mostly played in the "dead puck" era, but his five All-Star Team selections and two Lady Byngs should mean that he's a lock for the Hall.

2016: **Sergei Fedorov and John LeClair**.

Fedorov is a fairly obvious choice but LeClair might be a little controversial. He had a relatively short peak, but it was a heck of a peak. Like Kariya, his All-Star Team selections suggest that he meets the Hall's standards.

2017: **Alexander Mogilny, Dave Andreychuk, and any of Martin Brodeur, Teemu Selanne, and Jaromir Jagr who retire after the 2013–14 season**.

This is where we get into guesswork, since we don't yet have a complete list of players that will be eligible in 2017. Jagr, Brodeur, and Selanne are all absolute first-ballot locks; they just have to retire first. The Inductinator believes that Andreychuk and Mogilny's career totals will be enough to get them in, but if too many of the big three call it a career this summer, then one or both of them might be pushed back at least another year.

HAPPY TRAILS

HAPPY RETIREMENT, TEEMU

Closing Thoughts

Whatever you might think of the apparent standards that the Hockey Hall of Fame selection committee has, this analysis suggests that they are not as incongruous as is sometimes said. We can in no way assume that the factors discussed in this chapter are explicitly considered by the committee, however, they do illustrate that the selections are likely more consistent than the Hall of Fame is typically given credit for. This suggests that predictions made about future inductions using the implicit standards should be relatively accurate.

That being said, even if these standards were explicitly used by the Hall of Fame, this would not necessarily justify them. For example, as noted several times in this analysis, the selection committee does not seem to value strong defensive forwards adequately, nor do they recognize purely defensive defencemen among modern players. This is surprising given the "hockey insider" makeup of the committee, which (one would think) would recognize the value of such players better than some armchair analyst. But this does not seem to be the case.

Shot Quality

By Tom Awad

With the rise of shot-based metrics, hockey statisticians have split into two camps: those who believe that shot-based metrics give you such a large sample size that they tell you whatever you need to know, and those who believe in shot quality. Shot quality, in a nutshell, is the odds that a given shot will score. Nobody doubts that shot quality exists at an individual shot level; a rebound from the slot is easily 10 times more dangerous than a shot from the point with no screen, and everybody agrees on this. The debate is over whether, in the long run, shot quality evens out among teams, and is therefore irrelevant to take into account, or if it matters enough that it is a significant component of teams' success.

One of the problems with shot quality is that, unlike goals or shots, shot quality is not extremely well defined. Another is that statistics for it are not easily available. So the debate rages on with no end in sight.

While I'm not presumptuous enough to assume that I'll put an end to this debate, I'll at least attempt to answer a few of the more fundamental questions: Does shot quality exist? How important is it? How can I use it to improve my assessment of players and teams?

The Components of Shot Quality

There are a large number of unmeasured factors that go into the quality of a shot: the speed of the puck, whether anyone is screening the goaltender, and the exact location of the puck on the net among them. But there are four factors that we *can* measure and quantify that can be shown to have a direct impact on a shot's odds of going in. Those factors are the shot location, rebounds, power plays, and the game state. Between them, these factors can help us estimate a shot's odds of scoring, ranging from about 35–40% at the high end to 1–2% at the low end.

Shot Location

The location of the shot is by far the most important factor in determining a shot's odds of going in. It is obvious to anyone with even a passing familiarity with hockey that a closer shot has higher odds of going in. A closer shot will hit the net at higher speed, provide less time for the goaltender to react, and allow the shooter greater accuracy in where the shot will hit the goal. But how big is the impact? Pretty large, based on 2013–14 scoring data[2].

---

2 Acknowledgement: All raw data in this chapter is sourced from the *NHL*, http://www.nhl.com.

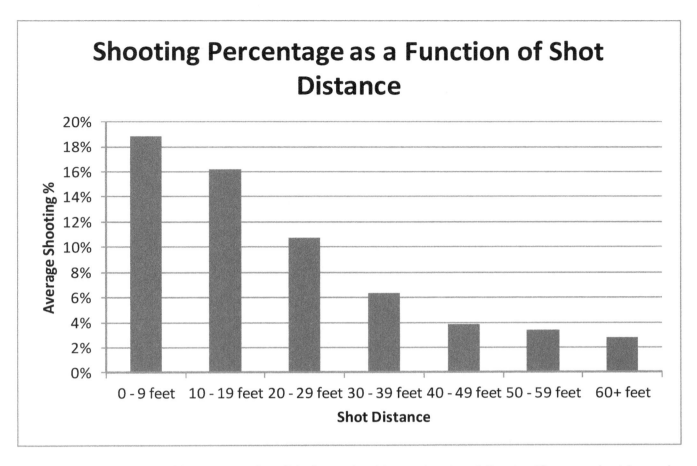

Shooting Percentage as a Function of Shot Distance

This result makes intuitive sense, but it is important to understand its significance: just based on distance alone, a shot has a seven times greater chance of going in if it is taken less than 10 feet from the net than if it was taken 60 feet or more. This is why, at an individual game level, shot totals do not necessarily give a complete picture of who dominated. The number of true scoring chances, defined approximately as shots with a 10% or more chance of scoring, is about one third of all shots, but they represent 70% of all goals.

For the last few seasons, the NHL has reported not just distance but also X/Y coordinates for their shots, and these paint an even clearer picture of the situation.

Odds of Scoring as a Function of Distance From Net

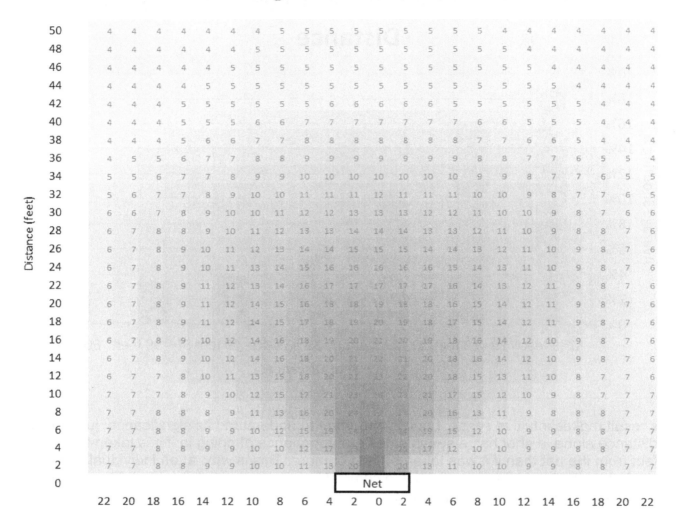

This graphic gives a very clear picture of where the best scoring areas are: directly in from of the net, at a distance of less than 30 feet. Obviously, your odds get even better if you get even closer than that. We already suspected this, of course, but the data bears it out.

Which leads to the question: if shots from 50 or more feet have such a small chance of scoring, why bother? Other than the occasional dump-in or line change, you'd think more players would hold out for a better shot, even if half the time they never get one. However, there is one good reason to take more distant shots.

Rebounds

Rebounds are defined as shots that are taken immediately after another shot, meaning the goaltender stopped the first shot but did not freeze the puck. As a general rule, rebounds are the most dangerous shots in hockey. Again, there are a number of practical reasons for this: the goaltender is often out of position from the first shot, and the rebound shooter is often planted in front of the net, waiting to pounce. Although rebounds only represent 6.7% of all shots taken in the NHL, they are responsible for 18% of goals, making them three times as dangerous as non-rebound shots.

Rebounds are also more dangerous the sooner they are taken after the original shot. The most dangerous rebounds occur within 2 seconds of the original shot, but even rebounds taken within 4 seconds of the original shot are still more dangerous than other shots.

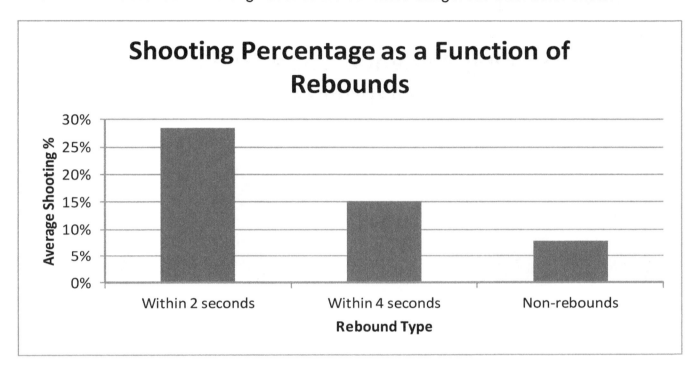

This answers our question from earlier: the real reason that teams will often bother to take a shot from a greater distance that has little chance of going in is that it offers a chance at rebounds. Just getting the puck close to the opposing net creates potential scoring opportunities. For once, the conventional hockey wisdom of "go to the net, good things will happen" turns out to be completely correct.

Unsurprisingly, the players who take the most rebounds also score a lot of goals. Last season, Zach Parise and Chris Kunitz led the NHL with 30 rebounds each, with Patrick Marleau in third place with 29. All three were among the top 25 goal-scorers in the league; more importantly, Marleau and Parise have been strong, consistent scorers throughout their careers, and even Kunitz was a 25-goal scorer before ever playing a single minute with Sidney Crosby. Another reason why these players get so many rebounds is that they all play with elite, playmaking centres: Crosby and Joe Thornton are two of the three top playmakers of the last decade (with Henrik Sedin) and Mikko Koivu is no slouch either.

Power Plays

Unlike shot distance, being on the power play doesn't represent anything directly measured about the game, it is a proxy for other things. In particular, we know that teams that are on the power play get more time to set up their shots and are more likely to have a screen in front of the goaltender. There is also the fact that players on the power play, on average, tend to be better shooters than the average NHL player, although that effect is small enough that it can be ignored. Top-six forwards, who get the most power-play time, are also those who take the most shots at even strength.

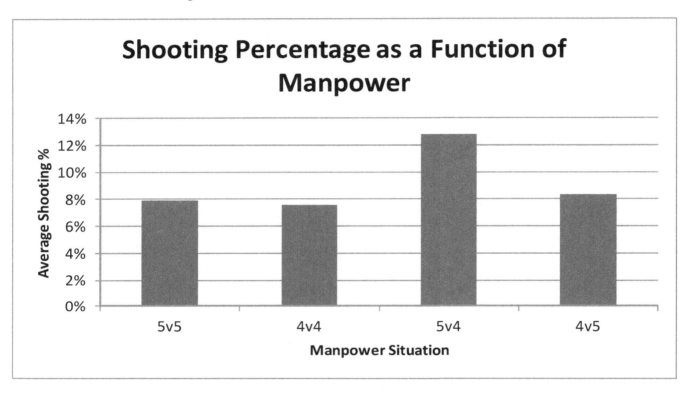

There are a few non-intuitive things that jump out from this table. The fact that power-play shots are the most likely to go in is not surprising. We expect power plays to be more productive, both from a shot volume and shooting percentage point of view, and the data bears that out. It is a little surprising to see shorthanded shots convert at a slightly higher rate than even-strength shots, but the fact is that many shorthanded shots tend to be breakaways or 2-on-1s where the shorthanded team has intercepted control of the puck. It is important to remember, however, that shorthanded shots are fairly rare. While teams at even strength average 29 shots per 60 minutes, shorthanded teams average only 8.4, so shorthanded goals are still rare (as everyone knows!). Teams on the power play, however, average 52 shots per 60 minutes. When you think about it, that's still less than 2 shots per full 2-minute power play!

Another odd artifact of the table above is that shots at 4v4 are slightly less likely than 5v5 to score. On the surface, this should be impossible: the entire point of 4v4 overtime was to create more open ice to increase the odds of scoring. The reason for this is simply that NHL teams play defensively when tied. This makes sense in regulation, since a tie at the end of 60 minutes produces an average of 1.5 points per team vs a single point for a regulation win/loss, but I don't have an explanation as to why this continues in overtime. Maybe some habits die hard?

Game Score

One of the most fascinating discoveries that emerged from the rise of shot-based analysis is that shots are not necessarily expected to be even for both teams at all points of the game. Teams that are playing from behind tend to outshoot their opponents, but these shots are of lower quality, on average, than those of the leading team.

What is interesting is that, while there is a small difference in other shot quality metrics, the score itself shows up as a factor in whether or not a shot will score. If a team has the lead, its shots are more likely to go in; if a team is trailing, its shots are less likely to go in, even taking shot distance, rebounds and power plays into account. The least dangerous shots are taken by teams when the score is tied as the incentive for teams in the NHL is to play for the tie (because of the charity point), both teams focus much more on preventing scoring opportunities than creating them.

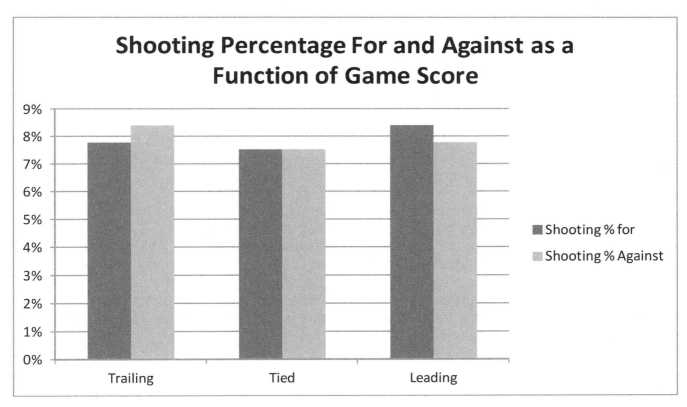

With better data, we should be able to quantify which in-game factors change based on the score: for example, do defencemen position themselves more aggressively when their team is trailing, allowing them to better join the offence but leaving themselves vulnerable to an odd-man rush? For now we will simply use the score as a proxy for how teams' play style affects how likely their shots are to score.

For a more in-depth analysis of how the game score affects team results, see the chapter on Score Effects.

Other Minor Factors

There are several other minor factors that can be measured that influence shot quality that I will simply list but not go into detail here because their impact is too small. The first is *giveaways*. Shots taken after a giveaway by the opposing team are more dangerous than regular shots, especially when the giveaway occurs in the team's defensive zone. The second is *shot type*. The type of shot taken affects its odds of going in. The most interesting of these are deflections and tip-ins, which are much *more* likely to score than regular shots, as well as wraparounds, which are much *less* likely to score than other, similar shots, especially when you take into account that wraparounds occur very close to the net.

There are also two "structural" factors that influence a shot's likelihood of scoring: the second period, where shots are more likely to go in because team benches are located further away from their net, leading to an increase in defensive breakdowns, and home ice advantage. These factors are interesting only from an academic point of view because they do not differ among teams or players. There are some players who don't play at all on the power play, but there are no players who don't play at all in the second period, or who play only on the road. Therefore, they are interesting only from a theoretical point of view, but won't help us in understanding the performance of players or teams.

The Bottom Line

There is a huge difference in quality between different shots and we now have enough data to tell the difference. Shots range in level of danger from almost harmless (1–2% chance of scoring) to extremely dangerous (30%+ chance of scoring). In the NHL, 41% of shots can be classified as "low risk", meaning they have less than a 5% chance of scoring, and these shots represent only 11% of the goals scored in the league. On the other hand, scoring chances, defined as shots with a 10% chance of scoring or more, represent 35% of the shots in the league but result in 70% of the goals. The bottom line is that there is a large and measurable difference in the quality of shots taken in the NHL.

Shot Quality for Players

Knowing the difference in quality between various shots is *interesting,* but is it *useful? What* information can be gleaned from this? How can this analysis be used to deepen our understanding or predict future performance?

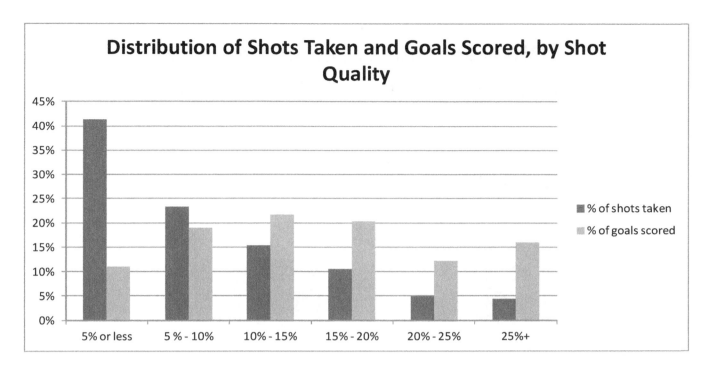

Distribution of Shots Taken and Goals Scored, by Shot Quality

First of all, *different players have different roles and those roles will affect the quality of shots they take.* To take the most obvious example, forwards and defencemen have very different positions, and this affects where they shoot from. During the 2012–13 season, at 5v5, forwards took 24,047 shots and scored 2,225 goals, for a total shooting percentage of 9.3%. Defencemen, meanwhile, took 8,386 shots and scored only 345 goals, a rate of only 4.1%. This doesn't mean that forwards are better shots than defencemen, rather, it reflects the fact that while the forwards shot from an average distance of 29 feet from the net, defencemen took their shots from an average distance of 50 feet.

Once we factor this in, we realize that, in fact, both forwards and defencemen converted their shots into goals at pretty much the expected rate.

Power Play Positions

This role differential becomes even more pronounced when we look at players' results on the power play, where teams have a defined setup that they try to execute regularly. Some players are known for simply setting up shop in front of the net, screening the goaltender, and pouncing on rebounds. In the current NHL, one player who specializes in this role is Wayne Simmonds. In 2013–14, Simmonds played 246 minutes at 5v4 and took 51 shots. However, 46 of those shots were taken less than 20 feet away from the net, and 12 of them were rebounds, which is what allowed Simmonds to score 12 power-play goals, giving him a power-play shooting percentage of 24%.

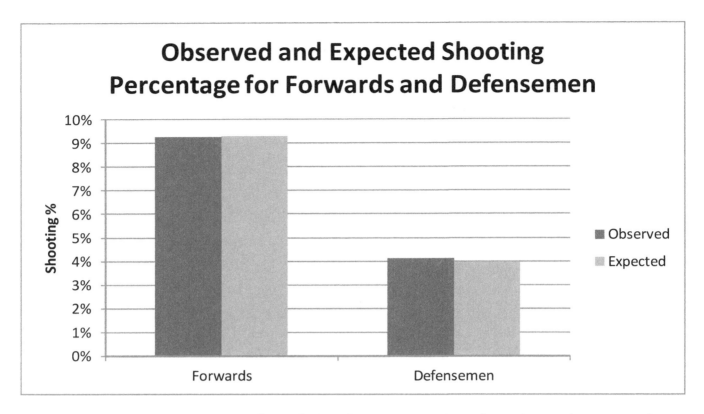

Observed and Expected Shooting Percentage for Forwards and Defensemen

At the other end of the spectrum, Brad Richards, a centre, plays the point on the power play for the New York Rangers, and thus almost all of his shots were from 40 feet away from the net or more. That's why he scored only a single goal at 5v4 in 56 shots (his two other goals were scored at 5v3).

Shot Quality for Teams

And so, we come to the final question, the question you've all been waiting for: is shot quality a major factor for teams' success? And the answer is…

A little bit, but not really.

Wait a minute! That's a cop-out!

OK, OK, let me explain.

First of all, differences in observed shot quality do not account for much of each team's overall results. In 2013–14, at 5v5, shot quality accounted for only 4.5% of teams' overall variance in results. By contrast, shot differential accounted for 39.7% of the overall variance, while shooting percentage differential (PDO) accounted for 55.8% of total results. In other words, shot differential accounted for less than one-twentieth of team's overall results. This is important, because every season some teams get outshot yet keep on winning, and their supporters often like to cite that they are "only allowing low quality scoring chances" or "waiting for good opportunities to shoot". The 2013–14 Colorado Avalanche are a good example of this. The Avalanche finished third in the league, surprising everybody (including themselves!), while getting outshot by 258 shots. Yet shot quality was not the reason, in fact, their shot quality was slightly *below* average. They were just running hot, much the same way they were running cold in 2012–13 when they finished 29th in the standings. The bottom line is that when teams get outshot but still win, shot quality is almost never the reason, usually, these teams get good goaltending, good shooting, or a massive dose of luck, and most likely some combination of all three.

Second of all, shot quality correlates pretty poorly with overall success. Here is a table of all 30 NHL teams, ranked by goal differential at 5v5 for the 2013–14 season. I have split their goal differential into the portion attributable to shot differential (Sh Diff) the portion attributable to shot quality (Sh Qual), and the portion attributable to shooting percentage differential (Sh %).

Team Goal Differential by Source, 2013–14

Team	Sh Diff	Sh Qual	Sh %	Total
Boston Bruins	18	1	44	62
Anaheim Ducks	11	6	35	52
Chicago Blackhawks	33	-2	8	39
St_ Louis Blues	15	4	20	38
Los Angeles Kings	28	-2	-2	24
San Jose Sharks	26	15	-20	22
Tampa Bay Lightning	10	0	12	22
Colorado Avalanche	-16	-5	38	17
Minnesota Wild	-1	6	6	11
Pittsburgh Penguins	5	3	4	11
Columbus Blue Jackets	-2	3	8	9
New York Rangers	18	-3	-7	7
Dallas Stars	5	-4	7	7
Phoenix Coyotes	-3	-11	18	5
Detroit Red Wings	1	-5	8	3
Vancouver Canucks	4	-5	0	-2
Philadelphia Flyers	-11	0	5	-6
Ottawa Senators	-1	-13	2	-11
Carolina Hurricanes	-3	-1	-9	-13
Winnipeg Jets	1	-1	-13	-13
Montreal Canadiens	-13	-2	2	-13
Toronto Maple Leafs	-38	6	17	-15
New Jersey Devils	8	9	-33	-16
Washington Capitals	-17	5	-7	-19
Florida Panthers	0	0	-27	-27
New York Islanders	-1	3	-30	-28
Calgary Flames	-9	-6	-17	-32
Nashville Predators	0	2	-34	-33

Edmonton Oilers	-28	-5	-9	-42
Buffalo Sabres	-37	2	-24	-59

As you can see, the teams that succeed tend to excel in shot differential and in percentages, not in shot quality. The top 5 teams averaged +21 in shot differential, +21 in shooting percentage differential, and only *+1* in shot quality. The same thing was true at the other end, where 7 of the 9 worst teams actually had a positive shot quality differential! Why is this?

In a nutshell, winning through superior shot quality does not seem to be an effective strategy in today's NHL. The best teams focus on possession, get a high volume of low quality shots on nets, and pounce on a defensive breakdown or a lucky bounce. And while they obviously try to prevent opposing scoring chances, in practice, the best way to do so is to deny them the puck in the first place.

One last thing to keep in mind is that the best players don't need to take the best shots. If you have the release of a Steven Stamkos, you don't need to wait until you're 15 feet from the net. Just shoot! Alexander Ovechkin is the perfect example of this type of player. Ovechkin has led the league in shots in 8 of his 9 seasons; this season, he had 26% more shots than the #2 player, Patrick Sharp. Ovechkin doesn't take many high-quality shots. You don't get that many shots by being picky. Ovechkin fires whenever he can, knowing that his shot is good enough that a fair number of them will turn into goals.

What About the Bruins?

Some teams do win on percentages, but that is mostly because of their superior shooting and goaltending skills, not because of shot quality. Over the last few years, the Boston Bruins have been the best example of this. From 2010–11 to 2013–14, the Bruins outshot their opponents by 598 shots at even strength; at an average shooting percentage of 8%, that would have translated to a 48-goal differential. Yet the Bruins have outscored their opponents by 177 goals! None of this showed up in the shot quality statistics; the average quality of chances by the Bruins and their opponents was the same. A difference of this magnitude cannot occur through luck alone. The Bruins clearly benefited from two elite goaltenders during this period, Tim Thomas and Tuukka Rask, and excellent finishing ability from Milan Lucic, Brad Marchand, David Krejci, and Patrice Bergeron.

Note that the Bruins were good at keeping down both the amount *and* the average quality of shots against when killing penalties, justifying their reputation as an elite defensive team. While the average NHL team allowed 50.5 shots against per 60 minutes, and these shots had an average shot quality of 12.0%, the Bruins allowed 49 shots per 60 minutes, and these shots only had an average shot quality of 11.6%.

The Persistence of Shot Quality

While shot quality is not a major element of teams' performance, it is at least a measurable one. Because it is a shot-based statistic rather than a goal-based statistic, it has a lot of data, and this means it is easier to separate the signal from the noise. The year-to-year persistence of shot quality at even strength is 0.44[3], which makes it one of the more stable team statistics.

Closing Thoughts

Shot quality remains one of the least understood areas of hockey research. Until there are standardized statistics to measure it, it will remain an area where data will be nebulous and people will not easily be able to compare notes. However, the baselines have been established. We know that location is the most important factor in determining a shot's odds of scoring, and we know that rebounds are the most dangerous shots as well as being a major justification for distant shots. We can also see that differences in shot quality explain the large and repeated differences between the shooting percentages of different players.

However, despite all this, we have come to the conclusion that shot quality, despite being a very real and measurable phenomenon, is *not* typically a major cause for teams' success or lack of it. Sabres fans looking to blame shot quality for their team's woes will have to look elsewhere.

---

3   Rob Vollman, "Hockey Abstract", 2013, Chapter 1, pg 4–5.

What Are Score Effects?

By Tom Awad

A few years ago, hockey analysts realized the importance of shot differential. In the years that have passed, shot differential has become one of the go-to metrics for quantifying the true talent and future success of both players and teams.

However, whenever shot differential is analyzed, it is often measured only when the score is "close", typically defined as when the score is tied or when there is a difference of only a single goal in the first two periods. The reason for this is fundamental: as soon as people started looking at shot differential, they realized that both shot differential and shooting percentage varied as a function of the score. The first references I can find to this effect come from Philip Myrland[4] and Tyler Dellow[5] way back in 2009. Teams that are trailing tend to outshoot their opponents, but their shots tended to go in less often. This effect was documented and confirmed extensively, by Gabriel Desjardins[6], myself[7], and others.

In this chapter, I will simply resume the known state of the art on this subject. My objective is to get more detailed data on how the score effect varies by score and by period as well as to better quantify its size.

The Big Picture

To get a truly accurate picture of how teams perform in different score situations, I have accumulated the data from the last three NHL seasons (2011–12, 2012–13 and 2013–14)[8]. This allows us to get a respectable sample size even on relatively rare situations, such as teams being down by 2+ goals in the first period. I have split all situations into five game states: when teams are down by 2+ goals, down by 1 goal, tied, up by 1 goal and up by 2+ goals. Obviously, because I am looking at the entire NHL, the down by 1/up by 1 and down by 2+/up by 2+ statistics will simply be mirror images of each other.

First of all, let's look at the overall picture, including the number of seconds per game (s/game), the goals (G), shots (S) and penalty minutes (PIM) for and against (F and A), per 60 minutes of play (/60), as well as the shooting (Sh%) and save (Sv%) percentages.

4   Phil Myrland, "Playing to the Score", *Brodeur is a Fraud*, January 5, 2009, Web, http://brodeurisafraud.blogspot.ca/2009/01/playing-to-score.html.
5   Tyler Dellow, "SF/SA Ratios in Different Goal States", *MC79 Hockey*, March 31, 2009, Web, http://www.mc79hockey.com/2009/03/sfsa-ratios-in-different-goal-states/.
6   Gabriel Desjardins, "Corsi and Score Effects", *Arctic Ice Hockey*, April 13, 2010, Web, http://www.arcticicehockey.com/2010/4/13/1416623/corsi-and-score-effects.
7   Tom Awad, "Shooting to the Score", *Hockey Prospectus*, September 13, 2009, Web, http://www.hockeyprospectus.com/puck/article.php?articleid=268.
8   Acknowledgement: All raw data is from *NHL* game files. http://www.nhl.com.

Team Results by Score, 5v5, 2011–12 to 2013–14

	s/game	GF/60	GA/60	SF/60	SA/60	PIMF/60	PIMA/60	Sh%	Sv%
Down by 2+	756	2.38	2.22	31.5	25.4	3.28	3.68	7.54	8.73
Down by 1	1032	2.36	2.24	30.6	27.2	3.12	3.40	7.70	8.26
Tied	2126	2.20	2.20	29.2	29.2	2.86	2.86	7.52	7.52
Up by 1	1032	2.24	2.36	27.2	30.6	3.40	3.11	8.26	7.70
Up by 2+	756	2.22	2.38	25.4	31.5	3.68	3.28	8.73	7.54

This table simply restates what I said above: teams that are trailing by 2+ goals outshoot their opponents by over 6 shots per 60 minutes. Put another way, they get about 55% of the overall shots, as good as the most dominant teams in the NHL. The Chicago Blackhawks and Los Angeles Kings, the two best teams in shot differential last season, got about 55.6% of all even-strength shots.

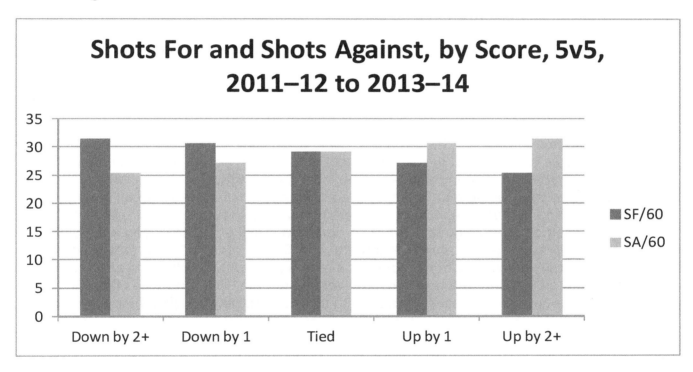

However, this shot dominance was counterbalanced by an almost equivalent drop in shooting percentage. While those teams did score 2.38 goals per 60 minutes, highest of all the game score situations, it wasn't as good as their shot totals would imply. Their shooting percentage was just 7.54%, lower than the overall even-strength shooting percentage of 7.82%, and much lower than the numbers achieved at other score levels. In fact, shooting percentage seems to drop in proportion to how far you are behind, with the large exception of tied scores, which we will get back to later. The bottom line is that teams that are trailing outshoot, teams that are leading get outshot, but the difference in the final goal numbers is not as large as one would assume from the shot differential.

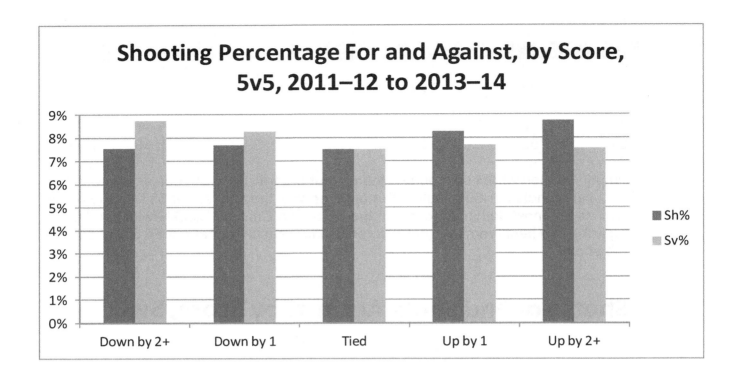

Shooting Percentage For and Against, by Score, 5v5, 2011–12 to 2013–14

It is important to note that teams trailing by 2+ goals are outscoring their opponents. This is significant since we assume that these teams are, on average, less skilled than their opponents, since they are nursing a two-goal deficit to begin with. Score effects have often been explained as the leading team going into a "defensive shell": they trade off a higher volume of shots against for lower quality scoring chances against, which is why the shooting percentage of their opponents goes down. The defensive shell effect has been analyzed on many occasions, including by Gabriel Desjardins[9] and David Johnson[10]. The theory behind the "defensive shell" is sound: when leading, it is reasonable to trade off goals against for goals for as long as you can reduce the overall volume of both. The problem is that, in practice, *this is not what we observe*. Teams with the lead are not reducing the number of goals being scored; in fact, they are allowing more goals than when they are tied or trailing! So the driving force must be coming from the opposite side, it is trailing teams that change their style of play when playing from behind, playing more aggressively and accepting the fact that they may be giving up more dangerous scoring opportunities.

To be clear, I'm not saying that teams in the lead don't play more defensively, they undoubtedly do, and it is logical for them to do so. I'm saying that the increased aggressiveness of trailing teams is even greater than the increased defensiveness of leading teams, resulting in an overall increase in goals scored when the score is not tied.

This is consistent with the fact that, in the NHL's point system, it is the trailing team that has the greater incentive. For a team in the lead, the difference between a regulation win and a

9   Gabriel Desjardins, "How Does the Defensive Shell Work?", *Arctic Ice Hockey*, March 14, 2011, Web, http://www.arcticicehockey.com/2011/3/14/2041124/how-does-the-defensive-shell-work.
10 David Johnson, "The theory behind the defensive shell game", *Hockey Analysis*, May 21, 2013, Web, http://hockeyanalysis.com/2013/05/21/the-theory-behind-the-defensive-shell-game/.

regulation tie is 2 points vs an expected 1.5 points, a difference of 0.5 points, since after a regulation tie you have a 50% chance of winning in overtime or in the shootout. However, for the trailing team, the difference between a regulation loss and a tie is 1.5 points; this is a huge incentive to play for the tie.

The other effect we can see from this table is that scoring is at its lowest when teams are tied. Again, this is consistent with the NHL's incentive system. If preserving the status quo gives you an average of 1.5 points, while a goal by either team gives you an average of 1 point, which will you play for? Ironically, while the NHL has officially abolished ties, its charity point system has created a strong, perverse incentive for teams to play for the tie during regulation.

Results by Period

Looking at the aggregate numbers tells us a lot, but it would be even more informative to look at the results by period. For example, we would not expect teams trailing by one goal in the first period to play in the same way as teams trailing by one goal in the third period.

First of all, to put these numbers in context, I will give overall numbers for the three periods:

Team Results by Period, 2011–12 to 2013–14

	s/game	GF/60	GA/60	SF/60	SA/60	PIMF/60	PIMA/60	Sh%	Sv%
First Period	1947	2.10	2.10	28.6	28.6	3.12	3.12	7.36	7.36
Second Period	1870	2.50	2.50	30.3	30.3	3.61	3.61	8.24	8.24
Third period	1886	2.19	2.19	27.8	27.8	2.79	2.79	7.86	7.86

This may come as a surprise to some of our readers, but there are 15% more goals scored per even-strength minute during the second period than during the first or third. While I have no hard data on why this is, the logical explanation to me is the position of the player benches versus the goaltender during the second period. Since the sides of the ice are swapped, the benches are further away from their own defensive zone, which makes line changes more precarious. There are more shots taken and the shots are more dangerous, so there are more goals scored.

The rate of penalties per period is also informative. In the second period, there are more penalties taken, another sign of potential defensive breakdowns. And, as per the conventional wisdom, the referees put away their whistles in the third, calling 17% fewer penalties than during the two previous periods.

Goals and PIM per Period, 5v5, 2011–12 to 2013–14

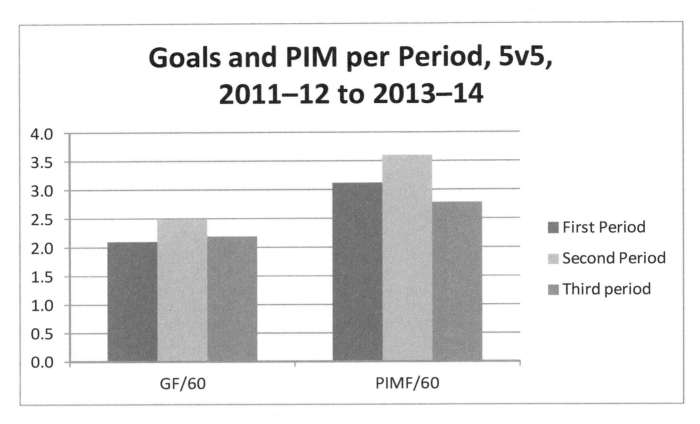

Legend:
- First Period
- Second Period
- Third period

Now that we have looked at the overall results per period, we are ready to see how the score affects team play differently per period.

Team Results by Score, First Period, 2011–12 to 2013–14

	s/game	GF/60	GA/60	SF/60	SA/60	PIMF/60	PIMA/60	Sh%	Sv%
Down by 2+	82	2.21	2.10	29.1	25.1	3.58	4.11	7.62	8.37
Down by 1	314	2.06	2.17	29.1	27.0	3.48	3.52	7.10	8.03
Tied	1155	2.09	2.09	29.1	29.1	2.81	2.81	7.18	7.18
Up by 1	314	2.17	2.06	27.0	29.1	3.52	3.48	8.03	7.10
Up by 2+	82	2.10	2.21	25.1	29.1	4.11	3.58	8.37	7.62

As we would expect, during the first period the score is tied almost 60% of the time. But even as of the first period, score effects are starting to show up: teams trailing by 1 goal are outshooting their opponents by 2 shots per 60 minutes, and teams trailing by 2+ goals are outshooting their opponents by 4 shots per 60 minutes. In both cases their shooting percentage is being significantly affected.

Team Results by Score, Second Period, 2011–12 to 2013–14

	s/game	GF/60	GA/60	SF/60	SA/60	PIMF/60	PIMA/60	Sh%	Sv%
Down by 2+	281	2.59	2.32	32.1	27.7	3.45	4.07	8.06	8.38
Down by 1	387	2.57	2.48	31.5	29.5	3.43	3.71	8.16	8.40
Tied	533	2.51	2.51	30.6	30.6	3.50	3.50	8.22	8.22
Up by 1	387	2.48	2.57	29.5	31.5	3.71	3.43	8.40	8.16
Up by 2+	281	2.32	2.59	27.7	32.1	4.07	3.45	8.38	8.06

The numbers for the second period are extremely similar to those for the first, except that shot totals and shooting percentages have gone up across the board.

Team Results by Score, Third Period, 2011–12 to 2013–14

	s/game	GF/60	GA/60	SF/60	SA/60	PIMF/60	PIMA/60	Sh%	Sv%
Down by 2+	393	2.26	2.17	31.6	23.8	3.09	3.32	7.15	9.11
Down by 1	330	2.39	2.04	31.1	24.5	2.39	2.93	7.67	8.30
Tied	439	2.10	2.10	28.0	28.0	2.23	2.23	7.50	7.50
Up by 1	330	2.04	2.39	24.5	31.1	2.93	2.39	8.30	7.67
Up by 2+	393	2.17	2.26	23.8	31.6	3.32	3.09	9.11	7.15

The third period is where we see the most massive score effects, and we now understand why the third period is typically excluded from "Corsi close" or "Fenwick close" numbers unless the score is tied. Teams down by a goal are outshooting their opponents by 6.5 shots per 60 minutes, and those down by 2 or more are outshooting them by almost 8! What is impressive is that it seems to be working: teams down by 1 scored 2.39 goals per 60 minutes, a higher rate than anything seen in the first or third period. As a reminder, I have excluded all empty-net, pulled goalie, or other irregular manpower situations from the data. These are truly 5v5, 2-goalie situations.

It is possible that we have a player-calibre bias here: when a team is down by 1 goal in the third period, it is likely that they will shorten their bench and play only their most talented scorers. We may simply be looking at the effect of better scorers being on the ice more often, but I would need more detailed data than what I have to establish this.

Penalties

A major observation from the tables above is that teams that are in the lead get called for more penalties than teams that are trailing. This was first pointed out by JLikens[11] in 2010 and, since his conclusions were both sound and straightforward, I will simply restate them here: this effect seems to be due more to referee bias than anything else.

In particular, look at the third period numbers: referees seem extremely hesitant to call penalties on teams that are trailing by 1 or on tied teams. In particular, teams that are trailing by 1 have 0.54 more penalty minutes called on their opponents, meaning their opponents get 5 minors for every 4 they get. This is only a difference of 0.05 goals per 60 minutes, but it means that one team out of 12 gets an extra two-minute power play in the third period, and (with a 20% success rate) one team out of 60 gets to tie the game purely out of officiating bias. The skew does not exist to the same extent for teams trailing by 2+ goals, indicating that it is probably more reflective of refereeing bias than of possession.

---

11 Tore Purdy (Jlikens), "Score Effects and Minor Penalties", *Objective NHL*, November 3, 2010, Web, http://objectivenhl.blogspot.ca/2010/11/score-effects-and-minor-penalties.html.

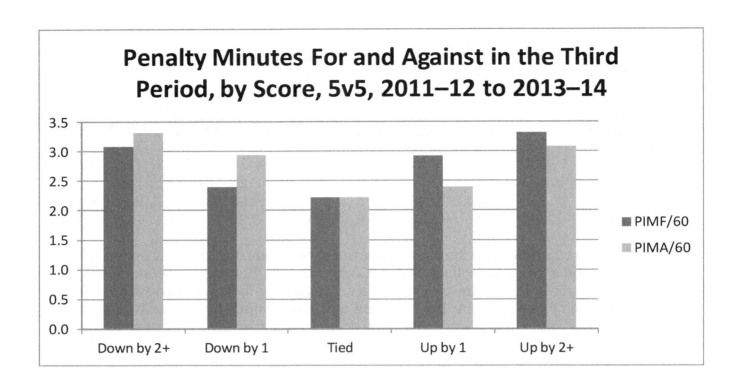

Penalty Minutes For and Against in the Third Period, by Score, 5v5, 2011–12 to 2013–14

Effect on Player Statistics

Since Corsi and Fenwick are such popular and important ways of judging players, anything that would corrupt those measures is important to factor in. Obviously, the most important adjustment is to always use "Corsi close" or "Fenwick close" when looking at shot metrics. Shot differential during the third period, unless the score is tied, is simply not representative of how well a player can help control the flow of play.

However, even these measures can be biased. Last year, at 5v5 during the first two periods, the Boston Bruins spent about 8 hours trailing, 21 hours tied and 16 hours leading (including, impressively, 6 hours with a 2+ goal lead!). This means that even their "shot differential close" was affected by -0.7 shots per 60 minutes, a fairly significant bias when the best team in the league outshoots their opponents by about 5 shots per 60 minutes. Note that this also explains a small sliver of why the Bruins' percentages were so good last season.

We could use only Corsi or Fenwick with the score tied, but a much better solution is to use score-adjusted Fenwick. Eric Tulsky[12] defined one way of adjusting for score effects, by comparing a team's performance in each of the situations to the league average. Delving into this too deeply would be outside of the scope of this chapter, but I would simply like to state that for both sample size and accuracy reasons, I believe that Tulsky's "score-adjusted Fenwick" is superior to "Fenwick close" for both player and team evaluation, although the second is obviously easier to calculate.

12 Eric Tulsky, "Adjusting for Score Effects to Improve Our Predictions", *Broad Street Hockey*, January 23, 2012, Web, http://www.broadstreethockey.com/2012/1/23/2722089/score-adjusted-fenwick.

Closing Thoughts

The main takeaways from this analysis are:

1. Teams play to the score. Teams playing from behind take more shots and they are less likely to score. Teams playing with the lead take fewer shots and they are more likely to score. Generally speaking, trailing teams play aggressively, take more shots and risk defensive breakdowns, while leading teams play conservatively but will pounce on the opportunities they do get.
2. When the score is tied, both teams play extremely defensively; in particular, shooting percentages are low for both teams. This is logical because of the incentives of the NHL's point system.
3. Score effects become more pronounced in the third period. Teams one goal down go from outshooting their opponents by 2 shots per 60 minutes to 6.5 shots per 60 minutes. Teams two goals down go from outshooting their opponents by 4 shots per 60 minutes to 8 shots per 60 minutes. Conversely, teams down by 2+ goals only score on 7.1% of their shots while teams up by 2+ goals score on 9.1% of their shots.
4. Referees also play to the score! Especially in the third period, they are hesitant to call penalties on teams when the score is tied or when a team is trailing by a single goal.
5. Teams trailing by a single goal in the third period actually score at a fairly high rate. It is open for further analysis to determine if this is because they ice better players at the end of games or if there are other factors at work.

What Makes Good Players Good? Part 1: Forwards

By Tom Awad

At its very core, the purpose of sports statistics is to determine who is good, who is better than whom, and by how much. In hockey, when it comes to teams, we are starting to have a pretty good idea of what makes for sustainable success in the NHL. Puck possession is a strong and persistent measure of a dominant team. Shooting percentage and goaltending are more transient, but have a talent component that can be measured over a long enough period of time.

However, when it comes to players, we are still somewhat in the stone age. For the longest time, players were measured primarily by goals and assists, which are crude, primitive measures that only captured the rawest offensive contributions, didn't account for role, teammates or position, and completely ignored defensive play. The next traditional statistic, plus-minus, is perfect in theory but useless in practice. While plus-minus reflects the fundamental information you want to know about a player (does he contribute to outscoring the opposition?), it is even more influenced by outside factors, like teammates and goaltending, and is too noisy to be of much use. Unlike baseball, much of which can be broken down into individual plays and analyzed in isolation, hockey is a fluid sport and statistics cannot easily capture the quality of players independently of the 11 other players on the ice.

In recent years, there has been an improvement in the quality of individual statistics. Goals Versus Threshold (GVT) wrapped up all traditional stats into a single, easy-to-use value, but it still has many of the limitations of traditional stats; it is better suited for broad strokes than precise analysis. Shot-based metrics, such as Corsi and Fenwick, and contextual statistics like zone starts and quality of competition, have given us a better idea of which players play how, and why they are getting the results they are. However, I want to go further. The biggest enemy of any statistical analysis is sample size: a single player gets about 25 hours of ice time over a single season and is on the ice for about 100 goals for each team, fewer than that at even strength. If there are differences in how well players are capable of converting shots into goals, they will not be clear over even an entire season. To clearly see talent differences, we want to aggregate all replacement level players together, all average players together, and all elite players together to clearly see, as my title states, "What makes good players good?"

Luckily, the sport of hockey has provided us with a very good proxy for how "good" a player is: ice time. Since better players should naturally get more ice time, by ranking players by ice time, we should get a good idea of the average statistics of first line players, second line players, and so on. Obviously, there may be a few individual cases where a player's ice time didn't correspond precisely to his talent level, for reasons of habit, injury, coach favoritism, or others. However, as a general rule, we expect that coaches will play their best players the most, and a cursory glance at the NHL's ice time leader list confirms this impression.

I will perform the analysis for forwards first, then I will do the same for defencemen and, finally, goaltenders.

2013–14 Season Results

To group forwards, I sorted them by ice time per game for the 2013–14 season. I then summed the players to divide them into four bins of equal ice time, so that "Tier 1" players represented 25% of the total ice time by forwards, with the same for Tier 2, Tier 3, and Tier 4. I then summed the results of what happened while they were on the ice.

Let's start with the raw results. In this and the chapter's other tables, TOI/GP refers to time on ice per game, while the other statistics are calculated per 60 minutes of play (e.g., GF/60). GF, GA and GD refer to the actual Goals For, Against and the Differential, while EGF, EGA and EGD refer to the expected results, and SF, SA and SD refer to shots. All data throughout this piece is sourced from NHL's official data[13].

Even-Strength Results by Tier, 2013–14

	TOI/GP	GF/60	GA/60	GD/60	EGF/60	EGA/60	EGD/60	SF/60	SA/60	SD/60
Tier 1	867	2.72	2.33	0.39	2.47	2.30	0.17	31.32	29.59	1.73
Tier 2	801	2.46	2.28	0.18	2.36	2.29	0.07	30.19	29.53	0.66
Tier 3	731	2.18	2.30	-0.11	2.20	2.23	-0.03	28.82	29.09	-0.26
Tier 4	567	1.73	2.10	-0.37	1.94	2.10	-0.16	26.28	27.87	-1.58

What does this table tell us? Obviously, Tier 1 players played more ice time per game, but the difference was not huge: only 66 seconds per game between Tier 1 and Tier 2, and another 70 seconds down to Tier 3. This is only even-strength ice time, the difference in special teams ice time will be more pronounced, as we will see below. We do see that the Tier 1 players obtained significantly better results than their brethren, a goal differential of 0.39 per 60 minutes of ice time. This means that, over the course of an 82-game season, a team obtaining the results of Tier 1 forwards would have a goal differential of 0.39 * 82 = +32 goals, which is good but not spectacular. By comparison, the Boston Bruins outscored their opponents by 87 goals. Remember that these Tier 1 players are taken from all teams in the league, so by definition there is almost no difference in goaltending.

More interesting is what led to this goal differential. We see that Tier 1 players had an average shot differential of +1.73 shots per 60 minutes. Obviously, we would expect this differential to be positive, but at an average even-strength shooting percentage of 8%, a difference of 1.73 shots per 60 minutes translates to 1.73 times 8% = 0.14 goals per 60 minutes. Tier 1 players outscored their opponents by 0.39 goals per 60 minutes. Where did the rest come from?

A minuscule amount came from shot quality. If we look at expected goal differential, we see that, weighing for shot quality, the expected goal differential is 0.17. That means that the rest of the difference, 0.22 goals per 60 minutes, comes from shooting percentage for and against. What did the shooting percentage of the various tiers of players look like?

---

13 Acknowledgement: All raw data for this chapter is from NHL.com, http://www.nhl.com.

Shooting Percentages, For and Against, 2013–14

	SF%	SA%
Tier 1	8.67	7.78
Tier 2	8.16	7.71
Tier 3	7.58	7.90
Tier 4	6.58	7.53

Well that's interesting! Tier 1 players shot a whole 2.1% better than Tier 4 players; put another way, their shots were 32% more likely to score. Given that each group took over 40,000 shots, that means that the 2.1% difference in shooting percentage of the Tier 1 players amounted to 40,000 times 2.1% = 840 extra goals. Clearly, while shooting percentages in the long term regress to the mean, they do not regress to the same mean for everybody.

We can see in the following chart what was the source of the goal differential for each tier of players. What jumps out from the chart is that for each tier, shot differential and shooting percentage differential are about equally responsible for players' results, and shot quality differential has a negligible role. In other words, when we try to understand why top forwards in the NHL are able to outscore other forwards, slightly less than half of it is due to outshooting them (which implies greater puck possession) and slightly more than half of it is due to better finishing ability. When we judge elite players by their Corsi results, we are neglecting the source of over half their dominance.

5v5 Source of Goal Differential, by Tier, 2013–14

	Shot Differential	Shot Quality Differential	Shooting % Differential
Tier 1	0.14	0.03	0.22
Tier 2	0.05	0.02	0.11
Tier 3	-0.02	-0.01	-0.08
Tier 4	-0.13	-0.03	-0.21

2012–13 Season Results

The next obvious question is: are these results typical or do we see similar results in other years? Obviously, our large sample size gives us confidence that our results should be repeatable from year to year, but there's nothing like checking, right? I ran the same analysis for the 2012–13 season. The results are:

Even-Strength Player Results by Tier, 2012–13

	TOI/GP	GF/60	GA/60	GD/60	EGF/60	EGA/60	EGD/60	SF/60	SA/60	SD/60
Tier 1	874	2.68	2.35	0.34	2.47	2.32	0.16	31.59	28.85	2.75
Tier 2	804	2.46	2.31	0.15	2.37	2.24	0.13	30.12	28.44	1.68
Tier 3	730	2.18	2.30	-0.12	2.19	2.28	-0.09	27.44	28.76	-1.32
Tier 4	565	1.77	2.07	-0.30	2.00	2.15	-0.15	25.20	27.63	-2.42

The results for the 2012–13 season are very similar to those for the 2013–14 season, as expected. Remember that the 2012–13 season was an abbreviated 48-game season, so the numbers are slightly more noisy.

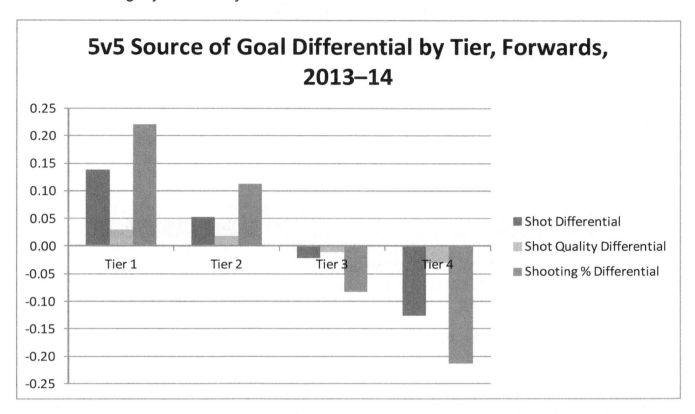

5v5 Source of Goal Differential by Tier, Forwards, 2013–14

- Shot Differential
- Shot Quality Differential
- Shooting % Differential

The shooting percentages also tell a similar story. Note that, this year, the shooting percentages against were higher for the higher tiers. Later, we will explore why, as a general rule, shooting percentages against are higher for upper tier players.

Shooting Percentages, For and Against, 2012–13

	SF%	SA%
Tier 1	8.49%	8.13%
Tier 2	8.16%	8.12%
Tier 3	7.93%	7.99%
Tier 4	7.01%	7.48%

On the whole, this means that for 2012–13, shooting percentage differential was as important as shot differential to Tier 1 players goal differential.

Three-Season Results

For completeness' sake, I looked up the numbers for 2011–12 as well to see what the values averaged out to:

Shooting Percentages, For and Against, 2011–12

	SF%	SA%
Tier 1	8.61%	8.15%
Tier 2	8.51%	7.86%
Tier 3	7.62%	7.81%
Tier 4	6.36%	7.44%

For those of my readers who really want to conquer sample size, I summed the results from the three seasons together, and instead of averaging them out per 60 minutes I am showing totals. This gives a better impression of how much data I'm using. The resulting table is the following:

Even-Strength Player Results by Tier, Forwards, 2011–12 to 2013–14

	GF	GA	GD	EGF	EGA	EGD	SF	SA	SD
Tier 1	9765	8549	1216	8946	8385	561	112882	106378	6504
Tier 2	9257	8505	752	8758	8394	364	111306	108236	3070
Tier 3	8312	8655	-343	8371	8531	-160	108491	109739	-1248
Tier 4	6747	8247	-1500	7666	8341	-674	102890	110220	-7330

Tier 1 players outshot their opponents by 6504 shots, and outscored them by 1216 goals. With an average even-strength shooting percentage of 8.23% over the three seasons, we would have expected them to outscore them by 6504 * 8.23% = 535 goals. Therefore, they generated an additional 681 goals through a combination of shot quality and shooting percentage differential. We can see from the above table that the expected goal differential for Tier 1, even taking into account shot quality, was just 561 goals. So the remaining 655 goals come from shooting percentage differential. This confirms my conclusion from above: Tier 1 players outscore the opposition through a combination of puck possession (shot differential) and finishing ability, with finishing ability accounting for slightly more than half of their overall results. The opposite is true of Tier 4 forwards, whose lack of finishing ability is the most important reason they get outscored.

5v5 Source of Goal Differential, by Tier, 2011–12 to 2013–14

	Shot Differential	Shot Quality Differential	Shooting % Differential
Tier 1	535	26	655
Tier 2	253	111	388
Tier 3	-103	-58	-183
Tier 4	-603	-71	-826

Factors Affecting Player Results

So far, we have seen the raw results of players and observed that higher tier players produce better outcomes when they are on the ice. But we also know that different types of players play in different situations, which affects their results in a major way. So the next question is: do Tier 1 players get easier or harder tasks than Tier 2, 3, and 4 players?

To answer this question, we will use Delta (see the Q&A chapter). One of the benefits of Delta is that all "circumstantial" statistics, zone starts, quality of competition and quality of teammates, can be expressed in goals. This allows us to quantify how much each tier of players benefits or is penalized by their roles.

Delta and Adjustments by Tier per 60 minutes, 2013–14

	Raw Delta	Delta ZS	Delta QoC	Delta QoT	Delta Adj
Tier 1	0.17	0.02	0.07	-0.05	0.21
Tier 2	0.07	0.01	0.03	-0.02	0.09
Tier 3	-0.03	-0.01	0.00	0.02	-0.02
Tier 4	-0.16	-0.01	-0.08	0.04	-0.21

These results are, instinctively, what we should have expected. Tier 1 players have slightly more difficult zone starts (positive Delta ZS), stronger competition (positive Delta QC), and stronger teammates (negative Delta QT). The zone starts and competition get progressively easier as we move to Tier 2, Tier 3 and Tier 4, and the teammates get progressively weaker as well. Above all, though, the most significant result is probably that the overall assignments are close to average for everybody, since stronger competition and stronger teammates almost balance out.

Also interesting is that zone starts are so close to neutral for all tiers. This is an important point, since most people assume that players with easier zone starts are weak players (to use the common term, they are "sheltered") while players who start exclusively in the defensive zone are excellent. This is incorrect, players' zone starts are established by the ratio of their offensive talents to their defensive talents, or to put it another way, how good are you are with the puck vs how good are you without the puck. Among the forwards with the most difficult zone starts on their team last season were Chicago's Brandon Bollig, Edmonton's Boyd Gordon, and Philadelphia's Adam Hall. These are solid defensive players but they are not first-liners. The forwards with the easiest zone starts were Phoenix's Mike Ribeiro, New York's Brad Richards, Carolina's Jeff Skinner, and Minnesota's Zach Parise. In many cases, these players could play a purely offensive role because the team had a solid defensive centre to take the defensive faceoffs: Kyle Brodziak in Minnesota, Brian Boyle in New York, and Manny Malhotra in Carolina.

The bottom line is that Tier 1 forwards, the ones that get the most ice time, do not have a leaning for defensive zone starts. Zone starts do affects players' results, however, and we need to take them into account. Players who start more often in the defensive zone will tend to have weaker Corsi and Delta ratings and, inevitably, +/-. This is not because they suck, it's because their job is hard.

Goals, Assists, and Points

I have intentionally started with more advanced statistics to illustrate the effects that elite players have on what happens while they are on the ice. In particular, looking at goal differential while a player is on the ice is more useful than looking at goals and assists, since offensively-minded players can pad their point totals by playing a more wide-open game that doesn't end up benefiting their team. However, it is still useful to look at goal (G/60) and assist (A/60) scoring rates, the latter of which is further divided into primary (A1/60) and secondary assists (A2/60) to see if we can notice a difference in performance between the tiers of players. The point percentage (Pts %) refers to that player's share of all on-ice scoring.

Even-Strength Goals, Assists and Points per Tier, Forwards, 2013–14

	GF/60	G/60	A1/60	A2/60	Pts/60	Pts %
Tier 1	2.72	0.84	0.69	0.42	1.95	71.7
Tier 2	2.46	0.71	0.62	0.38	1.71	69.6
Tier 3	2.18	0.59	0.50	0.34	1.44	65.8
Tier 4	1.73	0.46	0.38	0.26	1.11	64.0

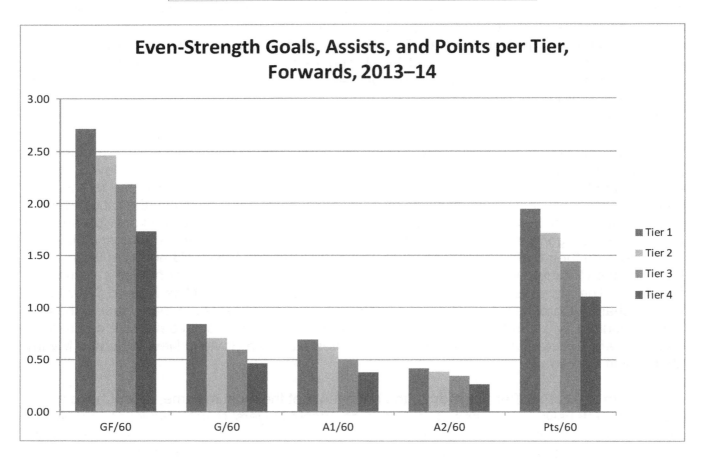

One of the interesting observations taken from looking only at even strength, per-ice-time numbers is that there's much less difference among NHL players than raw totals would suggest. The players in Tier 1 averaged about 57 points per 82 games played, while the players in Tier 4 averaged only a lowly 16 points per 82 games, a factor of about 3.5. However, the bulk of that difference was due to differences in ice time and in particular power-play time, which we will get back to later.

However, when looking at the above table, we see that Tier 1 players average 1.95 points per 60 minutes of even-strength ice time, while Tier 4 players average 1.11, a large difference but much smaller than the raw numbers would suggest. We also see in this table confirmation of what we have previously stated[14]: that the cutoff for being a top-six forward in the NHL is 1.7 points per 60 minutes of even-strength ice time. In fact, Tier 2 players averaged exactly 1.71 points per 60 minutes.

We have already seen above that more goals for (and, to a lesser degree, more goals against) are scored when top tier players are on the ice. What this table shows us is that those players are also more responsible for those goals. Tier 1 players scored a point on 72% of the goals scored while they were on the ice, while Tier 4 players scored a point on only 64% of goals. Tier 1 and 2 players were also slightly more likely to score goals or primary assists, while Tier 3 and 4 players obtained a slightly higher fraction of secondary assists. While these differences are not huge, they probably understate the reality: since Tier 4 players often play with other Tier 4 players, when a goal is scored, *somebody* has to be responsible for it, and it will rarely be a defenceman. Unlike on the power play, defencemen do not drive much of the offence at even strength. So the likely conclusion is that when upper tier and lower tier players play together, the upper tier players are doing most of the scoring.

Penalties

It is fairly obvious that good players score more points; after all, we are used to looking at the league's top scorers and know the names by heart. But do elite players take fewer penalties than their peers, or more? After all, there are top scorers in the mould of Martin St. Louis, but there are also others in the mold of Corey Perry. That being said, we might also guess that better players would be able to draw more penalties (PIM, penalties in minutes), since other players would have to get more physical with them to prevent them from creating scoring opportunities.

Penalties Taken and Drawn, per Tier, 2013–14

	PIM Taken/60	PIM Drawn/60	Net PIM/60
Tier 1	1.29	1.52	0.23
Tier 2	1.20	1.42	0.21
Tier 3	1.29	1.42	0.12
Tier 4	1.61	1.42	-0.19

This table is different from the ones before, in contrast to what we saw above, there is not a huge difference between Tier 1, 2, and 3 players; they all seem to draw slightly more penalties than they take. In fact, penalties don't seem to correlate very well with what we think of as "skill" players: Thomas Vanek, a player known mainly as a scoring threat, managed to take 16 minors last season and only draw 7, while Boston's Daniel Paille, who has averaged only 16 points per season during his four-year tenure in Boston, drew 13 while taking only 3.

The huge gap is between Tier 4 and everyone else. The Tier 4 players are the only ones with a negative net penalty differential (as a general rule, defencemen take more penalties than

14 Rob Vollman, "Top-Six Forwards, Part 1", *Hockey Prospectus*, December 10, 2009, Web, http://www.hockeyprospectus.com/puck/article.php?articleid=387.

forwards, so forwards will typically have a small positive net penalty differential and defencemen a slightly negative one). This difference is entirely due to their propensity to take more penalties. While 0.3 penalty minutes per 60 minutes may not seem like much, each penalty minute is worth about -0.1 goals to your team, which means that Tier 4 players contribute -0.04 goals per 60 minutes fewer than Tier 1, 2, and 3 players. Given three forwards on the ice at any one time, that means that a line of Tier 4 forwards is costing its team about 0.12 net goals per 60 minutes, which is not negligible when compared to the goal differential numbers above.

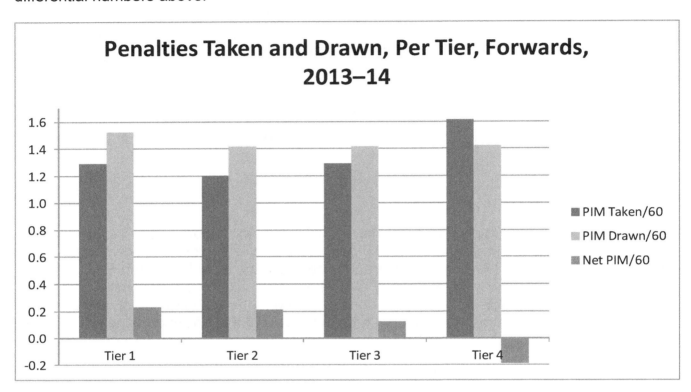

Power Play

So far we have seen how top tier players achieve better results than their peers at 5v5. Next we shall analyze how well these results translate to the power play. Instinctively, we should expect that their results would be just as good, or better, at 5v4 than at 5v5. For one thing, we know that elite players get the lion's share of ice time on the power play, as opposed to the more equal distribution we observe at even strength. As a practical matter, playing with the man advantage gives players more space to make their plays, a distinction which should favour the more skilled players.

In practice, this is exactly what we see:

5v4 Player Results by Tier, 2013–14

	TOI/GP	GF/60	GA/60	GD/60	EGF/60	EGA/60	EGD/60	SF/60	SA/60	SD/60
Tier 1	171	6.96	0.99	5.97	6.72	0.85	5.88	55.86	8.35	47.51

Tier 2	124	6.33	0.88	5.45	6.23	0.83	5.40	52.10	8.57	43.53
Tier 3	78	5.33	0.93	4.40	5.97	0.81	5.16	50.38	8.48	41.90
Tier 4	22	5.23	0.76	4.47	5.24	0.83	4.41	46.08	8.98	37.10

First of all, we see that the difference in ice time is *massive*. While Tier 1 players had 19% more even-strength ice time than Tier 3 players and 53% more even-strength ice time than Tier 4 players, on the power play they get over twice the ice time of Tier 3 players and almost 8 times the ice time of Tier 4 players.

The distribution of ice time within the tiers is also interesting. Tier 4 players are basically never used on the power play; the few that are are either aging stars who still have good hands but can't handle the rigour of a regular shift (Ray Whitney) or young players in limited roles who are given a chance to demonstrate their skills (Filip Forsberg).

Among Tier 3 players, it's a case of feast or famine. Certain Tier 3 players are power play specialists: Michael Ryder, Andrew Shaw, Alex Chiasson, and Erik Cole get "first line" power-play time even though they have a more limited role in other situations; typically these players will not kill penalties at all. Others, like Zack Smith or Carl Hagelin, see almost no power-play time; as we expect, these are defensive specialists who will be used more intensively on the penalty kill. Only three out of 130 Tier 3 players played more than 90 seconds per game on both the power play and penalty kill: Joel Ward and Artem Anisimov, both of whom missed being Tier 2 by just a few seconds, and Ryan Smyth.

By comparison, 80% of Tier 2 players were regular contributors to the power play (defined as more than 90 seconds per game) and 95% of Tier 1 players were. In fact, of 81 Tier 1 players, all but one of them played at least 72 seconds per game on the power play: Calgary's Matt Stajan.

What about the results themselves? They are, in fact, very similar to the even-strength results. Tier 1 players scored at a rate almost 30% higher than Tier 3 players (I will ignore Tier 4 players since there were so few of them with regular power-play roles), comparable to the 23% outscoring rate at even strength. What's really interesting is how those results were achieved, as compared to even strength:

5v4 Source of Goal Differential by Tier, Forwards, 2013–14

	Shot Differential	Shot Quality Differential	Shooting % Differential
Tier 1	0.40	0.02	0.09
Tier 2	-0.07	0.03	0.05
Tier 3	-0.26	-0.01	-0.76
Tier 4	-0.84	-0.16	0.06

In contrast to the results at even strength, Tier 1 forwards scored more goals on the power play mainly because they generated more shots on net. This shot differential came about, in part, because of more offensive zone starts. To begin with, zone starts on the power play are skewed. At even strength, 36% of zone starts are in the neutral zone, with 32% each in the offensive and defensive zone. On the power play, 77% of the faceoffs are in the offensive zone! Another 17% are in the neutral zone, leaving a microscopic 6% in the defensive zone. This is not surprising, as we know that teams on the power play have ownership of the puck at least 85% of the time. But Tier 1 players benefit from offensive zone starts even more disproportionately:

5v4 Delta and Adjustments by Tier, Forwards, 2013–14

	Raw Delta/60	Delta ZS/60	DeltaS/60
Tier 1	5.97	-0.20	5.77
Tier 2	5.45	-0.05	5.39
Tier 3	4.40	0.12	4.52
Tier 4	4.47	0.37	4.84

For readers who are not used to thinking in terms of Delta, this table indicates that Tier 1 players got power-play zone starts that were even more offensive (no pun intended!) than average, equivalent to an extra 0.2 goals per 60 minutes of power-play time, Tier 2 players got zone starts equivalent to an extra 0.05 goals per 60 minutes, while Tier 3 players got offensive zone starts that were more defensive by 0.12 goals per 60 minutes. This difference explains about one third of the shot differential between Tier 1 and Tier 2 players, and about half of the shot differential observed between Tier 1 and Tier 3 players.

Power-Play Goals, Assists and Points per Tier, 2013–14

	GF/60	G/60	A1/60	A2/60	Pts/60	Pts %
Tier 1	6.96	1.62	1.44	1.20	4.27	61.4
Tier 2	6.33	1.41	1.16	1.12	3.69	58.2
Tier 3	5.33	1.34	1.03	0.70	3.07	57.6
Tier 4	5.23	1.11	0.90	0.84	2.85	54.5

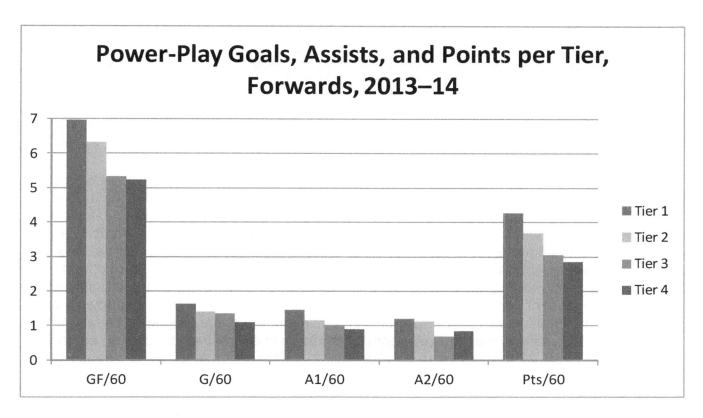

Power-Play Goals, Assists, and Points per Tier, Forwards, 2013–14

Scoring at 5v4 is about 2.5 times higher than at even strength, so players' point totals are higher. We see here the exact same distribution as we did at even strength: players scored points in direct proportion to their tier and upper tier players had points on a greater proportion of goals. Obviously, there could be some bias here, as lower tier players are more likely to have a job not involved in puck possession, such as screening the goaltender, a job which leads to a lot of power-play goals but doesn't earn a point other than through deflections or tip-ins.

Penalty Killing

Should elite forwards kill more penalties, or fewer? Both schools of thought have their adherents. On one side, the importance of shot blocking to modern penalty killing makes teams more hesitant to use their best forwards for this job, lest they get injured. On the other hand, your most skilled players are likely to be more skilled defensively as well, and killing penalties is a "high leverage" situation, one where having better players can lead to a large improvement in goal differential. There is also the opportunity cost of using elite players to kill penalties. It is an exhausting business and a player who has just spent 90 seconds playing at 4v5 will not be as fresh when the penalty is over and the teams return to balance.

In practice, the truth is somewhere in the middle. Top tier players do indeed kill more penalties than their peers, but not by much:

	TOI/GP	GF/60	GA/60	GD/60	EGF/60	EGA/60	EGD/60	SF/60	SA/60	SD/60
Tier 1	66	1.07	5.98	-4.91	0.98	6.02	-5.04	9.14	51.01	-41.87
Tier 2	50	1.20	6.31	-5.11	1.05	6.22	-5.17	9.52	52.21	-42.69
Tier 3	54	0.83	6.06	-5.24	0.82	6.33	-5.51	7.64	53.12	-45.48
Tier 4	42	0.58	6.33	-5.75	0.82	6.26	-5.44	8.11	52.23	-44.12

The first thing we notice is that all tiers of players spend between 42 and 66 seconds a game killing penalties, which is not a huge gap given what we saw on the power play. As before, the difference within tiers is instructive. The NHL has a lot of Tier 1 players who spend basically zero time on the penalty kill: Alexander Ovechkin, Phil Kessel, Evgeni Malkin, Patrick Kane, and others. On the flip side, there are many top line forwards, especially #1 centres, who also anchor their team's shorthanded unit: Anze Kopitar, Ryan Getzlaf, Tomas Plekanec, and Bryan Little are the most notable ones. But unlike the power play, where all the top players also got the most even-strength ice time, expert penalty killers are found up and down the depth chart The forward with the most shorthanded time in the entire league last season, Toronto's Jay McClement, was only eleventh on his team in even-strength ice time among forwards! And of the 27 forwards who played at least 10,000 seconds at 4v5 last season, 6 were Tier 1, 6 were Tier 2, 9 were Tier 3, and 6 were Tier 4. That's about as evenly distributed as you can get.

What's notable, however, is that the Tier 1 players clearly achieve better results while they are on the ice. Tier 1 players got outscored by 4.91 goals per 60 minutes, while Tier 4 players got outscored by 5.75 goals. In other words, Tier 1 players achieved a penalty-killing rate of about 83.6%, while Tier 4 players achieved the equivalent of 80.8% (normalizing 60-minute rates to 2 minutes). Digging even further, we see that the bulk of this difference came as a result of a greater number of shorthanded goals, with the Tier 1 players, teams scored almost twice as many shorthanded goals!

The conclusion seems to be that Tier 1 players are indeed better penalty killers than their peers, but because of the opportunity cost of using them, their shorthanded time is limited. They are probably used to kill penalties more in high-leverage situations, when up by one goal late in the game, for example. This could be an area of further study.

Closing Thoughts

I have thrown a phenomenal amount of numbers at you, so I thank you for sticking it out with me until here. What have we learned from this exercise?

1. Elite ("Tier 1") forwards get more ice time than weaker forwards, so ice time is a loose proxy for play skill. However, even-strength ice time is reasonably distributed among all players.
2. Tier 1 forwards outscore their opponents through a combination of better puck possession and better finishing ability. Of the two, finishing ability is slightly more

important.

3. Shooting percentage is highly correlated with player strength in all manpower situations and does not depend on shot quality.

4. There is little correlation between overall player strength and zone starts. However, there is a high positive correlation between player caliber and quality of opposition as well as quality of teammates.

5. Tier 1 forwards don't draw many more penalties, or take fewer penalties, than Tier 2 or Tier 3 players. However, Tier 4 players take more penalties.

6. Tier 1 and Tier 2 forwards get the lion's share of power-play time. Tier 4 forwards get virtually none.

7. The main driver of overall ice time for forwards is offensive ability. Almost all first line forwards also play regularly on the power play. However, a good defensive forward will get a reasonable amount of even-strength ice time and large amounts of penalty-killing ice time.

Author's Note: The methodology in this article was first published in the article "What Makes Good Player Good?" on Hockey Prospectus[15] *in 2010.*

---

15 Tom Awad, "What Makes Good Players Good?", *Hockey Prospectus*, September 28, 2010, Web, http://www.hockeyprospectus.com/puck/article.php?articleid=625.

What Makes Good Players Good? Part 2: Defencemen

By Tom Awad

In part 1 of this analysis, I ranked all NHL forwards by ice time, grouped them into four tiers and compared the results of each tier to see what distinguishes top tier forwards from other players. I will now repeat this analysis for defencemen. Because there are fewer defencemen than forwards, I will group them into three tiers rather than four. This also has the convenient feature of ranking defencemen in the way we tend to do it instinctively (top-two, top-four, top-six) even though that is not a strictly necessary part of my methodology.

Without further ado, let's jump in!

2013–14 Season Results

To group defencemen, I sorted them by ice time per game for the 2013–14 season[16]. I then divided them into three bins of equal ice time, so that "Tier 1" players represented 33.3% of the total ice time by defencemen, and the same for Tier 2 and Tier 3. I then summed the results of what happened while they were on the ice. Once again, the categories include time on ice per game (TOI/GP), followed by goals, even-strength goals, and shots (G, EG, S), for, against, and differential (F, A, D), all per 60 minutes (/60).

Even-Strength Results by Tier, Defencemen, 2013–14

	TOI/GP	GF/60	GA/60	GD/60	EGF/60	EGA/60	EGD/60	SF/60	SA/60	SD/60
Tier 1	1061	2.36	2.32	0.04	2.27	2.27	0.00	29.57	29.21	0.36
Tier 2	975	2.23	2.20	0.03	2.24	2.20	0.04	29.14	28.80	0.34
Tier 3	837	2.16	2.26	-0.09	2.16	2.23	-0.07	28.27	29.24	-0.97

What are the most interesting observations from this table? First of all, unlike forwards, the goal differential and expected goal differential results are not extremely different by group. While the difference between Tier 1 and Tier 4 forwards was 0.76 goals per 60 minutes and 0.33 expected goals per 60 minutes, the difference for defencemen is only 0.13 goals, six times less, and the difference in expected goals is 0.07. In fact, Tier 2 defencemen have a slightly better expected goal differential than Tier 1 defencemen! The difference in shot differential was slightly more pronounced, with a difference of 1.33 shots per 60 minutes, although at an average even-strength shooting percentage of 8%, that translates to only 0.11 goals per 60 minutes.

This all points to an important conclusion: **results at even strength are driven primarily by forwards**. This is not to say that offensive play is more important than defensive play; simply that, in the NHL, the players who contribute the most to outscoring the opposition at 5v5 are first-line forwards, not top-pair defencemen. We can see this in another way, by looking at the shooting percentages for the different tiers:

---

16 Acknowledgement: All data is from *NHL* game files, http://www.nhl.com.

Shooting Percentages For and Against, Defencemen, 2013–14

	SF%	SA%
Tier 1	7.98%	7.95%
Tier 2	7.64%	7.64%
Tier 3	7.65%	7.71%

Both shooting percentage for and shooting percentage against were slightly higher for the Tier 1 defencemen, possibly due to playing with and against stronger forwards. But overall, the numbers are extremely close: the spread from lowest to highest is seven times smaller than it was for forwards, indicating that defencemen don't seem to drive shooting percentages significantly in either direction.

Another important number: even-strength ice time for Tier 1 defencemen was 1061 seconds (17:41) per game, only 86 seconds more than Tier 2 defencemen (975 seconds, or 16:15). This is only 9% more. We will have to wait until we analyze special teams ice time to see if this is meaningful or not, since the special teams ice time could vary more (spoiler: it does!).

2012–13 Season Results

Once again, because some of these results are counter-intuitive, we should check to see if the 2013–14 season was typical or not. The easiest way is to run the same exercise for the 2012–13 season.

Even-Strength Defencemen Results by Tier, 2012–13

	TOI/GP	GF/60	GA/60	GD/60	EGF/60	EGA/60	EGD/60	SF/60	SA/60	SD/60
Tier 1	1066	2.41	2.30	0.12	2.33	2.27	0.06	29.21	28.66	0.56
Tier 2	983	2.21	2.34	-0.13	2.21	2.29	-0.08	27.95	28.79	-0.84
Tier 3	833	2.13	2.13	-0.01	2.19	2.18	0.01	28.02	27.89	0.12

Unsurprisingly, the results are extremely similar to those from 2013–14, with no real discernible pattern. Interestingly, during this season, the Tier 2 defencemen had the worst results, which simply corroborates what we had speculated earlier: defencemen do not strongly drive the results. There is a slight pattern, with Tier 1 defencemen having above-average results in both years, but little else.

Factors Affecting Player Results

We have seen that there are very few differences between the results of the three Tiers of defencemen. However, we know that player results are influenced by context. Is it possible that the best defencemen are getting ordinary results simply because they're being given extraordinarily difficult tasks? To find out, we once again turn to Delta. Delta indicates how heavily players' results are affected by the three major environmental factors: Zone Starts (ZS), Quality of Competition (QoC), and Quality of Teammates (QoT) . A note to those unused to Delta: Delta QoC correlates almost perfects with Corsi QoC, the only difference being that Delta QoC is expressed in goals and Corsi QoC is expressed in shots.

Delta and Adjustments by Tier per 60 minutes, 2013–14

	Raw Delta	Delta ZS	Delta QoC	Delta QoT	Delta Adj
Tier 1	0.00	-0.02	0.06	-0.02	0.02
Tier 2	0.04	0.00	0.01	-0.03	0.03
Tier 3	-0.07	0.01	-0.06	0.03	-0.09

The first observation is that, unsurprisingly, Tier 1 defencemen face the strongest competition, while Tier 3 defencemen face the weakest. Anyone who has analyzed Quality of Competition in the past would have expected this. The six defencemen who faced the strongest Delta Quality of Competition (Shea Weber, Roman Josi, Oliver Ekman-Larsson, T.J. Brodie, Erik Johnson, and Jan Hejda) were all Tier 1 defencemen, while of the six weakest, two (Jake Gardiner and Matt Bartkowski) were Tier 2, while the four others (Torey Krug, Jakub Kindl, Nick Leddy, and Brian Lashoff) were Tier 3.

The second observation is that, other than the Delta QoC, none of the other factors is very significant. Tier 1 Defencemen start slightly more than average in the offensive zone, but only enough to justify a difference of 0.02 goals per 60 minutes, a negligible amount. Even the quality of teammates did not vary much, which indicates that coaches are more likely to pair a top tier defenceman against the other team's top line than to pair him with their own top line.

Goals, Assists, and Points

So far we have observed strikingly little difference between the different tiers of defencemen, but there remain other aspects to be analyzed. Next I will turn my attention to the traditional stats: are top tier defencemen better at accumulating Goals and Assists than their less-used counterparts?

Even-Strength Goals, Assists and Points per Tier, Defencemen, 2013–14

	GF/60	G/60	A1/60	A2/60	Pts/60	Pts %
Tier 1	2.36	0.19	0.28	0.32	0.78	33.2%
Tier 2	2.23	0.14	0.24	0.28	0.66	29.7%
Tier 3	2.36	0.15	0.21	0.26	0.62	28.8%

Finally, we see a difference here. As we know, defencemen's offensive contributions at even strength are fairly limited; even an offensively-oriented defenceman scores fewer points per minute of even-strength ice time than a third-line forward. But we do see a difference between the tiers: Tier 1 defencemen scored 18% more points per minute of ice time than their Tier 2 brethren, and 26% more than Tier 3s. This seems to indicate that Tier 1 and Tier 2 defencemen are fairly similar in their defensive ability, but what gives one group slightly more ice time than the other is a difference in offensive ability. Next, we'll look at special teams data to see if that confirms our theory.

Power Play

Other than offensive results, we have seen little difference between the results of Tier 1 and Tier 2 defencemen, and only a slight difference with Tier 3 defencemen. However, when we look at the power play, we start to understand where the differentiation lies:

5v4 Results by Tier, Defencemen, 2013–14

	TOI/GP	GF/60	GA/60	GD/60	EGF/60	EGA/60	EGD/60	SF/60	SA/60	SD/60
Tier 1	155	6.32	0.96	5.36	6.26	0.83	5.43	52.19	8.55	43.65
Tier 2	64	5.53	0.72	4.81	6.09	0.78	5.31	51.55	8.58	42.97
Tier 3	42	5.73	0.66	5.07	5.63	0.80	4.82	48.62	8.91	39.70

Tier 1 defencemen get the bulk of the power-play time; indeed, they get almost as much power-play time as Tier 1 forwards. What's more, the team's results—especially the offensive results—are better with Tier 1 defencemen on the ice than with the others. Although, once again, the difference is smaller than with forwards: between Tier 1 and Tier 3 there is a difference of 0.29 goals per 60 minutes. By contrast, between Tier 1 and Tier 4 forwards there was a difference of 1.5 goals per 60 minutes!

It seems that playing on the power play is a core characteristic of the defencemen who get the most ice time. In fact, the 48 defencemen with the most ice time in the NHL last season also played at least 1:07 per game on the power play; not until we get to Jan Hejda do we find a defenceman who got his ice time mostly from even-strength and penalty-killing situations. Obviously, part of this is because getting power-play ice time contributes to total ice time. But of the 25 defencemen with the most even-strength ice time in the league, only two, Hejda and Dennis Seidenberg, played less than a minute per game on the power play. After that, however, we find many candidates, so it seems that offensive ability is required to be a "franchise" defenceman (Ryan Suter, Shea Weber, Alex Pietrangelo, and the like) but you can still be a #2 defenceman without it.

5v4 Goals, Assists and Points per Tier, Defencemen, 2013–14

	GF/60	G/60	A1/60	A2/60	Pts/60	Pts %
Tier 1	6.32	0.86	1.31	1.42	3.60	56.9%
Tier 2	5.53	0.68	1.03	1.16	2.86	51.8%
Tier 3	5.73	0.67	1.26	1.36	3.30	57.5%

Since Tier 1 defencemen are on the ice for more power-play goals, it is unsurprising to find that they score more points. This table underscores how important the power play is to defencemen's point totals: they score about five times more points per minute of power-play ice time than even-strength ice time, as compared to a ratio of about 2.2 for forwards. This is why point totals are such a poor metric for judging defencemen: the biggest factor that determines a defenceman's point totals is the amount of power-play ice time he gets, not his talent level or even who his power-play teammates are.

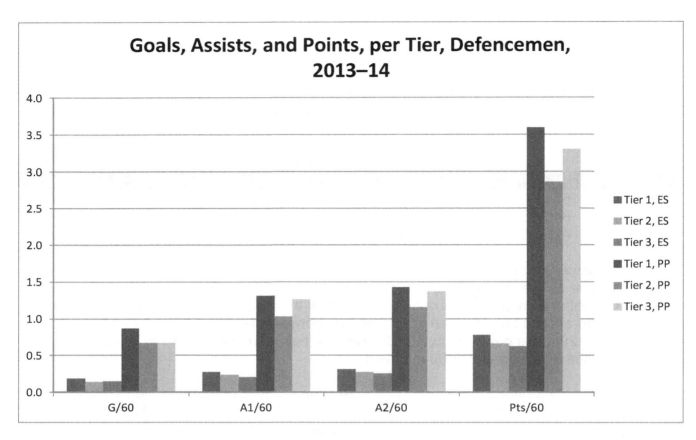

Goals, Assists, and Points, per Tier, Defencemen, 2013–14

The other interesting takeaway from this table is that Tier 3 defencemen's points are much higher than Tier 2. Some of this may be due to sample size issues: Tier 3 defencemen scored a total of 225 points, a number which may contain an uncertainty of 7%. The other possible explanation is that there are some defencemen who don't have the requisite skills to be Tier 1 or Tier 2, but have sufficient offensive skills to be power play specialists. Some of these are older stars: Sergei Gonchar, a Tier 1 defenceman at his peak, is now Tier 3 but can still contribute significantly at 5v4. Some are younger stars with offensive talent who are still maturing: 22-year-old Torey Krug led all Tier 3 defencemen with 19 power-play points last season and, by the playoffs, was getting top-four minutes. Others are on teams with a wealth of other quality defencemen: the Kings' Alec Martinez might have been a top-four defenceman on a weaker team, but playing on the same team as Willie Mitchell and Robyn Regehr, he is one of the better offensive options but not one of the better defensive ones.

Penalty Killing

This, we expect, should be the ultimate test of defencemen. While many teams staff the power play with four forwards and only one defenceman, letting a forward man one of the points, penalty killing is primarily the defencemen's responsibility, with defencemen getting exactly 50% of all penalty-killing ice time, as compared to 40% of even-strength ice time and only 32% of power-play ice time. This should be where we will be able to distinguish elite defensive players.

4v5 Results by Tier, Defencemen, 2013–14

	TOI/GP	GF/60	GA/60	GD/60	EGF/60	EGA/60	EGD/60	SF/60	SA/60	SD/60
Tier 1	134	0.97	6.02	-5.05	0.80	6.19	-5.39	8.22	51.71	-43.49
Tier 2	112	0.84	6.03	-5.20	0.79	6.24	-5.44	8.64	52.45	-43.81
Tier 3	67	0.86	6.57	-5.71	0.91	6.25	-5.34	8.79	52.67	-43.88

The first interesting fact to note is that both Tier 1 and Tier 2 defencemen get significant penalty-killing ice time. In fact, of the 57 Tier 1 defencemen in our sample, 39 of them spent more than 2 minutes a game killing penalties, and all but four of them spent at least 54 seconds per game on the ice with a man down. The outliers are well-known offence-only defencemen: P.K. Subban, Keith Yandle, Kris Russell, and Mike Green.

Secondly, we see that the goal differential is significantly better for Tier 1 and Tier 2 defencemen than for Tier 3. It is harder to draw conclusions from penalty-killing data than it is from even strength because the sample sizes are smaller, but that still represents a difference of almost 73 goals of goal differential (since Tier 3 players collectively played 111 hours of PK time, a difference of 0.66 goals per hour is 111 * 0.66 = 73 goals).

To confirm this difference, I wanted to compare the data from another season. Because the 2012–13 season was shortened by a lockout, I analyzed data from the 2011–12 season to see if I saw the same pattern.

4v5 Results by Tier, Defencemen, 2011–12

	TOI/GP	GF/60	GA/60	GD/60	EGF/60	EGA/60	EGD/60	SF/60	SA/60	SD/60
Tier 1	130	0.81	5.86	-5.05	0.76	5.87	-5.11	8.78	48.74	-39.96
Tier 2	121	0.76	5.87	-5.11	0.80	5.93	-5.13	8.86	49.15	-40.29
Tier 3	61	0.73	6.22	-5.49	0.78	6.07	-5.29	8.24	50.53	-42.30

The results are strikingly similar, primarily in that the penalty-killing results of Tier 3 defencemen are measurably worse than their Tier 1 and Tier 2 counterparts, and that at least some of that differential comes from increased shooting percentage against. In fact, combining the two seasons we see a fairly significant difference:

4v5 Shooting Percentages For and Against, Defencemen, 2011–12 and 2013–14

	SF%	SA%
Tier 1	10.29%	11.80%
Tier 2	9.29%	11.68%
Tier 3	9.25%	12.50%

Despite playing in front of the same goaltenders and against slightly weaker opposition, shots taken when Tier 3 defencemen were killing penalties were about 6% (12.5% vs. 11.8%) more likely to score than when other defencemen were playing. On top of the fact that they allowed 2% more shots against, this amounts to 8% more goals scored by the opposition.

This is the most conclusive evidence I can find for statistically significant penalty-killing skill, although it is important not to make too much of it either. Given that Tier 3 defencemen get about 20% of all penalty-killing ice time, this means the average NHL team gave up 1.6% (an 8% increase during 20% of the time) more power-play goals than they would have otherwise; given an average of 50 power-play goals per season per team, that is about 0.8 goals per season.

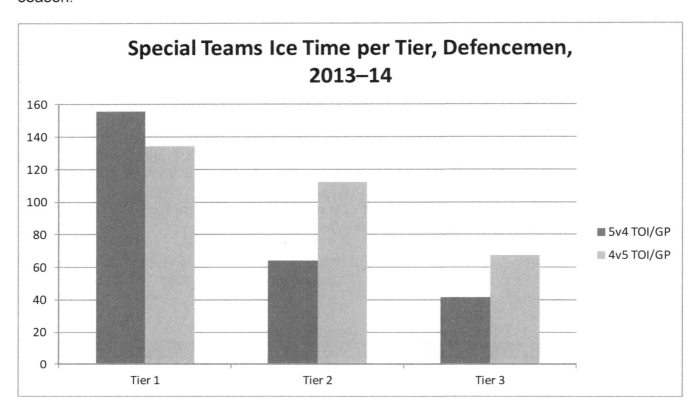

In the above graph, we see the distribution of ice time for defencemen, per tier. We can see visually that being a major contributor on the power play is only common for Tier 1 ("top-two") defencemen, while all top-four defencemen are expected to contribute regularly to penalty killing.

Penalties

We know that defencemen take more penalties than forwards. In large part, this is reflective of their role: defencemen are expected to strip opponents of the puck, impede them, block their progress, and generally make their lives miserable. Much of this necessarily involves pushing the rules as much as possible; too little interference and the opponents can score unimpeded; too much and you take a penalty. As we would expect, some are better at skirting the line than others:

Penalties Taken and Drawn, per Tier, Defencemen, 2013–14

	PIM Taken/60	PIM Drawn/60	Net PIM/60
Tier 1	1.10	0.72	-0.38
Tier 2	1.25	0.61	-0.64
Tier 3	1.42	0.67	-0.75

What we see here is a similar progression to what we saw for forwards, except that everyone is in the negatives: Tier 1 defencemen manage to only take 0.4 PIM per 60 minutes more than they draw; that's a net of -1 minor penalty per 300 minutes of ice time, while Tier 3 players are in the red by twice as much. Since an entire season's worth of ice time for a defenceman is approximately 27 hours (20 minutes * 82 games), then a Tier 3 defenceman will take about 5.5 net penalties more than a Tier 1 defenceman, at a cost to his team of 5.5 * 20% (average power-play success rate) = 1.1 goals per season. This is even more significant since we saw earlier that Tier 1 defencemen face a higher Quality of Competition, which would typically result in more penalties taken. So Tier 1 defencemen are being more disciplined despite facing more dangerous opponents.

Unlike many of the other stats, however, there is a huge variation here, even within a single tier. Some defencemen manage to still be net positive, including Ryan McDonagh, Dan Hamhuis and Jacob Trouba (all Tier 1), but also Jake Gardiner (Tier 2) and Winnipeg's Keaton Ellerby (Tier 3).

The worst offenders are also split among the tiers. I'm sure my readers will be shocked to learn that Dion Phaneuf had the worst metric among Tier 1 defencemen and second-worst overall, obtaining -44 net penalty minutes, while Kyle Quincey (Tier 2) had the worst score with -56 net penalty minutes. However, even among the best defencemen in the league (players like Ryan Suter, Shea Weber, Drew Doughty, Duncan Keith and Zdeno Chara) we find negative net penalties, though not at Phaneuf's levels.

Unlike many other stats, then, net penalties may have more to do with play style than overall skill. Also, the context of the penalty is not clear from the record: was it a scoring chance? A penalty may well be more desirable than the alternative in many cases. What we can say, however, is that overall Tier 1 defencemen seem to be able to make those decisions more judiciously than their counterparts.

Closing Thoughts

What are the important points to remember from this analysis?

1. There is not that much difference in even-strength results among different tiers of defencemen. Results at even strength seem to be driven primarily by forwards.
2. There is little correlation between defenceman ice time and Zone Starts. However, there is a high positive correlation between defenceman ice time and Quality of Opposition.
3. A top-two defenceman will typically play a significant role on the power play. A top-four

defenceman will typically play a significant role on the penalty kill.

4. When killing penalties, better defencemen are capable of reducing both the quantity of shots faced and their chances of scoring.
5. Defencemen, as a whole, take more penalties than they draw, but Tier 1 defencemen take fewer of them, despite facing more dangerous opponents.
6. Unlike forwards, where offensive ability was the main driver of ice time, there are many profiles of defencemen. The best defencemen are those that excel at both ends of the ice, but many defencemen in the NHL contribute despite being weaker in one set of skills.

What Makes Good Players Good? Part 3: Goaltenders

By Tom Awad

In Part 1 of this analysis, I ranked all NHL forwards by ice time, grouped them into four tiers and compared the results of each tier to see what distinguishes top tier forwards from other players. In Part 2, I did the same for defencemen. In Part 3, I will now do the same for goaltenders. Obviously, goaltenders should not be ranked by ice time per game; the best proxy for coaches' confidence in their goaltenders is the total amount of time that they get.

2013–14 Season Results

Because of the smaller number of goaltenders versus position players, I chose to group goaltenders into only two tiers: this also has the benefit of sorting them roughly into categories of starter and backup. To group the goaltenders, I sorted them by total ice time per game for the 2013–14 season. I then summed the players to divide them into two bins, so that "Tier 1" goaltenders represented 60% of the total ice time and Tier 2 represented 40% of the total ice time. I split them in this way to ensure that the majority of NHL starters fell into Tier 1.

Once again, all data is sourced from NHL game files, and the categories include goals, even-strength goals, and shots (G, EG, S), for, against, and differential (F, A, D), all per 60 minutes (/60). The additional categories are the team's shooting percentages for (SH%F) and against (SH%A).

Even-Strength Results by Tier, Goaltenders, 2013–14

	GF/60	GA/60	EGF/60	EGA/60	SF/60	SA/60	Sh%F	Sh%A
Tier 1	2.29	2.17	2.25	2.23	29.34	29.03	7.82%	7.48%
Tier 2	2.19	2.36	2.20	2.22	28.59	29.01	7.67%	8.14%

The most important take away from this table is, of course, the difference in shooting percentages against between the Tier 1 and Tier 2 goaltenders. While Tier 2 goaltenders allowed 8.14% of shots taken against them, equivalent to an even-strength save percentage of 91.9%, Tier 1 goaltenders allowed only 7.48% of the shots they faced, an even-strength save percentage of 92.5%. While this difference of 0.6% may not seem like much, it represents one goal every five games: out of 150 shots faced, a Tier 1 goaltender allowed a bit over 11 goals, while a Tier 2 goaltenders allowed a bit over 12. Usefully, the number of shots faced was identical for both, so workload cannot be used as a possible explanation.

There are also other interesting differences, including a difference of 0.7 shots for and 0.1 goals for per 60 minutes. Since it is unlikely that Tier 1 goaltenders are such spectacular puck handlers that they can affect goals for to such an extent, the more likely conclusion is that this is simply noise. We shall have to look at results of other seasons to see if this pattern is consistent or not.

76

2012-13 Season Results

Goaltending is often beset by sample size issues, so to attempt to address these as best I can, I will look at three seasons of data before making any major claims.

Even-Strength Results by Tier, Goaltenders, 2012–13

	GF/60	GA/60	EGF/60	EGA/60	SF/60	SA/60	Sh%F	Sh%A
Tier 1	2.25	2.12	2.22	2.20	28.18	28.24	7.99%	7.51%
Tier 2	2.25	2.44	2.29	2.30	28.76	28.67	7.84%	8.50%

For 2012–13, the results are even more discouraging for Tier 2 goaltenders. The difference in save percentages increased from 0.66% to 0.99%, making it worth 0.3 goals per game rather than 0.2. It is important to note that, unlike in 2013–14, the Tier 2 goaltenders faced shots that were 3% more dangerous on average. This is actually what we would expect if they are weaker due to score effects, weaker goaltenders are more likely to be trailing in the third period, when they will face fewer but more dangerous shots.

2011-12 Season Results

Having another full season of data never hurt anyone, so I also accumulated the results for the 2011–12 season. What is impressive is how close they are to the results of 2013–14, indicating to me that we have probably converged on a good estimate of the skill difference between the two groups.

Even-Strength Results by Tier, Goaltenders, 2011–12

	GF/60	GA/60	EGF/60	EGA/60	SF/60	SA/60	Sh%F	Sh%A
Tier 1	2.31	2.19	2.24	2.22	28.99	29.07	7.97%	7.55%
Tier 2	2.18	2.39	2.23	2.26	28.75	28.60	7.57%	8.35%

This is the season with the smallest difference between the two Tiers of goaltenders. While the difference in shooting percentages was 0.8%, once again the Tier 2 goaltenders faced shots that were 4% more challenging than their Tier 1 counterparts. Still, the Tier 1s were once again worth 0.16 goals per 60 minutes more than the alternatives.

We also see, once again, a difference in the shooting percentages for. Tier 1s had their skaters score on 8% of the shots they took, while Tier 2s only saw their teammates score on 7.6% of their attempts. This led to a difference in goal support of 0.13 goals per 60 minutes. Given this data, there is little doubt that there is something fishy going on. Tier 1 goaltenders' teammates seem to play better in front of them; what could be the cause of this?

Factors Affecting Player Results

One of the few factors that could have such a large impact is home-ice advantage, since we know that teams are more successful at home; among other things, their shooting percentage is higher. It turns out that there is a massive home/road start differential between Tier 1 and Tier 2 goaltenders:

Home and Road Starts per Tier, 2013–14

	Road Starts	Home Starts
Tier 1	703	816
Tier 2	526	413

Tier 2 goaltenders (typically backups) start 56% of their games on the road, while Tier 1s start only 46% of the time on the road. This explains some amount of the difference between the performances of the two groups. Some teams take this strategy to the extreme: Carey Price started 37 of Montreal's 41 home games last season but only 22 of their road games, while poor Peter Budaj started 17 times on the road but only 4 (!) times at home. Suddenly his 90.9% save percentage doesn't seem quite as terrible. A similar skew was seen between Semyon Varlamov (37 home, 23 road) and Jean-Sébastien Giguère (4 home, 15 road). All 19 NHL goaltenders that started 50 or more games last season started more often at home than on the road.

I had an inkling that the difference in usage went further than this, so I looked at back-to-back starts. It is well known that teams that play on back-to-back nights do worse on the second night, especially since over two thirds of back-to-back games are played on the road. Who do you suppose gets these difficult starts?

Home and Road Starts per Tier, 2013–14

	Road Starts	Home Starts	Road Starts B2B	Home Starts B2B
Tier 1	703	816	127	70
Tier 2	526	413	177	66

Despite getting only 38% of all goaltending starts, Tier 2 goaltenders got 58% of the most difficult starts, starting on the road on the second night of back-to-back games. They also got almost 50% of the fatigued home starts as well. Note that the fatigue I'm speaking of doesn't apply to the goaltender himself. When a backup goaltender gets the second start of back-to-back games, chances are he didn't play the night before. But a goaltender playing in front of a tired team will be less well defended. Over the last five seasons, the overall save percentage of teams on the road playing the second night of back-to-back games was 90.84%, lower than the 91.08% they achieved when they were not fatigued.

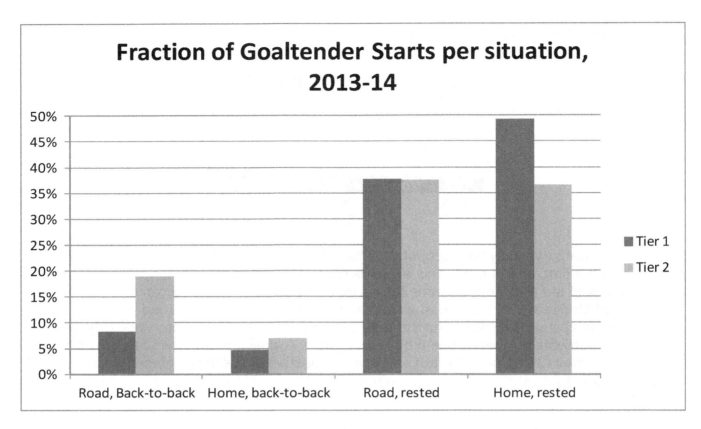

Fraction of Goaltender Starts per situation, 2013-14

This choice of starts does not fully explain the lower save percentage of Tier 2 goaltenders, but it does explain part of it, as well as why their teammates inexplicably score fewer goals in front of them.

Penalty Killing

I will skip over goaltenders' results on the power play, since their role is minimal and the data would be swamped by noise. There are only about 200 shorthanded goals scored in the entire NHL in a full season, which means we have less data about them than we have for an individual team.

However, goaltenders' penalty-killing numbers are of primary importance. Almost a quarter of all goals allowed in the NHL are scored while killing penalties, which means that a team's ability to prevent goals with a man disadvantage can make or break them.

4v5 Results by Tier, Goaltenders, 2013–14

	GF/60	GA/60	EGF/60	EGA/60	SF/60	SA/60	Sh%F	Sh%A
Tier 1	0.93	6.16	0.86	6.21	8.4	52.3	11.05%	11.78%
Tier 2	0.85	6.19	0.78	6.22	8.7	52.1	9.73%	11.87%

The huge difference in save percentages that we saw at even strength no longer shows up killing penalties. The results of the two tiers are almost indistinguishable from one another.

Possibly this was a single-season blip?

4v5 Results by Tier, Goaltenders, 2012–13

	GF/60	GA/60	EGF/60	EGA/60	SF/60	SA/60	Sh%F	Sh%A
Tier 1	0.64	6.20	0.68	5.97	7.8	48.0	8.17%	12.92%
Tier 2	0.67	6.14	0.75	6.01	7.8	48.6	8.67%	12.64%

It appears not! Above are the results for the 2012–13 season and in this case the Tier 2 goaltenders actually did better than the Tier 1s, although the difference is small enough that the two can be considered equal to within the margin of error. I ran the numbers for 2011–12 as well, just to be triply certain.

4v5 Results by Tier, Goaltenders, 2011–12

	GF/60	GA/60	EGF/60	EGA/60	SF/60	SA/60	Sh%F	Sh%A
Tier 1	0.79	5.95	0.78	5.82	8.7	48.7	9.08%	12.21%
Tier 2	0.74	5.96	0.78	6.14	8.7	50.3	8.54%	11.85%

Once again, the Tier 2 goaltenders did marginally better than their Tier 1 counterparts. Amazingly, despite a large and persistent difference in save percentages at even strength, it appears that there is no difference in skill between starters and backups while killing penalties.

To me, this was wildly counter-intuitive. In 2010, Gabriel Desjardins showed that penalty-killing save percentage was essentially random from year to year[17], and further studies have only confirmed this. However, this only proved that the sample size was too small. When even a starting goaltender allows only 30 penalty-killing goals per season, the standard deviation on those is 5.5. That is too much noise to observe any underlying skill, especially when the difference between an elite goaltender and an average one is only 1% of save percentage.

While I never would have expected that we have enough data to isolate a single goaltender's skill on the penalty kill, I assumed that, in aggregate, there would be a difference, especially on something as fundamental. Recently, another analysis, performed by CanesandBluesFan[18] came to the same conclusion as mine: there is no measurable difference between NHL goaltenders on the penalty kill.

The question then becomes: how far down the talent pyramid would this skill appear flat? If every NHL team called up its AHL starter, would the penalty-killing numbers budge? I believe more research is required to answer these questions.

---

17 Gabriel Desjardins, "Is it Possible to Determine Goaltender True Talent on the PK?", *Arctic Ice Hockey*, March 5, 2010, Web, http://www.arcticicehockey.com/2010/3/5/1312360/is-it-possible-to-determine.

18 CanesAndBluesFan, "Penalty Kill Save Percentage", *St. Louis Game Time*, April 30, 2014, Web, http://www.stlouisgametime.com/2014/4/30/5665790/penalty-kill-save-percentage.

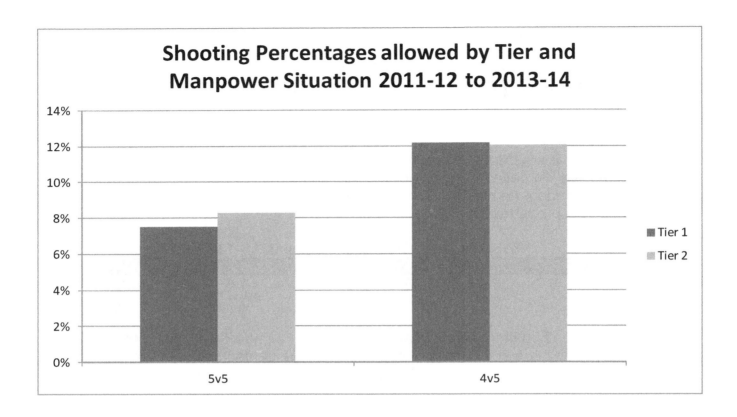

Penalties

I didn't think there was a ghost of a chance that there would be a skill difference between Tier 1 and Tier 2 goaltenders when it came to taking and drawing penalties, but I'd be doing my readers a disservice if I didn't at least look.

Penalties Taken and Drawn, per Tier, 2013–14

	PIM Taken/60	PIM Drawn/60	Net PIM/60
Tier 1	0.05	0.14	0.10
Tier 2	0.04	0.13	0.09

The bottom line is that goaltenders don't draw a lot of penalties, and they *really* don't take a lot of penalties. Per minute, they take about 25 times fewer penalties than forwards or defencemen. As expected, there is no measurable difference between Tier 1 and Tier 2 goaltenders. I won't bore you by showing you the results for other seasons: they look exactly the same.

Closing Thoughts

1. There is a difference of skill between Tier 1 and Tier 2 goaltenders in the NHL. The measured difference in save percentage between the two Tiers is 0.8%. If a Tier 1 goaltender starts 60 games during the season and faces 22 even-strength shots per

game, this corresponds to a difference of 60 * 22 * 0.8% = 10.5 goals over the course of the season.

2. Tier 2 goaltenders get the harder starts, starting more often on the road and more often on the second night of back-to-back games. This means the actual difference in skill between the two Tiers may be smaller than the measured difference.

3. There is no measurable difference between Tier 1 and Tier 2 goaltenders in penalty-killing save percentage.

Goaltending Analytics Revisited

By Rob Vollman

Goaltending seems to be the most obvious shadows upon which analytics can cast a bright light, but the only modern statistic consistently used in its evaluation is save percentage. Sure, it's now studied with the minor improvement of being restricted to even-strength situations, but is there nothing more that can be done to improve upon it?

In truth, there has been a great deal of analytic work in this area, enough to actually fill an entire book of its own. Introducing relatively few of them in the inaugural edition of *Hockey Abstract* was surely an oversight. At the risk of oversimplifying some of the more recent advances, I'll introduce and/or summarize as many of them as possible in this chapter, complete with references to further detail and as much hard-to-find data as possible.

But before we begin, let's be clear about how much evidence the "one stat argument" is built upon. Analytics has come a long way, both in goaltender evaluation and in answering goaltending-related questions, but the best starting point is definitely still save percentage. The upcoming advances achieve their full value when they're built upon save percentage, in order to focus in on specific areas.

Since studies that use save percentage are often based on the assumption that all shots are created equally, we'll explore the ways it can be adjusted for the quality of shots the goalie faces. We'll revisit quality starts and search for more specific talents, like drawing penalties, handling the puck, and performing in key situations such as in the shootout or in the clutch.

Going beyond goaltender evaluations, analytics can also answer broader questions, such as where goalies should be drafted, how much they should be paid, when they should be pulled, and how to project their future performance and/or translate their data from other leagues.

It's truly exciting how far hockey analytics has come in the study of goaltending. While no single advance is necessarily earth-shattering, they can have a compound effect when added together. A consistent goalie who faces high quality shots, is talented in the shootout, and who can handle the puck, draw penalties and thrive in the clutch can really move the needle far more than his save percentage might indicate.

Who are these goalies, what are these skills, and how can analytics help measure them? We'll begin by revisiting my own modest contribution to the field: quality starts.

Quality Starts

Forget evaluating goalies based on wins and losses. That's over! If the starting goalie stops at least a league average number of shots in a particular game, assuming he was sufficiently tested, then that's all that can be fairly expected of him.

Quality starts were formally introduced to hockey back in 2009, but the idea is much older than that. John Lowe introduced it to baseball back in 1985, which have been awarded to a starting pitcher any time he works at least six innings and allows three runs or fewer. I almost immediately applied the same concept to hockey, despite being just 10 years old and having to count them by hand using box scores in the newspaper. The 2009 version upon which I ultimately settled requires a .917 save percentage (or .913 prior to 2009–10), while playing at least as well as an emergency AHL call-up (88.5%) if he only faces 20 shots or fewer.

I doubt that I was the only one to conduct such experiments in the 24 years before its formal introduction in *Hockey Prospectus* because it's an idea that spread quickly. In just these past five years I've seen quality starts make their way through bloggers and the mainstream media, and into front offices and coaching staffs[19]. I've seen it sneak in to fantasy hockey pools on *ESPN*[20] and spread to other leagues such as the AHL[21], U.S. College hockey[22], and professional women's hockey[23]. It's such an intuitive idea that I often even see it being completely reinvented every season or two, most recently by Nick Emptage[24] as a "quality appearance." His version uses a tougher .9231 save percentage boundary and drops that second condition when there's a low volume of shots (as most versions do).

Despite its popularity, you can't actually find quality start data anywhere until it's published in various books, magazines, and websites at season's end. Calculating the data by hand is the only way to evaluate goalies this way mid-season. That's frustrating!

Fortunately, the season is over and we've got the data we need. The following leader board is based on the past three seasons combined, including all goalies who started at least 50 games. Even though that's a rather small and inadequate number of starts on which to grade a goalie (in my view), only 47 netminders made the cut, so be very cautious about the reliability of any drawn conclusions.

What should we be looking for? Obviously, a quality start percentage (QS%) below 50% is quite poor, anything over 60% will be among the league leaders, and the average for an NHL regular is 53.4%. Based on the average of every goalie with fewer than 10 starts in a season, the average for replacement-level goalies is 42.8%, but there is some selection bias involved in that criteria, since playing that poorly will generally limit you to 10 starts in the first place.

19 Chris Hall, "Goaltender Quality Starts", *Coach Chris Hall*, September 6, 2013, Web, http://coachchrishall.com/2013/09/06/goaltender-quality-starts/.

20 Tim Kavanagh, ""In the Crease: Quality Starts", *ESPN*, February 26, 2013, Web, http://espn.go.com/fantasy/hockey/story/_/page/inthecrease130226/fantasy-hockey-goalies-goaltender-rankings-analysis-quality-starts?src=mobile.

21 Geoffrey Detweiler, "Johan Backlund: Quality Behind Phantom Defense", *Broad Street Hockey*, June 24, 2010, Web, http://www.broadstreethockey.com/2010/6/24/1534707/johan-backlund-quality-behind.

22 Steve Racine, "Quality Starts and Michigan's 2012–13 Goaltending", *MGO Blog*, September 15, 2013, Web, http://mgoblog.com:8080/diaries/quality-starts-and-michigans-2012–13-goaltending-panic-and-run-around-screaming.

23 Mike Burse, "Clarkson Cup Predictions by the Numbers", *Women's Hockey Life*, March 18, 2014, Web, http://www.womenshockeylife.com/blogs_view_dsp.cfm?BlogId=1260&CatId=3.

24 Nick Emptage, "Your Goalie May Vary: Looking at Single-Game Save Percentages", *Puck Prediction*, October 5, 2013, Web, http://puckprediction.com/2013/10/05/your-goalie-may-vary-looking-at-single-game-save-percentages/.

One final element in the following leader board is the **really bad start** (RBS), which is sometimes known as blow-ups or disaster starts, which are awarded when a goalie fails to stop even 85% of the shots. A team has only a 10% chance of winning when their starting goalie fares that poorly. I've supplemented each goalie's RBS with how frequently he's pulled (for any reason), which is shown side-by-side in order to provide an idea which goalies coaches have had more patience with (relative to the team's other options).

Quality Starts, 2011–12 to 2013–14[25]

Goalie	Team(s)	Starts	QS	RBS	Pull	SV%	QS%
Brian Elliott	StL	81	56	9	4	.9267	69.1
Cory Schneider	Van/NJ	100	69	10	3	.9258	69.0
Tuukka Rask	Bos	114	78	16	6	.9294	68.4
Josh Harding	Min	59	39	9	8	.9221	66.1
Henrik Lundqvist	NYR	167	108	13	5	.9253	64.7
Jonathan Bernier	LA/Tor	74	47	7	5	.9216	63.5
Ben Bishop	StL/Ott/TB	93	59	12	8	.9228	63.4
Jhonas Enroth	Buf	57	36	8	4	.9177	63.2
Jonathan Quick	LA	154	97	23	8	.9188	63.0
Jimmy Howard	Det	149	93	22	9	.9171	62.4
Jaroslav Halak	StL/Wsh	110	68	15	11	.9209	61.8
Sergei Bobrovsky	Phi/CBJ	120	73	14	11	.9196	60.8
Ben Scrivens	Tor/LA/Edm	63	38	7	4	.9191	60.3
Kari Lehtonen	Dal	158	94	22	11	.9195	59.5
Pekka Rinne	Nsh	138	82	28	14	.9154	59.4
Carey Price	Mtl	161	95	23	6	.9180	59.0
Antti Niemi	SJ	175	103	21	14	.9163	58.9
Jonas Hiller	Ana	148	87	27	12	.9109	58.8
Semyon Varlamov	Col	145	85	21	7	.9173	58.6
Roberto Luongo	Van/Fla	128	75	14	10	.9182	58.6
Corey Crawford	Chi	139	80	20	12	.9139	57.6
Tim Thomas	Bos/Fla/Dal	101	58	10	7	.9157	57.4
Ryan Miller	Buf/StL	157	90	18	11	.9171	57.3
Mike Smith	Phx	161	92	21	15	.9203	57.1
Braden Holtby	Wsh	86	49	13	8	.9183	57.0
Ray Emery	Chi/Phi	67	38	8	5	.9075	56.7
Craig Anderson	Ott	134	75	19	12	.9172	56.0
Miikka Kiprusoff	Cgy	92	51	15	6	.9115	55.4
Jose Theodore	Fla	65	36	11	9	.9114	55.4
Michal Neuvirth	Wsh/Buf	55	30	8	3	.9105	54.5
Marc-Andre Fleury	Pit	159	86	23	8	.9152	54.1
Ilya Bryzgalov	Phi/Edm/Min	127	68	28	11	.9073	53.5
Jean-Sebastien Giguere	Col	62	33	8	3	.9137	53.2
Scott Clemmensen	Fla	50	26	12	4	.9027	52.0
Martin Brodeur	NJ	127	65	25	6	.9041	51.2
Al Montoya	NYI/Wpg	53	27	11	2	.9051	50.9

25 Acknowledgement: Raw game-by-game data for my Quality Start calculations came from the *NHL* http://www.nhl.com.

Niklas Backstrom	Min	105	53	19	11	.9104	50.5
Cam Ward	Car	112	56	19	9	.9106	50.0
Evgeni Nabokov	NYI	121	60	21	8	.9091	49.6
Steve Mason	CBJ/Phi	122	60	25	16	.9075	49.2
Ondrej Pavelec	Wpg	167	82	32	14	.9042	49.1
Devan Dubnyk	Edm/Nsh	110	54	19	8	.9105	49.1
Nikolai Khabibulin	Edm/Chi	55	27	10	8	.9082	49.1
Tomas Vokoun	Wsh/Pit	62	30	13	9	.9154	48.4
Jonas Gustavsson	Tor/Det	66	30	9	4	.9077	45.5
James Reimer	Tor	97	43	19	15	.9116	44.3
Mathieu Garon	TB	60	26	11	11	.9001	43.3

Minimum 50 Starts

Quality starts were explored in quite some depth in last year's book, as well as in several online articles over the past five years, so I'll make just a few quick observations before moving on to some newer ground.

- Brian Elliott rarely gets his due. Any time you can sign a goalie with his recent credentials for between $1.8 million (old contract) and $2.5 million (current contract), that's a major plus.
- You don't need analytics to appreciate the value of goalies like Tuukka Rask and Henrik Lundqvist, but now you can see why undervalued goalies like Cory Schneider and Josh Harding have been championed by the analytics crowd for years.
- The retirement line appears to begin at around 55.4%, where Miikka Kiprusoff and Jose Theodore reside. Jean-Sebastien Giguere and Martin Brodeur aren't far behind, at 53.2% and 52.0% respectively.

Shot Quality

One of the intuitive flaws with the "one stat argument" of evaluating goalies exclusively with save percentage is that it treats every shot equally. Whether it was a rebound, screened, taken from up close by Steven Stamkos or from a distance by Mike Brown, save percentage treats all shots as being equally dangerous. That just intuitively feels wrong, and why attempting to measure and account for the quality of those shots is an idea that pops up quite frequently.

A bucket of cold water was dumped on this topic years ago by the findings of two of the biggest names in hockey analytics, Tom Awad and Gabriel Desjardins. Awad[26] calculated that shot quality determines only 1.7% of a goalie's single-season save percentage in even-strength situations, and only 5.4% over three seasons. The impact is slightly higher on the penalty kill, where shot quality determines up to 2.9% of a goalie's save percentage in a single season, and a more decisive 19.9% over three seasons.

---

26 Tom Awad, "How Much Skill is There in Goaltending?", *Hockey Prospectus,* May 7, 2010, Web, http://www.hockeyprospectus.com/puck/article.php?articleid=558.

As for Desjardins[27], he later calculated that "shot distance—and by extension, long-run shot quality allowed—accounts for 5% of save percentage". The tiny upside established by two of the most careful minds in our business led most analysts to focus their energies elsewhere.

Enter Chris Boyle. His passion for that 5% edge led him to reignite the discussion by launching the "Shot Quality Project" on Sportsnet[28] this past season. Many of his findings, such as a heat map that displays the location of all of a goalie's shots, clearly show a difference in the quality of shots faced by Henrik Lundqvist and Tuukka Rask.

Boyle's approach is reminiscent of the Defence-Independent Goaltending Rating (DIGR)[29], which was introduced at the MIT Sloan Analytics Conference in 2011. Its mission is to calculate what each goalie's save percentage would be had they faced the same quality of shots.

As for me, I put together a chart[30] of all the goalies who have faced at least 1,000 shots over the past three seasons, and related save percentage to average shot distance. A quick glance suggests that there's at least the possibility of a slight relationship between the two.

Shot Distance vs Save Percentage, 2011-12 to 2013-14

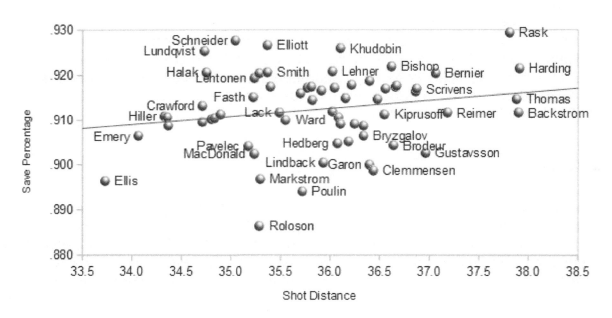

Rask and Lundqvist may have comparable save percentages but Boston's goalie enjoys an

27 Gabriel Desjardins, "Shot Distance Allowed as a Team Talent", *Arctic Ice Hockey*, October 24, 2011, Web, http://www.arcticicehockey.com/2011/10/24/2506209/shot-distance-allowed-as-a-team-talent.
28 Chris Boyle, "Shot quality reveals Rask's true value", *Sportsnet*, November 19, 2013, Web, http://www.sportsnet.ca/hockey/shot-quality-reveals-rasks-true-value/.
29 Michael E. Schuckers, "DIGR: A Defense Independent Rating of NHL Goaltenders using Spatially Smoothed Save Percentage Maps", *St. Lawrence University* and *Statistical Sports Consulting*, March 4, 2011, Web, http://myslu.stlawu.edu/~msch/sports/Schuckers_DIGR_MIT_2011.pdf.
30 Acknowledgement: Shot distance data from *Extra Skater*, http://www.extraskater.com.

extra three and a half feet with which to see shots coming, on average. Is it possible that distance plays a factor in save percentage? It's hard to be certain from just this view, given the inconsistency in how accurately shot locations are recorded from city to city.

How significant is the shot distance recording bias? Several analysts have taken a run at quantifying it over the years, most notably Alan Ryder[31] in 2007, Ken Krzywicki[32] in 2009, or the aforementioned 2011 study by Desjardins. Unfortunately, the worst transgressors and the calculated extents seem to change every time.

Despite the limitations imposed by this recording bias, I've informally used something that I call **home plate save percentage** when comparing goalies who face different levels of shot quality. It's named after a region in front of a goalie that's shaped like a home plate in baseball. If you draw lines from the goal posts to the two defensive zone faceoff dots, and then straight up to the top of the faceoff circles, a straight line connecting them both will create a zone where the most dangerous shots generally occur.

Most goalies face about 44% of their shots from inside the home plate area, posting a save percentage of about .855 on the shots that were taken from within and .958 on those from the outside. Since goalies face these shots in different ratios, and some of them excel at one type of shot more than the other, it can be interesting to consider them separately. If nothing else, it places goalies on more of an equal footing to compare apples to apples and oranges to oranges, instead of comparing two baskets of miscellaneous fruits (which can include some real watermelons, in some cases).

The following table features each goalie's shots, goals, and save percentage (SV%) from outside the home plate area in the first few columns, and then from within the home plate area in the last few. The percentage of shots that were taken from inside the home plate area (HP%) is included in between the two sets of data.

Home Plate Save Percentage, 2011–12 to 2013–14[33]

Goalie	Team(s)	Shots	Goals	SV%	HP%	Shots	Goals	SV%
Henrik Lundqvist	NYR	2550	103	.960	46.3	2203	252	.886
Thomas Greiss	SJ/Phx	700	39	.944	44.0	551	64	.884
Brian Elliott	StL	1234	50	.960	43.4	945	110	.884
Cory Schneider	Van/NJ	1573	55	.965	45.5	1314	154	.883
Tuukka Rask	Bos	1987	81	.959	38.7	1255	148	.882
Jaroslav Halak	StL/Wsh	1574	67	.957	45.4	1308	162	.876
Braden Holtby	Wsh	1617	83	.949	42.0	1173	148	.874
Devan Dubnyk	Edm/Nsh	1816	102	.944	47.5	1641	209	.873
Kari Lehtonen	Dal	2518	102	.960	45.8	2126	275	.871
Jose Theodore	Fla	1054	60	.943	43.6	816	107	.869
Jhonas Enroth	Buf	1115	59	.947	41.7	796	105	.868

31 Alan Ryder, "Product Recall Notice for Shot Quality", *Hockey Analytics*, June 1, 2007, Web, http://hockeyanalytics.com/2007/06/product-recall-notice-for-shot-quality/.
32 Ken Krzywicki, "Removing Observer Bias from Shot Distance", *Hockey Analytics*, September 1, 2009, Web, http://www.hockeyanalytics.com/Research_files/SQ-DistAdj-RS0809-Krzywicki.pdf
33 Acknowledgement: Data obtained from *Super Shot Search*, http://somekindofninja.com/nhl/.

Ben Bishop	StL/Ott/TB	2275	53	.977	34.5	1196	158	.868
Nikolai Khabibulin	Edm/Chi	2713	101	.963	44.3	786	104	.868
Mike Smith	Phx	778	39	.950	50.3	2162	286	.868
Anton Khudobin	Bos/Car	855	27	.968	42.7	638	85	.867
Evgeni Nabokov	NYI	1786	90	.950	47.4	1610	217	.865
Sergei Bobrovsky	Phi/CBJ	2047	80	.961	42.4	1505	203	.865
Ryan Miller	Buf/StL	2808	124	.956	43.2	2135	288	.865
Jason Labarbera	Phx/Edm	621	36	.942	40.9	429	58	.865
Jimmy Howard	Det	2298	93	.960	44.0	1809	246	.864
Roberto Luongo	Van/Fla	1984	66	.967	46.6	1733	241	.861
Semyon Varlamov	Col	2544	96	.962	44.5	2040	284	.861
Michal Neuvirth	Wsh/Buf	1009	49	.951	45.8	851	120	.859
Robin Lehner	Ott	1034	39	.962	39.8	685	97	.858
Eddie Lack	Van	549	21	.962	47.8	503	72	.857
Jonathan Quick	LA	2306	86	.963	41.4	1629	234	.856
Corey Crawford	Chi	2093	83	.960	45.1	1716	248	.856
Tim Thomas	Bos/Fla/Dal	1728	69	.960	43.3	1321	191	.855
Ray Emery	Chi/Phi	1056	50	.953	47.3	949	138	.855
Al Montoya	NYI/Wpg	919	46	.950	47.1	818	119	.855
Victor Fasth	Ana	2788	109	.961	41.8	418	61	.854
Antti Niemi	SJ	583	24	.959	41.8	2002	292	.854
Craig Anderson	Ott	2463	93	.962	42.1	1788	262	.854
Carey Price	Mtl	2708	87	.968	43.1	2052	301	.853
Jonas Hiller	Ana	2200	92	.958	45.4	1829	269	.853
Justin Peters	Car	742	30	.960	45.6	623	92	.852
Cam Ward	Car	1964	88	.955	43.0	1480	219	.852
Karri Ramo	Cgy	583	21	.964	46.6	508	76	.850
Ben Scrivens	Tor/LA/Edm	1264	49	.961	40.0	842	126	.850
Jean-Sebastien Giguere	Col	1069	40	.963	43.9	835	125	.850
Miikka Kiprusoff	Cgy	1534	65	.958	43.0	1156	174	.850
Marc-Andre Fleury	Pit	2425	75	.969	45.2	1998	302	.849
Jonathan Bernier	LA/Tor	1488	46	.969	39.9	988	151	.847
Peter Budaj	Mtl	768	29	.962	45.0	628	96	.847
Scott Clemmensen	Fla	907	53	.942	45.0	741	114	.846
Mathieu Garon	TB	898	54	.940	43.9	702	108	.846
Tomas Vokoun	Wsh/Pit	1065	32	.970	41.4	753	116	.846
Martin Brodeur	NJ	1709	81	.953	44.8	1388	216	.844
Dan Ellis	4 Teams	655	35	.947	48.9	628	98	.844
Ondrej Pavelec	Wpg	2657	123	.954	45.6	2231	350	.843
Pekka Rinne	Nsh	2357	85	.964	39.5	1542	243	.842
James Reimer	Tor	1841	78	.958	39.9	1223	193	.842
Josh Harding	Min	1049	27	.974	39.9	695	110	.842
Ilya Bryzgalov	Phi/Edm/Min	864	43	.950	45.5	1513	241	.841
Anders Lindback	Nsh/TB	1998	88	.956	43.1	722	115	.841
Steve Mason	CBJ/Phi	2147	93	.957	41.0	1489	242	.838
Carter Hutton	Nsh	583	20	.966	43.6	451	74	.836
Joey MacDonald	Det/Cgy	620	25	.960	46.4	536	88	.836

Jonas Gustavsson	Tor/Det	1118	46	.959	44.7	904	151	.833
Dwayne Roloson	TB	539	28	.948	52.1	587	100	.830
Niklas Backstrom	Min	1770	62	.965	39.3	1147	196	.829
Kevin Poulin	NYI	595	30	.950	46.1	509	87	.829
Johan Hedberg	NJ	680	28	.959	41.0	473	82	.827
Jacob Markstrom	Fla/Van	662	31	.953	46.5	575	100	.826

It shouldn't be any surprise to see Henrik Lundqvist on top of virtually any measurement that takes shot quality into account. Some of the league's most undervalued goalies share the top of the list with him and Tuukka Rask, although I'll admit that it's a surprise to see Devan Dubnyk up there. On the flip side, Dubnyk's save percentage outside the home plate area is the 5th worst. Consider his position on the following chart, which maps each goalie's save percentage by location.

Save Percentage by Location, 2011–12 to 2013–14

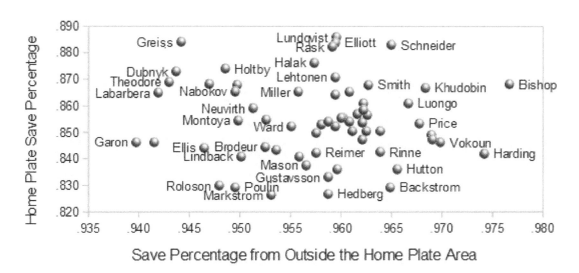

Dubnyk is not alone among goalies who do surprisingly well from close up, but who struggle on shots from a distance. While the instinct might be that this is a result of size over skill, Jose Theodore, Jason LaBarbera, and especially Thomas Greiss fit the same profile.

Another interesting result is Brian Elliott, who is located in almost the exact same position as Henrik Lundqvist and Tuukka Rask, the goalies who are the very best at shots taken in the home plate area. Cory Schneider is actually just as effective at the tough shots as they are, but has the advantage of being above average at the lower quality shots, too.

Actually, it's time to be a bit more precise with our language. Each of these models is actually studying the *location* of the shots, not the *quality*. In reality, there's a lot more to the quality of a shot than just its location, like whether it was a rebound, screened, or taken by a sniper rather than an enforcer, and so on. David Johnson[34] even found that save percentages were

---

34 David Johnson, "Zone Start effects on Goalie Save Percentage", *Hockey Analysis*, April 26, 2012, Web, http://hockeyanalysis.com/2012/04/26/zone-start-effects-on-goalie-save-percentage/.

significantly higher within a few seconds of a faceoff, suggesting such shots were of lower quality, regardless of distance.

One of the reasons some of these factors are ignored is because there are too few to study. There are only about 1.5 rebound shots per team per game, for example. The lack of data limits how reliably a goalie's rebound control can be measured and decreases the likelihood that superior handling of rebounds will affects a game's (or even a season's) outcome. Therefore, only the most thorough goaltending analysts, like Phil Myrland[35] for example, have invested any time studying rebounds.

The more important remaining aspect of shot quality is probably the quality of the shooters. Intuitively, there has to be a quality difference when facing the top playoff teams, relative to the basement dwellers. The following chart shows a slight downward slope in each goalie's save percentage as the average shooting percentage of their opponents goes up.

Opponent Quality and Save Percentage, 2011–12 to 2013–14

These are some fascinating results. For example, consider Carolina's Justin Peters (now with Washington) and Cam Ward. Opponents are equally likely to score against either goalie, but that actually results in a drop in their shooting percentage in those facing Peters. And consider new teammates Roberto Luongo and Al Montoya in Florida. Although one goalie's save percentage is far better than the other's, that difference might actually be explained by the quality of opposing shooters.

And what about a player's own team? Whether it's by luck, skill or design, it makes sense to test the idea that a team's defensive play can reduce the overall quality of the shots allowed, however that's defined, even if it's simply by allowing shots from a greater average distance.

Consider the Boston Bruins, for instance. All of their goalies were on the right-hand side of the

---

35 Phil Myrland, The Value of Rebound Control", *Brodeur is a Fraud*, April 21, 2009, Web, http://brodeurisafraud.blogspot.ca/2009/04/value-of-rebound-control.html.

shot distance chart earlier this chapter. Tim Thomas won the Vezina and the Conn Smythe in Beantown before struggling through a merely average season (at best) in Florida and Dallas. Even if that can be chalked up to his age and/or taking a year off, what about Tuukka Rask? His dominant numbers as a Bruin rival those of the legendary Dominik Hasek. Unless you believe they are equally talented, how could that be explained without team effects?

One way to look for team effects is to study what happens to save percentages when goalies change teams. Phil Myrland and Vic Ferrari[36] both looked into that years ago and found the net effect to be no more than one or two goals a season, tops, even once adjusted for scorekeeper bias.

Not only did Tore Purdy[37] also confirm that save percentage scarcely changes when a goalie changes teams, but he also approached the question by comparing the save percentages of starting goalies to their backups. If there's a strong team effect then they should be correlated, but he found that the difference was scarcely greater than what could be simulated randomly. Therefore, team effects are currently felt to be a minimal component of shot quality.

In the end, the two most prominent components of shot quality appear to be the location of the shot and the quality of the shooter. Therefore, I created my own modest attempt at visualizing this using what I called a **goalie usage chart**, which maps these two factors. Specifically, the horizontal axis is the average distance of the shots they faced, with the average shooting percentage of the opposing teams they face on the vertical axis. In this chart, each goalie's circle is sized based on his shooting percentage relative to league average, with shaded meaning it was above average (which is good) and white being below (which is not as good).

36 Vic Ferrari, "The Shot Quality Fantasy", Irreverent Oiler Fans, July 24, 2009, Web, http://vhockey.blogspot.ca/2009/07/shot-quality-fantasy.html.
37 Jlikens, "Team Effects and Even Strength Save Percentage", Objective NHL, May 10, 2011, Web, http://objectivenhl.blogspot.ca/2011/05/team-effects-and-even-strength-save.html.

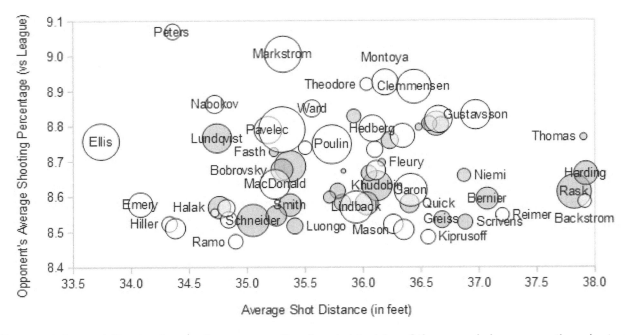

Goalie Usage Chart, 2011–12 to 2013–14

Minnesota's and Boston's goalies are on the far right side of the graph because the shots they face are at the greatest distance (without accounting for recording bias), with Toronto not far behind. They are also at the lower end of the chart in terms of the average shooting percentages of the opponents, which results in potentially the easiest assignments in the NHL. Their save percentages are consequently good, especially in the case of Josh Harding and Tuukka Rask.

Comparing Rask to Lundqvist once again highlights the talents of the latter, who faces shots from closer up (recording bias aside) and faces teams with slightly higher shooting percentages, and yet performs just as well overall. There is not a single goalie with an above-average save percentage who faces both closer shots and tougher competition than Lundqvist. In fact, there are only a few goalies who face equal or slightly greater competition than Lundqvist and yet maintain above-average save percentages, and each of them enjoy at least an extra foot and a half to see their shots.

Here's the entire leader board for every goalie who has faced at least 1,000 shots over the past three seasons (Shots), including their save percentage (SV%, league average .914), average shot distance (Dist), average shooting percentage of their opponents (SH%), and a crude estimate of the average difficulty (Difficulty) of a goalie's assignment.

The difficulty is based on adding the standard deviations of each of the latter two factors, which isn't an appropriate statistical practice, but simply something to paint a rough picture of which goalies are facing tougher playing conditions. Imagine a line that runs through the upper left corner of the previous chart, down through the bottom right corner, and the goalies below should be listed in approximately that order.

Difficulty of Goaltending Assignments, 2011–12 to 2013–14[38]

Goalie	Team(s)	Shots	SV%	Dist	SH%	Difficulty
Justin Peters	Car	1366	.911	34.4	9.07	4.45
Jacob Markstrom	Fla/Van	1268	.897	35.3	9.01	2.98
Dan Ellis	4 Teams	1284	.896	33.7	8.76	2.83
Evgeni Nabokov	NYI	3397	.910	34.7	8.86	2.56
Henrik Lundqvist	NYR	4753	.925	34.7	8.77	1.84
Jose Theodore	Fla	1893	.912	36.0	8.92	1.58
Cam Ward	Car	3410	.910	35.6	8.85	1.57
Ondrej Pavelec	Wpg	4931	.904	35.2	8.79	1.53
Al Montoya	NYI/Wpg	1737	.905	36.2	8.93	1.45
Dwayne Roloson	TB	1126	.886	35.3	8.79	1.41
Ray Emery	Chi/Phi	2005	.906	34.1	8.58	1.16
Scott Clemmensen	Fla	1648	.899	36.4	8.91	1.09
Ryan Miller	Buf/StL	4943	.917	35.9	8.83	1.03
Victor Fasth	Ana	1001	.915	35.2	8.73	1.01
Eddie Lack	Van	1052	.912	35.5	8.74	0.82
Kevin Poulin	NYI	1104	.894	35.7	8.75	0.65
Johan Hedberg	NJ	1153	.905	36.1	8.79	0.61
Sergei Bobrovsky	Phi/CBJ	3552	.920	35.3	8.68	0.58
Brian Elliott	StL	2179	.927	35.4	8.69	0.57
Jonas Hiller	Ana	4045	.911	34.3	8.52	0.49
Jaroslav Halak	StL/Wsh	2882	.921	34.8	8.57	0.38
Nikolai Khabibulin	Edm/Chi	1564	.909	34.4	8.51	0.36
Joey MacDonald	Det/Cgy	1157	.902	35.2	8.64	0.35
Corey Crawford	Chi	3809	.913	34.7	8.56	0.31
Devan Dubnyk	Edm/Nsh	3458	.910	34.8	8.57	0.31
Carey Price	Mtl	4727	.918	36.2	8.76	0.20
Jhonas Enroth	Buf	1922	.915	36.5	8.80	0.20
Craig Anderson	Ott	4275	.917	36.6	8.81	0.18
Martin Brodeur	NJ	3097	.904	36.7	8.82	0.18
Ilya Bryzgalov	Phi/Edm/Min	3511	.906	36.3	8.77	0.18
Peter Budaj	Mtl	1397	.911	36.1	8.73	0.15
Ben Bishop	StL/Ott/TB	2703	.922	36.6	8.81	0.12
Tomas Vokoun	Wsh/Pit	1792	.917	36.7	8.80	0.04
Jason Labarbera	Phx/Edm	1050	.910	34.8	8.54	0.04
Jean-Sebastien Giguere	Col	1926	.914	35.8	8.67	-0.01
Jonas Gustavsson	Tor/Det	2022	.903	37.0	8.83	-0.07
Marc-Andre Fleury	Pit	4423	.915	36.2	8.70	-0.19
Cory Schneider	Van/NJ	2887	.928	35.1	8.53	-0.20
Mike Smith	Phx	4875	.921	35.4	8.58	-0.23
Braden Holtby	Wsh	2790	.917	36.1	8.67	-0.29
Michal Neuvirth	Wsh/Buf	1860	.909	36.1	8.67	-0.30
Kari Lehtonen	Dal	4677	.919	35.2	8.55	-0.31

38 Acknowledgement: Raw shot distance data for my calculations came from *Extra Skater* http://www.extraskater.com.

Semyon Varlamov	Col	4584	.917	35.8	8.62	-0.37
Pekka Rinne	Nsh	3899	.916	35.7	8.60	-0.43
Karri Ramo	Cgy	1092	.911	34.9	8.47	-0.48
Anton Khudobin	Bos/Car	1510	.926	36.1	8.63	-0.62
Jimmy Howard	Det	4107	.917	35.8	8.58	-0.64
Roberto Luongo	Van/Fla	3718	.917	35.4	8.52	-0.70
Anders Lindback	Nsh/TB	1586	.900	35.9	8.57	-0.88
Robin Lehner	Ott	1719	.921	36.0	8.58	-0.90
Mathieu Garon	TB	1619	.900	36.4	8.62	-1.02
Antti Niemi	SJ	4791	.916	36.9	8.66	-1.21
Jonathan Quick	LA	3935	.919	36.4	8.58	-1.29
Tim Thomas	Bos/Fla/Dal	3049	.915	37.9	8.77	-1.51
Carter Hutton	Nsh	1034	.909	36.3	8.52	-1.56
Steve Mason	CBJ/Phi	3667	.909	36.3	8.51	-1.78
Jonathan Bernier	LA/Tor	2476	.920	37.1	8.59	-1.91
Thomas Greiss	SJ/Phx	1251	.918	36.7	8.53	-1.92
Miikka Kiprusoff	Cgy	2691	.911	36.6	8.49	-2.15
Ben Scrivens	Tor/LA/Edm	2106	.917	36.9	8.53	-2.19
Josh Harding	Min	1744	.921	37.9	8.66	-2.29
James Reimer	Tor	3064	.912	37.2	8.55	-2.37
Tuukka Rask	Bos	3242	.929	37.8	8.61	-2.56
Niklas Backstrom	Min	2917	.912	37.9	8.58	-2.86

Minimum 1000 Shots

Not to keep beating the Lundqvist drum, who I also named as the league's best goalie in last year's book, but just look at that. By these two measurements, he has the 5th hardest job in the NHL and yet the 5th highest save percentage. Sergei Bobrovsky, Brian Elliott and Jaroslav Halak, who are ranked 18th, 19th, and 21st respectively, are the only ones among those with the 30 most difficult assignments who are even close.

In my opinion, the quest for shot quality is one of the most intriguing and compelling ideas in the world of goalie analytics today, but is currently being discouraged by inconsistently recorded data, overlapping influences, and a relatively small overall significance. I look forward to when the league introduces systems to more accurately measure the location of a shot, and potentially its speed, which will make these studies even more worthwhile.

Ultimately, we know intuitively that not all shots are equal and, once the quality of the data improves, the ongoing attempts to accurately determine and adjust for the quality of those shots could finally prove to be a meaningful part of goalie evaluation.

Shootout Specialists

Is the shootout simply a random coin toss? There are plenty of studies that have demonstrated so, especially for the players, but not for the goalies given their much larger sample of data. Recent evidence has suggested that there could be a persistent ability here, and one that might be great enough to move the needle in the standings enough to warrant some attention.

The Penguins have gone 45–19 in the shootout thanks to Fleury stopping 158 of 205 shots (77.1%), for example, and the Rangers have gone 48–33 with Henrik Lundqvist stopping 234 of 310 (75.5%). Is this really just a random result or is there some persistence?

To informally answer that for myself, I used a quick and dirty (yet handy) trick to overcome issues with small sample sizes. I grouped the 50 goalies with inadequate sample sizes into five groups of goalies with adequate sample sizes. In this case, that means dividing all of 2013–14's goalies who have faced at least 10 shots in their careers into five even categories (of 10) based on how well they performed in the shootout prior to this season. Then we can see if that matches what each group did in 2013–14. Some individuals will have done better, some will have done worse, but if there truly is an element of persistence to this data, then the averages of each group will remain at least somewhat similar.

In this case, the five combined groups of goalies have save percentages of .747, .695, .650, .626, and .551, respectively. If there is some persistence to this, then each group's 2013–14 results should be comparable, or at least go in that same order but closer to the league average (.672). And, sure enough, the five sets of goalies posted shootout save percentages of .715, .688, .671, .609 and .630 in 2013–14. Four of the five groups finished closer to league average and retained their order, which suggests that there's some predictability here.

Could there be enough value here for teams to invest a little extra cap space to acquire goalies who are good at the shootout? If so, here is the all-time shootout data for all the active goalies who have faced at least 10 shots over the past three seasons and have also faced at least 50 all-time.

All-time Shootout Save Percentage, Active Goalies[39]

Goalie	Team(s)	W	L	Shot	Goal	SV%
Marc-Andre Fleury	Pit	45	19	205	47	.771
Semyon Varlamov	Wsh/Col	18	11	94	23	.755
Henrik Lundqvist	NYR	48	33	310	76	.755
Antti Niemi	Chi/SJ	32	21	179	47	.737
Tim Thomas	Bos/Fla/Dal	36	30	234	64	.726
Kari Lehtonen	Atl/Dal	36	23	207	57	.725
Jimmy Howard	Det	19	21	143	40	.720
Ben Bishop	StL/Ott/TB	11	10	88	25	.716
Josh Harding	Min	14	10	73	21	.712
Ryan Miller	Buf/StL	50	30	279	81	.710
Pekka Rinne	Nsh	23	23	175	51	.709
Corey Crawford	Chi	20	18	129	38	.705
Jonathan Quick	LA	36	22	206	61	.704
Carey Price	Mtl	21	24	156	47	.699
Tuukka Rask	Bos	15	14	111	34	.694

39 Acknowledgement: Raw shootout data for my calculations came from the *NHL* http://www.nhl.com.

Martin Brodeur	NJ	42	30	244	75	.693
Jaroslav Halak	Mtl/StL/Wsh	19	20	129	40	.690
Jonas Hiller	Ana	20	22	182	57	.687
Jonas Gustavsson	Tor/Det	8	9	53	17	.679
Jose Theodore	5 Teams	22	17	134	43	.679
Roberto Luongo	Van/Fla	34	41	264	87	.672
James Reimer	Tor	7	9	54	18	.667
Michal Neuvirth	Wsh/Buf	8	7	51	17	.667
Craig Anderson	4 Teams	20	17	129	44	.659
Steve Mason	CBJ/Phi	15	24	132	46	.652
Brian Elliott	Ott/Col/StL	15	16	108	38	.648
Evgeni Nabokov	SJ/NYI	30	30	214	76	.645
Peter Budaj	Col/Mtl	19	22	145	52	.641
Ondrej Pavelec	Wpg	15	19	119	43	.639
Sergei Bobrovsky	Phi/CBJ	11	11	66	24	.636
Mike Smith	Dal/TB/Phx	21	27	158	59	.627
Nikolai Khabibulin	Chi/Edm	14	24	138	52	.623
Ilya Bryzgalov	5 Teams	24	32	201	76	.622
Scott Clemmensen	NJ/Tor/Fla	11	15	95	36	.621
Cam Ward	Car	11	25	107	41	.617
Devan Dubnyk	Edm/Nsh	9	13	75	29	.613
Jean-Sebastien Giguere	Ana/Tor/Col	21	29	155	62	.600
Ray Emery	Ott/Chi/Phi	7	15	74	30	.595
Cory Schneider	Van/NJ	6	13	64	26	.594
Jason LaBarbera	4 Teams	12	11	79	34	.570
Niklas Backstrom	Min	22	33	182	80	.560
Curtis Sanford	StL/Van/CBJ	5	11	50	22	.560

Minimum 50 Shots

The first observation is that being good at hockey doesn't necessarily mean that a goalie will be good in the shootout. The best regulation-time goalies in the league are sprinkled almost evenly throughout the list, mixed in with journeymen and backups. As Eric Tulsky[40] discovered in his recent study, "save percentage during play is worthless as a predictor of the shootout."

Once you calculate a confidence interval, arguably only three or four goalies are definitively better than average at the shootout: Fleury, Lundqvist, Niemi, and Thomas, and potentially only Backstrom is worse. That's not very many clear cut cases, but it's a lot more than you can say for shooters, none of whom have sufficient success and/or sample size to be confidently considered either above or below average.

Could this result be achieved by random chance? Probably not. The results of Michael Lopez's[41] more careful study found that only 11 times in 10,000 simulations did a situation like this occur through random variation.

---

40 Eric Tulsky, "Ilya Bryzgalov and the Shootout", *Broad Street Hockey*, February 10, 2012, Web, http://www.broadstreethockey.com/2012/2/10/2787082/ilya-bryzgalov-shoot-out-philadelphia-flyers.
41 Michael Lopez, "NHL shootouts aren't random. So let's stop calling them that.", *Stats by Lopez*, March 12, 2014, Web, http://statsbylopez.com/2014/03/12/nhl-shootouts-arent-random-so-lets-stop-calling-them-that/.

All of this suggests that a gifted shootout goalie can potentially be worth a couple of extra points in the standings. Look at New Jersey, with Schneider and Clemmensen at the bottom of the list, and remember that the Devils were 0–13 on the shootout last year and will probably finish poorly again no matter how well their shooters do. What would it be worth for them to secure a shootout specialist in nets?

— DEVILS IN THE SHOOTOUT —

2014 RECORD: 0-13

Toronto's ex-coach Ron Wilson explicitly switched goalies for the shootout back in the 2007–08 season, replacing Vesa Toskala, who was miserable at the shootout, with Curtis Joseph. It was the fourth time such a switch had occurred, according to TSN[42], but it has never paid off.

Don't give up. A popular analytics blogger known simply as Frank[43] calculated that a single shootout goal is worth 0.368 wins. Since a shootout win results in two points in the standings instead of just one, 0.368 extra wins is worth exactly 0.368 extra points in the standings. Given how relatively rare the shootout occurs and how small the predictable difference is between even the best and the worst goalies, it's possible that we're only talking about a single point in the standings per season. That, however, is still worth about a million dollars, according to hockey's 3-1-1 rule. Maybe that's an investment New Jersey will find is worth making.

---

42 Staff, "Wilson's Golie Switch Makes For an Interesting Debate", *TSN*, October 22, 2008, Web, http://www.tsn.ca/nhl/story/?id=253404.

43 Frank F, "Is a Goalie's Shootout Performance Meaningful?", *That's a Clown Hypothesis, Bro!*, January 1, 2014, Web, http://clownhypothesis.com/2014/01/01/is-a-goalies-shootout-performance-meaningful/.

Other Skills

While quality starts, shootout talent, and shot quality don't move the needle very much in goaltender evaluation individually, together they can start to add up.

There are a variety of other areas where goalies can distinguish themselves one from the other. For instance, some goalies are better at handling the puck or drawing penalties, while others appear to be superior in clutch situations. How can we measure these?

Puck Handling

Studies about puck handling have been quite modest in scope, and normally centre around Martin Brodeur, who is widely considered the best by quite some margin. The future Hall of Famer has recorded 10 points over the past three seasons, while only Kari Lehtonen (9), Henrik Lundqvist (7), Pekka Rinne (6), and Mike Smith (6) have more than half as many.

Bruce McCurdy[44] rigorously compared Brodeur's puck handling with that of Philadelphia's Ilya Bryzgalov over the course of their five-game playoff series in 2012. Looking at each goalie's percentage of good passes, giveaways, clearing plays, fielding the puck (generally behind the net) and so on, he speculated on the effect a goalie's puck handling can have on shot suppression, maintaining the game's flow, preventing penalties and injuries, and on both opposition and own-team strategy. He didn't reach any firm conclusions, but certainly laid the foundation for future work in this area.

The only other study of which I'm aware is courtesy of Phil Myrland[45], who attempted to quantify the effect puck handling can have on shot suppression in a Brodeur-based study of his own. He reasoned that a good puck handler can prevent about a shot per game, but reached no conclusion on the potential quality of the remaining shots.

Drawing Penalties

Drawing penalties is an easier topic to cover now that the *Extra Skater*[46] website makes the data readily available for study. Over the past three seasons combined, the league leaders are Carey Price and Kari Lehtonen, both of whom have drawn 27 more penalties than they've taken themselves. That's quite a bit more than the next highest ranked goalies, Niklas Backstrom (21) and Tim Thomas (20), the only other netminders with a penalty differential of at least 20.

On the other end of the spectrum, Mike Smith has taken 15 penalties, the most of any goalie

---

44 Bruce McCurdy, "Tender Touches: An attempt to measure Martin Brodeur's puckhandling impact", *Edmonton Journal*, May 25, 2012, Web, http://blogs.edmontonjournal.com/2012/05/25/tender-touches-an-attempt-to-measure-martin-brodeurs-puckhandling-impact/.

45 Phil Myrland, "Estimating Brodeur's Shot Prevention", *Brodeur is a Fraud*, October 30, 2008, Web, http://brodeurisafraud.blogspot.ca/2008/10/estimating-brodeurs-shot-prevention.html.

46 Acknowledgement: Penalty data for goalies from *Extra Skater* http://www.extraskater.com.

by quite some margin, but he has also drawn 23, which is tied with Backstrom for third. Other undisciplined goalies include Ben Scrivens, who has taken 8 penalties and drawn 10, Evgeni Nabokov, who has taken 8 penalties and drawn 9, and the only two goalies significantly into negative territory, Ray Emery and Karri Ramo, who have each taken 4 more penalties than they've drawn.

Given that a team has just under a one-in-five chance of scoring on a power play, that makes goalies like Price and Lehtonen arguably worth up to two goals per season. That's worth some consideration.

Clutch Play

Do some goalies have the ability to crank it up a notch when the game is tight, especially in critical games? There's plenty of anecdotal evidence, which is why most fans believe so, but is there enough on which to base analytic conclusions?

Even though it makes perfect sense, from a human nature perspective, that certain types of athletes perform better under pressure, it's not easy to identify and measure such players in the NHL with statistics. After all, there are 1.64 million hockey players worldwide, according to the IIHF's most recent survey[47], of which only 983 played in the NHL last year. I imagine it would be quite difficult to be among the best 0.06% in the world at something if you lacked the ability to marshal your talents in critical moments.

The larger problem is that we don't know who the clutch players are until long after the fact. After all, how frequently do clutch situations truly occur? If too broad a definition is assigned, then the end result will be no different from a goalie's overall statistics, and a narrow definition will result in too little data on which to draw any meaningful conclusions.

For example, assume a definition was conceived that resulted in roughly 10% of the average goalie's action being defined as a clutch situation. Given that it can take several seasons to figure out how good a goalie is overall, that means it could take several decades to figure out which ones are good in the clutch, by which point their careers are over and the information is useless.

And that's just one of many problems with trying to measure clutch play. Phil Myrland[48], who studied the question over five years ago, ultimately concluded with a long list of reasons why further study was practically impossible. Score and team effects can cloud the picture just as much as the small sample sizes, for instance, which can also confound the ability to figure out what predictive value it may have.

That's not to say that the area is being ignored within the analytics community. Matt Pfeffer[49] has recently begun to post each goalie's save percentages in "high leverage situations", for

47 IIHF, "Survey of Players", 2013, Web, http://www.iihf.com/iihf-home/the-iihf/survey-of-players/.
48 Phil Myrland, "Clutch Play", *Brodeur is a Fraud*, December 2, 2009, Web, http://brodeurisafraud.blogspot.ca/2009/12/clutch-play.html.
49 Matt Pfeffer, "The season's most clutch goalies", *Hockey Prospectus*, April 9, 2014, Web, http://www.hockeyprospectus.com/the-seasons-most-clutch-goalies/.

example, but ultimately wound up with a list that included James Reimer, Ryan Miller, and Ilya Bryzgalov instead of the usual suspects.

Ultimately, Myrland's concluded his study on clutch play by writing that, "I don't think the evidence suggests it is particularly significant or that it is accurately estimated by observers." I'd agree with that and add the point that it isn't being accurately estimated by analytics either.

Goaltending Q & A

There are a lot of other interesting ways that analytics has been applied to the field of goaltending, such as where goalies should be drafted, how much they should be paid, and when they should be pulled for an extra attacker.

Here are a handful of such questions and, once again at the risk of oversimplification, summaries of the latest research and current thinking of the analytic community.

1. How are goalies affected by workload?

One of the most common unanswered questions in the field of goaltending is to what extent a goalie's save percentage is influenced by shot volume. Do goalies get "into a groove" and post better save percentages when they're facing a lot of shots and, by extension, can season-to-season variations in individual save percentages be explained by changes in shot volumes?

The question of whether or not a goalie's save percentage is related to shot volume is actually quite complex, even though the trend is obvious on an individual game basis, and has been anecdotally observed at the season level. This past season, for example, Jonathan Bernier went from the Kings to the Leafs, a low shot volume team to a high shot volume team, and saw his save percentage rise from .912 in 62 career games to .922 in 55 games. We've also seen everyone from Tomas Vokoun to Roberto Luongo post insane save percentages on high shot volume teams, and it seems that many goalies post their career-high save percentages the same season they face their highest shot volumes.

The question is: is this relationship between shot volume and save percentage real and, if so, how much of it is a matter of a goalie getting in to a groove and playing better?

Tyler Dellow[50] can quickly address the second part of that question. He's the analyst that first established that save percentages don't drop with every minute that elapses without a shot. That is, despite anecdotal evidence from the goalies themselves, netminders don't actually get cold from lack of action. At least, not in a way that can be measured with analytics.

As for the key part of the question, many fans have seen a chart similar to the following. In simplistic terms, it shows an increase in a goalie's individual game save percentage based on

---

50 Tyler Dellow, "Does Save Percentage Fall as Time Elapses?", *MC79 Hockey,* February 21, 2006, Web, http://www.mc79hockey.com/?p=2447.

the number of shots he faced that night.

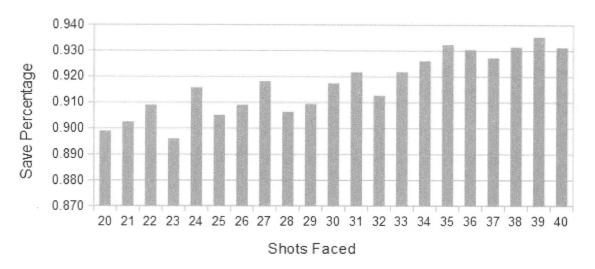

I have a lot of concerns about this approach, however, most notably the following:

- Recording bias. While every single goal will be counted, shots will be recorded more generously by some scorekeepers than by others. And, obviously, those with fewer shots recorded will have lower save percentages, even if they were in actuality just as effective as anybody else. In essence, if every goalie was identical, recording bias alone could still create a chart like that all by itself (if the effect was dramatic enough).

- Score effects. Teams protecting leads late in the game tend to take fewer shots. That means the losing goalie, who will presumably already have a lower save percentage than the winning goalie, will wind up facing fewer shots through the final frame. That will artificially push goalies with lower save percentages to the left side of the chart and those with higher save percentages to the right.

- Goalies getting replaced. If a goalie is playing poorly, then he is removed from this sample, and this is more likely to occur when the goalie is facing a high volume of shots. Therefore, goalies facing a low volume of shots are more likely to still include these struggling performers, which will pull their average save percentages down.

- Selection bias. The mix of goalies facing 40 shots per night is not the same mix of goalies facing 20 shots a night, nor are the shooters involved. Certain teams, opponents, and goalies are being represented more in one group than the other.

- Special teams play. Shots are taken at different rates in different manpower situations, and their shooting percentages can vary too.

Let's take a closer look at that first concern about recording bias. I'm bothered by both the inconsistency in which the data is being recorded and that shots on goal are being used as the proxy for a goalie's workload. After all, a goalie has to work just as hard to set himself up for all attempted shots, whether they actually reach him or not. Interestingly, this was the exact purpose for which former Buffalo Sabres goalie coach Jim Corsi invented the statistic that bears his name today.

Consider the following chart, which maps the average number of *attempted* shots a goalie faces per night against his save percentage, using every goalie to face at least 1,000 attempted shots over the past three seasons. If there's a relationship, then it's not one that's obvious to the naked eye.

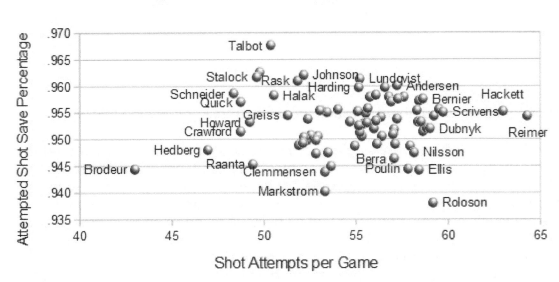

Overall, the goalies who face relatively fewer shots, like Jonathan Quick, Corey Crawford, Jimmy Howard and anyone who plays for the New Jersey Devils, fare no better nor worse than those who routinely get shelled, like Toronto's goalies.

This chart also nicely highlights one of my other main concerns, team effects. Look at all the New Jersey Devils on the left side of the chart (Martin Brodeur, Johan Hedberg, Cory Schneider), and all the Toronto Maple Leafs on the right (James Reimer, Jonathan Bernier, Ben Scrivens). Even if we did find some kind of relationship between a goalie's workload and their save percentages, how would we know that it wasn't just a consequence of the team's defensive system?

In my view, there are just too many variables to answer this question easily. I do know of one analyst who has made a valiant attempt to control for as many of these factors as possible, Shane Beirnes[51]. His conclusion was that "there is a clear relationship between save

---

51 Shane Beirnes, "Bernier's Save Percentage II", Personal Blog, February 22, 2014, Web, http://shanebeirnes.wordpress.com/2014/02/22/berniers-save-percentage-ii/.

percentage and shot volume. This relationship appears on both a season-by-season and game-by-game basis", but he also added that this "does not mean that shots *cause* higher save percentages. More work needs to be done to determine why this relationship exists." Hear hear.

Bonus Question 1a: What about the number of consecutive games a goalie faces, does that affect his numbers?

No, at least not in a way that could be discovered by two separate studies completed by Phil Myrland[52] and Jonathan Willis[53].

2. When should goalies be pulled for the extra attacker?

When trailing by a single goal, the analytically correct time to pull the goalie for an extra attacker is with about three minutes left in the game. That figure, which comes courtesy of David Beaudoin and Tim B. Swartz's[54] definitive work on the topic, is double the conventional wisdom.

That's why fans of analytics rejoiced when Patrick Roy successfully pulled the goalie for an extra attacker with two and a half minutes left in Colorado's first round match-up with the Minnesota Wild last year. Despite it being established as the right move analytically long ago, very few coaches have been willing to give it a try. Until now.

When you really think about it, it makes intuitive sense to pull a goalie that early. After all, a team that's trailing late in the game has very little chance of winning the game, and it doesn't really matter much if the deficit is one goal or two. Allowing another goal really doesn't alter a team's fate that dramatically. On the other hand, scoring a goal will tie the game, which essentially gives the trailing team a 50% chance of winning.

Therefore, if a team pulls its goalie, failure causes its chance of winning to drop only slightly, while success vaults it all the way up to 50%. As it stands, empty net goals are only two-and-a-half times more common than equalizers. How great does that ratio need to be before this strategy is no longer worthwhile?

On the other hand, the reluctance of the coach to pull the goalie for an extra attacker also makes sense. If a coach's decisions follow conventional wisdom and they don't work out, no one is going to blame him. But if he takes a risk and it blows up in his face, then he has to face some angry questions from fans, media, and the front office. Just ask Claude Noel!

Thankfully, this strategy is now much safer for coaches to emulate, thanks to rookie coach and Hall of Famer Patrick Roy, someone whose fame and incredible success this season

52 Phil Myrland, "Goalie Fatigue", *Brodeur is a Fraud*, August 19, 2008, Web, http://brodeurisafraud.blogspot.ca/2008/08/goalie-fatigue.html.
53 Jonathan Willis, "Do Goalies Wear Down From Playing Too Many Games?", *The Score*, September 14, 2009, Web, http://blogs.thescore.com/nhl/2009/09/14/do-goalies-wear-down-from-playing-too-many-games/.
54 David Beaudoin and Tim B. Swartz, "Strategies for Pulling the Goalie in Hockey", *Simon Fraser University*, Web, http://people.stat.sfu.ca/~tim/papers/goalie.pdf.

earned him the freedom to try his own approach, one that he tested in his days in the Quebec Major Junior league. Now that he has succeeded, other NHL coaches were finally permitted to safely follow suit.

Incidentally, there are plenty more analytic gems that are just waiting for the next Roy to come along and prove them.

3. Do goalies have a tendency to bounce back after bad games?

In last year's Stanley Cup Final, Don Cherry[55] loudly asserted that Henrik Lundqvist has the ability to bounce back from bad games. He was absolutely right in that one instance, but do goalies really play better after having a bad game and, if they do, does Lundqvist's ability to do so exceed that of the average goalie?

To answer that, I looked at the last three years worth of game-by-game data for how goalies played right before a really bad start (as a control measure), and how they performed in their next game afterwards. Only the starts that occurred within at most three days of that really bad start were considered, and remember that such starts are defined as a game where the goalie fails to stop at least 85% of the shots he faced.

The results? Over the past three seasons combined, NHL goalies had an average save percentage of .9176 before a really bad start, but fell to a .9143 save percentage afterwards. As for Henrik Lundqvist, he actually fell from .9289 before a really bad start to .9192 in the following game.

That's one of the things I love about analytics. In many cases there's no need to guess about whether certain things are true or not because they can simply be checked. And there doesn't appear to be any evidence that goalies in general, or Lundqvist in particular, play any better than usual after a really bad start. In fact, it seems that at least a portion of whatever caused the bad game in the first place tends to continue.

4. Should goalies be drafted early?

In general, no. When you compare the historical probability of success of goalies drafted early versus those drafted late, the advantage is much smaller than it is for forwards and defencemen (except for the stay-at-home variety). Therefore, teams are better off investing its early picks on skaters.

That was the conclusion Kent Wilson[56] reached when he first studied the topic back in 2008. His concern was that the drafted goalie will either be the best player on your team or won't play in the NHL at all. The margin of difference between a strong goalie and a mediocre one is very small and not likely one that scouts can easily pick up upon. That's not the case with forwards and defencemen, whose skills are a little easier to separate at that age, and can at least contribute on the depth lines if they aren't a direct bull's eye.

---

55 Author's note: Regrettably, I could not find this clip on CBC's website.
56 Author's note: Regrettably, I could not find a reference to this study.

Wilson isn't alone here, the problem also having been more recently examined by analysts like Richard Pollock[57] and Scott Reynolds[58], who reached similar conclusions. It's difficult to evaluate a goalie's true talent even after years in the NHL, and virtually impossible in the years preceding it.

5. How much should a team spend on goaltending?

Given questionable high-profile contracts, like those awarded to Rick DiPietro, Ilya Bryzgalov and Roberto Luongo, not to mention more recent big investments in Jonathan Quick and Henrik Lundqvist, it's natural that one of the more frequent goaltending questions for the analytics community is how much teams should spend in nets. In fact, this question was even featured in the best-seller *Stumbling on Wins*[59], whose authors argued that there is too small a difference between one goalie and another to warrant big investments.

To be more precise, the predictable difference in goalies is too small to justify big contracts. If a team knew with certainty who was going to win the Vezina, that goalie would be worth all the money he could fit in a wheelbarrow.

That's something of a paradox in the world of goaltending. Great goalies are of almost incomparable value, but you only really know who they were in hindsight. Consider this past season, when three of the league's top goalies carried cap hits under $3.0 million: Semyon Varlamov, Ben Bishop, and Jonathan Bernier. That's not a situation that would be typical of the league's leading scorers (unless they're on an entry-level contract), because that's a lot easier to predict. Of course, we do have some idea who the better goalies will be, like Tuukka Rask and Henrik Lundqvist, for example. But, as a general rule, teams are better off investing their money where it's less of a gamble.

I love the way that Gabriel Desjardins[60] demonstrated this concept after the 2009–10 season. He calculated the combined save percentage of the 20 goalies with the richest contracts, some of whom had great years and some of whom didn't, and observed that they outperformed the remaining 42 by only a .924 to .918 margin. Multiply that by a goalie's average workload over an entire season, and the result is about six fewer goals against.

According to hockey's 3-1-1 rule, a difference of six goals means that these top 20 goalies are each only worth gambling about an extra $2.0 million. In other words, if a team can't secure a great goalie for around $3.85 million, then they should sign one of the best available average goalies for a lot less and invest the difference in their skaters. More often than not, the team will be better off. Especially if that average goalie is the one that has the Bishop-like season!

Why is it so hard to find the great goalies? Because luck plays such a huge factor in a goalie's

57 Richard Pollock, "Selecting a Goaltender", *Hockey Prospectus*, May 13, 2009, Web, http://www.hockeyprospectus.com/puck/article.php?articleid=125.
58 Scott Reynolds, "Goalies in the First Round", *Gospel of Hockey*, June 21, 2009, Web, http://gospelofhockey.blogspot.ca/2009/06/for-those-that-havent-read-kents-old.html.
59 David J. Berri and Martin B. Schmidt, "Stumbling on Wins", Chapter 3, 2010.
60 Gabriel Desjardins, "Are Expensive Goaltenders worth the Money?", *Arctic Ice Hockey*, March 8, 2010, Web, http://www.arcticicehockey.com/2010/3/8/1312090/are-expensive-goaltenders-worth.

save percentage. Awad[61] found that luck was 66% responsible for a goalie's save percentage in any single season. Only after three seasons does the effect of skill start to rival that of random variation.

That's why it can take four years or more to determine a starting goalie's true talent, according to a study by Gabriel Desjardins[62]. Even if a goalie plays 40 games, sees 1,000 shots and posts a .925 save percentage, then there's still a 30% chance he's actually league average or worse. That's too great a risk to justify a bank-breaking contract!

When it comes to goaltender evaluation, teams need to get an edge any way they can. In my view, Brian MacDonald's recent research has really become the leading word on this matter. In an approach covered in great detail on his website[63] and in *Hockey Prospectus 2013–14*, MacDonald establishes confidence intervals around each goalie's most likely save percentage, which can be used to calculate the likelihood that his performance will be worthy of an added investment.

Also, bear in mind that strong goalies are more important to some teams than to others. Those that expose their goalies to a lot more shots are going to get more value out of their goalies than tight defensive teams who allow fewer. That means that a generous contract could be (slightly) easier to justify for Toronto than it could be for New Jersey.

As an aside, this reminds me of another intriguing idea from Phil Myrland[64], who calculated the **win threshold** as the save percentage that a goalie requires in order for his team to break even goal-wise. Some teams outshoot opponents by such a wide margin, and/or score on such a high degree of their own shots, that their own goalie doesn't have to do much in order to win. The formula is (shots against – goals for) / shots against.

Some teams may find that they'll get along just find with a replacement-level goalie. How good are they anyway? Gabriel Desjardins[65] took the first look at this years ago and found that the average save percentage of a replacement-level goalie was about .9078. The research that has come since, including Bruce Peter's[66] recent comprehensive study of the topic, has pegged that as probably being on the high end.

In the end, the calculations may be simple, but the correct valuation of goalies is not. That's why analytics are often used to argue against big contracts for all but those absolutely proven

61 Tom Awad, "How Much Skill is There in Goaltending?", *Hockey Prospectus,* May 7, 2010, Web, http://www.hockeyprospectus.com/puck/article.php?articleid=558.

62 Gabriel Desjardins, "Fooled by Randomness: Goaltender Save Percentage", *Arctic Ice Hockey*, April 20, 2010, Web, http://www.arcticicehockey.com/2010/4/20/1429278/fooled-by-randomness-goaltender.

63 Brian MacDonald, "Goalies", *Greater Than Plus/Minus*, Web, September 26, 2013, http://www.greaterthanplusminus.com/p/goalies.html.

64 Phil Myrland, "The Win Threshold", *Brodeur is a Fraud*, October 10, 2009, Web, http://brodeurisafraud.blogspot.ca/2009/10/win-threshold.html.

65 Gabriel Desjardins, "What do NHL Gms think if replacement level goaltending?", *Arctic Ice Hockey*, February 24, 2011, Web, http://www.arcticicehockey.com/2011/2/24/2006968/what-do-nhl-gms-think-is-replacement-level-goaltending.

66 Bruce Peter, "What Should We Expect From NHL Goaltenders?", *Habs Eyes on the Prize*, May 10, 2012, Web, http://www.habseyesontheprize.com/2012/5/10/3010919/what-should-we-expect-from-nhl-goaltenders.

to be elite, like Henrik Lundqvist and Tuukka Rask. There are so many capable starting goalies in the NHL, and so few who are demonstrably elite, so it's a lot easier to make a mistake with a high-priced deal than to actually land someone who is worth big money. So unless you have a crystal ball, the smart money is invested in skaters instead.

6. Is there a goalie projection model?

One of the main reasons people study hockey analytics is in an attempt to understand the past well enough to set reasonable expectations of the future. After all, what use is all this analysis if it can't help establish what we can expect from today's goalies?

However, I'm only familiar with one serious attempt to project a goalie's future performance based on his previous NHL data, and it was developed just this past season. The small sample sizes, high year-to-year variances, and all the confounding factors, like team effects, special teams, recording bias, shot quality and quality of opponents, have been scaring off analysts from tackling this topic for years.

Enter a brave *Hockey Graphs* analyst named Garik[67]. He developed a three-step projection model that takes a goalie's even-strength save percentage over the past four years, regresses the data to the league average, and applies an aging curve.

There are a few key differences between this and the player projection model introduced in last year's *Hockey Abstract*. First, no historical data is used, nor are historical players with comparable statistics used to project a goalie's future performance. Given how even-strength save percentage data is only available for the past decade, this limitation is unavoidable. And, given the use of both regression and an age curve, it is also unnecessary.

Secondly, this system weights the data using the Marcel model popularized by baseball's Tom Tango. "Marcel" means that instead of weighing all the previous three seasons equally, or weighing it in a 3/2/1 or 4/2/1 ratio, it weights the data in a 5/4/3 ratio. That is, the most recent season is multiplied by 5, the year before by 4, and the year before that by 3, and then the entire sum is divided by that total (12). Since Garik's system uses four seasons, the ratio is actually more at the halfway point between the two methods, multiplying the current season by 5, previous season by 3, and the season before that at 2.5 and 1.5, respectively, before dividing by the same 12.

The results? The most recently published calculations this April project the top goalies to be Tuukka Rask (.9207), Cory Schneider (.9180), Sergei Bobrovsky (.9165), Anton Khudobin (.9164), and Semyon Varlamov (.9162), with Henrik Lundqvist in 9th with .9155.

This system is still very new, but it's an interesting and promising start.

---

67 Garik, "Forecasting Future Goalie Performance with Four Year Hockey Marcels", *Hockey Graphs*, February 3, 2014, Web, http://hockey-graphs.com/2014/02/03/forecasting-future-goalie-performance-with-four-year-hockey-marcels/.

7. Is there an AHL-to-NHL translation model for goalies?

Predicting NHL performance by translating data from other leagues is one of my favourite innovations, which is probably why I went on for 25 pages on the topic last year. Despite all of my work for skaters in creating age curves, separating goals and assists, updating translation factors in over a dozen different leagues, and adjusting for manpower, ice time, and scoring levels, I've never published anything related to goaltending. Why?

Simply put, translating data from other leagues to the NHL isn't nearly as easy for goalies as it is for skaters, mostly because the sample sizes are just too small and the variance too high. See for yourself in the following chart, which includes the save percentages for every goalie to move from the AHL to the NHL, and play at least 20 games in each, since the 2005 lockout. If you see a pattern, then your eye is sharper than mine.

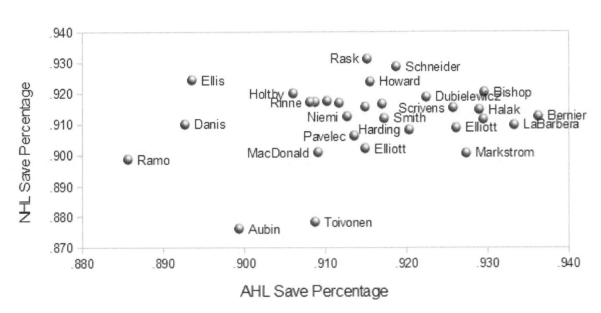

AHL vs NHL Save Percentages, 2005–06 to 2012–13

Goalies like Ondrej Pavelec, Brian Elliott, Jimmy Howard, and Tuukka Rask all had nearly identical AHL save percentages, but with significantly different results in the NHL. Consider goalies like Jonathan Bernier and Jason LaBarbera, who dominated the AHL, and yet performed worse in the NHL than their peers who struggled, like Dan Ellis, Braden Holtby, and Pekka Rinne. There's just no way to use this data to predict how the next goalies will perform.

Gabriel Desjardins, who first pioneered the translation process for skaters, took a crack at goalie translations himself, in the early days of *Hockey Prospectus*[68]. His efforts were largely stumped by the fact that teams don't have patience for AHL goalies, and even the briefest cold streak will get them relegated to the bench, or back to the AHL. That means that the only goalies with a decent sample size were those that either played really well after making the

---

68 Gabriel Desjardins, "The Impossibility of Projecting Goaltenders", *Arctic Ice Hockey,* January 27, 2011, Web, http://www.arcticicehockey.com/2011/1/27/1917934/the-impossibility-of-projecting-goaltenders.

jump or who played for awful teams. That skews the analysis.

Other have taken a run at the problem more recently, most notably Bruce McCurdy[69] and Stephan Cooper[70], but with similarly disappointing results. Applying the same process that is used for players, the lack of a decent sample size led Cooper to conclude that "the relationship between the AHL performance and the NHL performance proved to be pretty much random."

Interestingly, Cooper did find an 8% difference in how much more difficult NHL shots are relative to AHL shots. That's about the same difference that exists between better and weaker NHL goalies, suggesting that a solid AHL goalie is no worse than a weak NHL one.

An idea borrowed from baseball and ingeniously applied to hockey gave us yet another perspective on the topic, as Rob Pettapiece[71] took an intriguing look at AHL goalies by singling out how they performed against NHL players. That's similar to how college baseball pitchers are judged based on how they perform against college hitters who have been drafted by major league teams.

In this case, Pettapiece defined an NHL player as anyone in the AHL who played games in the NHL that same season, and then calculated each goalie's save percentage exclusively in shots taken by such players. It's a fascinating idea that I didn't even think was possible with the available data.

The sample sizes are really far too small on which to base any conclusions, but nevertheless quite fascinating. Pettapiece's AHL findings are the first two columns and I've added each goalie's subsequent performance in the NHL in the last two columns.

AHL Save Percentage vs NHLers, and NHL Performance, 2011–12

Goalie	Team(s)	Shot	SV%	Shot	SV%
Eddie Lack	Van	529	.922	1052	.912
Jeff Zatkoff	Pit	390	.921	582	.912
Michael Leighton	Phi	552	.920	26	.808
Jacob Markstrom	Fla/Van	403	.918	1046	.891
Dustin Tokarski	Mtl	475	.918	93	.946
Cedrick Desjardins	TB	326	.917	86	.884
Cam Talbot	NYR	468	.917	560	.941
Robin Lehner	Ott	375	.915	1565	.919
Danny Taylor	Cgy	527	.915	68	.912
Kevin Poulin	NYI	521	.912	942	.892

Six of these goalies faced a reasonable sample size of shots in the NHL the following season.

69 Bruce McCurdy, "Projecting goalie performance", *Copper and Blue*, October 21, 2008, Web, http://www.coppernblue.com/2008/10/projecting-goalie-performance.html.
70 Stephan Cooper, "AHL to NHL Translations: Save Percentage", *Habs Eye on the Prize*, July 11, 2012, Web, http://www.habseyesontheprize.com/2012/7/11/3147551/ahl-to-nhl-translations-save-percentage.
71 Rob Pettapiece, " Looking at AHL Goaltenders vs NHL Players", *NHL Numbers*, July 16, 2012, Web, http://nhlnumbers.com/2012/7/16/looking-at-ahl-goaltenders-vs-nhl-players.

Of them, Kevin Poulin was expected to fare the worst, and he almost did (Jacob Markstrom was negligibly worse). However, Eddie Lack and Jeff Zatkoff were expected to outperform Cam Talbot and Robin Lehner, and did not. Interesting yes, but useful, maybe not.

Long story short, no, despite the problem being attacked by a variety of analysts in several different ways, there isn't currently a method to translate a goalie's AHL data into its NHL equivalent.

Closing Thoughts

Despite the fact that even-strength save percentage is almost universally used to evaluate goaltenders, that's not to say that there hasn't been any progress is the area of goaltending analytics. An entire book could be dedicated to the topic, and it was quite a challenge to introduce and summarize so many important concepts so briefly in a single chapter.

The walk away lesson is that even-strength save percentage gets you most of the way there, but there are dozens of methods to focus in on specific aspects of a game and improve those evaluations. Each one doesn't mean much by themselves, but can really move the needle when they're all used together.

Knowing which goalies are facing the toughest shots, whether that's defined by shot location, the skill of the shooter or otherwise, is a concept that's growing in importance as the quality of the data improves. Also knowing which goalies can reliably close the door in the shootout, who can consistently post quality starts, who can draw penalties and who can handle the puck, are all examples of recent advances that can help squeeze that little bit of extra value when evaluating goalies. Therefore, it pays to study more than just the save percentages.

Team Essays

By Rob Vollman

Once applied, what do the various analytic approaches say about each of today's NHL teams? To answer that we'll take a high-level, two-page look at each club for the 2014–15 season in such a way that each viewpoint can be combined with traditional analysis and updated as circumstances change.

When Bill James wrote the second book in his *Baseball Abstract* series in 1978, he organized that edition into team-based sections. His book eventually became the collection of team-based essays and statistical collections for which it is known.

It makes sense to continue in the footsteps of his winning formula and to pave the way for a similar format in *Hockey Abstract*. As such, this next section will take a quick analytic look at each team using player usage charts, shot-based data, and the other latest statistical developments.

There are some concerns with this approach that need to be kept in mind, however. First of all, this perspective ignores the traditional aspect of the analysis that can only come with closely watching all 82 games as well as speaking with the analysts, coaches, scouts, players, and front offices involved with each team. The information will therefore be presented in a fashion that can be easily combined with whatever such analysis the reader may acquire elsewhere.

Secondly, this point-in-time analysis could be potentially useless a year from now, and possibly much sooner, as rosters undergo significant changes. Comprehensive coverage is therefore best shared in an online format that can be easily updated as situations develop. That's why this analysis will be limited to the information of greatest significance, and/or what is most likely to endure, and will focus primarily on the process behind the perspective rather than on the results themselves.

Please do not approach this with the mindset that it is comprehensive, even from an analytic viewpoint, nor that it is being presented as being definitive. It is intended only as an informed interpretation of certain data from a certain perspective. With those important caveats in mind, let's review the two primary analytic tools that will be used in our team-based analysis: player usage charts and the new Hockey Abstract checklist.

Player Usage Charts

Player usage charts are unquestionably one of the most popular innovations coming out of the world of hockey analytics today, and why not? At a single glance they provide most of the context required to put a player's performance in the appropriate context.

While they're useful at the individual level to sort out the influence playing conditions can have on someone's numbers, they're even more handy at the team level. It can quickly established who is going to be tasked with taking on the top opponents, who is going to form the key scoring line, and who is on the checking line together with how effectively the team will likely match up in each situation.

Before we get into the nuts and bolts of player usage charts, here are a few updates for those already familiar with the tool and who plan to skip ahead

First of all, these charts are for the 2014–15 season using the roster as they stood in mid-July. It also includes all restricted free agents and those under contract but playing abroad. It will not include unsigned unrestricted free agents nor any transactions that occurred in late July or beyond.

While last year's book included five seasons worth of data, these charts will include only the last three. That will not only make them more consistent with the rest of this book but will also avoid including data that is simply too old to be relevant. And while there are several available tools that can provide player usage data on a single-season basis, remember how unreliable information can be in such small doses. Three years is really the minimum number of seasons required to start forming an opinion about a player's usage and/or effectiveness in this context, especially since one of them was only 48 games.

This season, defencemen are denoted in italics to make it easier to distinguish them from forwards. While forwards can often be assigned shifts based on the zone in which a play is about to start, most defencemen normally have a fairly even balance, and are instead assigned shifts primarily to match up against certain opponents. That's why there's usually a bigger spread in quality of competition for defencemen than there is for zone starts.

Other things to be on the lookout for include:

- Players who are anywhere near the minimal cut-off (20 games), which is a very small sample size.
- Anyone whose usage has changed considerably over the past three years, including both young players who are getting tougher jobs (e.g., T.J. Brodie and Cam Fowler) or older players who don't really carry the tough minutes anymore.
- Those who played most of the previous three seasons on a team with either very different zone start percentages or a much different possession-based standard.
- Also remember that the circles are relative to one's teammates, so be mindful of who everyone is being compared against. A shaded circle on the Blackhawks is more difficult to achieve than the same-sized one of the Sabres.
- The scale is different from team to team so that they're easier to read, be very mindful of that.
- To avoid getting too crowded, only the players of the highest significance are included. This will very occasionally leave out some enforcers and depth players.
- Question the value of players that are assigned the tough minutes but have huge white bubbles. Just because someone plays the tough minutes doesn't mean that he should!
- As always, look for players with unusually out-of-place circles, such as shutdown

players with nicely shaded circles, or sheltered players with white ones.

Now that the veteran readers are all set, let's take a look back at what player usage charts actually are and where they came from.

Background

When introducing player usage charts to someone new, the Vancouver Canucks are the most common example,. After all, who hasn't wondered how the Sedin twins went from being point-a-game players in their mid-20s to Art Ross, Hart Memorial, and Ted Lindsay award winners in their older age, and then right back down again upon coach Alain Vigneault's departure? Especially since Vigneault's arrival in New York coincided with Mats Zuccarello's point explosion!

That's when a look at Vancouver's player usage chart has always come in handy. Even at a quick glance, it's easy to see how the Sedin twins, and their linemate Alex Burrows, start the great majority of their shifts in the offensive zone and against secondary opponents. That leaves a player like Ryan Kesler to take on the top-line opponents, like Jonathan Toews and Sidney Crosby, and players like Manny Malhotra to handle the pucks dropped in the defensive zone.

It should be absolutely no surprise that the Sedin's scoring totals would absolutely flourish under such conditions, and that Burrows could go from someone who scored 52 points in his first 206 games to someone who scored 51 in his first season alongside them. Unfortunately, the fun was over when Vigneault left town, forcing Vancouver's top line to start carrying more weight. Their scoring predictably dropped, with Burrows reverting back to his old pace with just 15 points in 49 games.

How exactly do player usage charts work? Ideally, they are easy to understand with very minimal explanation, but it never hurts to have the following details readily available.

The horizontal axis features the player's **offensive zone start percentage**, which is the percentage of all shifts he started in that zone. It's important to remember that the perhaps poorly-named statistic does not include shifts that started in the neutral zone, nor on-the-fly changes. Think of it more as a representation of whether a player is used primarily for his offensive or defensive talents.

The advantage of an offensive zone start is obvious. Starting in the offensive zone means that subsequently winning a face-off generally leads directly to a shot on goal, whereas in the defensive zone, it would need to be carried out and the offensive zone gained before a shot could even be attempted. As such, each offensive zone start has been calculated to be worth an extra 0.8 shots in a player's shot-based plus/minus (0.4 shots for and the 0.4 that goes against the opponents).

On the vertical axis, you'll find the player's **quality of competition**, which is the average plus/minus of one's opponents over 60 minutes, except that it is based on attempted shots (Corsi) instead of goals. This plus/minus is also measured relative to the team's other players, giving each team roughly the same number of players over zero as there are under. Those who face the top lines will be at the top of the chart, while those with the easier task of facing mostly depth lines will be at the bottom.

Other methods of measuring the average quality of one's competition do exist, but they rarely differ significantly. We can use goals or shots, for example, and there's also a growing trend to use the average ice time of one's opponents, instead of their average shot-based or goal-based plus-minus, as innovated by Eric Tulsky of *Broad Street Hockey*. That approach tends to favour the competition of those on the top scoring lines instead of the league's top defensive players.

Finally, there are those big circles around each player's name. This is a representation of how well the team did with that player on the ice, in terms of possession. A big, shaded circle means the team does very well, while a white one means they're frequently getting stuck in their own zone, and/or playing without the puck. These circles are calculated using a proxy based on the attempted shot differential (per minute) when that player is on the ice relative to when he's not. That means that there should be roughly the same number of shaded bubbles as white bubbles. A player on a great team would have to be even better than his teammates in order to earn a shaded bubble, while a player on a far weaker team would at least have a lower bar to climb over.

What does it all mean? A team's top shutdown players are at the top of the chart, angling towards the left, while its top scoring line is on the far right, angling down towards the middle. The latter will consequently have shaded circles far larger than the former, whose may even be white.

The checking line is on the left side, generally hovering around the horizon, and tend to have big white circles. That's partly because of their defensive zone usage, but also because they would probably be on one of the top lines instead if they were more complete players. Those below that line are generally depth players, such as enforcers, rookies, and AHL call-ups.

In the end, these charts put all the other statistics into the proper context. Whether they're basic stats, like goals, assists and plus/minus, or of the more non-traditional shot-based variety. Statistics can be highly misleading unless you understand the situations in which a player was typically used. That's the ultimate beauty of player usage charts.

Personally, I've been really excited about player usage charts ever since I first introduced them on Arctic Ice Hockey[72] back in the 2011 off-season. I was impressed with how quickly they caught on, both within the analytic community (including its grouchier members), but also among mainstream media and even NHL front offices.

Even after three years, they're constantly being refined and developed, and being used by a wider audience. I already know of three tools that allow everyone to build their own charts online, including Robb Tufts' customizable tool on my own *Hockey Abstract* website[73], a

72 Rob Vollman, "Winnipeg OZQoC Graphs", *Arctic Ice Hockey*, Web, June 20, 2011,
    http://www.arcticicehockey.com/2011/6/20/2233834/winnipeg-ozqoc-graphs.
73 Robb Tufts, "Player Usage Charts", *Hockey Abstract*, Web, http://www.hockeyabstract.com.

classic version on Greg Sinclair's *Ninja Greg* website[74], and most recently on *Extra Skater*[75], one of the best analytic websites since *Behind the Net* (where all of my forthcoming data comes from).

And that's about all there is to know about player usage charts!

The Hockey Abstract Checklist

A brand new design for this book is a system to quickly evaluate where an organization currently stands in all the key areas that could affect their position in the standings. That includes factors such as coaching, special teams, goaltending, depth, and specific key positions, such as a team's top four or scoring line.

The categories themselves were determined by figuring out (1) what aspects of a team's play correlates most closely with its winning percentage, (2) how it can be measured with analytics, and (3) how consistent (predictive) the measurement is from season to season.

For example, knowing how closely related possession is with winning, how to measure it using a shot-based proxy, and how reliably it persists from year to year, creates confidence not only in its inclusion in our checklist as a point of great relevance, but in the score assigned to each team.

In this first season, we'll have only three possible scores for each category:
- A star indicates that this team is among the two or three league leaders in the given category, like the New York Rangers for goaltending or the Los Angeles Kings in possession, for example.
- A checkmark indicates that the team possesses the quality in question to an extent that would be competitive among the 16 playoff teams.
- A blank space means that the team has not focused on this area and may not have it adequately covered. (Either that, or the phone rang while I was writing and the distraction caused me to skip that space.)

While the values I've selected are based on the latest research of considerable volume, not to mention my experience writing team-level analysis with *Hockey Prospectus* for several years, they may not always be correct. This can happen for any number of reasons, such as my information being out of date, my missing some key insights that can't yet be measured with analytics, or my interpretation of the data simply being faulty. In each case, it is easy to correct the value as new information comes to light and to arrive at a more updated, high-level view for each team.

Here are the categories I've selected and how they're measured:

---

74 Greg Sinclair, "Player Usage Charts", *Super Shot Search*, Web, http://somekindofninja.com/nhl/usage.php.
75 Darryl Metcalf, Extra Skater, Web, http://www.extraskater.com.

1. Possession

The measurable team aspect of the game with one of the strongest correlations to winning is the time spent in possession of the puck. Unlike other equally strong aspects, such as shooting and save percentages, time of possession is quite persistent from game to game, month to month, and year to year.

That's a big reason why the Stanley Cup champion consistently ranks at the top of the league in the regular season, as do about three of the four Conference Finalists. That's also why it's the ideal measurement with which to begin the checklist.

How is time of possession measured? In the absence of a stopwatch-based reading like the NHL kept at the turn of the century, attempted shots are used as a proxy. The logic is that the percentage of attempted shots a team takes is roughly equal to the percentage of time it had the puck and/or was in the opposing zone.

It's important to consider possession in close-game situations only, as teams tend to sit back and yield the play when they're protecting a late lead. And since certain players are better at driving possession than others, it's also important to factor in any major roster changes that can affect the team in one direction or another.

Close Game Team Possession Percentages (Corsi)[76]

Team	2011–12	2012–13	2013–14	Average
Los Angeles	54.9	58.0	57.3	56.5
Chicago	53.5	55.5	55.6	54.8
Boston	53.5	55.0	55.0	54.4
St. Louis	54.5	52.4	53.1	53.5
New Jersey	51.1	55.6	54.6	53.5
Detroit	54.0	54.1	51.3	53.0
Vancouver	53.2	52.8	52.0	52.6
Ottawa	51.8	53.4	52.2	52.3
San Jose	51.1	52.1	53.8	52.3
Pittsburgh	55.0	48.8	49.7	51.5
NY Rangers	48.5	52.6	53.2	51.3
Dallas	49.2	50.0	41.3	50.2
Arizona	49.7	50.5	49.8	49.9
Florida	50.1	49.3	49.7	49.8
Winnipeg	50.3	49.6	49.4	49.8
Philadelphia	51.2	47.5	49.2	49.6
Carolina	48.4	52.0	49.3	49.5
NY Islanders	48.0	51.7	49.6	49.5
Colorado	50.7	47.3	47.4	48.7
Montreal	47.3	53.4	47.2	48.6
Tampa Bay	47.4	44.9	51.5	48.5
Anaheim	48.2	46.9	49.8	48.5

76 Acknowledgement: Possession data came from *Extra Skater* http://www.extraskater.com.

Columbus	47.1	46.3	50.9	48.3
Washington	49.3	47.9	47.6	48.3
Calgary	48.4	47.4	45.8	47.2
Nashville	45.4	44.9	49.5	46.8
Minnesota	44.0	48.4	48.2	46.6
Edmonton	47.0	43.5	43.5	44.9
Toronto	47.9	43.5	42.1	44.6
Buffalo	48.6	43.7	41.0	44.5

2. The Shootout

The shootout is incredibly important to a team's position in the standings. Just ask the New Jersey Devils, whose 0-13 record likely cost them one of the final playoff positions last year.

Unfortunately, a team's shootout record is subject to a great deal of luck and can therefore be quite unpredictable. That being said, evidence explored in the goaltending chapter suggests that there is some persistence on the goal prevention side of the equation, and it also stands to reason that teams with more capable shooters from which to choose are in a better position to win than those teams with fewer.

3. Goaltending

Nothing destroys pre-season projections to a greater extent than goaltending. It can be enormously difficult to predict, but no single player has a greater influence on the ultimate outcome of an NHL season than the starting goalie. Take the Tampa Bay Lightning, for instance, who defied the consensus pre-season expectation that they would miss the playoffs. Who would have guessed that Ben Bishop, who had a .913 save percentage in 45 previous NHL games, would be a Vezina finalist?

While that particular case may have been hard to predict, some teams have more of an advantage than others between the pipes. Even-strength save percentage and quality start percentage are just two of the many factors that can be used to rate a team's starting goalie and the depth behind him.

Even-Strength Save Percentages, 2011–12 to 2013–14[77]

Team	Starter	ESSV%	Backup	ESSV%	3:1 Avg
Boston	Rask	.938	Svedberg	.938	.938
NY Rangers	Lundqvist	.932	Talbot	.940	.934
Los Angeles	Quick	.926	Jones	.949	.932
NY Islanders	Halak	.930	Johnson	.938	.932
Carolina	Khudobin	.931	Ward	.916	.927
Columbus	Bobrovsky	.931	McElhinney	.916	.927
St. Louis	Elliott	.932	Allen	.911	.927
Toronto	Bernier	.928	Reimer	.922	.927
Arizona	Smith	.929	Dubnyk	.917	.926

77 Acknowledgement: Raw goaltending data from the NHL, http://www.nhl.com.

San Jose	Niemi	.925	Stalock	.932	.926
Tampa Bay	Bishop	.929	Nabokov	.916	.926
Buffalo	Enroth	.929	Neuvirth	.916	.926
Washington	Holtby	.929	Peters	.916	.926
Minnesota	Harding	.928	Backstrom	.921	.926
Ottawa	Anderson	.926	Lehner	.924	.925
Anaheim	Andersen	.928	LaBarbera	.914	.924
Vancouver	Miller	.924	Lack	.921	.923
Montreal	Price	.925	Budaj	.917	.923
Florida	Luongo	.926	Montoya	.912	.923
Detroit	Howard	.928	Gustavsson	.907	.923
New Jersey	Schneider	.926	Clemmensen	.911	.922
Nashville	Rinne	.924	Hutton	.917	.922
Dallas	Lehtonen	.925	Lindback	.910	.921
Calgary	Hiller	.922	Ramo	.919	.921
Edmonton	Scrivens	.923	Fasth	.915	.921
Pittsburgh	Fleury	.917	Greiss	.930	.920
Colorado	Varlamov	.925	Berra	.898	.918
Chicago	Crawford	.923	Raanta	.896	.916
Philadelphia	Mason	.917	Emery	.913	.916
Winnipeg	Pavelec	.913	Hutchinson	.958	.913

4. Penalty Kill

A team's penalty killing has a decent correlation with winning percentage, but not a great deal of persistence. How reliably can a team's shorthanded play be predicted?

The main tool at our disposal is the number of attempted shots a team allows per 60 minutes. It can sometimes produce unexpected results, but there's actually quite a bit of value in the approach. When I used this method early last season to rank each team for a Bleacher Report[78] article, it's failure to perfectly match the current penalty-killing percentage standings resulted in 163 reader comments questioning my sanity. The concerns were all about how the teams with the best penalty-killing percentages in the league could possibly be in the bottom third, like Toronto (21st), Washington (22nd), Pittsburgh (24th), Tampa Bay (25th), and Colorado (27th). Well, this strict ranking by attempted shots allowed actually proved accurate in four of those most controversial cases, who ultimately finished 28th, 16th, 5th, 23rd, and 24th respectively.

While it may not be perfect, this approach can also be applied here to get an accurate read of where each NHL team might find itself ranked at the end of this season (after taking major roster changes into account).

---

78 Rob Vollman, "Ranking Every NHL Team's Penalty Kill in 2013–14", *Bleacher Report*, November 11, 2013, Web, http://bleacherreport.com/articles/1840695-ranking-every-nhl-teams-penalty-kill-in-2013-14.

Attempted Shots Allowed per 60 Minutes on the Penalty Kill[79]

Team	2011–12	2012–13	2013–14	Average
New Jersey	80.0	71.8	85.2	80.2
Philadelphia	84.5	81.4	82.2	82.9
Vancouver	87.4	80.7	83.1	84.3
St. Louis	87.7	82.0	85.4	85.6
Boston	87.7	78.2	91.5	86.9
Minnesota	92.3	77.8	86.7	87.2
Ottawa	91.2	87.5	85.0	88.0
Pittsburgh	78.9	87.8	100.0	88.8
Columbus	86.1	83.0	96.2	89.6
Montreal	82.9	87.8	98.3	89.9
Los Angeles	90.4	90.4	93.8	91.7
Detroit	93.6	88.0	93.1	92.2
Calgary	93.5	90.7	93.3	92.8
Florida	93.7	88.4	95.6	93.2
NY Rangers	97.9	90.3	89.5	93.2
Winnipeg	99.7	83.1	94.2	94.3
NY Islanders	96.8	89.2	94.9	94.4
Colorado	85.8	100.8	102.4	95.3
Carolina	102.9	98.4	86.9	95.8
San Jose	101.2	89.8	94.3	95.8
Chicago	99.9	91.4	94.6	95.9
Edmonton	87.2	97.1	107.4	97.0
Nashville	106.2	90.3	96.2	98.7
Buffalo	95.3	98.7	102.1	98.9
Toronto	100.8	86.3	105.2	99.0
Anaheim	97.0	92.7	105.6	99.3
Tampa Bay	102.5	97.8	102.3	101.4
Dallas	100.4	106.0	100.0	101.6
Arizona	103.9	93.2	104.9	101.8
Washington	99.5	103.2	116.0	106.9

5. Power Play

A team's power-play percentage may have a weaker correlation with the team winning percentage than its penalty killing, but it is more persistent and predictable. The same metric for penalty killing can be used as a starting point to measure power plays (i.e., attempted shots per 60 minutes), which can be further focused with a closer look at some of the individual players, in the fashion described in the power play specialist chapter.

Attempted Shots per 60 Minutes on the Power Play[80]

Team	2011–12	2012–13	2013–14	Average
San Jose	119.9	110.7	117.6	116.9
Pittsburgh	115.4	97.3	107.6	108.4

79 Acknowledgement: Penalty killing data came from *Extra Skater* http://www.extraskater.com.
80 Acknowledgement: Power play data came from *Extra Skater* http://www.extraskater.com.

Vancouver	105.8	92.8	103.9	101.9
Anaheim	102.5	100.7	101.0	101.5
St. Louis	103.2	100.7	97.2	100.2
Washington	93.0	94.8	107.8	99.4
Ottawa	97.0	103.4	98.3	98.9
Philadelphia	96.7	95.1	103.3	98.8
Detroit	101.0	101.0	92.9	98.0
Boston	95.3	87.4	104.5	97.1
Los Angeles	93.3	97.6	99.8	96.8
Carolina	94.5	92.6	98.0	95.4
NY Islanders	91.0	97.4	96.7	94.7
Columbus	98.6	83.4	95.9	94.5
NY Rangers	85.9	81.7	105.6	92.5
Winnipeg	92.5	85.6	94.8	91.9
Dallas	81.0	85.5	103.5	91.5
Arizona	81.0	85.6	101.7	90.2
Montreal	88.8	87.2	92.9	89.9
Toronto	88.1	84.9	94.4	89.8
Chicago	85.1	84.0	97.4	89.4
Minnesota	87.8	94.1	87.3	89.0
Buffalo	97.1	83.5	84.7	89.0
Colorado	93.8	82.8	80.4	85.8
Florida	92.2	78.1	82.7	85.6
Calgary	86.0	83.8	85.9	85.5
New Jersey	82.4	87.3	75.5	81.0
Nashville	78.2	81.4	82.9	80.8
Edmonton	80.4	73.9	85.2	80.8
Tampa Bay	81.1	72.9	78.1	78.0

6. Scoring Line

When a team is down by a goal late in the game, who does it put on the ice, and what's their relative chance of scoring?

Rating a team's scoring line involves taking a closer look at the individual analytics of its most likely options. This includes everything from their even-strength scoring rate, their possession numbers, their shooting, their passing, the level of competition they typically face, the portion of their shifts that begin in the offensive zone, how effective they are at winning faceoffs and drawing penalties, and so on. In each case, I'm using my own experience studying this types of analytics for each of the given players over the years.

It's important to note that not every team focuses on building an elite scoring line, which is generally the most expensive part of the entire roster, instead choosing to spread out their scoring over several lines. While those teams may not get a check mark in this category, the additional savings should help them achieve a few gold stars elsewhere on the checklist.

7. Shutdown Line

The flip side of the previous category's question is who will hop the boards to face the top opposing scorers when protecting a late lead, and how effectively will they neutralize their opponents.

This is where a lot of the individual analytics are applied, in much the same way as the scoring line evaluation, but with (slightly) less of an emphasis on the offensive aspect of the game and more on their defensive play.

8. Forward Depth

While not as important as their scoring or shutdown lines, the league's best teams usually manage to use their remaining cap space and roster positions to get that little bit of extra value out of their depth lines. The goal is to have at least one more effective checking line and some strong secondary scoring.

In last year's *Hockey Abstract*, the league's most underrated players were identified using a variety of cutting-edge analytics. They included players who are versatile do-it-all players, can play tough minutes, drive possession, draw penalties, win faceoffs and have good contractual value. Those same methods, which correctly predicted Frans Nielsen's breakout season, can help project which teams have the depth edge in 2014–15.

9. Top Pairing, and
10. Second Pairing

A team's top two defencemen are arguably the most important skaters on the entire team. Based on an analysis I completed for *Hockey Graphs*[81] last season, most teams keep them together and usually in a balanced fashion.

Some teams deploy its top two defencemen together to form a top shutdown pairing, which generally proves effective, while a select few have the particular talent required to use them as a scoring-focused pairing instead, like in Chicago, Ottawa, and Los Angeles. Less effective are those teams who split them up onto separate shutdown and scoring-focused units, but it has been known to work.

Regardless of how teams have deployed their top defencemen, we can use all of the previously mentioned individual analytics to project how effectively their top four will perform.

11. Defensive Depth

A team has only half as many defencemen as forwards in its lineup on any given night, making it particularly important to have strong defensive depth. Losing two forwards carries far less impact than losing two defencemen, after all.

Earning a check mark in this category indicates not only that a team has a strong third pairing, and additional options available in reserve, but also that it possesses players who can step up into the top four in either an offensive or a defensive fashion in temporary injury-triggered situations.

12. Coaching

As we saw last year, the coaching staff can theoretically move the needle by up to 8 points in the standings, in one direction or another. It's possible that teams like Colorado and Tampa Bay would have been complete flops this past season with someone different at the helm, for instance.

While analytics are really in their infancy in this department, it isn't completely without tools. Indeed, the nine coaches who were fired since the season began had an average ranking of 18.4 out of 30 in last year's study, while those whose teams made the Conference Finals averaged 6.5.

Only three of the nine dismissed coaches were in the upper half of the league, Philadelphia's Peter Laviolette was 6th, Pittsburgh's Dan Bylsma was 9th and Nashville's Barry Trotz was 11th, suggesting that we can at least make a first attempt at evaluating this important aspect of a team's success. Two of those three coaches, incidentally, have been immediately re-hired on different teams this season.

---

81 Rob Vollman, "How Do Teams Use Their Top Defensemen", *Hockey Graphs*, June 26, 2014, Web, http://hockey-graphs.com/2014/06/26/how-do-teams-use-their-top-defensemen/.

Here is the leader board for active coaches, including their current team, the number of NHL games they have coached (GC), the points their teams have earned (PTS), the number of points that exceeded expectations (xPTS), and the rate per game (xPTS/G). I have been trying to secure the data to include each coach's experience in other leagues, but have thus far been unable to.

Active Coaches for 2014–15, All-Time[82]

Team	Coach	GC	PTS	xPTS	xPTS/G
STL	Ken Hitchcock	1240	1492	131.3	.106
CHI	Joel Quenneville	1293	1589	114.0	.088
BOS	Claude Julien	778	956	95.7	.123
ANA	Bruce Boudreau	517	686	93.4	.181
DET	Mike Babcock	868	1092	74.3	.086
NSH	Peter Laviolette	759	866	69.4	.091
LA	Darryl Sutter	1039	1152	69.2	.067
ARI	Dave Tippett	868	1050	68.3	.079
WSH	Barry Trotz	1196	1274	67.6	.057
MTL	Michel Therrien	592	664	63.7	.108
NYR	Alain Vigneault	888	1036	59.0	.066
DAL	Lindy Ruff	1247	1395	52.2	.042
SJ	Todd McLellan	458	599	50.9	.111
CGY	Bob Hartley	780	872	50.6	.065
COL	Patrick Roy	82	112	40.0	.488
TOR	Randy Carlyle	664	763	38.0	.057
TB	Jon Cooper	98	114	24.6	.251
OTT	Paul MacLean	212	236	16.5	.078
CBJ	Todd Richards	335	356	14.2	.042
PHI	Craig Berube	79	94	13.9	.176
MIN	Mike Yeo	212	234	12.0	.057
NJ	Peter DeBoer	458	480	9.2	.020
CAR	Bill Peters	0	0	0.0	.000
VAN	Willie Desjardins	0	0	0.0	.000
PIT	Mike Johnston	0	0	0.0	.000
NYI	Jack Capuano	277	275	-1.2	-.004
FLA	Gerard Gallant	142	122	-1.4	-.010
WPG	Paul Maurice	1119	1128	-9.1	-.008
EDM	Dallas Eakins	82	67	-11.7	-.142
BUF	Ted Nolan	389	377	-13.3	-.034

There are other analytical ways to measure coaches that are under development, most of which involve a closer look at his player usage. For example, Michael Parkatti recently won a contest held by the Edmonton Oilers entitled *Hackathon*[83] which invited fans to predict how many points various players would score and to conduct a predictive analysis in an additional

---

82 Acknowledgement: Raw coaching data for my calculations from *Hockey Reference*, http://www.hockey-reference.com.

83 Ryan Dittrick, "Oilers announce winner of Hackathan 2.0", Edmonton Oilers, May 29, 2013, Web, http://oilers.nhl.com/club/news.htm?id=672358.

field of choice.

While I beat him on the predictive side of things, he edged me with a thought-provoking analysis of the effects of coaching strategy in terms of line matching, line composition, and zone starts. He won an opportunity to work with the team's Analytics Working Group, while I got an autographed Taylor Hall jersey. Which still hasn't arrived. Sigh.

There are still those who are far more skeptical in how much influence a coach can ultimately have in the standings. For example, Nick Emptage[84] recently completed a study of all 41 coaching changes over the past few years, and found that on the whole they had no clear impact on a team's subsequent performance in the short run, and an average increase of just 1.5 points the following season. So it is still very much in question how significant the coaching staff's influence can be in the standings.

13. Prospects

There are generally three things that can blow a set of projections out of the water: goaltending, coaching, and the sudden explosion of young talent. To an extent, that's exactly what happened in Tampa Bay and Colorado, and what failed to happen in Buffalo and Edmonton.

As such, at least some provision must be made for teams whose youth have the potential to explode. The small sample sizes and the relative scarcity of data in other leagues make it a challenge to accurately predict which teams have strong organizational strength and which ones don't, but using tools such as NHL translations can help establish each team's rough positioning.

Not Included

There are a number of factors that were not included:

- Each team's shooting abilities, which can be important but very hard to predict. It can be considered (to an extent) when judging a team's power play and/or top scoring line.
- The likelihood of injuries, which is almost impossible to predict (though it does go up with age) and has minimal correlation to a team's position in the standings, as Thomas Crawshaw[85] once established.
- The front office and their ability to adapt to changing circumstances. A team with a front office strong enough to make the right moves throughout the season probably built a team strong enough to measure well before the season begins, too.
- Faceoffs just missed the cut, in a relatively agonizing decision. They do have some impact on a team's winning percentage, and there is a degree of predictive persistence to it, it just wasn't significant enough to warrant the additional complexity. It's factored in when evaluating each player's performance instead.

---

84 Nick Emptage, "How Much Difference Do NHL Coaches Makes?", *NHL Numbers*, November 15, 2013, Web, http://nhlnumbers.com/2013/11/15/how-much-difference-do-nhl-coaches-make.
85 Thomas Crawshaw, "The Pain Game: 5-year analysis", *Springing Malik*, July 2, 2013, Web, http://springingmalik.blogspot.ca/2013/07/the-pain-game-5-year-analysis-200809_2.html.

- Team discipline, which is simply not persistent enough, and can be factored into the individual player evaluations.

Despite these and other limitations, this new checklist should product a high-level foundation for how the teams currently measure up.

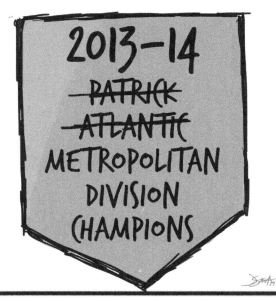

Closing Thoughts

Team-level predictions are notoriously unreliable, whether they're based on analytics or on traditional analysis. Too many things can occur throughout the course of a season to confound a team projection, such as injuries, major transactions, hot goaltending, quickly developing rookies, unusual coaching decisions, and puck luck, just to name a few. Only an online website that can be updated with all the major developments throughout the course of a season can have any chance of accurately projecting what is to come.

That's why the focus of this next section isn't so much on forecasting the outcome of the next season, but on providing demonstrations on how certain analytics can be used to shed light on what might come to pass in 2014–15.

In last year's *Hockey Abstract*, the player usage charts were provided for each team but without any context or interpretation at all. Between this year's quick interpretation and the new Hockey Abstract checklist, a reasonably useful view can be crafted for each team, and in such a way that it can be easily updated with new information, or to reflect any traditional analysis that goes beyond the level of insight that this analytic perspective can provide.

Don't get too fixated on the results and stay focused on the process. If you have additional data, or an alternative interpretation of the existing data, then it is perfectly reasonable to take out a pencil and adjust the checklist appropriately. In fact, that should be an excellent exercise for the future, when the same processes can be used to handicap the outcome of 2015–16 and beyond.

Anaheim Ducks

Defying both their mainstream and analytic critics, the Ducks actually improved on their 2012–13 performance to record a franchise record 116 points, and pushing the eventual Stanley Cup champions to their limit in the Conference semi-finals.

This is, however, not a strong possession team and was heavily reliant on solid shooting percentages from Corey Perry and, Hart Trophy runner-up, Ryan Getzlaf. Though he couldn't secure enough secondary scoring to replace the retired Teemu Selanne and departing free agents Dustin Penner and Mathieu Perreault, GM of the year Bob Murray did score a coup in acquiring Ryan Kesler via trade to centre the team's re-tooled shutdown line. The Ducks should remain just a small step back of the league's elite teams.

Anaheim Ducks - Player Usage

Star coach Bruce Boudreau deploys his team almost flawlessly, structuring the entire line-up around Ryan Getzlaf and Corey Perry, one of the most effective top line duos in the entire NHL. Was Dany Heatley acquired to play on their left side this season? If not, Kyle Palmieri might be a better choice than Matt Beleskey, but both options are still gambles.

The success of the scoring line depends on the ability of the top shutdown line to effectively shoulder the tough minutes against the top opponents. It has been excellent these past two seasons and should remain so with the incomparable Ryan Kesler joining Andrew Cogliano as Saku Koivu's replacement at centre. But who will replace Daniel Winnik on the other wing? The newly-signed Nate Thompson is a defensive-minded player, but not of the top-six variety. Jakub Silfverberg has been gradually developing into a solid top-six, two-way forward, but didn't get as much Calder attention as he deserved in 2012–13 and may be the superior option (assuming he is eventually re-signed).

Sometimes, gritty depth players are left off the player usage chart because they stretch it so far down. That's the case with Tim Jackman, the lone veteran amongst a staggering abundance of young bottom-six talent. None of them look particularly impressive so far, but there's just too much talent to be a complete bust. Rickard Rakell and Pat Maroon could be the two most intriguing options.

As for the blue line, the big story has been the rapid development of Cam Fowler into a complete top-pairing defenceman. Ben Lovejoy's equally surprising success as a top-four option and Hampus Lindholm's quick start should help replace Sheldon Souray, whose career may be over, and reduce the demands on Francois Beauchemin, who may soon begin to decline. Clayton Stoner's high-cost signing appears to be unnecessary with several superior third-pairing defencemen under contract, like Vatanen.

Score	Category	Notes
	Possession	It's not a possession team, but becoming less of a weakness.
	The Shootout	Anaheim lost a few weapons and have unknowns in goal. The remaining scoring threats are solid, but not elite.
	Goaltending	Andersen, Gibson (and LaBarbera) are unproven.
	Penalty Kill	Ducks fell to 28th in attempted shots allowed per minute last year, but Kesler will help.
✔	Power Play	One of the league's top power plays is always top 10 in creating chances, but they still lack a secondary threat.
☆	Scoring Line	It doesn't get much better than top two-way stars Perry and Getzlaf, no matter who is on their wing.
✔	Shutdown Line	Kesler should replace Koivu beautifully, Cogliano is good, but there's still a question of who replaces Winnik on the wing.
	Forward Depth	There's not a lot of scoring but there is a great deal of upside in a large collection of young players.
✔	Top Pairing	Fowler and Beauchemin are solid at both ends of the ice.
✔	Second Pairing	Lovejoy and Lindholm should be passable but unspectacular.
✔	Defensive Depth	The Ducks have expensive but usable third-pairing options in Allen, Stoner, Fistric, and Vatanen.
☆	Coaching	Boudreau is highly underrated.
✔	Prospects	The team is very well stocked top to bottom.

Assessment: A solid playoff team but probably not a divisional champion.

Arizona Coyotes

It's a team with a new name but potentially the same result. Though they are without any obvious holes, the Arizona Coyotes are merely average in most areas and light on star power. They are likely to remain a playoff bubble team and a late slide could leave them just barely on the outside once again.

Interestingly, the Coyotes had eight players with at least 40 points last year. That deep but essentially mediocre offence will have to get by with only Sam Gagner to replace Radim Vrbata and Mike Ribeiro on the scoring line. It will be fascinating to see how coach Dave Tippett deploys the remainder of the team's forwards.

Arizona Coyotes - Player Usage

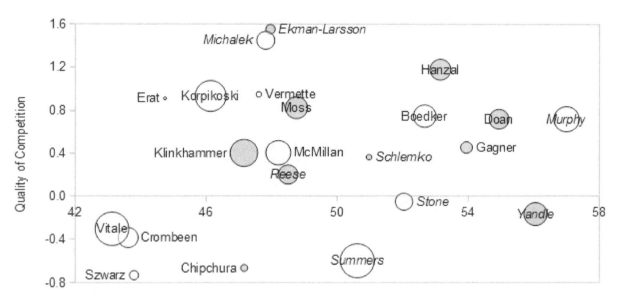

Perhaps no team is as dependent on their top two shutdown defencemen as Arizona is on young two-way star Oliver Ekman-Larsson and shot-blocking master Zbynek Michalek. There's quite a bit of a usage gap between those two and the value-priced likes of David Schlemko and shrewd pickup Dylan Reese. The blue line's fate could therefore hinge on the rapid development of youngsters Brandon Gormley and Connor Murphy.

Keith Yandle plays a very specific role on the blue line, and plays it well. In fact, I often consider him the prototype of a puck-moving defenceman who effectively logs big minutes exclusively in scoring-focused situations against secondary opponents. This strategy's success relies on having work horses like Ekman-Larsson and Michalek, which is also why the model is effective with Boston's Torey Krug, for example.

Up front, the Coyotes had one of the league's top shutdown lines in 2012–13 with Boyd

Gordon, David Moss and Rob Klinkhammer, but the line was dismantled upon Gordon's departure. Moss was moved to a scoring line, while Klinkhammer was shuffled down the depth chart in favour of Lauri Korpikoski, who has often left the team at a possession-based disadvantage. Antoine Vermette can be effective in a shutdown role but the newly-acquired Joe Vitale and B.J. Crombeen are strictly checking line wingers for Kyle Chipchura's line.

Sam Gagner may help replace some of the lost offence with the departure of Radim Vrbata and Mike Ribeiro. Mikkel Boedker is the highest scorer of the remaining players, but is not a strong possession player. Veterans Shane Doan and Martin Erat may actually be the team's best scoring line options, despite the latter's lack of goal scoring lately. Tough two-way centre Martin Hanzal is another scoring line option, if Gagner is moved to the wing.

The Coyotes are also gambling on Devan Dubnyk as the team's backup goalie despite a truly awful season. It's actually not that big of a risk given his previous success and the fact that steady veteran Mike Smith can easily start well over 60 games a season.

Score	Category	Notes
	Possession	Coyotes are typically just below average, but were simply terrible in 2012–13.
	The Shootout	Gagner will help replace Vrbata, but overall they're not a strong shootout team, especially in nets.
✔	Goaltending	Smith's .929 even-strength save percentage over the past three years is fifth among goalies with at least 100 starts.
	Penalty Kill	Michalek is excellent and Vermette is good, but the team is always in the bottom third in preventing shots.
	Power Play	They took a huge step forward last year, but there are just not enough scoring threats for Yandle to work with.
	Scoring Line	The Coyotes' scoring is spread out over several lines of 40-point players.
	Shutdown Line	There is potential to build around Vermette, but it doesn't look promising.
✔	Forward Depth	The bottom six is shaping up very nicely.
✔	Top Pairing	Ekman-Larsson is highly underrated and Michalek is one of the league's better shutdown veterans.
✔	Second Pairing	Yandle is the best at what he does.
	Defensive Depth	It's in the hands of rookies or value-priced journeymen.
✔	Coaching	Tippett is a solid coach who can make a lot out of very little.
✔	Prospects	Murphy or Gormley could play a prominent role on defence, and Domi could be close.

Assessment: Arizona is a playoff bubble team at best.

Boston Bruins

The Bruins have thus far resisted the urge to panic after a disappointing seven-game second round loss to the Montreal Canadiens. Wholesale changes are completely unnecessary on what remains the best team in the East and possibly in the entire league.

The Bruins won the President's Trophy and finished top three in both goals scored and in fewest goals against. Tuukka Rask won the Vezina Trophy, Patrice Bergeron won the Selke Trophy, and Zdeno Chara was a finalist for the Norris Trophy. While GM Peter Chiarelli has some work to do in signing several restricted free agents, their only noteworthy losses this summer were Jarome Iginla, backup goalie Chad Johnson, and fourth line agitator Shawn Thornton.

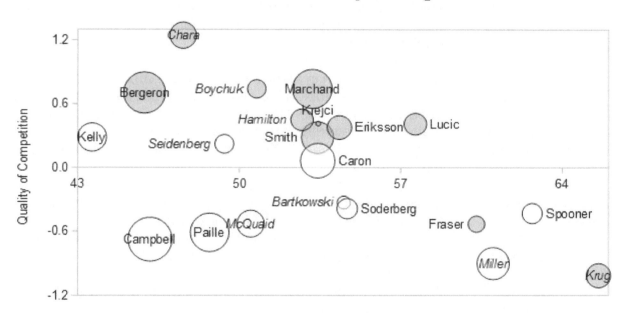

Boston Bruins - Player Usage

Patrice Bergeron is the league's best shutdown forward and the usage chart clearly demonstrates why. He takes on the team's top opponents, most frequently in the defensive zone, and yet he's the very definition of a possession monster. He has amazing chemistry with Brad Marchand and new arrival Reilly Smith on a tremendous shutdown line.

Iginla's departure opens up a spot alongside Milan Lucic and leading scorer David Krejci on the top scoring line, most likely for veteran Loui Eriksson.

The fact that each player's possession numbers are measured relative to their teammates casts Boston's remaining forwards in the worst possible light. Their checking line of Chris

Kelly, Gregory Campbell, and Daniel Paille could nevertheless stand to improve, and Carl Soderberg's secondary scoring line will be largely in the hands of the team's youth.

Zdeno Chara and whoever is fortunate enough to skate alongside him, most likely puck-moving youngster Dougie Hamilton, form a fantastic two-way shutdown pairing. Johnny Boychuk is an underrated and physical second pairing defenceman, and ideally Dennis Seidenberg can be effective for at least one more year in that role. Young Torey Krug plays the sheltered scoring-focused role almost to perfection, much like Keith Yandle does in Arizona, with either Matt Bartkowski or the huge Adam McQuad as the depth option most likely to prove effective alongside him.

Finally, the Bruins have settled on rookie Niklas Svedberg to replace Chad Johnson as Tuukka Rask's backup, with star prospect Malcolm Subban knocking at the door.

Score	Category	Notes
☆	Possession	The Bruins are arguably the best possession team in the East.
	The Shootout	Rask is capable, but there's not much in the way of shooters.
☆	Goaltending	If anyone can challenge Lundqvist for the title of league's best goalie, it's last year's Vezina winner.
✔	Penalty Kill	There's a solid defensive core built around Chara and Marchand, which is always top ten in preventing shots.
✔	Power Play	The power play took a big step forward into the top ten thanks in part to newcomers like Soderberg and Smith (and Iginla).
✔	Scoring Line	It should remain effective even without Iginla.
☆	Shutdown Line	Bergeron is the best in the game and Marchand complements him perfectly.
	Forward Depth	This is a rare aspect of Boston's roster that is merely average.
✔	Top Pairing	Chara is one of the best two-way defencemen in the game, but he's 37 years old and without a star partner.
	Second Pairing	The Bruins are adequate behind Chara, but not exceptional.
	Defensive Depth	There are several options, but other than Krug they may all be replacement level at best.
☆	Coaching	Julien is a highly accomplished coach with a great staff.
✔	Prospects	There are prospects of potential impact at every position.

Assessment: The Bruins are the best team in the East and ready to contend for the President's Trophy once again.

Buffalo Sabres

The good news is that the Sabres have far too exceptional a collection of blue chip prospects to remain in the league's basement for long. The bad news is that five of their six major summer acquisitions (Brian Gionta, Josh Gorges, Andrej Meszaros, Zac Dalpe, and Tyson Strachan) were negative possession players, and all but one of their eight departures (Christian Ehrhoff, Ville Leino, Jamie McBain, Henrik Tallinder, Cory Conacher, Alexander Sulzer, and Matt d'Agostini) were positive. It looks like we have our early front runner for the "Connor McDavid Sweepstakes".

Buffalo Sabres - Player Usage

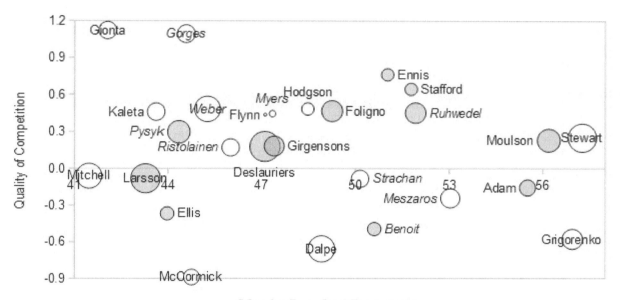

Offensive Zone Start Percentage

Buffalo's top forwards are mostly scoring line options, some of whom will therefore have to be drafted into shutdown roles instead. Matt Moulson and Chris Stewart will play the wings on that top scoring line, the former because of his exceptional talent, and the latter because he's incapable of playing elsewhere. Expect last year's team-leading scorer Cody Hodgson to be the centre, until someone like Mikhail Grigorenko develops into the role.

The Sabres will be leaning on Tyler Ennis for the top shutdown line. The team's only other forward who has faced a higher average quality of competition over the past three years is veteran right winger Brian Gionta. The problems are that he's even smaller than Ennis and that the 35-year-old can no longer carry a shutdown line, based on his weak possession numbers.

Buffalo has a number of checking line forwards from which to choose to complete that line, the best of which is probably tough young winger Marcus Foligno. That actually leaves the

Sabres with far better forward depth than most teams, thanks to promising youngsters like Zemgus Girgensons, Johan Larsson, Nicolas Deslauriers, and Luke Adam along with veterans Brian Flynn, Torrey Mitchell, Matt Ellis, and tough guy Patrick Kaleta.

The blue line has undergone quite an overhaul. Although he hasn't lived up to his promise, Tyler Myers is probably the team's best defenceman. Josh Gorges will probably also be thrust into a top shutdown role, for which he's probably not best suited.

That may not be ideal, but there is really no one else who has established themselves as top-four blue line options. Usage and possession data suggest that veterans Mike Weber, Andre Benoit, Tyson Strachan and even Andrej Meszaros are depth options only, and not exactly great ones at that, other than Benoit. There should therefore be ample opportunity for prospects like Mark Pysyk, Rasmus Ristolainen, Nikita Zadorov, Jake McCabe, and Chad Ruhwedel to have a considerable impact this season.

With Ryan Miller gone, it will be exciting to finally see Jhonas Enroth step out of the shadows and get a shot as the team's starter, assuming he can beat out Michal Neuvirth for the job. The clock is ticking, because the Sabres have several young goalies knocking on the door.

Score	Category	Notes
	Possession	You probably didn't need to buy *Hockey Abstract* to figure out where Buffalo stands with regards to possession.
	The Shootout	Sabres have unknowns in goal and few (if any) proven shooters.
	Goaltending	Enroth is highly underrated but unproven, as is Neuvirth.
	Penalty Kill	Gionta and Gorges could help a penalty kill that finished a fairly customary 23rd in attempted shots allowed per minute.
	Power Play	Hopefully Moulson can help a team that has ranked 25th and 23rd in attempted shots per minute the last two years.
	Scoring Line	This would only be a secondary scoring line on most teams (except for Moulson).
	Shutdown Line	It could rank among the league's worst shutdown lines.
✔	Forward Depth	Between great prospects and well-chosen veterans, this is a rare area of strength for the Sabres.
	Top Pairing	Myers and Gorges could make a fine second pairing.
	Second Pairing	You know Nolan will try Meszaros here, which will only work if the prospect with whom he's paired is truly exceptional.
✔	Defensive Depth	The checkmark is for having too many talented prospects to completely miss, not for their three below-average veterans.
	Coaching	It could be boom or bust for Nolan this year.
☆	Prospects	A staggering collection of talent guarantees that Buffalo simply can't stay in the basement for long.

Assessment: Paging Connor McDavid!

Calgary Flames

Surprisingly, the departure of Jarome Iginla, Jay Bouwmeester, Miikka Kiprusoff, and Alex Tanguay did little to nothing to hurt the team's winning percentage last year, which actually went up despite being on the losing end of more close games than anyone but the Devils. Losing Mike Cammalleri, Lee Stempniak, Chris Butler, and T.J. Galiardi could have a comparably minor effect this year.

It will nevertheless be another long, cold winter in Calgary this season. Despite a good coaching staff, a top-notch first pairing and capable goaltending, the Flames have very few players that can score and/or effectively play the tough minutes. The good news is that their incredible organizational strength will make its presence felt soon enough, especially if Connor McDavid is added to the collection at year's end.

Calgary Flames - Player Usage

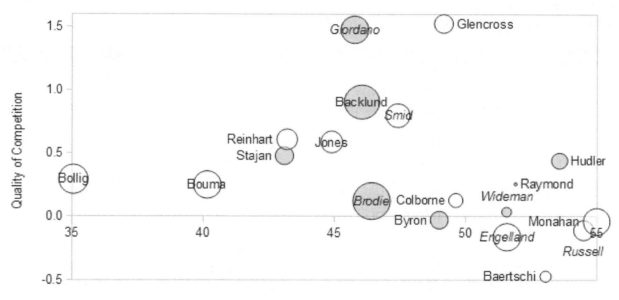

A couple of seasons ago, former Calgary GM Jay Feaster dismissed my player usage chart presentation with a casual shrug that they were already using them. Clearly they aren't because they have very few players who can take on top opponents and all of their summer signings require relatively sheltered minutes in order to be effective. I didn't mean his dismissal as a criticism, because there are more ways to build a team than in this possession-based model, but it does raise those valid concerns.

One area where there are no concerns is that awesome top pairing with Mark Giordano and T.J. Brodie. The former was a valid dark horse Norris selection last year and the latter successfully made the largest single-season leap in quality of competition of any defenceman in the league.

That gives the Flames the freedom to play their remaining defencemen in more sheltered roles in the offensive zone and against secondary lines, which is quite fortunate given how badly most of them need it to remain effective, like puck-movers Dennis Wideman and Kris Russell, tough guy Ladislav Smid, and high-priced free agent signing Deryk Engelland.

Up front, Curtis Glencross and Jiri Hudler will be relied upon for scoring, either with Sean Monahan if he's ready (someone will have to move to wing), or the newly-signed Mason Raymond if he's not.

As for the shutdown line, Mikael Backlund has been one of Calgary's best-kept secrets (even from themselves). He takes on tough minutes and gives the team that same edge up front that Giordano does on the blue line. It's just hard to find anyone that can effectively play alongside him against top opponents, like perhaps David Jones and Matt Stajan moved to the wing?

Given their questionable defence, the Flames were wise to upgrade their goaltending situation by signing Jonas Hiller to join Karri Ramo. Hiller's analytics once suggested a huge upside that has yet to manifest itself. It's not too late!

Score	Category	Notes
	Possession	The Flames are not built for possession and moving ever further away.
	The Shootout	Hiller's a capable goalie, but the team has no real scoring threats.
	Goaltending	Hiller has a big upside, but he and Ramo's numbers are in the mediocre .920 range (at even strength).
	Penalty Kill	The exceptional Giordano makes Calgary respectable.
	Power Play	Flames have finished 22nd or 23rd in attempted shots per minute for 3 straight seasons, but with unpredictable results.
	Scoring Line	This depends on Glencross' health and Monahan's development to even achieve adequacy.
	Shutdown Line	Who can play with Backlund against the top opponents?
✔	Forward Depth	This is where the prospects can make their presence felt.
✔	Top Pairing	The Giordano/Brodie pairing is the team's greatest strength.
	Second Pairing	Wideman is possibly the team's only other legitimate top-four defenceman.
	Defensive Depth	There remains just three veterans, all with poor possession numbers, two of whom require sheltered minutes.
✔	Coaching	Hartley is an underrated coach who may surprise us.
✔	Prospects	This is one of the deepest pools of talent, including several forwards who could have a significant impact right away.

Assessment: The Flames are still in the draft lottery mix.

Carolina Hurricanes

The Hurricanes did a fantastic job rebuilding their blue line last summer, but missed the playoffs yet again because of a scoring slump and a disappointing, injury-plagued season from goalie Cam Ward.

A new coaching staff, a new starting goalie in Anton Khudobin (hopefully), and a return to form from top scorers like Eric Staal and Alexander Semin just might be enough for a nearly identical team to jump from second last in the Metropolitan division to a team with a fighting chance for the playoffs.

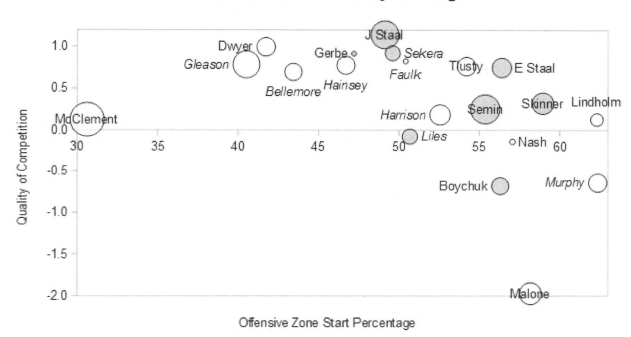

Carolina Hurricanes - Player Usage

Last summer, Carolina provided a textbook example of how to improve a struggling blue line. Andrej Sekera was acquired from Buffalo and proved to be an effective and affordable top pairing option to nicely complement Justin Faulk. Ron Hainsey was a surprisingly effective and value-priced top-four defenceman, and found chemistry with physical AHL call-up Brett Bellemore. Tim Gleason was moved to Toronto for an overpriced but effective number four option in John-Michael Liles. Gleason was even brought back this summer as someone who can ideally play a veteran defensive role on a low-cost third pairing, with either the physical Jay Harrison or the team's speedy young puck-mover Ryan Murphy. Nicely done.

The savings the Hurricanes managed to find on the blue line helps pay the salaries of their four highest scoring forwards Alexander Semin, Jeff Skinner, and the Staal brothers Eric and Jordan, who all play for a combined cap hit of $27 million. The first three are excellent scoring line options who could really break out this year, while a solid shutdown line that includes the underrated Nathan Gerbe can be built around the younger Staal brother. While Patrick Dwyer might be likely to remain on that line, his weaker possession numbers suggest that he might be more effective facing more secondary opponents on a new checking line built around the recently-signed defensive specialist Jay McClement, who replaces Manny Malhotra.

Jiri Tlusty's and young Elias Lindholm's weaker possession numbers also suggest that they'd be better off in the bottom six, where players like Riley Nash have been effective, though for Lindholm such a move would likely only prove temporary. Zach Boychuk might be worth a try in the bottom six as well.

Finally, the prospect of seeing Anton Khudobin finally replace mediocre veteran Cam Ward as the starting goalie is an exciting one. A breakout season both in nets and from their scoring line is probably their only chance of making a return to the postseason.

Score	Category	Notes
	Possession	The Hurricanes were effective possession-wise only once in the past five years, back in 2012–13.
	The Shootout	Carolina is potentially among the league's worst.
	Goaltending	Khudobin has been fantastic, but in a small sample size, and Ward has been mediocre at best.
✔	Penalty Kill	People thought I was crazy when I praised them last year, but they can kill penalties. McClement joining the Staal brothers while Khudobin gets more starts will only make them better.
	Power Play	The Hurricanes are exactly 13th in attempted shots per minute every year, but they're just not going in.
✔	Scoring Line	It was an off year, but Eric Staal, Semin, and Skinner are all valid top scoring line threats.
✔	Shutdown Line	Jordan Staal is one of the league's best defensive forwards, and Gerbe is an underrated value-priced complement.
	Forward Depth	The Hurricanes could use some more forward depth.
✔	Top Pairing	Sekera was the perfect addition to play with Faulk.
	Second Pairing	Can Hainsey be effective again, this time with Liles?
	Defensive Depth	They do have eight reliable defencemen, but six of them are below average in terms of possession.
	Coaching	Peters hasn't had a lot of success as a head coach, but Carolina could use a dose of whatever he learned in Detroit.
	Prospects	The cupboard isn't completely bare, but there's a minimal likelihood of anyone moving the needle this year.

Assessment: There are scenarios where Carolina can make the playoffs, but quite a few things will need to break their way.

Chicago Blackhawks

The Chicago Blackhawks are the best team in the league, at least in my view, and came within an overtime loss of competing for the Stanley Cup for the third time in four seasons.

This team has a strong commitment to possession-based play, constantly cycling out those players who have struggled, like Brandon Bollig, Michal Handzus, Sheldon Brookbank and Brandon Pirri, for those who haven't, like Kris Versteeg, Brad Richards, and David Rundblad.

Of those who have at least 20 career games under their belts, the only players on their roster who are below water in possession are the tough minutes defensive pairing of Niklas Hjalmarsson and Johnny Oduya, and the two checking line youngsters who get buried in the defensive zone, Marcus Kruger and Ben Smith.

Chicago Blackhawks - Player Usage

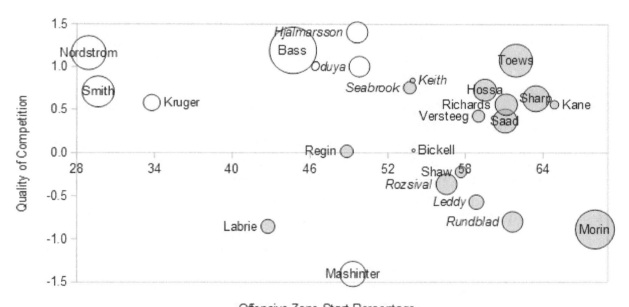

Offensive Zone Start Percentage

Duncan Keith's Norris-winning season alongside long-time partner Brent Seabrook is partly thanks to Hjalmarsson and Oduya handling a heavier share of the duties against top opponents and in the defensive zone. The former pair's superior possession numbers are reflective of this more favourable deployment, more time behind Chicago's star forwards, and of course their own greater abilities at driving possession.

A player usage chart also helps demonstrate one of the key differences between top two-way, possession-driving forwards like Jonathan Toews, Marian Hossa and Patrick Sharp, and more exclusively scoring-focused stars like Patrick Kane. With the ice tilted in his favour (through more shifts started in the offensive zone and fewer against the top lines), Kane can fully unleash his offensive talents, much in the same way they expect from the Brad Richards.

Chicago's challenge has always been to use their remaining cap space as carefully as possible to fill the remaining depth positions. Up front, they should get solid secondary scoring from several youngsters, like two-way talent Brandon Saad, gritty Andrew Shaw and possibly Jeremy Morin, not to mention veterans like Kris Versteeg and Bryan Bickell.

As for blue line depth, Nick Leddy has developed into a solid puck-moving option on the third pairing, and could partner up with either the defensively responsible 36-year-old Michal Rozsival or the promising Swedish puck-mover David Rundblad.

The only aspect of the roster that can be considered average is the goaltending. Corey Crawford has been a perfectly serviceable starter for three of his four seasons, and though rookie backup Antti Raanta was less than impressive in 25 games with Chicago (and 14 in the AHL), he was downright dominant in his final two seasons in Finland.

Score	Category	Notes
☆	Possession	Few teams, if any, can match Chicago's possession-based play.
✔	The Shootout	Crawford is solid, and Toews and Kane are both elite.
	Goaltending	Crawford's .923 even-strength save percentage over the past three seasons is below average, and Raanta is an unproven backup.
✔	Penalty Kill	The Blackhawks are all over the map, but improving. Toews and Hjalmarsson can guide them to an effective season.
	Power Play	They are improving, but unpredictable. They have the talent to be a lot better than middle-of-the-road, as they have been.
☆	Scoring Line	Richards and Kane together could be awesome.
☆	Shutdown Line	Toews is among the best and most teams would even be lucky to build a line around Hossa or Sharp.
☆	Forward Depth	Chicago has several potential 20-goal scorers in its bottom six and a decent young checking line.
☆	Top Pairing	Norris Trophy winner Keith and Seabrook are always among the league's best pairing.
✔	Second Pairing	Oduya and Hjalmarsson are given a more challenging assignment than most top pairings (including their own).
✔	Defensive Depth	Leddy could probably crack the top four on most teams, and both Rozsival and Rundblad are good 6/7 options.
☆	Coaching	Either Quenneville or Hitchcock is the league's best coach.
✔	Prospects	It's not a deep pool, but Teravainen and Rundblad could both have an immediate impact.

Assessment: Chicago looks like the odds-on Stanley Cup favourite.

Colorado Avalanche

Colorado shocked pundits, both mainstream and those who rely on analytics, with 112 points to finish atop the Central division, thanks to a dominant 41-11-7 record in games decided by a single goal and/or empty netter. However, its lack of depth and possession-based play was exposed by the Minnesota Wild in the first round, bringing its Cinderella season to a swift conclusion.

Deciding that the problem was actually inexperience, GM Joe Sakic acquired veterans Jarome Iginla, Brad Stuart, Daniel Briere, and Jesse Winchester. If the problem was actually their possession-based play, then losing two of their strongest such players in Paul Stastny and P.A. Parenteau, not to mention depth defencemen Cory Sarich and Andre Benoit, for four players who are below average in this regard is a step in the wrong direction.

Colorado Avalanche - Player Usage

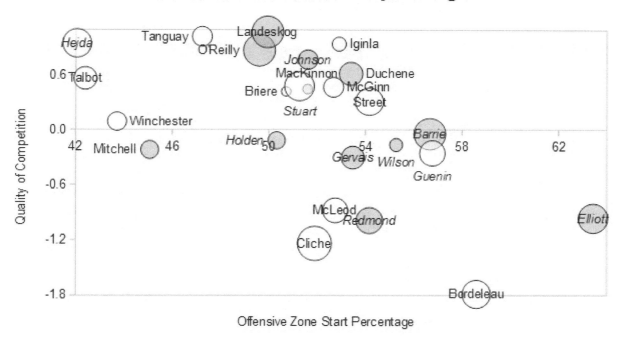

Colorado's forward core enviably features four players aged 18 to 23 who all scored between 23 and 28 goals, as well as 63 to 70 points. Add in the return to health of 35-year-old playmaker Alex Tanguay and the addition of his former Flames linemate Jarome Iginla through free agency, who scored 30 goals and 61 points for Boston last year, and the Avalanche should be flush with scoring line options this year.

The impact of Paul Stastny's departure to free agency is therefore not so much the lost scoring, but what it could mean to the shutdown line. Which of these six players will be called upon to face top opponents in key defensive situations? My best guess is Ryan O'Reilly,

Gabriel Landeskog, and Matt Duchene.

On the bright side, Sakic's moves have helped address the depth concerns. Skilled 36-year-old Daniel Briere playing alongside Jamie McGinn can help provide some secondary scoring, while Jesse Winchester should be an upgrade over the likes of Marc-Andre Cliche, Cody McLeod, and Patrick Bordeleau on the checking line, with veterans Max Talbot and John Mitchell.

Colorado's blue line greatly exceeded my expectations last year. Granted, Erik Johnson was already a solid two-way top pairing defenceman, but who could have foreseen Andre Benoit and Nick Holden as legitimate top-four options? They were 30 and 26 years old respectively, with a combined 48 games of prior NHL experience.

This year, the Avalanche are going for the shotgun method, having acquired as many defencemen as possible, and hoping that a few will once again step forward. Tyson Barrie is the logical choice from a puck-moving perspective (assuming he re-signs), and big 36-year-old bruiser Jan Hejda from a shutdown perspective. Don't count on Brad Stuart or Nate Guenin to be anything more than defensive-minded third pairing options.

Score	Category	Notes
	Possession	This is plainly not a team that cares about possession.
	The Shootout	Varlamov has been exceptional, but in a marginal sample size. There are too few proven shooters.
	Goaltending	Varlamov was a legitimate Vezina finalist last year, but can he do it again? And is Berra a capable backup?
	Penalty Kill	This team is unique in how exclusively they use certain forwards, like Cliche and Talbot, but they finished in the bottom fifth in attempted shots allowed per minute once again.
	Power Play	Colorado was third last in attempted shots per 60 minutes, but were saved with some hot shooting.
✔	Scoring Line	Colorado has many fast, young scoring threats complemented by solid veterans.
	Shutdown Line	Losing Stastny hurts.
✔	Forward Depth	Sakic took some meaningful steps to address this hole.
	Top Pairing	Johnson might be the team's lone top pairing option, but a solid two-way one at that. Don't make Hejda play here again.
✔	Second Pairing	There's no question that a strong pairing will step forward.
☆	Defensive Depth	Colorado has arguably 10 NHL-calibre defencemen, although they are primarily third pairing options.
✔	Coaching	Let's see Roy do that again!
	Prospects	The young players that you already see are basically what you get.

Assessment: Colorado is a playoff bubble team that is quite unlikely to defend its division title.

Columbus Blue Jackets

Columbus enjoyed its second playoff appearance in franchise history and it was no fluke. The Blue Jackets have been taking huge steps towards a consistent possession-based game and should remain in the mix this coming season.

Columbus Blue Jackets - Player Usage

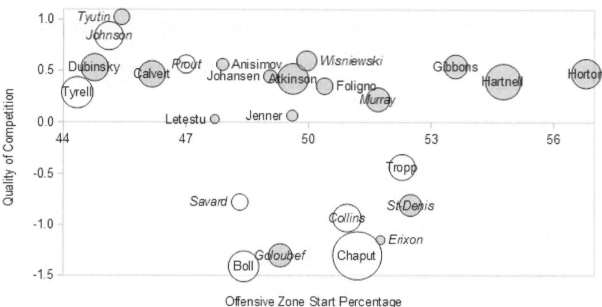

Offensive Zone Start Percentage

The big move this summer was swapping veterans with Philadelphia, sending R.J. Umberger away for potentially the final piece needed for their scoring line, Scott Hartnell. While unlikely to be as effective without Giroux, Hartnell is a gritty, possession-driving leader who could complement Nathan Horton perfectly. The critical piece of that top scoring line is its centre, Ryan Johansen, who still hasn't signed. Despite being used against the top lines, he unexpectedly led the team in scoring last year by 12 goals and 12 points.

How will Umberger's absence affect the shutdown line? It remains capably centred by Brandon Dubinsky, who is potentially the team's most valuable forward. He is a classic and tough do-it-all, possession-driving player. Matt Calvert and Nick Foligno are two tough and capable options to play the wing, and there's always the versatile Artem Anisimov.

As for secondary scoring, Columbus has a pair of undersized skilled players in Cam Atkinson and Brian Gibbons, not to mention 21-year-old Boone Jenner, and versatile and underrated, two-way veteran Mark Letestu.

I'm convinced that coach Todd Richards keeps Jack Johnson on the top pairing just to annoy the hockey analytics crowd. He's a black hole of possession that leaves the Blue Jackets without the puck whenever he's on the ice. Why not try the highly underrated James Wisniewski, who is perfectly capable as an offensive-minded top pairing defenceman? Fedor Tyutin is a solid two-way veteran who could easily play alongside and is quite used to carrying the torch in defensive zone situations, and against top opposing lines. Johnson might then become more effective in a second pairing role with 21-year-old Ryan Murray, the second overall selection the 2012 entry draft.

In nets, the Blue Jackets are fortunate to have 2013's Vezina winner Sergei Bobrovsky, whose numbers are matched by very few, and exceeded only by the league's elite like Tuukka Rask and Henrik Lundqvist.

Score	Category	Notes
✔	Possession	Only Chicago has fewer regulars with below-average possession numbers over the past three years.
	The Shootout	Bobrovsky is below average, and the mediocre Mark Letestu could be the team's best shooter.
✔	Goaltending	Former Vezina winner Bobrovsky has the third best even-strength save percentage over the past three years, among those with 100 starts.
	Penalty Kill	The Blue Jackets took a step back last year, but they are still competitive.
	Power Play	They had surprising results, but the underlying analytics are still below average. Hartnell could help.
✔	Scoring Line	Assuming Horton is healthy and Johansen re-signs, Hartnell might be that final missing piece.
	Shutdown Line	Dubinsky is the perfect man to centre this line, but who will play the wings?
✔	Forward Depth	Columbus hasn't ignored youth and talent in their quest for size and grit.
	Top Pairing	Get Johnson off the top pairing!
✔	Second Pairing	Columbus has at least two solid top-four defencemen in Tyutin and Wisniewski, and Murray's almost there.
	Defensive Depth	They're still waiting for some youngsters to reach their potential.
	Coaching	Few coaches have had as many near misses as Richards.
✔	Prospects	Columbus has an above average pool, and plenty of opportunities available for them.

Assessment: Columbus should remain in the mix for one of the final playoff positions again this season.

Dallas Stars

Last summer, the Dallas Stars underwent a complete overhaul from top to bottom, even replacing the coach (with Lindy Ruff) and the general manager (with Jim Nill). The result was a return to the postseason, after being one of the last teams eliminated from the race for five straight seasons. Expect them to continue to build on that success this season.

The scoring was led by the incomparable duo of Jamie Benn and Tyler Seguin, who each scored at least 34 goals and 79 points. No other Stars forward earned more than 35 points last year, prompting Nill to trade for Jason Spezza and to sign Ales Hemsky this summer.

Dallas Stars - Player Usage

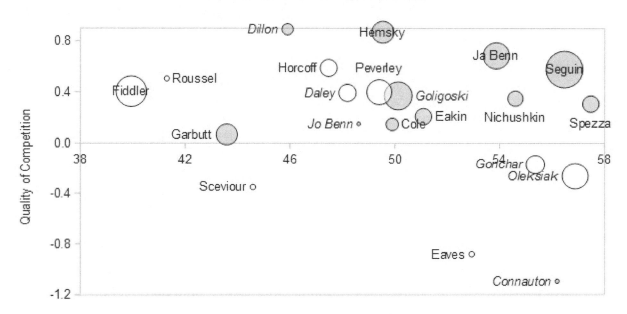

Offensive Zone Start Percentage

Spezza is coming off a rough season in Ottawa, where he just couldn't find scoring line chemistry with anyone, at least not until Hemsky was acquired at the trade deadline. So Dallas secured them both! But should they be split up? Hemsky is quite capable of playing on the top two-way line with Benn and Seguin, which would allow the big 19-year-old Valeri Nichushkin to play on a more sheltered scoring line alongside Spezza instead.

Dallas is going to need a lot more from their veterans like Vernon Fiddler, Sergei Gonchar, Shawn Horcoff, and Erik Cole this season. Along with Ray Whitney, who was released to free agency, these five players cost a combined $21.3 million, and did not provide fair value despite all but Fiddler enjoying relatively sheltered assignments.

Unless things improve, the Stars are going to continue to rely more on gritty winger Ryan Garbutt and agitator Antoine Roussel, who is one of the league's few tough guys who can carry a regular and defensively responsible shift. The star of the bottom six is 23-year-old two-way gem Cody Eakin, who will likely see himself promoted to the top six, especially with Rich Peverley's future so uncertain.

Dallas is taking a bit of a risk going into the season with a top four composed of puck-mover Alex Goligoski, long-time second pairing option Trevor Daley, tough young defender Brenden Dillon and Jamie Benn's older brother Jordie, but blue line upgrades aren't easy to perform. Goligoski, acquired from Pittsburgh in the James Neal and Matt Niskanen trade, is the team's clear number one defenceman, and the strongest possession-driving force on the blue line.

In Kari Lehtonen, the Stars can expect consistent but average goaltending. This summer Nill secured 6'7" Swede Anders Lindback, who struggled the past two seasons in Tampa Bay, to serve as Lehtonen's backup until prospect Jack Campbell is ready.

Score	Category	Notes
✔	Possession	The team's first step towards possession-based hockey was a successful one, and now it's taking its second.
☆	The Shootout	Lehtonen is sensational, and Seguin leads a growing collection of several strong recently-acquired shooters.
	Goaltending	Lehtonen is consistent and capable, but doesn't really move the needle. Lindback is a risky choice as backup.
	Penalty Kill	The Stars' 22nd place finish in fewest attempted shots allowed per minute was actually their best in recent times.
✔	Power Play	Seguin guided the Stars to second place in attempted power-play shots. Spezza and Hemsky will help that continue.
✔	Scoring Line	Hemsky and Spezza are great acquisitions, and Nichushkin has tremendous potential.
✔	Shutdown Line	Seguin and Benn are one of the league's best duos, but are less effective when essentially serving as the shutdown line.
	Forward Depth	Can their high-priced veterans bounce back?
	Top Pairing	Goligoski is potentially the team's only established top pairing defenceman.
✔	Second Pairing	The Stars have several decent top-four defencemen.
	Defensive Depth	Gonchar is almost finished, and the prospects aren't quite there yet.
✔	Coaching	Ruff proved to be a great fit for Dallas.
✔	Prospects	Dallas' system is top ten by any measure.

Assessment: Dallas is certainly a playoff team, but not likely one who will earn a home seed.

Detroit Red Wings

Despite an injury parade that placed the matter into considerable question most of the year, the Red Wings did indeed manage to qualify for the postseason for the 23rd consecutive season. They were subsequently brushed aside in five games in their opening round series with Boston.

Detroit may no longer be one of the league's dominant teams, but it does have the potential for one more deep run if youngsters like Gustav Nyquist, Tomas Tatar, Riley Sheahan, and Tomas Jurco can develop while Henrik Zetterberg and Pavel Datsyuk are still on top of their games.

Detroit Red Wings - Player Usage

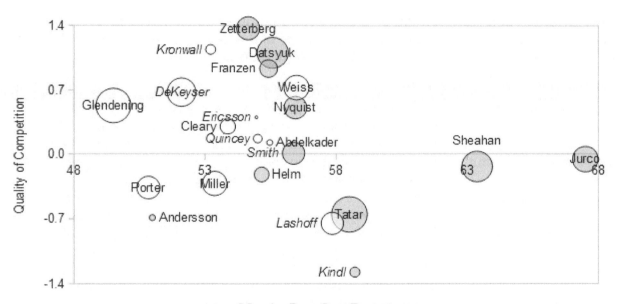

Offensive Zone Start Percentage

Zetterberg and Datsyuk lost time last year to back and knee problems respectively, but, if healthy, they could still absolutely dominate opponents and once again form one of the league's best two-way shutdown lines. Johan "the Mule" Franzen complements them well.

Gustav Nyquist's impressive scoring display last year was not a result of having received preferential playing conditions. He led the team with 28 goals in 57 games while facing top-six opponents in both zones, although he was boosted by some great shooting luck. In contrast, Tomas Tatar, Riley Sheahan, and Tomas Jurco were sheltered last season, being used more exclusively in the offensive zone and against secondary competition, but given their possession numbers, was that really necessary? The Red Wings have historically leaned perhaps too heavily on their veterans and should advance their younger players a little faster. With the departure of Daniel Alfredsson, David Legwand, and Todd Bertuzzi the scoring line

148

will finally be focused on their young talent.

There may be some concerns with Detroit's bottom six, however. Stephen Weiss' struggles have been well-established, but players like Danny Cleary, Luke Glendening, and Drew Miller (the team's leading forward in ice time) weren't necessarily any better. Newly-signed Kevin Porter might not help much either. Their best checking line options probably include speedy veteran Darren Helm and gritty winger Justin Abdelkader, while promising young Swede Joakim Andersson might provide some secondary scoring.

On the blue line, Niklas Kronwall is starting to fill the massive skates of Nicklas Lidstrom as the team's top defenceman. He's a highly physical, puck-moving defenceman who is not far back of the league's elite. The bad news is that he's largely alone as an effective top-four option. Rookie Danny DeKeyser was used far too ambitiously, as was veteran Kyle Quincey, leaving the physical Jonathan Ericsson as possibly the only defender somewhat capable of taking on top opponents. Perhaps Brendan Smith could handle a tougher assignment?

Jimmy Howard is definitely coming off a bad season, but he doesn't always get his due for finishing among the league's better goalies in three of the past five years. Jonas Gustavsson is not an ideal backup, but will suffice until Petr Mrazek is ready.

Score	Category	Notes
✔	Possession	Detroit has always been the prototypical example of a possession team, thanks to Zetterberg and Datsyuk, but do have some concerns on the checking line and blue line.
✔	The Shootout	Howard is capable in nets and Gustavsson is usable. Datsyuk is among the league's best shooters.
✔	Goaltending	Howard's .928 even-strength save percentage over the past three years ranks sixth among those with 100 starts.
✔	Penalty Kill	They rarely use their best penalty killers Datsyuk and Zetterberg, using secondary players like Helm instead.
✔	Power Play	They had an off year, in my view, but Datsyuk is one of the greats and works well with Zetterberg and Kronwall.
	Scoring Line	It will be in the hands of unproven youngsters.
☆	Shutdown Line	If healthy, Zetterberg and Datsyuk are the best in the league.
	Forward Depth	There are too many weaknesses in the bottom six.
✔	Top Pairing	Kronwall is the team's only legitimate top-pairing defenceman, but Ericsson should suffice as his partner.
	Second Pairing	The Red Wings are short on effective top-four defencemen.
	Defensive Depth	Detroit is capable beyond the top four, but not deep.
☆	Coaching	Babcock and his staff are well known for being the best.
☆	Prospects	Detroit has a wealth of young players capable of having an immediate and significant impact.

Assessment: This is a playoff team with a significant upside, unless injuries strike again.

Edmonton Oilers

It was argued in last year's *Hockey Abstract* that the Oilers may have been the league's worst team in 2012–13, and while they would enjoy some improvement, they were still quite unlikely to qualify for the postseason. That interpretation was in stark conflict with mainstream analysts, who were ultimately shocked by Edmonton's 28th place finish.

The good news is that the prime years of Taylor Hall, Ryan Nugent-Hopkins, and Jordan Eberle need not be wasted as Edmonton has continued to take several positive steps, and may have finally achieved legitimate playoff bubble status.

Edmonton Oilers - Player Usage

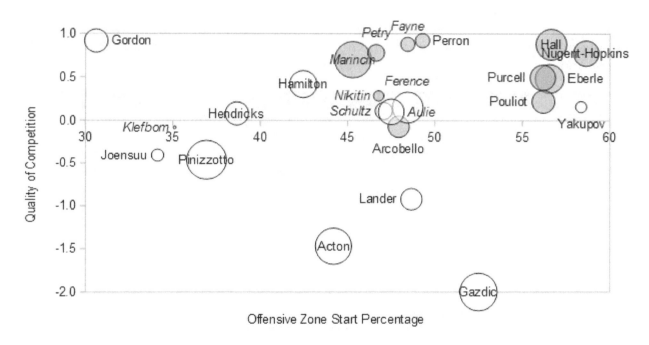

The Oilers finally addressed their blue line issues this summer. Mark Fayne should be an effective top pairing shutdown defenceman, especially if he's alongside the highly underrated Jeff Petry. Slovakian rookie Martin Marincin was very promising in his short stint alongside Petry, and could be a legitimate top-four defenceman, as could Nikita Nikitin, if he lives up to the incredible promise he showed in 2011–12 in Columbus. And, assuming he is re-signed, Justin Schultz could nicely fill a Keith Yandle or Torey Krug type of role as a big-minutes but sheltered puck-moving defenceman, a situation in which Andrew Ference might still remain a positive contributor as support. At least one of Oscar Klefbom and Keith Aulie should be a usable depth option.

Having acquired Teddy Purcell for Sam Gagner and signing free agent Benoit Pouliot, the Oilers now easily have two full lines of solid scoring options, all but one of whom (Nail

Yakupov) are solid possession-driving players. There are only two problems, one being that only one of them is a centre (Nugent-Hopkins), and the other being that at least three of them will need to make the adjustment into more of a two-way shutdown line that handles the top opponents and a more balanced mix of offensive and defensive zone play. Their incredibly underrated superstar Taylor Hall is one natural fit for that job.

The development of that legitimate top-six shutdown line will take some pressure off of Boyd Gordon, who is far better suited to centering a checking line. The bottom six is nevertheless one of Edmonton's greatest challenges, having historically been filled with tough guys and AHLers who get badly dominated by their opponents. Mark Arcobello could nevertheless centre a nifty secondary scoring line with Pouliot (or Yakupov should he continue to fall into disfavour), but neither Jesse Joensuu nor Matt Hendricks appear to be the answer for Gordon's checking line.

In nets, Edmonton is gambling that Ben Scrivens and Viktor Fasth will succeed where Devan Dubnyk, Jason LaBarbera, and Ilya Bryzgalov recently failed. For what it's worth, Dubnyk's career even-strength save percentage going into last season was .9204 in 128 starts, while Scrivens and Fasth currently combine for .9211 in 98 starts.

Score	Category	Notes
	Possession	Edmonton is moving in the right direction, but have an incredibly long way to go.
	The Shootout	There are unknowns between the pipes, but they also have a couple of decent shooters like Eberle and Hendricks.
	Goaltending	Scrivens and Fasth are promising, but untried, and with below average NHL results thus far.
	Penalty Kill	Gordon was a key addition, but the Oilers finished second last in attempted shots allowed per minute.
	Power Play	The Oilers improved from 29th in attempted shots per minute to 24th. Nugent-Hopkins and Hall are both excellent, however.
✔	Scoring Line	The Oilers have no shortage of possession-driving scoring threats.
✔	Shutdown Line	It takes some faith, but I believe that an effective two-way line can be built around Hall and Nugent-Hopkins.
	Forward Depth	While they do have some secondary scoring threats, the checking line continues to be a significant concern.
✔	Top Pairing	Yes, Fayne and Petry can do the job, in my view.
	Second Pairing	It's no longer unrealistic for the Oilers to hope for an effective top four.
✔	Defensive Depth	They have plenty of reasonable third pairing options.
	Coaching	Edmonton's coaching selections can be hard to understand.
✔	Prospects	They have nothing left at forward beyond the recently-drafted Draisatl, but still have plenty of defencemen on the way.

Assessment: The Oilers may have a shot at the playoffs. Finally.

Florida Panthers

It was a disappointing season in the sunshine state, even relative to the team's modest expectations. Florida finished second last and has only made the playoffs once since 2000, back when Pavel Bure led the league in goals.

Last summer, the team tried a number of value-priced signings but, this year, new owner Vinnie Viola has allowed GM Dave Tallon to open the wallet up wide. He ultimately invested over $15 million in Jussi Jokinen, Dave Bolland, Derek MacKenzie, Shawn Thornton, and Willie Mitchell, the gamble being that only the first is a positive puck possession player.

Florida Panthers - Player Usage

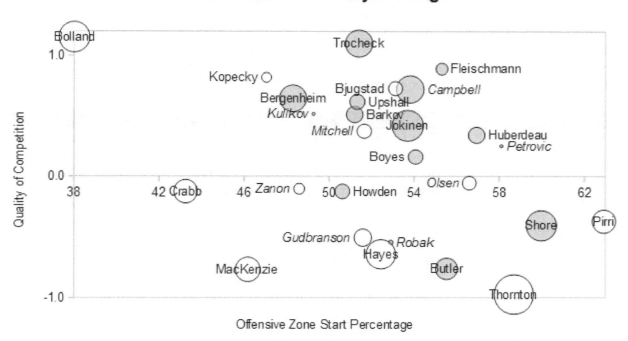

The Panthers are apparently being re-built into a competitive team from the ground out. In Roberto Luongo, for example, they finally have capable goaltending, instead of former stars with one skate in retirement. And on the blue line, they have Brian Campbell who is one of the league's top ten defencemen, in my view. He's an incredible possession-driving top pairing defenceman who has always made his partner look great, whether it was Jason Garrison, Filip Kuba, or Tom Gilbert. It could be Dmitry Kulikov's turn next.

Tallon no doubt picked up Willie Mitchell to be the tough, veteran, defensive-minded presence for a second pairing that could feature first overall selection Aaron Ekblad. Mike Weaver would have been a far more affordable option, and would probably have proven more capable against top-six opponents, but Mitchell's Stanley Cup ring undoubtedly figured into the decision. The rest of the blue line will be filled by a handful of (thus far) underachieving prospects, like Colby Robak, Eric Gudbranson, and maybe Dylan Olsen.

It will be fascinating to see how new coach Gerard Gallant deploys his diverse collection of forwards. It's going to be hard to put together an effective scoring line, for example, when his highest scoring player last year was 6'6" rookie Nick Bjugstad and his 38 points. While he'll likely never achieve that distinction again, Bjugstad could be an excellent source of secondary scoring alongside the likes of Scottie Upshall.

Brad Boyes and Jussi Jokinen, the only two 20-goal scorers last year, are more obvious choices for the scoring line. Boyes once scored 76 goals over two combined seasons for the Blues, while Jokinen, who was once available on waivers for far less than his current deal, has the team's best possession numbers. Jonathan Huberdeau will need a rebound season to fend off 18-year-old Aleksander Barkov for the final spot.

As for the shutdown line, Dave Bolland has been brought in to take over Marcel Goc's duties in the defensive zone and against top opponents, but at the risk of his being historically hammered possession-wise. Sean Bergenheim could help address that issue, if he stays healthy, but has a career high of just 29 points. That's where Thomas Fleischmann comes in, who has been an effective top-six winger for four years before last year's disappointment—he could provide this line with a much-needed offensive bite.

Score	Category	Notes
	Possession	The Panthers actually weren't too far below water possession-wise, but their recent moves might really sink them.
✔	The Shootout	Jokinen is a good acquisition to join Boyes as top shooters, and Luongo is about average in nets.
✔	Goaltending	Luongo's .926 even-strength save percentage over the past 3 years is even with Quick. Montoya is a good backup.
	Penalty Kill	Florida were league average in shots allowed, but the loss of Weaver and Goc will hurt.
	Power Play	Campbell is exceptional and, ideally, Jokinen will help prevent the Panthers from finishing at the bottom again.
	Scoring Line	This is more of a secondary scoring line.
	Shutdown Line	It's an uphill battle but Gallant might make something work.
✔	Forward Depth	Panthers might have been better off trying players like Shore and Trocheck instead of getting Thornton and MacKenzie.
✔	Top Pairing	Campbell and my grandma would be an effective top pairing.
	Second Pairing	Kulikov is the only other proven top-four option.
✔	Defensive Depth	Ekblad is just one of a half-dozen prospects.
	Coaching	Gallant struggled in Columbus but was great in the QMJHL.
✔	Prospects	Ekblad's the blue chip prospect in an otherwise average system.

Assessment: The Panthers took expensive moves in the wrong direction this summer, but Luongo, Campbell, and their plentiful youth could lift this team into the hunt anyway.

Los Angeles Kings

The Kings, top possession team in the league last year, won the Stanley Cup for the second time in three seasons, what a triumph for the analytics movement! Of course, if they hadn't outscored their opponents 31 to 12 in the seven elimination games along the way, then the narrative may have been written quite differently indeed.

Los Angeles Kings - Player Usage

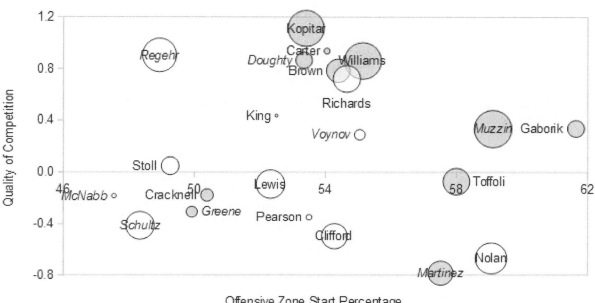

What makes the Kings such an effective puck possession team? The fact that the most notable characteristic of virtually all of their top players is their commitment to possession. It can have an almost compound effect as they take to the ice together.

One of the pitfalls for such teams is that it can sometimes be difficult to consistently translate that possession advantage into scoring. That's a problem that has certainly affected the Kings at various stretches of the regular season. That's why it's so exciting to have a full season with Anze Kopitar and Marian Gaborik playing together in the top six. Kopitar is one of the league's most complete players, a Selke finalist who led the team in scoring for the seventh straight season, and someone who absolutely dominates the possession game, even against the league's top opponents.

Gaborik's arrival meant that the Kings could now roll two full scoring lines. Gaborik has traditionally been more of a scoring line option, being used more often in the offensive zone, and less frequently against the top lines. Justin Williams is also more on the scoring-focused end of the spectrum, and is one of the game's strongest possession players—his Conn Smythe was yet another perceived vindication for the analytics movement. Jeff Carter is a two-way sniper, captain Dustin Brown is more of a gritty, do-it-all option, while Mike Richards' poor possession play makes him stand out on a player usage chart like a sore thumb. Either 22-year-old secondary scoring option Tyler Toffoli or physical, two-way winger Dwight King could easily steal his spot in the top six. Beyond those two, however, I have never had a strong impression of this team's forward depth.

The Los Angeles blue line is often celebrated, but Drew Doughty is its only truly exceptional performer. Jake Muzzin has good size, a good shot, and has posted solid possession numbers, but generally wasn't used very frequently against the top lines, nor in the defensive zone. Puck-moving Slava Voynov is probably the team's only other top-four defenceman right now. By default Robyn Regehr, whose days as an effective and physical defensive presence against top players are clearly behind him, will probably be relied upon more than he should be. Matt Greene and rookie Brayden McNabb also both offer a physical, stay-at-home presence similar to Regehr's, and will most likely line up alongside Alec Martinez on the sheltered third pairing.

Score	Category	Notes
☆	Possession	The Kings are the most cited example of the full power of a possession-based team.
✔	The Shootout	Quick is solid in nets, and Stoll is one of the league's better shooters.
✔	Goaltending	Quick's .926 even-strength save percentage over the past three years ranks seventh among those with 100 starts, and Jones posted a mighty .949 in 18 starts.
✔	Penalty Kill	The Kings kill penalties by committee, and quite effectively.
✔	Power Play	Imagine Gaborik and Kopitar together for a full season!
☆	Scoring Line	Could they have an Art Ross contender if Kopitar is used on the scoring line with Gaborik and Williams?
✔	Shutdown Line	Brown is due for a bounce back season.
	Forward Depth	I may be alone in this, but I've never been impressed by this team's bottom six.
☆	Top Pairing	Doughty is potentially the league's best two-way defenceman.
	Second Pairing	The Kings actually aren't that strong beyond Doughty.
✔	Defensive Depth	They are fairly deep, however.
☆	Coaching	Sutter could be the most accomplished active coach never to have won the Jack Adams.
	Prospects	There's never a check mark, but they still somehow produce solid rookies every year anyway.

Assessment: The Kings certainly have the potential for a third Cup in four seasons, and a potential dynasty in the making.

Minnesota Wild

Minnesota's franchise model is to secure as many elite players as are available, and then to use value-priced players and prospects to fill the balance of the roster. It's the right strategy for them, and they've been highly effective on both fronts.

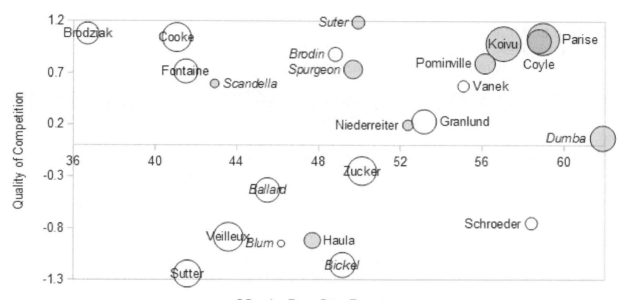

Minnesota Wild - Player Usage

Offensive Zone Start Percentage

Minnesota's top four doesn't get nearly enough credit, other than their superstar Ryan Suter, who takes up well over half the blue line payroll all by himself. Jared Spurgeon, for example, is a strong, two-way defenceman who often gets overlooked because of his small size. Marco Scandella might actually be Suter's equal in shutting down top opponents, and can help reduce his needlessly excessive workload. And Suter's own 21-year-old partner Jonas Brodin is a solid option in his own right.

There is a depth issue on the blue line, though. Matthew Dumba is ready to be brought along slowly thanks to those four, but there's no effective option with whom he can play.

As for the forwards, may I play coach for a moment? Zach Parise and Mikko Koivu are the two giant circles in the top right. That means they are used mostly in the offensive zone and are absolutely dominating top line opponents. They are exceptional two-way players. So why, then, is the checking line of Kyle Brodziak, Matt Cooke, and Justin Fontaine taking on the top lines when the play starts in the defensive zone? Those white circles mean that they're the ones being dominated. Consider using the checking line against secondary opponents instead, and shifting Koivu and Parise into a more balanced role in both zones.

The arrival of Thomas Vanek makes this strategy more viable because a strong scoring line can easily be built around him instead. It would be exciting to see him work with young Mikael Granlund, whose scoring has developed far faster than the rest of his game, along with young power forward Charlie Coyle. It's tempting to put 30-goal man Jason Pominville on that line instead, but his possession numbers are strong, and in the past he has proven quite capable of playing the more valuable shutdown role. So I'd keep him with Parise and Koivu. All of that still leaves strong secondary scoring from young players, like Nino Niederreiter and Erik Haula.

Regardless of how the players are ultimately deployed, the team's goaltending could have a huge bearing on the standings. Last year, my conviction was that the Wild were a playoff bubble team and that Josh Harding could make the difference. It was a bold claim to make for what was a relatively unknown backup, but it was accurate back then, and could be accurate now. If Harding (or Kuemper) can play well this year, they can remain competitive.

Score	Category	Notes
	Possession	The Wild started off strong, but gave up last year's experiment with possession-based play quite quickly.
☆	The Shootout	Parise, Vanek, and Koivu are all among the league's best shooters. They can be deadly if Harding can play and is the real deal. They're sunk with Backstrom in goal.
	Goaltending	Harding and Kuemper are both solid, but the former's status is uncertain and the latter is untried. Backstrom's best days are behind him.
✔	Penalty Kill	The Wild have been in the league's top fifth in fewest attempted shots allowed per minute for two seasons running, but the puck kept going in.
	Power Play	Minnesota is hoping that Vanek can be the difference maker.
✔	Scoring Line	The younger players have the potential to help Vanek score.
☆	Shutdown Line	Parise and Koivu form the nucleus of a top notch line.
	Forward Depth	The Wild have a mixed bag that could produce good results, if deployed correctly.
✔	Top Pairing	Brodin is not perfect, but with Suter he's good enough.
✔	Second Pairing	Scandella and Spurgeon are two of the most underrated defencemen in the league and should be used more.
	Defensive Depth	Dumba could be ready, but none of the veterans are up to par.
	Coaching	Yeo's stock is definitely rising.
	Prospects	Minnesota needs to re-stock the prospect shelves.

Assessment: The Wild are a likely playoff team, but will require solid goaltending and improved depth to truly become a threat.

Montreal Canadiens

Montreal went all the way to the Eastern Conference final for the second time in five seasons (and since the 1993 Stanley Cup). Their story begins with goalie Carey Price, who kept the mediocre possession team in the game on the nights they got shelled, and with P.K. Subban, the star puck-moving defencemen on whom their scoring relies.

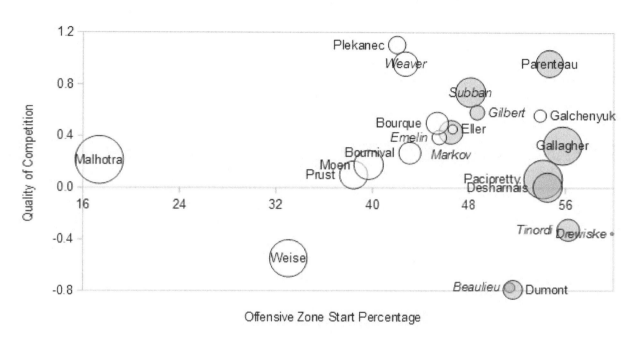

Montreal Canadiens - Player Usage

The biggest reason for optimism in Montreal is its much improved defensive corps. Normally, Florida's is not the blue line to raid but Montreal found two value-priced gems in two-way veteran Tom Gilbert and stay-at-home 36-year-old Mike Weaver.

The Canadiens also made the right decisions on who to keep and who to release, even if re-signing puck-moving veteran Andrei Markov used up the long-term dollars that were required to keep Josh Gorges. Alexei Emelin, prospects Jerred Tinordi and Nathan Beaulieu, and even journeyman Davis Drewiske will likely all prove to be better depth options than Francis Bouillon and Douglas Murray. Of course, none of this means a thing without Subban.

Up front, all of Montreal's strong possession-based players are on a single scoring line. Underrated sniper Max Pacioretty scored 39 goals last year, including a league-leading 11 game winners, thanks in part to great chemistry with 5'7" playmaker David Desharnais. Hard-working young grinder Brendan Gallagher fought his way into the final spot, but may need to yield it to newly-acquired P.A. Parenteau, a gifted possession-based player in his own right.

The Habs have several other forwards capable of providing some secondary scoring, like Alexander Galchenyuk, Lars Eller, Rene Bourque, rookie Jiri Sekac (whose scoring translates to about 30 points in the NHL), and speedy Michael Bournival, but none of them are particularly strong possession players, nor accustomed to taking on top opponents. That poses a bit of a problem for Tomas Plekanec, whose scoring has already dipped from having to almost single-handedly take on all the top opponents in defensive zone situations. Who will play alongside him, especially with Brian Gionta's departure to Buffalo in free agency?

Manny Malhotra always stretches out a player usage chart, because he's generally only used in the defensive zone. His checking line will be formed with some combination of Travis Moen, Brandon Prust and Dale Weise, all of whom will get buried in the defensive zone and absolutely bombed possession-wise. The key is for the rest of the team to take advantage of the greater number of offensive zone opportunities these players afford them.

The Habs are curiously deep in backup goaltending with Peter Budaj, Dustin Tokarski, and even Joey MacDonald on board. Is there something about Carey Price's health that we don't know?

Score	Category	Notes
	Possession	A return to Montreal's possession success in 2012–13 might be one of this team's final missing ingredients.
	The Shootout	Price is solid in nets, but not quite good enough to earn a check mark in the absence of better shooting.
✔	Goaltending	Price had a great year, but he usually finishes around the league average. They have good depth.
✔	Penalty Kill	They actually allowed more shots per minute than the year before, but Weaver can help them return to form.
	Power Play	Subban and Markov are awesome, but the team usually ranks between 16th and 20th in attempted shots per 60 minutes.
✔	Scoring Line	All of their best possession players are on a single and effective scoring line.
	Shutdown Line	Who will play with Tomas Plekanec?
	Forward Depth	This looks good only when you ignore the possession numbers.
✔	Top Pairing	Subban is truly an incredible talent.
✔	Second Pairing	Having Markov makes both pairings an offensive threat.
✔	Defensive Depth	This problem has finally been addressed.
✔	Coaching	Therrien has been extended for four more years.
✔	Prospects	Montreal's organizational strength is mostly on the blue line.

Assessment: Despite a few potentially serious holes, the Habs should remain a playoff team.

Nashville Predators

The Predators missed the playoffs in consecutive seasons for the first time in a decade and finally chose to part ways with long-time head coach Barry Trotz. New coach Peter Laviolette, who may prove to be a brilliant choice as replacement, has a much stronger team, but some challenging questions on how to best deploy its players.

Nashville Predators - Player Usage

Offensive Zone Start Percentage

The most fascinating aspect of Nashville's player usage chart isn't what's there, but what isn't. There are only seven players who are below average possession-wise, two of whom will be in the AHL. That is an interesting development on what hasn't historically been a possession-based team.

Also notice the absence of players accustomed to taking on the top lines, of which there are only four. And guess what? Three of them are among the five who are below average in possession. With Norris finalist and leading scorer Shea Weber as the only player proven to be effective against star opponents, that means the Predators could be on the losing side of the action when the top lines are on the ice, but dominate against the other three. It should be an interesting season!

Of course, that rough impression can't be taken for fact, as the blue line is rapidly becoming capable of skating with the league's best. Roman Josi and Seth Jones are skilled and rapidly developing defencemen, the former of whom will likely serve on Weber's top pairing, and the latter with shot blocking veteran Anton Volchenkov. Two more skilled and exciting young players, undersized puck-mover Ryan Ellis (assuming he re-signs) and 6'4" Swede Mattias

Ekholm, can continue to develop on a more sheltered third pairing.

It's not just the blue line where the Predators are blessed with some exciting young prospects. Calle Jarnkrok and Filip Forsberg, who were acquired in deadline deals for David Legwand and Martin Erat respectively, headline a collection of players that can provide excellent secondary scoring in the bottom six. That's especially fortunate given their lack of elite options on the top scoring line. In Derek Roy, Mike Ribeiro, James Neal, and Craig Smith, the Predators are going to quantity over quality.

If there's a greater concern, then it's with the shutdown line. Neither of their two-way veterans Mike Fisher (who is injured) and Olli Jokinen have been particularly effective in that role for years, while giant faceoff specialist Paul Gaustad and the gritty Eric Nystrom are more accustomed to checking line roles against the secondary lines. Gabriel Bourque and 37-year-old Matt Cullen might actually be superior checking line options anyway.

Whether or not they address those concerns, as usual their success may once again depend on goaltender Pekka Rinne and his return to Vezina (or even league average) form.

Score	Category	Notes
	Possession	Nashville is finally headed in the right direction.
✔	The Shootout	Rinne is a solid shootout goalie, and Cullen is among the league's better shooters.
	Goaltending	Rinne's numbers haven't been great lately.
	Penalty Kill	The Predators allow an above average number of shots, and Rinne hasn't exactly been stealing the show.
	Power Play	Weber is awesome, but will Neal be effective without Malkin? Predators ranked 26th in attempted shots per minute.
	Scoring Line	Neal and Ribeiro may help, but they are without elite scorers.
	Shutdown Line	There are not enough options who are proven to be effective against top opponents.
✔	Forward Depth	They have young and strong possession-driving talent.
✔	Top Pairing	Weber is potentially the league's best defenceman.
✔	Second Pairing	Volchenkov is a wise addition to work with their abundance of skilled young players.
	Defensive Depth	It's effective, but not deep enough if it's hit by injuries.
✔	Coaching	Laviolette is a potentially brilliant coaching selection.
✔	Prospects	The Predators had great drafts and acquired some great prospects when moving veterans at the trade deadlines.

Assessment: Nashville could compete for one of the final playoff spots.

New Jersey Devils

Is there a strong puck possession team that *hasn't* had strong results recently? Yes, the New Jersey Devils. Despite consistently finishing among the league leaders in possession-based metrics, terrible shooting, inadequate goaltending, and a dismal record in close games have left them out of the playoffs both times since their 2012 Stanley Cup run. I can't possibly imagine this slump stretching to three seasons.

New Jersey Devils - Player Usage

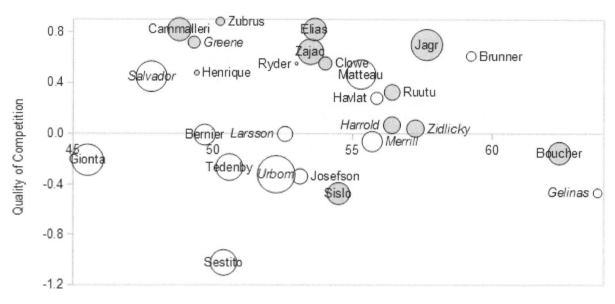

Offensive Zone Start Percentage

The downfall of great possession teams is usually the percentages. Since they tend to generate more scoring opportunities than their opponents, they can only lose when their opponents capitalize on a larger percentage of theirs. Cory Schneider can help address that. Applying his save percentage to Martin Brodeur's shots over the past two seasons would have prevented a whopping 36 goals against. Of course, Schneider can't play all the games, and some of Brodeur's starts will go to the team's mediocre backup Scott Clemmensen.

While the Devils might be better off without Brodeur, the same is not true of all their aging stars. Scoring legend Jaromir Jagr, consistent two-way star Patrik Elias, and defensive specialist Dainius Zubrus are all critical possession-driving top-six components, especially alongside shutdown centre Travis Zajac, young two-way goal scoring leader Adam Henrique, and newly-signed sniper Mike Cammalleri.

New Jersey also has incredible forward depth and can expect solid secondary scoring from three-time 30-goal scorer Michael Ryder and six-time 20-goal scorer Martin Havlat. Power forward Ryane Clowe and veteran agitator Tuomo Ruutu are solid possession players who

162

have a couple of 20-goal seasons apiece. That still leaves skilled Swiss forward Damien Brunner and several young prospects that may soon make mediocre checking line options like Steve Bernier and Stephen Gionta unnecessary, not to mention enforcers like Tim Sestito and Cam Janssen.

So where is New Jersey's soft spot? The blue line. Andy Greene is an exceptional and underrated top pairing defenceman, but he may struggle in the absence of Mark Fayne, or anyone else who can compete at that level. Bryce Salvador is the only other blue liner with experience taking on the top lines, but his recent performance has been ravaged by age and injury.

The situation isn't entirely grim, however, as Marek Zidlicky remains a usable puck-moving option on the second pairing, and the team has several strong prospects who are a year away at most, including big Jon Merrill, power-play quarterback Eric Gelinas, and Adam Larsson. If they develop exceptionally fast, then New Jersey will be a lot more than merely a threat for the playoffs, but possibly for the Stanley Cup itself.

Score	Category	Notes
☆	Possession	The Devils are the best and perhaps only example of a dominant possession team being unable to translate their advantage into goals. If they ever figure this out, watch out!
	The Shootout	Going 2-20 the past two years wasn't entirely bad luck because this team has no good goalies nor shooters.
✔	Goaltending	The team will be far better off with the highly underrated Schneider taking over most of Brodeur's starts.
☆	Penalty Kill	This is possibly the best penalty kill in the league, and could be even better with Schneider taking over for Brodeur.
	Power Play	The only time the Devils can't generate shots is on the power play, although a lot of them did go in last year.
✔	Scoring Line	Cammalleri can help get one more year out of Jagr.
✔	Shutdown Line	New Jersey is the model that other teams emulate.
✔	Forward Depth	No team is this deep in secondary scoring.
	Top Pairing	Greene might struggle without Fayne.
	Second Pairing	Zidlicky could be the only other usable top-four option.
	Defensive Depth	New Jersey's young talents might still be a year away.
	Coaching	DeBoer must shoulder some of the blame for Florida's and New Jersey's struggles.
	Prospects	There is great potential on the blue line, but not for this year.

Assessment: This is crazy. New Jersey has got to make the playoffs this time for sure. Right?

163

New York Islanders

The Islanders are a young team entering their prime, are led by one of the game's greatest offensive weapons, and have taken their goaltending from among the league's worst to one of the best. If their blue line holds up, then this team could be one of the Eastern Conference's strongest threats for years to come.

New York Islanders - Player Usage

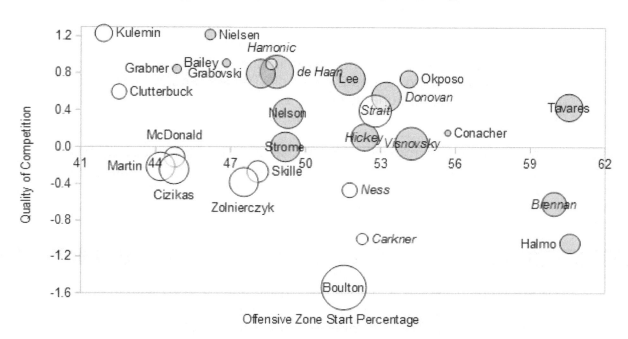

Offensive Zone Start Percentage

New York's success is all about unleashing John Tavares. Yes, the team does have other scoring threats, like last year's goal scoring leader Kyle Okposo, but in general, if you shut down Tavares then you shut down the Islanders. That's a big reason why GM Garth Snow picked up Mikhail Grabovski, a divisive player beloved by the analytics community, but loathed by the mainstream. Regardless of where you stand on the debate, the bottom line is that Grabovski's teams get more chances and goals than their opponents when he's on the ice, even against the top lines or in the defensive zone, and that's what winning games is ultimately all about.

The Islanders are also bringing along several young players in whom the secondary scoring will depend. Ryan Strome, Brock Nelson, Anders Lee, and even 5'8" Cory Conacher have all demonstrated the ability to score at other levels and to properly conduct possession-based hockey in their brief tours in the NHL.

And even though Tavares gets all the press, Frans Nielsen is the key player that makes the system work. The undervalued veteran is a classic do-it-all player who plays a tight two-way game against the league's best, and that's what gives Tavares the easier assignments required to keep scoring. Speedy Austrian Michael Grabner, a former 34-goal scorer, is the ideal complement for Nielsen, and the Islanders also picked up Nik Kulemin for further assistance. The veteran Russian may not be the best player in terms of possession, but he's accustomed to taking on top opponents in tough defensive-zone situations.

Kulemin's arrival allows Joshua Bailey to be moved to a bottom six checking line with big hitter Cal Clutterbuck. Bailey is an upgrade over the likes of big hitter Matt Martin, enforcer Eric Boulton, and journeymen Colin McDonald, Harry Zolnierczyk, and Jack Skille. The Islanders may not be a playoff team if any of these guys ever have to play regularly.

The blue line remains this team's chief weakness, one that had to rely on Andrew MacDonald far more than it should have last year. Lubomir Visnovsky is the big name here, but he's turning 38 and has missed 85 games over the past three seasons. When healthy, he's an excellent puck-moving and possession-oriented influence, but not the team's best defenceman. That honour goes to rugged 23-year-old Travis Hamonic, in my view. He plays the big minutes against the top opponents in both zones. In that regard he could be well-complemented by young puck-mover Calvin de Haan.

Of the many remaining options from which to choose, Thomas Hickey and Matt Donovan strike me as the best, followed by prospects like big Griffin Reinhart and offensive powerhouse Ryan Pulock. Whoever makes the team, at least their job will be much easier playing in front of Jaroslav Halak and Chad Johnson instead of Evgeni Nabokov, Anders Nilsson, and Kevin Poulin.

Score	Category	Notes
	Possession	Can the Islanders re-capture 2012–13's success?
✔	The Shootout	Halak is a solid upgrade in nets, and Nielsen is potentially the league's best in the shootout.
✔	Goaltending	Halak and Johnson could be one of the league's best duos.
	Penalty Kill	Grabner and Neilsen are good, but overall the team is generally between 15th and 18th at attempted shots allowed per minute.
	Power Play	Tavares is incredible, but overall the team is a little below average on the power play.
✔	Scoring Line	Just get Tavares the right wingers and he'll do the rest.
✔	Shutdown Line	This is one of the league's most underrated shutdown lines.
✔	Forward Depth	It's solid, assuming the right players are used.
	Top Pairing	It's a stretch, but Hamonic and de Haan ought to work.
	Second Pairing	Is Visnovsky healthy? Are the rookies ready?
	Defensive Depth	Replacement-level options aren't really options at all.
	Coaching	Capuano's teams haven't won a playoff series at any level since 2001.
✔	Prospects	Several youngsters could have an immediate impact for the Islanders this year.

Assessment: If the blue line holds up then this is a playoff team for sure.

New York Rangers

The Rangers have the same chocolate-covered candy coating, but it's wrapped around a much smaller peanut. New York's talent has been eroded this summer on the blue line, the checking line, and in terms of secondary scoring. It's not likely enough to knock them out of the playoffs, but the loss of their previously enviable depth should remove them as a legitimate Stanley Cup threat.

New York Rangers - Player Usage

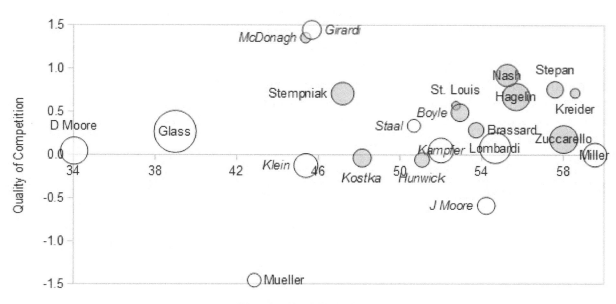

Do you notice anything unusual about New York's player usage chart? It's a great way to visually express coach Alain Vigneault's unique line and zone matching style, how it got two teams to the Stanley Cup finals over the past years, and what its consequences might be to individual players.

For example, it may have seemed like New York's $7.8 million man disappeared in the playoffs, but Rick Nash is playing "the Kesler minutes", and sometimes a player's scoring can drop off when he's tasked with taking on the top opponents. Scoring on just three of a whopping 83 shots can have an impact as well.

The logic behind this usage is that it paves the way for other players to play primarily in the offensive zone against easier competition. That's how Mats Zuccarello can go from a fringe NHLer with 34 points in 67 games to the team's leading scorer while playing "the Sedin minutes". The question is whether or not Martin St. Louis will be able to score without Steven Stamkos, especially at age 39. Chris Kreider has the tremendous speed and size to complete that line, but he's not a centre.

166

The final ingredient in Vigneault's system is a checking line to bury in the defensive zone, but he has lost big Brian Boyle and gritty Derek Dorsett. Tanner Glass is far from an adequate replacement on Dominic Moore's wing, which is symptomatic of the team's problem in the bottom six in general.

That leaves Vigneault two of Carl Hagelin, strong two-way playmaker Derek Stepan, and possession-driving veteran Lee Stempniak to distribute among the top six in some fashion, with the remaining player to provide secondary scoring alongside Derick Brassard. There is nothing but rookies, AHLers, and Matthew Lombardi beyond them.

The blue line may have some depth issues. That's why Ryan McDonagh and Dan Girardi will be taking on one of the league's toughest assignment for yet another season. The former is the puck-mover and the team's true number one, while Girardi throws hits, blocks shots, and does whatever is required to shut down top opponents. Ideally he'd be on the second pairing, but neither Marc Staal nor the newly-signed 38-year-old Dan Boyle would handle those top line duties any better than he can. In fact, Boyle's days as even a top-four, puck-moving defenceman might be coming to an end soon, and there's no one else on the roster that can relieve him. It's hard to imagine, but Mike Kostka and Matt Hunwick might actually be the team's best options for the third pairing. Well, at least they have the league's best goalie playing behind them.

Score	Category	Notes
✔	Possession	After a questionable three seasons, the Rangers should be back among the league leaders for the third straight year.
✔	The Shootout	Lundqvist is arguably the league's best shootout goalie, but the Rangers need more shooters.
☆	Goaltending	The best goalie in the business is locked in long term.
✔	Penalty Kill	This team has been making steady improvements.
	Power Play	What a tremendous leap forward! Is it for real?
✔	Scoring Line	Who needs size when you have skill?
✔	Shutdown Line	Nash and Hagelin are good possession-based players.
	Forward Depth	The bottom six is somewhat lacking.
✔	Top Pairing	McDonagh and Girardi are relied upon too heavily.
✔	Second Pairing	Staal and Boyle might suffice.
	Defensive Depth	The Rangers better hope to avoid blue line injuries.
☆	Coaching	Vigneault could practically trademark his zone-matching system, which got the most out of both Vancouver and New York.
	Prospects	There's no one who will really impact the standings this year.

Assessment: The Rangers remain a playoff team, but lack the depth to win the Cup.

Ottawa Senators

I really misjudged the Senators last year. Although their underlying analytics were fantastic, they were a young team that were greatly dependent on good goaltending and a couple of star players. They are now a year older and wiser, but are without one of those star players, Jason Spezza, and are still without a way to consistently shut down the top teams.

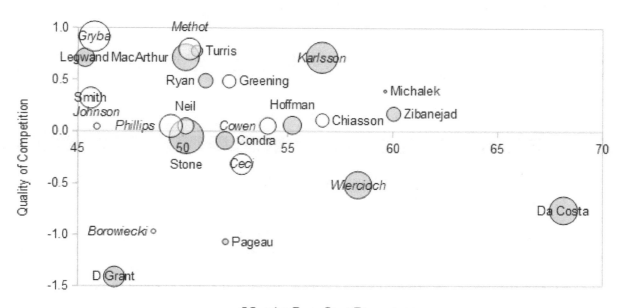

Ottawa Senators - Player Usage

Offensive Zone Start Percentage

One key piece of this team that's working perfectly is its top shutdown line of Bobby Ryan, Kyle Turris, and Clarke MacArthur. They're all between 25 and 29 years of age, scored between 23 and 26 goals and 48 to 58 points, and have solid possession numbers against top opponents and in both zones. All three were also given up on by their former teams, so give Ottawa credit for knowing undervalued talent when they see it.

The other key piece is superstar defenceman Erik Karlsson, the one shining light on an otherwise dark blue line. Karlsson may not be the toughest defensive hurdle for an opponent to face, but the Senators invariably dominate when the Swedish speedster is on the ice, even when playing big minutes against top opponents. Since that's what hockey's all about, does it even matter how he does it?

Last year, Marc Methot won the linemate lottery, but his skill doesn't warrant top pairing duty with Karlsson, or maybe even top-four duty altogether. But the Senators are without a clear shutdown defenceman. They've been strangely assigning the toughest minutes to depth option Eric Gryba, which is an astonishing show of support that has gone thus far unrewarded. But what else can coach Paul MacLean do? Veteran Chris Phillips can't effectively take on top-six opponents anymore, and there's still no reason to believe that huge Jared Cowen can be an effective top-four presence either. Perhaps they can try 6'5" puck-mover Patrick Wiercioch, who has been successful in carefully sheltered minutes that are soon going to be needed to develop Cody Ceci instead.

Up front, the newly-signed David Legwand will be tasked with replacing Spezza on a new scoring line with Milan Michalek and possibly 21-year-old Mika Zibanejad. Despite those two having 33 goals and 72 points between them last year, they are the highest scoring options available. While that may not be ideal, at least the Senators have a lot of young players with good possession numbers ready to provide secondary scoring, like perhaps Stephane Da Costa, Jean-Gabriel Pageau, speedy Mike Hoffman, or Mark Stone, with blue chip prospect Curtis Lazar not far behind.

The checking line will however be manned by gritty veterans, like tough guy Chris Neil, Colin Greening, a big guy with an even bigger contract, centre Zack Smith, and my favourite option, Erik Condra.

Score	Category	Notes
✔	Possession	Even through all the roster changes, the Senators have always found a way to stay above water possession-wise.
	The Shootout	Turris could be their best shooter, and their goaltending is below average.
	Goaltending	The Anderson/Lehner tandem is about average.
✔	Penalty Kill	They were third in fewest attempted shots allowed per minute last year, and killed 88.0% of penalties in 2012–13.
	Power Play	Karlsson is incredible, but losing Spezza will hurt.
	Scoring Line	Ottawa will need to rely on its defensive play.
✔	Shutdown Line	This is one of the league's most underrated top two-way lines.
✔	Forward Depth	The Senators are flush with promising young players and reasonably capable checking line veterans.
✔	Top Pairing	Karlsson has proven that he can dominate with any partner.
	Second Pairing	Do they even have another proven top-four defenceman?
	Defensive Depth	No comment.
✔	Coaching	MacLean won the Jack Adams in 2012–13.
	Prospects	They have a roughly average system without anyone likely to significantly affect their fortunes this season.

Assessment: Don't be deceived like I was last year by the possession numbers and the wealth of young talent, because this is a playoff bubble team at best, with a weak blue line and difficulty scoring.

Philadelphia Flyers

The Flyers have the amazing Claude Giroux, fantastic special teams, had seven players that scored 20 goals last year, and made the playoffs for the 17th time in 19 seasons before taking the eventual Stanley Cup finalists to within a single deciding game seven goal. So why am I so sour on their outlook for 2014–15?

Philadelphia Flyers - Player Usage

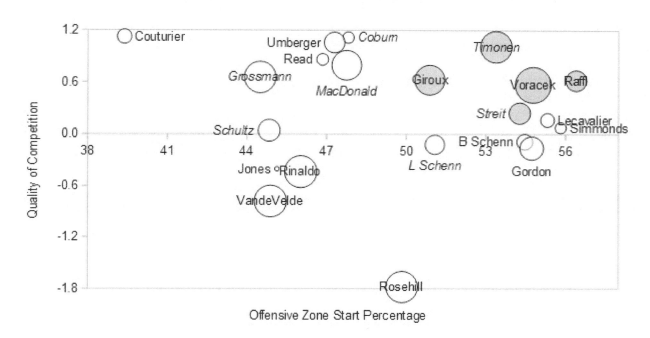

There is no error on that player usage chart, the Flyers have just five players with positive possession numbers over the past three seasons. Five! Let's see if there's a way to make this roster work.

First of all, all five are on the right side of the chart, which is where the team's top line scorers are usually found, so at least there are no concerns with Claude Giroux's line. He's an almost incomparable two-way talent and possession-driving force that works perfectly with Jakub Voracek, an offensive force finally hitting his prime. Whoever replaces Scott Hartnell on this line is in for a real scoring surge, most probably Wayne Simmonds.

Next, we have puck-moving veterans Kimmo Timonen and Mark Streit, who are 39 and 36, respectively. They can still do the job, they just need some strong, young defensive players to help them with the heavy lifting. In the case of the top pairing with Timonen, that's Braydon Coburn, the team's clear number one defenceman. Although his offensive game never quite materialized, he has proven that he can reliably handle the top opponents in key defensive situations.

170

As for the second pairing, well that's a little more of a problem. Andrew MacDonald, Nick Grossmann and Luke Schenn are among the worst defencemen in the league possession-wise. They also stand to make a combined $12 million this year! Nick Schultz is paid more reasonably, but is otherwise no better. The Flyers have to hope that at least one of them can handle a top-four assignment.

The top shutdown line might be less of a problem, despite those below-average possession numbers. Matt Read, 21-year-old Sean Couturier, and the newly-acquired R.J. Umberger are all accustomed to playing in the defensive zone and against top lines, and should be able to hold the fort long enough to keep Giroux concentrating on scoring. Given that this line combined for just 53 goals and 111 points last season, some secondary scoring from the bottom six will be important. Ideally, Vincent Lecavalier can bounce back and 23-year-old Brayden Schenn can start to realize his potential, in a more sheltered situation.

As for the checking line, Michael Raffl's possession numbers suggest he could be a real shining light, especially if gritty prospect Scott Laughton is ready to make the jump.

Is Steve Mason the real deal in nets? He better be, because even if this best-case scenario all comes to pass, it will still require some lights-out goaltending to sneak into the playoffs one more time.

Score	Category	Notes
	Possession	It has been a couple of seasons since the Flyers have been an effective puck possession team.
	The Shootout	Giroux and Read aren't bad shooters, but their goaltending is below average.
	Goaltending	A few good months isn't enough to alter the analytic outlook of a goalie who was among the league's worst for years.
☆	Penalty Kill	They consistently give up the fewest chances, thanks to stars like Couturier. The only concern is if Mason struggles.
☆	Power Play	Giroux could be the league's best power play specialist, and gets good help from Voracek and Simmonds.
✔	Scoring Line	The Flyers can count on Giroux.
	Shutdown Line	It has the potential to surprise.
	Forward Depth	I never thought I'd be unimpressed with the forward depth of a team that had seven 20-goal scorers, but I am.
✔	Top Pairing	Does Timonen have one more year left in him?
	Second Pairing	This could be a disaster.
	Defensive Depth	The Flyers are investing big money on some of the worst possession defencemen in the league.
	Coaching	A good start for Berube, but how will he do in a full season?
	Prospects	Laughton could certainly have an impact this year, but not necessarily a dramatic one.

Assessment: While it's certainly possible that Berube can make this lineup work, it's more likely going to be a disaster.

Pittsburgh Penguins

The Penguins made the playoffs for the eighth straight season, but a second round exit led to the release of both GM Ray Shero and coach Dan Bylsma. Already one of the league's strongest adopters of analytics, Pittsburgh and its new GM Jim Rutherford re-built the team's depleted depth with a focus that was as much on possession numbers as it was on cost efficiency.

Pittsburgh Penguins - Player Usage

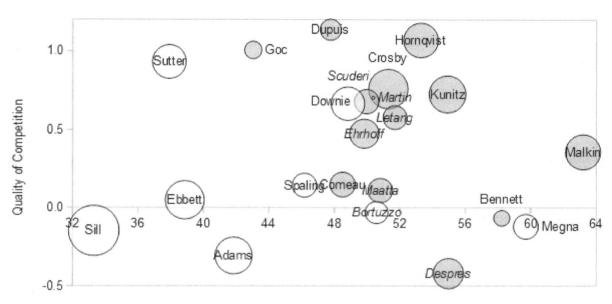

Offensive Zone Start Percentage

The team is obviously built around its two superstar centres, who could by themselves offer Stanley Cup contention for all but the league's worst teams. A player usage chart nicely demonstrates how Sidney Crosby is used for the shutdown line, taking on all the top opponents in both zones, while Evgeni Malkin is the captain of the scoring line, playing primarily in the offensive zone against second lines. Normally this would make Malkin the Art Ross champion, but that just goes to further demonstrate Crosby's incredible offensive talent.

And who are the lucky players that get to boost their scoring by playing alongside them? James Neal and Jussi Jokinen are gone, but 35-goal veteran Chris Kunitz and a healthy two-way veteran Pascal Dupuis remain, while shot-taking, possession-driving star Patric Hornqvist has been added. 22-year-old Beau Bennett would also be an intriguing addition to the top six, and at $0.9 million, a value-priced one at that.

The Penguins once had a depth issue, but virtually all of their summer moves were towards cost-effective possession-based hockey. Marcel Goc, Blake Comeau, and Steve Downie were all added for under $3.0 million total, which is a tremendous value. Goc in particular is the kind of gem that could take significant defensive pressure off of Crosby. Potentially, only the durable checking line of Brandon Sutter, Nick Spaling, and Craig Adams will finish this season below-water possession-wise.

Injuries stung the Penguins' blue line last year, as their top pairing defencemen Paul Martin and Kris Letang combined to play just 76 games. Martin is the two-way work horse, while Letang's elite puck-moving skills made him a Norris finalist in 2012–13. It will nevertheless be hard for Letang to earn his massive contract, even if he's 100%.

The team lost veterans Brooks Orpik, Matt Niskanen, and Deryk Engelland this summer, who signed elsewhere for a combined $14.1+ million (wow!). However, that blow is cushioned by having acquired the best available free agent defenceman, Christian Ehrhoff, and by the surprisingly quick development of 20-year-old prospect Olli Maatta, who is recovering from off-season shoulder surgery. Hopefully, WHL scoring sensation Derrick Pouliot, who is also having surgery, will develop just as quickly.

Stay-at-home veteran Rob Scuderi is not strong in the possession game and should be considered a third pairing option (albeit an expensive one), much like Robert Bortuzzo and Simon Despres.

Score	Category	Notes
✔	Possession	The historically average Penguins have made incredible strides through free agency this summer.
☆	The Shootout	Fleury could be the league's best shootout goalie, and they have Malkin and Crosby to score the goals.
	Goaltending	There are only four goalies who have started 100 games over the past three years and have a worse even-strength save percentage than Fleury's .917, but Greiss is a solid backup.
✔	Penalty Kill	2012–13 was an off year, and they gave up too many shots last year, but Martin, Dupuis, and Adams are solid overall.
☆	Power Play	Crosby, Malkin, Kunitz, Hornqvist, Letang, Ehrhoff, oh my!
☆	Scoring Line	Hornqvist will likely outscore Neal this season.
☆	Shutdown Line	Crosby is the best player in the game.
✔	Forward Depth	It's not super deep, but they added three solid free agents.
✔	Top Pairing	Ehrhoff was the best available free agent defenceman.
✔	Second Pairing	Maatta gives them up to five top-four defencemen.
✔	Defensive Depth	Several young players can step in, if injuries strike again.
	Coaching	Johnston's WHL success suggests a huge upside, but at the risk of having no NHL track record.
	Prospects	They have an average system with few players likely to steal a top spot this year, barring more injuries.

Assessment: With improved goaltending, this team would be a Stanley Cup favourite.

San Jose Sharks

Don't panic! Despite San Jose's postseason struggles, most teams would happily exchange rosters with a team that made the playoffs every time but once over the last 16 seasons, and who outscored the eventual Stanley Cup champions 17-8 through the first three games of its first round series. True, the Sharks are not without their flaws, like an aging core, questionable depth, and average goaltending at best, but this is not a team that needs to rebuild.

San Jose Sharks - Player Usage

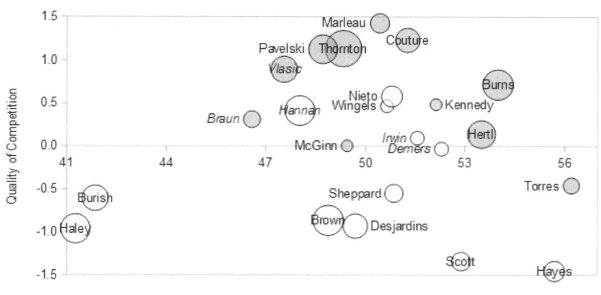

The Sharks are known for their exceptional strength down the middle and a possession-based top six that is almost without equal. They had three 70-point players last year and Logan Couture was on pace as well. All four of these two-way stars would be perfectly capable of serving on an elite shutdown line, but ultimately the honour generally goes to Couture, the only one not in his 30s, and Patrick Marleau.

Despite all the trade rumours, that leaves Joe Thornton, the league's second leading active scorer, as the centre on the scoring line. He is still one of the league's premier playmakers, and made a quick scoring sensation out of Czech rookie Tomas Hertl. Joe Pavelski's team-leading 41 goals and 79 points suggest that he may have taken over as the team's greatest offensive threat, however.

Brent Burns will likely move back to the blue line, especially with the departure of declining veterans Dan Boyle and Brad Stuart. He's a huge puck-moving defenceman that will need to be paired up with a strong defensive presence, so it's fortunate that San Jose has perhaps the league's best shutdown defenceman, Marc-Edouard Vlasic. Jason Demers can be slotted in as the puck-mover on the second pairing, and Justin Braun the defensive presence.

While the top lines look fine, both up front and on the blue line, the depth could be an issue, especially on the defence. They have only Scott Hannan, Matt Irwin, and Swiss puck-moving rookie Mirco Mueller on defence, and only slightly more options up front. Big hitter Tommy Wingels took a big step forward, speedy Matt Nieto had a great rookie season, and James Sheppard went on a tear down the stretch and through the playoffs, but none of their possession numbers are that great. The Sharks will have to hope for a bounce back season from Tyler Kennedy, and a healthy Raffi Torres, and try to avoid using some of the more dubious checking line veterans that they've accumulated lately.

Score	Category	Notes
☆	Possession	A strong core up the middle keeps the Sharks consistently among the league's best possession teams.
✔	The Shootout	Niemi is an exceptional shootout goalie, but the team could use more scoring threats of its own.
	Goaltending	Niemi and Stalock form a usable but unspectacular tandem.
✔	Penalty Kill	The Sharks have had consistently effective penalty killing.
☆	Power Play	Couture, Thornton, Marleau, Pavelski, and company have led the league in shots for three years, and by a wide margin.
✔	Scoring Line	Thornton is still one of the game's finest playmakers.
☆	Shutdown Line	They are rich with strong, two-way, possession-based stars.
	Forward Depth	It's possible the Sharks can salvage a decent bottom six.
✔	Top Pairing	Vlasic is potentially the league's best shutdown defenceman.
✔	Second Pairing	Braun and Demers could make a nifty second pairing.
	Defensive Depth	Blue line depth could be the team's greatest weakness.
✔	Coaching	Playoff disappointments aside, McLellan has been one of the most consistently effective regular seasons coaches for years.
	Prospects	The Sharks need to start re-stocking the shelves before their core players get too old.

Assessment: The San Jose Sharks remain a threat for the division title.

St. Louis Blues

The Blues have drawn Chicago, Los Angeles, and San Jose in the first round over the past three seasons, while teams like the Rangers have drawn Ottawa, Washington, and Philadelphia. Some teams get all the breaks! Then again, if you're not good enough to beat the league's best, you'd just be prolonging the inevitable by facing a softer team in the first round anyway. So, is the addition of Paul Stastny enough to get the Blues to that elite level?

St. Louis Blues - Player Usage

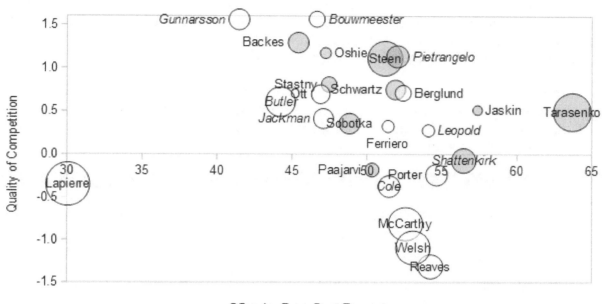

Offensive Zone Start Percentage

Paul Stastny was the best available free agent. He can do it all, effectively taking on top opponents in both zones. St. Louis is very lucky to have a player like Stastny, especially since they already have three others.

Yes, the Blues could very well have had the best shutdown line in the league last year with David Backes, T.J. Oshie, and Alexander Steen. They combined for 81 goals and 179 points last year, divided almost evenly. The shot-taking Steen was the key to that success, getting off to a white hot start, and landing a major new contract. And 22-year-old Jaden Schwartz, their highest remaining scorer, is also the kind of possession-driving, two-way forward that would be effective on a shutdown line.

Two of these players can therefore be unleashed onto what will no doubt be the league's strongest scoring line defensively. They'll be joined there by 22-year-old Vladimir Tarasenko, a sixth 20-goal scorer, and potentially the strongest possession driving player of the entire lot.

The team's secondary scoring should also undergo a huge improvement over Chris Stewart, Derek Roy, and Brenden Morrow. First there's Patrick Berglund, who may not be a strong possession player, and is a little overpaid, but is responsible defensively, and has twice topped 20 goals and 45 points. The Blues also went off the board to get two of the best available players from Europe, whose NHL translations suggest about 40 points apiece, Joakim Lindstrom and Finnish playmaker Jori Lehtera. Magnus Paajarvi also deserves more consideration, as he is only 23, has decent possession numbers, and scored 34 points in his rookie season. The Blues also have prospects Dmitrij Jaskin and Ty Rattie.

On the blue line, Carl Gunnarsson is about to enjoy the same boost as Jay Bouwmeester. Both of them played incredibly tough minutes on weak blue lines before coming to St. Louis. Of course, only one of them can play with potential Norris candidate Alex Pietrangelo on the top pairing. That means that Gunnarsson will most likely do the heavy lifting on the second pairing with sheltered but highly effective puck-mover Kevin Shattenkirk. That finally allows gritty Barret Jackman and Chris Butler to be slotted in where they'll be more effective, which is in a defensive depth role with the likes of Ian Cole and Jordan Leopold. The only concern is that six of these eight defencemen have negative possession numbers.

I'm not sure about the checking line either, especially with Vladimir Sobotka in the KHL, because neither Steve Ott nor Maxim Lapierre are the strongest possession players. Though Brian Elliott deserves credit for his numbers, there's also a concern in goal. He's unproven over the long haul and is without an experienced backup.

Score	Category	Notes
☆	Possession	Stastny makes one of the league's best even better.
	The Shootout	Oshie finally has some help (Lehtera), now all they need is someone who can stop the opponents.
	Goaltending	Elliott's numbers are comparable to Lundqvist's, but in fewer than half as many starts, and with only Allen as a backup.
☆	Penalty Kill	A great blue line with Pietrangelo, Bouwmeester, and Jackman, and great forwards like Backes, Oshie, and Stastny.
✔	Power Play	They took a step back last year, but Stastny will help boost a power play quarterbacked by Shattenkirk and Pietrangelo.
✔	Scoring Line	They could have the strongest scoring line defensively.
☆	Shutdown Line	It was potentially one of the league's best last year.
✔	Forward Depth	They have solid secondary scoring, but a worrisome checking line.
☆	Top Pairing	Bouwmeester is the perfect complement to Pietrangelo, a potential Norris candidate.
✔	Second Pairing	Gunnarsson can help Shattenkirk step up into the top four.
	Defensive Depth	St. Louis has eight experienced defencemen, but only two have positive possession numbers.
☆	Coaching	Hitchcock is arguably the league's best coach, with success virtually everywhere he's gone.
	Prospects	St. Louis is ranked dead last by more than one pundit.

Assessment: The Blues may finally be a Stanley Cup threat.

Tampa Bay Lightning

How did Tampa Bay manage to record over 100 points and qualify for the playoffs for only the second time in seven seasons, given the absence of Steven Stamkos to injury, and Martin St. Louis to a deadline deal? With unexpectedly lights-out goaltending from Ben Bishop and the rapid development of a roster half-composed of rookies, both guided by first-year NHL coach Jon Cooper. What can they accomplish this year, with that extra season of experience and a blue line upgraded through free agency?

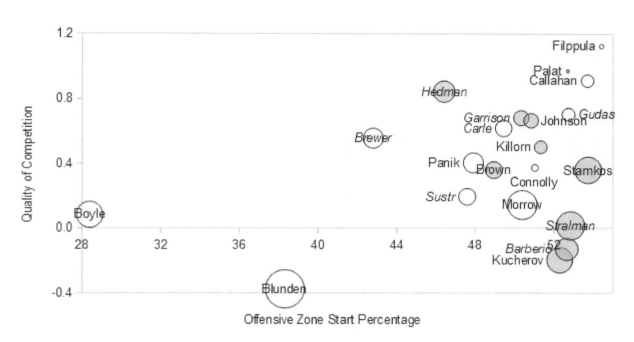

Tampa Bay Lightning - Player Usage

Although the Lightning are potentially quite deep in scoring, the key to their offence is unleashing Steven Stamkos and the top line in the absence of his long-time playmaking winger Martin St. Louis. That should be an easy assignment, given that he's probably the league's best sniper. Three young options include undrafted 5'8" forward Tyler Johnson, who had 70 goals in 137 AHL games, 50 points in his rookie NHL season, and solid possession numbers. There's also Nikita Kucherov, who scored almost a goal a game in short stints in the QMJHL and AHL, and was also strong possession-wise in his rookie campaign, albeit in a far more sheltered assignment. The most exciting option is obviously Jonathan Drouin, the second overall selection in the 2013 entry draft, who spent last year dominating the QMJHL.

Of course, the key to keeping Stamkos focused on scoring is to build a shutdown line that can effectively take on the league's top opponents while flashing an offensive game of their own. Valtteri Filppula was a pleasant surprise centring that line last year, scoring 25 goals and 58 points. Ondrej Palat, my choice for the Calder, and the team's leading scorer once St. Louis left, is the strongest two-way player among the team's young players and a natural fit for this duty. That leaves Ryan Callahan, a classic do-it-all player. His possession numbers haven't been great, but he scored 29 goals and 54 points while placing fourth in Selke voting in 2011–12.

That leaves secondary scoring primarily in the hands of Alex Killorn, who scored 41 points, and J.T. Brown, who scored just four goals on 113 shots and averaged about four shots a game in his last year in the USHL, both of whom are good possession players. There could be concern about the checking line, however. Richard Panik, 6'7" giant Brian Boyle, and veteran Brenden Morrow have been hammered recently, although at least in Boyle's case it's partly because he's been buried in the defensive zone.

Victor Hedman is the unheralded star of the blue line, an excellent puck-moving defenceman that will benefit greatly from the free agent acquisition of Jason Garrison and Anton Stralman. Matthew Carle will also benefit from their arrival, being relieved of some of the tougher minutes with which he has struggled, and moved back to the puck-moving second pairing role at which he has succeeded in the past. That also allows rugged Radko Gudas to throw hits and block shots as a depth piece with Eric Brewer or Mark Barberio, rather than playing the tough minutes against the top lines. This improved blue line should take enough pressure off of goalie Ben Bishop in order for him to steal the show again.

Score	Category	Notes
✔	Possession	Tampa Bay is quite unpredictable. They've been both very good and very bad possession-wise recently.
	The Shootout	If Bishop is the real deal in nets then Tampa Bay could go from being awful to being somewhat competitive.
✔	Goaltending	Bishop was a surprise Vezina finalist, and he better do it again, because Nabokov is strictly a backup at this point.
	Penalty Kill	Callahan will help, but the Bolts remain below average overall.
	Power Play	They generally finish near the bottom of the league in attempted shots per minute, and are now without St. Louis.
✔	Scoring Line	Even without St. Louis, Stamkos can be effective, especially with his choice of exceptional young talent.
	Shutdown Line	Most of their talent is more scoring-oriented.
	Forward Depth	There's a wealth of secondary scoring depth, but the defensive play could be suspect.
✔	Top Pairing	They got Hedman some help through free agency.
✔	Second Pairing	Carle will be more effective back on the second pairing.
✔	Defensive Depth	They have eight defencemen with NHL experience.
✔	Coaching	Though he doesn't have the longest track record, Cooper was a defensible pick for last year's coach of the year.
✔	Prospects	Even with all the rookies already in the lineup, there are actually plenty more on the way, most notably Drouin.

Assessment: All the young players give the Lightning a high ceiling, but also a low floor. They should make the playoffs with strong defensive play and/or stellar goaltending.

Toronto Maple Leafs

Toronto was the battleground between the analytics crowd and the mainstream. Neither side should claim victory, because both "camps" got it wrong. After all, the Leafs did keep winning without puck possession for over 100 games (going back to last season), but their late collapse highlighted some very serious flaws. In my view, that collapse could just be a small taste of what's yet to come.

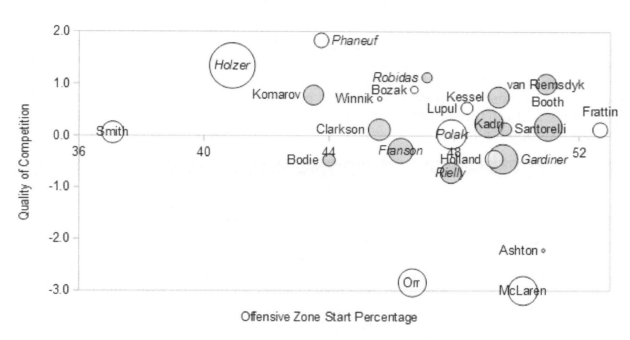

Toronto Maple Leafs - Player Usage

Everybody likes to pick on Toronto, but they do have a good scoring line. Phil Kessel and James van Riemsdyk are a perfect partnership, a pair of 30-goal scorers who combined for 584 shots last season. Kessel is the speedy sniper who focuses exclusively on scoring, while van Riemsdyk is the kind of well-rounded player who handles the bigger picture.

Who would complement these two the best? Joffrey Lupul has worked well in the past (in between injuries), while Nazem Kadri has great possession numbers and can draw penalties. Is he ready for top line duty? If not, then there's always Tyler Bozak, the strongest defensively of the three, but consider his particularly strong offence last year simply a bonus, and not something to expect every year.

Regardless of who is selected, the Leafs have gone off the board to put together some good value players to provide secondary scoring. Petri Kontiola is a playmaking centre with potential for 40 points, David Booth is a strong possession-driving veteran poised for a bounce back season, and Mike Santorelli is a reasonably well-rounded player who once scored 20 goals.

The problem is that this is a team that has never really had a shutdown line. Even experienced checking line players like Jay McClement, Nikolai Kulemin, and Dave Bolland are all gone. It could be time to embrace David Clarkson. He's a perfectly solid checking line winger, it's just that such players normally aren't paid $5.25 million. He might work best with shutdown specialist Daniel Winnik and Leo Komarov, a value pickup who did well in this role in 2012–13.

Dion Phaneuf is another player who just got a big contract and now he might finally get the help he needs to continue taking on one of the league's toughest assignments, which he has proven an inability to handle by himself. Stephane Robidas has always been highly underrated in this role, and the 37-year-old could be just the ticket, if he's healthy.

Carl Gunnarsson used to handle the tough minutes alongside Phaneuf, but Roman Polak is no upgrade. He struggles just as badly but against the depth lines. Someone from among "the sheltered three" needs to be challenged with top-four duties, whether that's 6'5" Cody Franson, Jake Gardiner, or smooth-skating rookie Morgan Rielly. They have all been able to move the puck and win the battles against the depth lines, now it's time to test their skills against top-six opponents.

Score	Category	Notes
	Possession	Toronto is the antithesis of a puck possession team.
	The Shootout	Toronto has several strong shooters in Bozak, Lupul, and van Riemsdyk, but will struggle in nets.
✔	Goaltending	Good goaltending is a necessity for Toronto. Bernier had a great year, and Reimer is as good as backups get.
	Penalty Kill	The Leafs were already among the worst teams at killing penalties, and now only one of their top eight and three of their top 12 most-used players are back this year.
	Power Play	Lupul, Kessel, and even Franson are impressive, and they had a great year, but they don't consistently generate opportunities.
✔	Scoring Line	Toronto has two 30-goal men on their top-notch scoring line.
	Shutdown Line	Winnik, Komarov, and Clarkson might just work.
	Forward Depth	Toronto has nicely assembled some secondary scoring, but defensive play will be a problem.
✔	Top Pairing	Is Robidas too old and broken down to help Phaneuf?
	Second Pairing	It's time for Franson and Gardiner to be challenged.
	Defensive Depth	There's not much beyond Rielly and Polak.
✔	Coaching	Though not one of the league's greats, give Carlyle his due for getting a lot out of several very different teams.
	Prospects	Toronto's system is a little below average at the moment.

Assessment: It's hard to justify playoff contention for Toronto using analytics, but they're better than last year.

181

Vancouver Canucks

Vancouver's story is that of a dominant team on its downward arc that brought in coach John Tortorella in a quest to squeeze just one more playoff appearance out of the team GM Mike Gillis built, before having to step back and re-tool. Nothing worked, the team had its worst finish since 1999, and now everybody's gone and they're starting anew.

Vancouver Canucks - Player Usage

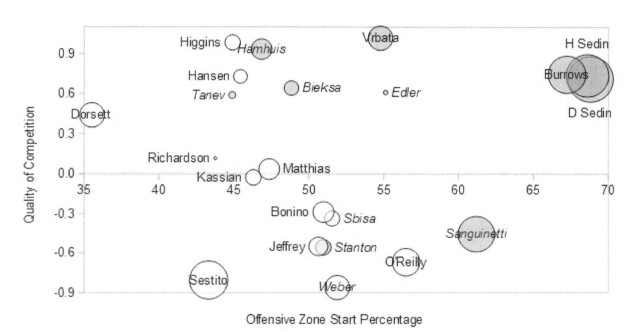

Former coach Alain Vigneault has a very distinctive player usage style and the decline in the Sedins' scoring from 85 points in 48 games to 87 in an 82-game season demonstrates what can happen when it's dismantled. The Swedish twins, who remain strong scoring line players, had to start taking on top line opponents and occasionally working defensive zone shifts, which took a bite out of their ability to produce. New GM Jim Benning acquired Radim Vrbata, one of only two 20 goal scorers on the team, to help re-ignite the pair next season.

The key to the Sedins' scoring success has always been the space they're given by Ryan Kesler's shutdown line taking on the top opponents, but now he's gone. Alexandre Burrows is a strong and gritty defensive player who can fit in this role, but has just 39 points in 96 games over the past two seasons. Chris Higgins is a good fit who has a little more offensive bite. With 17 goals, he is actually the leading returning scorer, and began his career with three straight 20-goal seasons. Do they intend for Bonino, their other newly-acquired 20-goal scorer, to centre this line? That will provide some offensive bite but probably won't work from either a defensive or a possession stand point.

The team's checking line is more about grit than about sound defensive play. Derek Dorsett was acquired from the Rangers, and gritty Zack Kassian was actually Vancouver's fifth leading scorer. Rounding out the bottom six, the Canucks also have speedy Dane Jannik Hansen, checker Brad Richardson, who won the Cup with Los Angeles in 2012, and 6'4" Shawn Matthias. Could prospect Bo Horvat be ready this year?

As for the Canucks' blue line, it held up nicely despite being hit by injuries last year. Dan Hamhuis is one of the league's strongest top pairing shutdown defenceman, but the team needs bounce back seasons offensively from tough guy Kevin Bieksa and well-rounded 6'4" Swede Alexander Edler, who both previously established their scoring at twice this level.

Chris Tanev's surprising establishment as a defensive-minded top-four defenceman gave Benning the confidence to deal Jason Garrison and his salary to Tampa Bay. Although their other big name defencemen are paid about the same, and Edler was infamously -39, Garrison was the right choice. He was the highest scorer of the group, but the weakest in terms of possession. The savings helped bring aboard Ryan Miller, who may not prove as effective as Roberto Luongo, but is used to facing the amount of rubber he's likely to see this year in Vancouver.

Score	Category	Notes
✔	Possession	The Canucks are probably at the minimum standard to be considered effective possession-wise.
	The Shootout	Miller is a solid shootout goalie, but Burrows leads too small a cast of average shooters at best.
	Goaltending	Don't expect Miller to be any better than Luongo, but Lack could be an effective backup.
✔	Penalty Kill	A consistently highly effective penalty kill will have to get by without Kesler.
✔	Power Play	The Canucks have been in the top fifth in creating changes two of the past three seasons, but aren't getting results.
✔	Scoring Line	Vrbata could help re-ignite the still offensively potent Sedins.
	Shutdown Line	Kesler's absence will be felt.
	Forward Depth	The Canucks bottom six is looking a little thin.
✔	Top Pairing	The underrated Hamhuis can work with almost anyone.
✔	Second Pairing	The Canucks have always had a reliable top four.
	Defensive Depth	They have several options, but none of them are that capable.
	Coaching	Desjardins has no track record in the NHL, but was simply fantastic in the AHL and WHL. He has a big upside!
	Prospects	Horvat is the most intriguing prospect in an otherwise below-average pool.

Assessment: A playoff berth isn't likely, but it's not completely out of the question either.

Washington Capitals

The Capitals narrowly missed the playoffs for the first time in six seasons. GM George McPhee and coach Adam Oates are gone, replaced by Brian MacLellan and long-time Predators coach Barry Trotz. The Capitals have excellent size and their players are all in their prime, but this is could be one of the worst possession teams in the league.

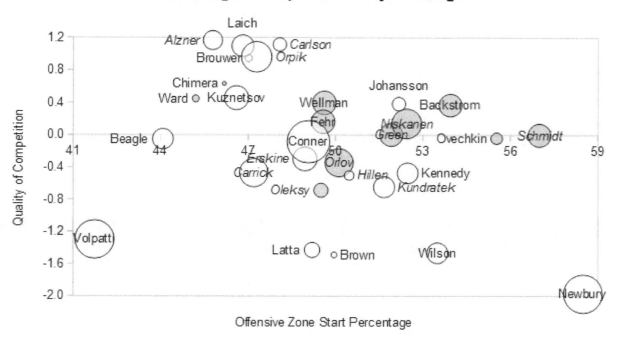

Washington Capitals - Player Usage

Alexander Ovechkin, along with his playmaker Nicklas Backstrom, and puck-moving defenceman Mike Green, is much-maligned for his poor defensive play, but that's not his job. The scoring line is kept focused on generating offence, and is consequently sheltered from playing against top lines, or in the defensive zone. It's a well-publicized fact that they were badly outscored last year, but they were not outshot nor outplayed, and can be relied upon to do their job this year, which is to score goals.

The season was a lot kinder to three two-way veterans, Joel Ward, Jason Chimera, and Troy Brouwer, all of whom recorded career highs in scoring, thanks to the right combination of good play, favourable circumstances, and good fortune. While a dip in their scoring is to be expected, two of them could be used with Brooks Laich on a shutdown line. Laich was an effective player who averaged 48 points a season for five years, but hasn't been the same since his groin injuries. He has scored just 19 points in 60 games over the past two years, and has really been dominated in that tough shutdown role, but the Capitals don't really have any other options at centre.

The remaining veteran(s) can help the exciting 22-year-old rookie Evgeny Kuznetsov on a secondary scoring line. The Russian didn't look great in his 17-game stint last year, but will also get help from 6'4" Eric Fehr, who has the best possession numbers of anyone not on the top line. He topped 30 points for the second time in his career. If Kuznetsov isn't ready, then they'll likely stick with Marcus Johansson, a playmaker who earned 44 points for the second time last year.

Washington's blue line was hit hard with injuries last year. The team resorted to 19-year-old Connor Carrick and 22-year-old Nate Schmidt, but they weren't quite ready. That's one reason why MacLellan signed free agents Brooks Orpik and Matt Niskanen at considerable cost ($11.25 million combined). Orpik is a defensive-minded defenceman who was in way over his head on Pittsburgh's top pairing, while Niskanen is a good possession-based, puck-moving defenceman, but one that has normally been used quite carefully a little further down the depth chart. Their arrival is welcomed by John Carlson and Karl Alzner, who are much better value at just under $6.8 million combined. They're solid defencemen, but have been struggling with an excess of tough minutes.

Beyond those six, plus Green, the Capitals still have another five defencemen, of which 23-year-old Dmitry Orlov is certainly the strongest option. The remainder are mostly gritty veterans like Jack Hillen, John Erskine, and Steven Oleksy. It's the same thing up front, with players like Aaron Volpatti, Michael Latta, Jay Beagle, and Tom Wilson. Well, at least the Hershey Bears will be awesome.

Score	Category	Notes
	Possession	Washington has been on a downward slide for about five years, and is among the league's weaker possession teams.
	The Shootout	The goaltending is somewhat of an unknown, and Backstrom leads a group of mediocre shooters at best.
	Goaltending	I believe that Holtby can be much more than the average goalie he appears to be, and he has two good backups.
	Penalty Kill	The Capitals finished last and second last in attempted shots allowed per minute the past two seasons.
☆	Power Play	Ovechkin and Backstrom are incredible on the power play.
☆	Scoring Line	Don't be distracted by plus/minus or the occasional defensive lapse because Ovechkin and Backstrom are among the best.
	Shutdown Line	Can Laich bounce back? He has decent wingers.
	Forward Depth	They have decent secondary scoring and size, but are suspect defensively.
✔	Top Pairing	The extra help will make Alzner and Carlson more effective.
✔	Second Pairing	It came at a steep cost, but Orpik and Niskanen will help.
✔	Defensive Depth	The Capitals apparently want *all* of the league's defencemen.
✔	Coaching	Trotz got the most out of some questionable Predators teams.
✔	Prospects	Kuznetsov is one of the league's most exciting rookies, and there are a couple more on the way.

Assessment: The Capitals will be fighting for one of the final playoff spots.

Winnipeg Jets

The Winnipeg Jets missed the playoffs for the 13th time in its 14-season franchise history, but did manage to finish about .500 for the third straight season for the first time, and played at a 96-point pace with new coach Paul Maurice. They stood firm this summer, believing in their solid top six, their usable top four, and their shaky depth, but what they really needed to make the playoffs was a new goalie.

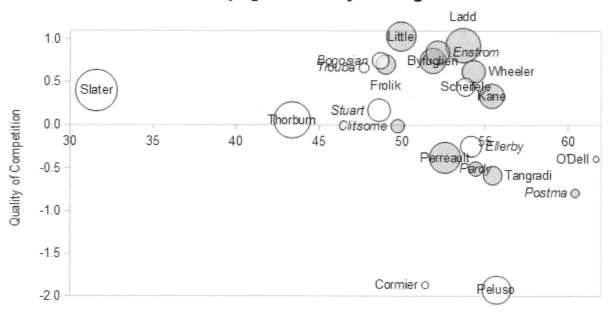

Winnipeg Jets - Player Usage

The most impressive aspect of the Jets' roster last season, at least to me, was their shutdown line. Bryan Little and Andrew Ladd combined for 46 goals and 118 points, and could have received some Selke consideration for their defensive play. They play a dominant possession game against top opponents in both ends. To a lesser extent, Michael Frolik is another sound two-way player and earned his third 40-point season last year.

The scoring line is similarly unheralded and has equally impressive possession numbers, but are used in the offensive zone more often and less frequently against the top lines. Speedy Evander Kane takes a lot of shots and could return to the 30-goal pace he set in 2011–12, especially with the help of 6'5" playmaker Blake Wheeler, who led the team with a career high 28 goals and 69 points last year.

Huge defenceman Dustin Byfuglien has fit in perfectly since being moved up front to the scoring line. He's not the best defensively, but has scored 53–56 points in three of the past four seasons. And, despite his generally bad plus/minus, they do tend to dominate the play when he's on the ice. If he's moved back to the blue line, then I'd like to see Mathieu Perreault tried on the top line. He has dominated opponents throughout his career in the bottom six and deserves to be challenged with some real competition. The alternative is for him to centre a strong secondary line that could feature 21-year-old star Mark Scheifele.

Toby Enstrom is the team's number one defenceman and potentially the team's only legitimate top pairing option since Byfuglien was moved up front. He's a complete player who will ideally bounce back offensively to the back-to-back 50-point seasons he enjoyed before the move to Winnipeg. Zach Bogosian is a big, tough player who is trying to fashion himself into a top shutdown defenceman with offensive upside, but is really better suited to a second pairing. He may soon be passed on the depth chart by 20-year-old Jacob Trouba, a complete defenceman who wasn't sheltered at all in his rookie season. Who will round out the top four? Two-way veteran Grant Clitsome is probably the most interesting option.

The Jets do have some blue line depth, including tough defensive veterans like Mark Stuart, Adam Pardy, and 6'5" Keaton Ellerby, those with a bit more offensive upside like Paul Postma, and puck-moving prospect Joshua Morrissey.

Score	Category	Notes
	Possession	Winnipeg is not a strong possession team, but has roughly held their own for the past five seasons.
	The Shootout	Wheeler and Ladd are among several great shooters, but Pavelec's sub-standard goaltending could negate that.
	Goaltending	Pavelec could be the league's worst starting goalie, and his backup has played 3 NHL games.
✔	Penalty Kill	They had a great season and are a little above average now.
	Power Play	The Jets consistently finished between 16th and 18th in attempted shots per 60 minutes over the past three seasons.
✔	Scoring Line	Their scoring totals match up with almost anyone's.
✔	Shutdown Line	Little and Ladd are highly underrated Selke possibilities.
	Forward Depth	Perreault was a good signing, but who else do they have?
	Top Pairing	Moving Byfuglien up front means Enstrom is the only legitimate top pairing defenceman.
	Second Pairing	Bogosian and Trouba are the only other two top-four defencemen, and are below average possession-wise.
✔	Defensive Depth	The Jets have an assortment of depth options.
	Coaching	Maurice is capable, but hasn't been known to move the needle very far.
	Prospects	The Jets aren't without potential stars, but have no one with the potential impact of Trouba or Scheifele.

Assessment: For want of a goaltender, the Jets remain a playoff bubble team a year longer.

Who is the Best Goal Scorer?

By Rob Vollman

The question of the league's best goal scorer appears to have a relatively simple answer and without the requirement for any form of sophisticated analytic work. After all, we already have a statistic that measures which player is the best at scoring goals—goals!

Furthermore, the question appears to boil down to only two players, since the league's goal-scoring title has gone to either Alexander Ovechkin or Steven Stamkos in six of the last seven seasons. They are the only two players with over 100 goals over the past three seasons, with 121 and 114 respectively. Given that Stamkos has played 37 fewer games, his 82-game average exceeds Ovechkin's 56.0 to 48.6. No other NHLer is higher than Pittsburgh's Evgeni Malkin (40.5) and James Neal (40.3), both of whose totals might have been boosted by the game's best playmaker, Sidney Crosby.

So I guess this study is done. Next Chapter. But wait! Even if the question ultimately does boil down to Ovechkin vs Stamkos, there is still much that can be learned from the analysis. For example, not only is it a wonderful sample case of how analytics can be used in hockey, but the same thinking process can be used to find the best goal scorers on a particular team or applied to similar types of questions.

Furthermore, since this book is intended to be as timeless as its *Baseball Abstract* inspiration, it can be applied in future seasons when Stamkos and Ovechkin's goal scoring dominance begins to fall into doubt.

There is also a lot more to this question than just looking at which players score the most goals per game. For instance, do these two players get the same opportunities, whether at even strength or on the power play? And this refers not just to the number of minutes in each manpower situation, but whether they start in the offensive zone, against the same level of opponents, and with the same quality of playmakers as linemates.

Truly building a case for one sniper over the other requires examining their player usage, comparing their linemates Nicklas Backstrom to Martin St. Louis, and breaking down each player's scoring by ice time and manpower situation. This process is further confused by the fact that Ovechkin's style is to attempt as many scoring opportunities as possible, while Stamkos is known for converting on a higher percentage of his chances than anyone else in the league. And what about the questions of coaching styles and consistency? If Ovechkin is so great, why did he average only 35 goals a season from 2010 until the 2012 lockout?

As a process is devised to compare these two goal scorers, we will also identify and compare these two to the game's other great snipers. This will help establish where they stand relative to the rest of the league and where their greatest future threats may be coming from. Let's begin!

Accounting for Manpower Situation

The first issue to address is the fact that Stamkos scores at a higher rate at even strength but that Ovechkin is the more effective scorer with the man advantage, and by a slightly larger margin. So who is the better goal scorer overall?

At first glance, this may be one of the easiest differences between the two to sort out. Stamkos has averaged 1.71 goals per 60 minutes at even strength over the past three seasons, the highest in the league by a very comfortable margin. The next highest player, Max Pacioretty, scores at less than 85% that rate. Ovechkin himself ranks sixth, with 1.26 goals per 60 minutes.

On the power play, the roles are reversed. Ovechkin leads the league with 3.55 power play goals per 60 minutes, is followed by James Neal at 3.26, and then Stamkos is third with 2.94. That means that Stamkos has a 0.45 goal scoring rate advantage at even strength, while Ovechkin is up 0.56 on the power play. But these two should not be weighed evenly, since a team spends a far greater portion of their game at even strength than on the power play. Nine times more, in fact.

That isn't to say that even-strength goal scoring is nine times more important than power-play scoring, however. While goal scoring is essentially the primary purpose of a power play, it is only one of many priorities at even strength. Theoretically, a player could have a lower scoring rate at even strength because he's tasked with duties other than scoring goals, such as throwing hits or neutralizing opponents. While that's unlikely to be the case when comparing Ovechkin to Stamkos, quite frankly, one could still use that argument to claim that the power play is a truer test of a player's goal scoring talents.

The higher importance of goal scoring on the power play relative to other manpower situations is also a reason why pure goal scorers get as much power-play time as they can handle, and are assigned only an average share (and sometimes less) at even strength.

For example, over the past three seasons, Ovechkin has played only 3.7 minutes at even strength for every minute on the power play, one of the lowest rates in the league. Fellow Russians Evgeni Malkin (3.58) and Ilya Kovalchuk (3.54), and rookie Alex Chiasson (3.52) are the only players with a lower ratio, although the aforementioned James Neal isn't far behind (3.73).

By comparison, Stamkos plays 4.54 minutes at even strength for every minute on the power play, which is a little more typical of the league's top offensive talents. That may not mean that Ovechkin is a better goal scorer, but instead that goal scoring is a higher share of his overall value as a player than it is for Stamkos, at least relative to the team's other options.

We should use both pieces of information to determine which player is the best overall goal scorer, but what's the exact ratio to use when comparing even-strength to power-play scoring? That's an interesting question and an important one to a growing subset of the analytics movement who prefer precision over arbitrarily chosen numbers. Although it's being left as an open question here, it should be acknowledged that the selected ratio could arbitrarily tilt the debate in one direction or another.

Fortunately, it doesn't matter for our current purposes because even when a ratio unfavourable to him is chosen, such as 3.7, Stamkos still bests Ovechkin by the comfortable margin of 1.97 to 1.74 goals per 60 minutes. All that the usage of a lower ratio really did was allow Neal to increase his lead over Pacioretty for third place, 1.59 to 1.52.

The following table looks at Stamkos, Ovechkin, and all NHL players with an even-strength scoring rate (ESG/60) of at least one goal per 60 minutes over the past three seasons. The weighted scoring rate (WG/60) uses the more typical ratio of 4.5-to-1 even-strength to power-play scoring rate (PPG/60).

Individual Weighted Goal Scoring Rate, 2011–12 to 2013–14

Player	Team(s)	GP	G	G/82	PPG	PPG/60	ESG	ESG/60	WG/60
Steven Stamkos	TB	167	114	56.0	31	2.94	82	1.71	1.93
Alexander Ovechkin	Wsh	204	121	48.6	53	3.55	68	1.26	1.67
James Neal	Pit	179	88	40.3	38	3.26	50	1.15	1.53
Max Pacioretty	Mtl	196	87	36.4	18	1.78	68	1.44	1.51
Jeff Carter	CBJ/LA	175	74	34.7	26	2.92	47	1.12	1.45
Corey Perry	Ana	205	95	38.0	27	2.33	67	1.24	1.44
Evgeni Malkin	Pit	166	82	40.5	23	1.86	59	1.34	1.43
Phil Kessel	Tor	212	94	36.4	24	2.09	70	1.17	1.34
Gustav Nyquist	Det	97	32	27.1	6	1.52	26	1.30	1.34
Joe Pavelski	SJ	212	88	34.0	29	2.50	57	1.07	1.33
Curtis Glencross	Cgy	145	53	30.0	14	2.47	37	1.08	1.33
Tyler Seguin	Bos/Dal	209	82	32.2	20	1.98	62	1.19	1.33
Jonathan Toews	Chi	182	80	36.0	12	1.28	62	1.31	1.31
Joffrey Lupul	Tor	151	58	31.5	17	2.39	41	1.06	1.30
Brad Marchand	Bos	203	71	28.4	10	2.12	53	1.12	1.30
John Tavares	NYI	189	83	36.0	24	2.16	59	1.09	1.29
Chris Kunitz	Pit	208	83	32.7	28	2.22	55	1.07	1.28
Logan Couture	SJ	193	75	31.9	22	2.25	49	1.06	1.27
Marian Hossa	Chi	193	76	32.3	17	1.96	53	1.12	1.27
Jeff Skinner	Car	177	66	30.6	20	2.17	46	1.06	1.26
Patrick Sharp	Chi	184	73	32.5	18	1.76	54	1.15	1.26
Rick Nash	CBJ/NYR	191	77	33.1	13	1.33	59	1.24	1.26
Jordan Eberle	Edm	206	78	31.0	20	1.90	57	1.09	1.24
Alexander Steen	StL	151	56	30.4	13	1.79	42	1.12	1.24
Sidney Crosby	Pit	138	59	35.1	16	1.64	43	1.14	1.23
Marian Gaborik	3 Teams	170	64	30.9	12	1.33	52	1.19	1.22
Michael Ryder	3 Teams	210	69	26.9	19	2.08	49	1.01	1.21
Jarome Iginla	3 Teams	204	76	30.5	18	1.75	58	1.06	1.19
Jamie Benn	Dal	193	72	30.6	10	1.01	60	1.23	1.19
Michael Grabner	NYI	187	48	21.0	3	1.75	40	1.04	1.17

86 Acknowledgement: Raw games, goal, and ice time data came from the *NHL* http://www.nhl.com.

Pascal Dupuis	Pit	169	52	25.2	2	1.45	46	1.11	1.17
Mathieu Perreault	Wsh/Ana	172	40	19.1	8	1.84	32	1.00	1.15
Mike Cammalleri	Mtl/Cgy	173	59	28.0	14	1.62	45	1.03	1.14
Bobby Ryan	Ana/Ott	198	65	26.9	11	1.49	52	1.06	1.14
Evander Kane	Wpg	185	66	29.3	9	1.29	55	1.11	1.14
Jason Pominville	Buf/Min	211	74	28.8	17	1.45	54	1.04	1.12
Jiri Tlusty	Car	195	56	23.5	6	1.22	48	1.10	1.12
Sean Monahan	Cgy	75	22	24.1	3	1.14	19	1.12	1.12
Andrew Ladd	Wpg	208	69	27.2	11	1.19	58	1.09	1.11
Tomas Tatar	Det	91	23	20.7	3	0.90	20	1.14	1.10
Jakub Voracek	Phi	208	63	24.8	16	1.35	47	1.02	1.08
Kyle Palmieri	Ana	131	28	17.5	2	0.72	26	1.11	1.04
Raffi Torres	Phx/SJ	123	25	16.7	2	1.06	23	1.02	1.03
Matt Read	Phi	196	57	23.8	5	0.77	46	1.06	1.01

Minimum 20 goals, 1.00 even-strength goals per 60 minutes

Among those with at least 20 goals over the past three seasons, there are 44 players who have averaged at least one even-strength goal for every 60 minutes played. Setting the goal scoring bar so low allowed the inclusion of secondary players like Raffi Torres, but it also permitted young potential snipers like Gustav Nyquist, Sean Monahan, Tomas Tatar, and Kyle Palmieri to be considered. Who knows, they may one day be the focal point of this kind of analysis.

Even Strength and Power Play Scoring Rates of Top Goal Scorers, 2011–12 to 2013–14

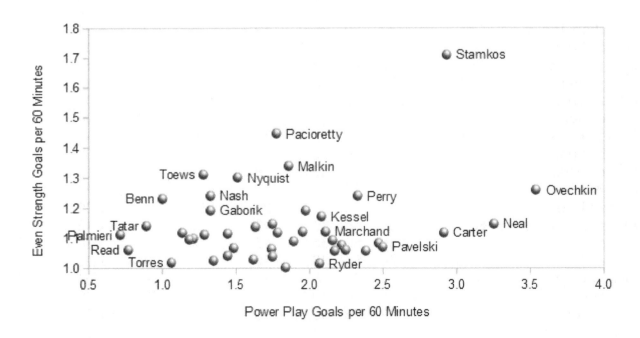

Almost any way you look at this data, Stamkos has a considerable lead over everyone in the group, arguably including Ovechkin himself. Even the next best players in each situation, Neal and Pacioretty, score at less than 80% of his clip. Unless an explanation can be found for his incredible scoring rate (other than his natural talent), then we have a clear leader.

You may have noticed that we have skipped over shorthanded situations. Even though such situations are defensive in nature, it can still be advantageous to have a goal scoring threat. However, the added effort and complexity of accounting for shorthanded scoring likely isn't worth the relatively minor impact it would have on our totals—although fans of either Brad Marchand or the Blackhawks might disagree.

Accounting for Opportunity

Despite establishing that Stamkos has been the superior goal scorer using our manpower-adjusted formula, our work is definitely not yet complete. Without considering how players are used, it is possible that one player's scoring totals are being boosted by starting most his shifts in the offensive zone and/or against secondary opponents, while those of another are being limited due to playing two-way hockey against the game's top players. Reverse their roles, and those scoring totals could be reversed as well.

It turns out that's not the case, in our two-player debate at least. Ovechkin has among the most offensively-oriented assignments in the entire league. While Stamkos doesn't exactly have it rough, his conditions are nowhere near as favourable as Washington's top star, and his scoring totals could soar even higher if they were.

However, many of the previously identified top goal scorers do handle some pretty tough assignments that are no doubt deflating their scoring totals. Almost certainly not to the extent that they'd contend with Stamkos and Ovechkin for the Rocket Richard Trophy, but more than enough to make quite a dent in their numbers.

Player usage charts are a great way to visualize how players have been used and whether their scoring totals might have been boosted. Although they are explained in more detail in the Team Essays chapter, the brief explanation is that the horizontal axis represents the percentage of shifts they start in the offensive zone, the vertical axis has an estimate of their average skill of their opponents, and the circles indicate how well the team performs when they're on the ice.

The following player usage chart includes all of the top goal scorers, which we have already defined as those who have averaged at least one goal per 60 minutes of even-strength play over the past three seasons. The density of the players in the middle prevented including labels for Jamie Benn and Jiri Tlusty (the shaded and unshaded circles between Brad Marchand and Chris Kunitz), and Gustav Nyquist (the shaded circle between Jakub Voracek, Tyler Seguin, and Jordan Eberle). Notice that these top goal scorers aren't all used in similar fashion.

Player Usage of Top Goal Scorers, 2011–12 to 2013–14

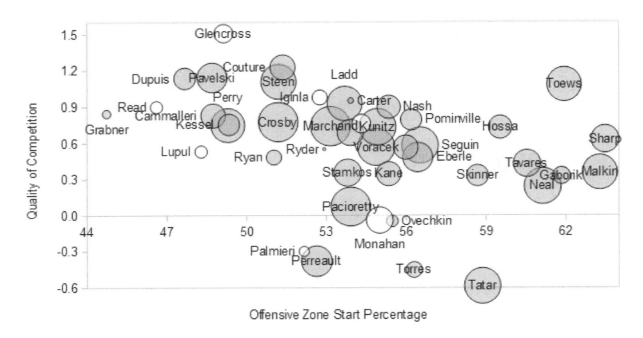

Offensive Zone Start Percentage

Top goal scorers are typically used in slightly offensive-minded fashion, generally against top-six opponents, and are almost always on the winning side of the possession game. However, there are some notable exceptions:

- Some of them are used more exclusively in the offensive zone, like Evgeni Malkin, Marian Gaborik, James Neal, John Tavares, Jeff Skinner, and three Blackhawks, Patrick Sharp, Jonathan Toews, and Marian Hossa.
- Others are used more frequently in the defensive zone, such as Michael Grabner, Matt Read, Pascal Dupuis, Joffrey Lupul, Joe Pavelski, Mike Cammalleri, Corey Perry, Curtis Glencross, and Phil Kessel.
- Some are secondary players used more frequently against depth-line opponents, such as Tomas Tatar, Raffi Torres, Mathieu Perreault, Kyle Palmieri, Sean Monahan and, surprisingly, Alexander Ovechkin. Steven Stamkos is not that far removed from this group, either.
- There are a few snipers who are on the losing side of the possession game, such as Sean Monahan, Curtis Glencross, Jiri Tlusty (unlabeled), Jarome Iginla, Joffrey Lupul, Matt Read, and Kyle Palmieri.

Not everything is exactly as it appears, however, when including players from different teams on the same usage chart, because not all teams spend the same amount of time in the offensive zone. The Chicago Blackhawks, for example, spend most of their time in the offensive zone, while the Toronto Maple Leafs rarely have any players higher than 50%. That's the reason why three Blackhawks are all on the right side of the chart, while so many Flames and Maple Leafs are on the left side.

In these cases it is helpful to look not only at the absolute offensive zone start percentage but where each player ranked among the team's forwards. The following table summarizes just that, following up each player's scoring rate with their offensive zone start percentage (ZS%), their average quality of competition (QoC), and where the average ranking (Rk) among their team's forwards over the past three seasons. The list itself is ordered by each player's approximate position among their team's forwards, in an equal combination of both measurements, from the most difficult assignment to the easiest.

Take Michael Grabner and John Tavares of the New York Islanders, for example. Grabner started 42.3%, 49.0%, and 45.0% of his shifts in the offensive zone over the past three seasons, respectively, which ranked 3rd, 7th, and 1st lowest among Islanders forwards. Tavares, in contrast, started 58.7%, 61.2%, and 62.6% in the offensive zone, respectively, which ranked 14th, 12th, and 15th. A similar pattern holds up for the quality of competition, indicating that Grabner was used in a defensive-minded fashion, while Tavares was used primarily to score. Common sense suggests that this may have had a significant influence on their respective scoring totals.

Difficulty of Assignment for NHL's Top Goal Scorers, 2011–12 to 2013–14

Player	Team(s)	GP	ESG	ESG/60	ZS%	Rk	QoC	Rk
Michael Grabner	NYI	187	40	1.04	44.7	3.7	0.84	2.7
Pascal Dupuis	Pit	169	46	1.11	47.7	6.7	1.14	2.3
Brad Marchand	Bos	203	53	1.12	53.2	7.3	0.74	1.7
Joe Pavelski	SJ	212	57	1.07	48.7	6.3	1.14	3.0
Corey Perry	Ana	205	67	1.24	49.3	5.7	0.75	3.7
Logan Couture	SJ	193	49	1.06	51.4	7.7	1.23	2.3
Alexander Steen	StL	151	42	1.12	51.2	8.0	1.11	3.0
Andrew Ladd	Wpg	208	58	1.09	53.7	8.3	0.93	3.0
Matt Read	Phi	196	46	1.06	46.6	6.3	0.90	5.3
Jeff Carter	CBJ/LA	175	47	1.12	53.9	8.3	0.95	3.2
Bobby Ryan	Ana/Ott	198	52	1.06	51.0	8.0	0.48	4.7
Curtis Glencross	Cgy	145	37	1.08	49.1	9.7	1.51	3.1
Jiri Tlusty	Car	195	48	1.10	54.3	8.0	0.76	4.7
Marian Hossa	Chi	193	53	1.12	59.5	7.7	0.73	5.3
Jonathan Toews	Chi	182	62	1.31	61.9	10.0	1.08	3.3
Jamie Benn	Dal	193	60	1.23	53.9	10.3	0.69	3.3
Rick Nash	CBJ/NYR	191	59	1.24	55.3	10.3	0.90	4.0
Joffrey Lupul	Tor	151	41	1.06	48.3	10.3	0.53	4.3
Mike Cammalleri	Mtl/Cgy	173	45	1.03	48.7	10.2	0.83	4.7
Chris Kunitz	Pit	208	55	1.07	54.9	11.3	0.73	4.3
Sidney Crosby	Pit	138	43	1.14	51.2	10.3	0.78	5.3
Michael Ryder	3 Teams	210	49	1.01	52.9	10.3	0.55	5.7
Jeff Skinner	Car	177	46	1.06	58.7	10.0	0.33	6.0
Tyler Seguin	Bos/Dal	209	62	1.19	56.5	11.7	0.58	4.3
Jason Pominville	Buf/Min	211	54	1.04	46.2	11.7	0.79	5.0
Jarome Iginla	3 Teams	204	58	1.06	52.8	11.7	0.98	5.3

87 Acknowledgement: Raw zone start and quality of competition data came from the *Behind the Net* http://www.behindthenet.ca.

Patrick Sharp	Chi	184	54	1.15	63.5	11.0	0.63	6.0
Jakub Voracek	Phi	208	47	1.02	54.9	11.0	0.57	6.3
Jordan Eberle	Edm	206	57	1.09	56.4	12.0	0.48	5.3
Evander Kane	Wpg	185	55	1.11	55.3	10.7	0.35	6.7
Gustav Nyquist	Det	97	26	1.30	56.0	11.5	0.57	6.0
Steven Stamkos	T.B.	167	82	1.71	53.8	10.0	0.36	7.7
Phil Kessel	Tor	212	70	1.17	49.3	12.0	0.75	6.0
Marian Gaborik	3 Teams	170	52	1.19	61.8	11.7	0.33	7.3
Kyle Palmieri	Ana	131	26	1.11	52.2	9.0	-0.30	10.5
John Tavares	NYI	189	59	1.09	60.5	13.7	0.43	6.3
Sean Monahan	Cgy	75	19	1.12	55.0	10.0	-0.04	11.0
Mathieu Perreault	Wsh/Ana	172	32	1.00	52.6	12.0	-0.38	10.7
Tomas Tatar	Det	91	20	1.14	58.9	8.5	-0.58	14.5
Max Pacioretty	Mtl	196	68	1.44	53.9	13.7	0.07	9.7
Raffi Torres	Phx/SJ	123	23	1.02	56.3	13.5	-0.45	10.5
James Neal	Pit	179	50	1.15	61.1	14.7	0.24	9.7
Alexander Ovechkin	Wsh	204	68	1.26	55.5	14.3	-0.05	10.3
Evgeni Malkin	Pit	166	59	1.34	63.3	16.3	0.36	8.7

Minimum 20 goals, 1.00 even-strength goals per 60 minutes

So why isn't Grabner used with John Tavares on the scoring line, incidentally? The speedy Austrian scored 34 goals in his rookie season back in 2010–11, including six while shorthanded, which demonstrates his potential value. In limited and defensive-oriented action alongside the likes of Frans Nielsen, he has scored only 48 goals in the three seasons since then.

This information shouldn't be taken as a criticism of those snipers handling the easier assignments at the bottom of the list, by the way. After all, it makes a great deal of sense that players like Ovechkin and Malkin would be deployed in such a way to maximize scoring. That's why it must be a testament to Grabner's defensive abilities that the same isn't done for him and for many others at the top of the list.

As for Stamkos, the difficulty of his assignment is a little below the middle of the pack, suggesting that he could score even more goals if his ice time were tilted to its maximum possible extent, like it is for Ovechkin. It certainly reinforces his case in our two-player comparison.

At first glance, this approach also seems to be making the case for players like Pascal Dupuis and Corey Perry, but the problem with those arguments is obvious—they both play with one of the game's great playmakers, Sidney Crosby and Ryan Getzlaf, respectively. Their centres boost their scoring, potentially in a similar fashion to Martin St. Louis and Nicklas Backstrom for Stamkos and Ovechkin. Is there a way to control for that?

Accounting for Linemates

There may be a way to identify each sniper's key playmaker, but how do we measure how good they are? Any assists they generate could have as much to do with the goal scorer's own talents than it does that playmaker's ability to get him the puck. How do we separate the credit?

In last year's *Hockey Abstract*, we introduced a new statistic called *setup passes*, which is defined as any pass that results in a shot. Since this isn't officially counted by the NHL, we have to rely on an estimate that's based on primary assists and the team's shooting percentage when the target player is on the ice, both of which are available on such websites as *Behind the Net* and *Extra Skater*.

The passing estimate isn't completely accurate and wouldn't be conclusive even if it were (since it doesn't consider the quality of those shot opportunities), but it should suffice in providing at least a high-level impression of which of our goal scorers are getting the pucks on their sticks most frequently.

The following table shows the average number of setup passes each of the relevant playmakers made per game (Pass/G) over the past three seasons. This player was selected based on whomever was credited with the most primary assists on the player's goals, with ties broken by whomever has the best numbers. That primary assist information is available in the game logs posted at *Hockey Reference*[88].

Passing Rates for Linemates of the NHL's Top Goal Scorers, 2011–12 to 2013–14

Player	Best Playmaker	Team(s)	GP	Pass	Pass/G
James Neal	Evgeni Malkin	Pit	166	748	4.51
Chris Kunitz	Sidney Crosby	Pit	138	604	4.38
Pascal Dupuis	Sidney Crosby	Pit	138	604	4.38
Jeff Skinner	Eric Staal	Car	209	809	3.87
Jiri Tlusty	Eric Staal	Car	209	809	3.87
Joe Pavelski	Joe Thornton	SJ	212	815	3.84
Jakub Voracek	Claude Giroux	Phi	207	786	3.79
Corey Perry	Ryan Getzlaf	Ana	203	764	3.77
Kyle Palmieri	Ryan Getzlaf	Ana	203	764	3.77
Gustav Nyquist	Henrik Zetterberg	Det	173	601	3.47
Evander Kane	Blake Wheeler	Wpg	210	704	3.35
Jordan Eberle	Taylor Hall	Edm	181	593	3.27
Joffrey Lupul	Phil Kessel	Tor	212	658	3.10
Mathieu Perreault	Alexander Semin	Wsh	186	556	2.99
Rick Nash	Derek Stepan	NYR	212	619	2.92
Tyler Seguin	Patrice Bergeron	Bos	203	592	2.92
Brad Marchand	Patrice Bergeron	Bos	203	592	2.92
Marian Gaborik	Derek Stepan	NYR	212	619	2.92
Tomas Tatar	Riley Sheahan	Det	44	125	2.85

88 Acknowledgement: Assist data from the game files at *Hockey Reference*, http://www.hockey-reference.com.

Jason Pominville	Thomas Vanek	Buf	194	533	2.75
Andrew Ladd	Bryan Little	Wpg	204	558	2.74
Alexander Steen	T.J. Oshie	StL	189	513	2.71
Max Pacioretty	David Desharnais	Mtl	208	557	2.68
Jamie Benn	Tyler Seguin	Dal	209	557	2.67
Patrick Sharp	Marian Hossa	Chi	193	508	2.63
John Tavares	Matt Moulson	NYI	204	526	2.58
Jonathan Toews	Patrick Sharp	Chi	184	473	2.57
Alexander Ovechkin	Nicklas Backstrom	Wsh	172	433	2.52
Steven Stamkos	Martin St. Louis	TB	206	516	2.50
Curtis Glencross	Jarome Iginla	Cgy	204	505	2.48
Bobby Ryan	Teemu Selanne	Ana	192	468	2.43
Jeff Carter	Mike Richards	LA	204	494	2.42
Evgeni Malkin	James Neal	Pit	179	433	2.42
Michael Grabner	Kyle Okposo	NYI	198	476	2.41
Jarome Iginla	Milan Lucic	Bos	207	493	2.38
Marian Hossa	Jonathan Toews	Chi	182	429	2.36
Michael Ryder	Loui Eriksson	Dal	191	437	2.29
Phil Kessel	Tyler Bozak	Tor	177	372	2.10
Logan Couture	Patrick Marleau	SJ	212	435	2.05
Sean Monahan	Lee Stempniak	Cgy	181	363	2.00
Mike Cammalleri	Lee Stempniak	Cgy	181	363	2.00
Sidney Crosby	Chris Kunitz	Pit	169	339	2.00
Raffi Torres	Shane Doan	Phx	196	379	1.94
Matt Read	Sean Couturier	Phi	205	319	1.55

While certainly not any kind of definitive proof, this data at least creates a basis for the argument that the goal scoring credentials of various Penguins, Hurricanes, and Ducks have been boosted by the playmaking talents of Sidney Crosby, Evgeni Malkin, Eric Staal, and Ryan Getzlaf, respectively. A study of each player's scoring totals with and without (WOWY) their linemates, which is available from David Johnson's *Hockey Analysis* website, could help establish its validity one way or the other.

As for Stamkos and Ovechkin, their playmakers are virtually tied, but surprisingly nowhere near the top of the list. Apparently, vaunted passers like St. Louis and Backstrom get them the puck no more frequently than their counterparts on other teams, and actually a little bit less. Is it possible that their playmaking reputations have been boosted by Stamkos and Ovechkin?

While the answer to that question is outside the scope of this analysis, it does bring back to mind a study from a chapter in last year's book about the league's best playmaker. Post-expansion history was searched for players with unusual one-time (or two-time) goal scoring totals, with the theory being that the temporary boost could have been thanks to an elite playmaker. Could the same theory work in reverse?

Digression: Can Goal-Scoring Linemates Boost Assist Totals?

For the purposes of entertaining those who enjoy historical digressions as much as I do, last year's study has been reproduced, but looking instead for players who had a large one-time boost in assists.

Specifically, we compared every post-expansion player for the largest difference (Diff) between their single-season career high in assists (Best), and their next best season (2nd). Once again, the theory is that such a temporary boost might be explained by the presence of an elite goal scoring talent playing alongside them. Let's see if that holds up!

Biggest Differences Between Single-Season Career High Assists and Second Highest, 1967–68 to 2013–14[89]

Season	Playmaker	Team	Best	2nd	Diff	Goal Scorer
1992–93	Pat LaFontaine	Buffalo	95	51	44	Alexander Mogilny
1992–93	Dmitri Kvartalnov	Boston	42	7	35	Adam Oates
1970–71	Tom Webster	Detroit	37	2	35	Various
1978–79	Bob MacMillan	Atlanta	71	39	32	Guy Chouinard
1970–71	Murray Hall	Vancouver	38	6	32	Wayne Maki
1980–81	Mario Faubert	Pittsburgh	44	7	31	Rick Kehoe
1985–86	Wayne Gretzky	Edmonton	163	135	28	Jari Kurri
1982–83	Tapio Levo	New Jersey	40	13	27	Don Lever
1985–86	Kjell Dahlin	Montreal	39	12	27	Mats Naslund
1981–82	Chris Valentine	Washington	37	10	27	Bob Carpenter
1990–91	Dave Capuano	Vancouver	31	5	26	Steve Bozek
1968–69	Dick Sarrazin	Philadelphia	30	4	26	Andre Lacroix
2005–06	Nolan Baumgartner	Vancouver	29	3	26	Markus Naslund
1980–81	Jacques Richard	Quebec	51	26	25	Marc Tardif
1992–93	Alexander Semak	New Jersey	42	17	25	Claude Lemieux
1991–92	Claude Vilgrain	New Jersey	27	2	25	Stephane Richer
1971–72	Rick Foley	Philadelphia	25	1	24	Bobby Clarke
1976–77	Tim Young	Minnesota	66	41	23	Ernie Hicke
2006–07	Daniel Briere	Buffalo	63	41	22	Jason Pominville
1984–85	Brent Sutter	NY Islanders	60	38	22	Mike Bossy
1984–85	Brian MacLellan	Los Angeles	54	32	22	Marcel Dionne
1970–71	Bryan Campbell	Chicago	37	15	22	Bobby Hull
1979–80	Dale Hoganson	Quebec	36	14	22	Real Cloutier
1979–80	Ron Chipperfield	Edm-Que	23	1	22	Various
1985–86	Scott Bjugstad	Minnesota	33	12	21	Dino Ciccarelli
1988–89	Bob Joyce	Boston	31	10	21	Ken Linseman
1995–96	Roman Oksiuta	Van-Ana	28	7	21	Various
1980–81	Kent Nilsson	Calgary	82	62	20	Eric Vail
1977–78	Tom Edur	Col-Pit	45	25	20	Jean Pronovost
1992–93	Nikolai Borschevsky	Toronto	40	20	20	Dave Andreychuk

---

89 Acknowledgement: Raw goal data for my calculations came from *Hockey Reference*: http://www.hockey-reference.com.

1988–89	Marc Habscheid	Minnesota	31	11	20	Neal Broten
1979–80	Rich LeDuc	Quebec	27	7	20	Real Cloutier
1980–81	Danny Geoffrion	Winnipeg	26	6	20	Morris Lukowich
2002–03	Jaroslav Bednar	LA-Fla	22	2	20	Various
2010–11	Linus Omark	Edmonton	22	2	20	Magnus Paajarvi
1979–80	Bob Fitchner	Quebec	20	0	20	Various

Since 1967 expansion.

This method doesn't appear to be very successful at finding the best goal scorers, especially compared to the reverse study last year. While there are some decent snipers on this list, the absences of Brett Hull, Phil Esposito, Mike Gartner, Jaromir Jagr, Guy Lafleur, Teemu Selanne, and Luc Robitaille, are quite conspicuous.

Last year, we widened the search by looking at the biggest gaps between first and third, in case a playmaker was paired up with a goal scorer for up to two seasons. At least that method picks up Lafleur (via Pete Mahovlich).

Biggest Differences Between Single-Season Career High Assists and Third Highest, 1967–68 to 2013–14[90]

Season	Playmaker	Team	Best	3rd	Diff	Goal Scorer
1992–93	Pat LaFontaine	Buffalo	95	51	44	Alexander Mogilny
1985–86	Wayne Gretzky	Edmonton	163	125	38	Jari Kurri
2000–01	Espen Knutsen	Columbus	42	4	38	Geoff Sanderson
1970–71	Murray Hall	Vancouver	38	1	37	Wayne Maki
1977–78	Harold Phillipoff	Atlanta	36	0	36	Bill Clement
1970–71	Tom Webster	Detroit	37	2	35	Various
1979–80	Blair MacDonald	Edmonton	48	15	33	Wayne Gretzky
1980–81	Mario Faubert	Pittsburgh	44	11	33	Rick Kehoe
1974–75	Pete Mahovlich	Montreal	82	50	32	Guy Lafleur
1978–79	Bob MacMillan	Atlanta	71	39	32	Guy Chouinard
1988–89	Rob Brown	Pittsburgh	66	34	32	Mario Lemieux
1976–77	Roland Eriksson	Minnesota	44	12	32	Steve Jensen
1981–82	Chris Valentine	Washington	37	5	32	Bob Carpenter
1975–76	Jean Potvin	NY Islanders	55	24	31	Clark Gillies
1978–79	Robert Palmer	Los Angeles	41	10	31	Marcel Dionne
1985–86	Kjell Dahlin	Montreal	39	8	31	Mats Naslund
1992–93	Nikolai Borschevsky	Toronto	40	10	30	Dave Andreychuk
2011–12	Adam Henrique	New Jersey	35	5	30	Ilya Kovalchuk
1967–68	Mike McMahon	Minnesota	33	3	30	Wayne Connelly
1981–82	Greg Theberge	Washington	32	2	30	Dennis Maruk
1990–91	Dave Capuano	Vancouver	31	1	30	Steve Bozek

Since 1967 expansion.

Interesting! While I'm as much of a fan of digressions into historical trivia as the next guy, let's wrap up this chapter's actual analysis, which is finding today's top goal scorer.

---

90 Acknowledgement: Raw goal data for my calculations came from *Hockey Reference*: http://www.hockey-reference.com.

Other Considerations

We've established a process to appropriately weigh a player's even-strength and power-play scoring rates, taken playing conditions and level of opportunity into account, and gotten an idea of whose totals may have been boosted by having an elite playmaking linemate. So far, a stronger case has been built for Stamkos than for Ovechkin, without any other player currently establishing themselves as part of the debate.

There are, however, a few things that could be examined in greater detail in the future. For instance, if Ovechkin had finished on top, then the questions of coaching systems and/or consistency could be considered, given how his goal scoring totals slumped from 2010 through 2012, under coaches Bruce Boudreau and Dale Hunter.

There's also the question of which players might have boosted their totals with empty net goals, and to what extent. Marian Hossa, for instance, leads the league with eight empty net goals, out of 76 total, over the past three seasons. Max Pacioretty, Jarome Iginla, Blake Wheeler, and David Backes have each scored seven. Among the top goal scorers being studied, empty net goals have boosted scoring by about 3.7%, on average, with only Hossa sitting above 10%. This would be an interesting topic for further study! As for the two players we're examining mostly closely, Stamkos and Ovechkin have each scored three.

Finally, instead of just the question of how much a player scores, the question of *how* they score could be examined in more detail. For instance, Ovechkin has led the league in shots eight times out of nine seasons, but Stamkos has him dominated in career shooting percentage, 17.5% to 12.3%. They are essentially at opposite ends of the following table, which ranks our top goal scorers by their shooting percentage (SH%, ASH%)

Since it's intended to accurately record how much each of the league's top goal scorers have shot over the past three seasons, this table considers all attempted shots (AttS), including those that hit the post, missed the net, were deflected wide, or were blocked altogether. The average distance of those shots (Dist) is also included to get another indication of who is taking high quality shots from up close and who is firing away from just about anywhere.

Shooting Information for the NHL's Top Goal Scorers 2011–12 to 2013–14[91]

Player	Team(s)	GP	G	Shot	Dist	SH%	AttS	Atts/G	ASH%
Curtis Glencross	Cgy	145	53	279	26.7	19.0	493	3.40	10.8
Steven Stamkos	T.B.	167	114	584	28.9	19.5	1059	6.34	10.8
Brad Marchand	Bos	203	71	407	28.1	17.4	678	3.34	10.5
Jonathan Toews	Chi	182	80	522	21.6	15.3	766	4.21	10.4
Mathieu Perreault	Wsh/Ana	172	40	228	25.9	17.5	419	2.44	9.5
Raffi Torres	Phx/SJ	123	25	168	32.6	14.9	270	2.20	9.3
Jordan Eberle	Edm	206	78	513	25.2	15.2	878	4.26	8.9
Sean Monahan	Cgy	75	22	140	32.3	15.7	250	3.33	8.8

91 Acknowledgement: All raw shot data for my calculations came from *Extra Skater.* http://www.extraskater.com.

Chris Kunitz	Pit	208	83	561	26.1	14.8	949	4.56	8.7
Jiri Tlusty	Car	195	56	384	28.0	14.6	658	3.37	8.5
Gustav Nyquist	Det	97	32	218	29.1	14.7	387	3.99	8.3
Matt Read	Phi	196	57	378	31.5	15.1	692	3.53	8.2
Corey Perry	Ana	205	95	686	24.2	13.8	1167	5.69	8.1
Michael Ryder	3 Teams	210	69	478	29.5	14.4	860	4.10	8.0
Joffrey Lupul	Tor	151	58	425	26.3	13.6	722	4.78	8.0
Sidney Crosby	Pit	138	59	458	26.7	12.9	750	5.43	7.9
John Tavares	NYI	189	83	636	24.5	13.1	1087	5.75	7.6
Marian Gaborik	3 Teams	170	64	430	24.6	12.1	859	5.05	7.5
Michael Grabner	NYI	187	48	419	28.6	11.5	657	3.51	7.3
Joe Pavelski	SJ	212	88	624	31.1	14.1	1208	5.70	7.3
Jason Pominville	Buf/Min	211	74	579	34.4	12.8	1025	4.86	7.2
Bobby Ryan	Ana/Ott	198	65	495	29.4	13.1	908	4.59	7.2
Mike Cammalleri	Mtl/Cgy	173	59	468	32.2	12.6	816	4.72	7.2
Marian Hossa	Chi	193	76	606	28.9	12.5	1051	5.45	7.2
Evgeni Malkin	Pit	166	82	629	27.9	13.0	1144	6.89	7.2
Max Pacioretty	Mtl	196	87	719	32.5	12.1	1210	6.17	7.2
Jarome Iginla	3 Teams	204	76	594	30.8	12.8	1065	5.22	7.1
Jeff Carter	CBJ/LA	175	74	573	29.5	12.9	1036	5.92	7.1
Logan Couture	SJ	193	75	629	30.0	11.9	1089	5.64	6.9
James Neal	Pit	179	88	703	30.0	12.5	1275	7.12	6.9
Tomas Tatar	Det	91	23	190	30.6	12.1	336	3.69	6.8
Andrew Ladd	Wpg	208	69	574	29.2	11.8	1005	4.83	6.8
Phil Kessel	Tor	212	94	761	31.7	12.4	1407	6.64	6.7
Alexander Ovechkin	Wsh	204	121	909	35.7	13.3	1818	8.91	6.7
Jamie Benn	Dal	193	72	592	30.2	12.2	1092	5.66	6.6
Tyler Seguin	Bos/Dal	209	82	697	32.5	11.8	1240	5.93	6.6
Pascal Dupuis	Pit	169	52	451	31.5	11.5	799	4.73	6.5
Rick Nash	CBJ/NYR	191	77	740	30.7	10.4	1200	6.28	6.4
Jakub Voracek	Phi	208	63	554	32.3	11.4	1008	4.85	6.3
Kyle Palmieri	Ana	131	28	273	26.2	10.3	464	3.54	6.0
Patrick Sharp	Chi	184	73	683	33.4	10.7	1216	6.61	6.0
Alexander Steen	StL	151	56	474	35.0	11.8	961	6.36	5.8
Jeff Skinner	Car	177	66	643	29.8	10.3	1130	6.38	5.8
Evander Kane	Wpg	185	66	728	31.0	9.1	1290	6.97	5.1

Minimum 20 goals, 1.00 even-strength goals per 60 minutes.

Among the league's top goal scorers, Stamkos is one of only four players to score on at least 10% of his attempted shots, while Ovechkin's 8.91 attempted shots per game is 2.57 more than Stamkos, and indeed 1.79 more than Neal in second place. It's quite interesting to see where on that spectrum the league's other top scorers fall in.

Ovechkin's shots were taken from an average distance of 35.7 feet, the highest on the entire table. Alexander Steen, another player well known for taking shots from anywhere and everywhere, is next at 35.0 feet. These two players are also the only two to have at least half of their attempted shots blocked or miss the net, at 50.0% and 50.7%, respectively. Stamkos had only 44.9% of his shots blocked or sail wide.

In terms of shot distance, Jonathan Toews is the lowest on the list, getting as close as 21.6 feet for his average shot, quite a bit closer than net-crashing Corey Perry, who is in second place at 24.2 feet. It is perhaps no surprise that Toews joins Stamkos as one of the four players to score on over 10% of attempted shots and why only 31.9% of his shots get blocked or sail wide, the lowest on the list by quite some margin.

To the eye, there certainly appear to be all sorts of relationships between shots taken per game (Shot/G), the percentage that are blocked and/or miss the net (Block/Miss), the average shot distance (Avg Dist), and a player's shooting percentage (SH%). Although it's not the topic of this chapter, let's quickly see what they are, at least for this group of top goal scorers.

Correlation Between Shooting Factors, 2011–12 to 2013–14

	Shot/G	Block/Miss	Avg Dist	SH%
Shot/G	1.00	0.19	0.20	-0.48
Block/Miss	0.19	1.00	0.58	0.00
Avg Dist	0.20	0.58	1.00	-0.32
SH%	-0.48	0.00	-0.32	1.00

Interesting! First of all, there's an understandably close relationship between the average distance from which a player shoots and whether the shots are ultimately blocked or sail wide. That makes a great deal of intuitive sense, given that it's harder to aim from a greater distance, which also gives defenders more space to block a shot. That's certainly consistent with what we observed about Ovechkin and Steen.

The next closest relationship is between the number of shots a player takes and their shooting percentage. Basically, the more shots a player takes, the lower his shooting percentage will be. That also makes sense because that greater volume of shots suggests that he is attempting shots from further away, which we have seen, or from more difficult angles.

Of course, that doesn't help determine who is the best goal scorer. Quite frankly, it doesn't matter whether someone peppers the net from anywhere and everywhere, like Ovechkin, or whether they feel it is best to get up close, like Toews. All that matters is who is most effective at getting the puck across the red line, regardless of how they do it. And we already have that answer.

Closing Thoughts

The league's best goal scorer right now is almost certainly Steven Stamkos based on analytics of the past three seasons. Seems obvious? Perhaps, but even an analysis that confirms a result that was already reached by the majority of fans and analysts subjectively still has value.

For example, not only did we demonstrate that Stamkos is the league's best goal scorer, but we also helped reveal why. He scored at the highest rate at even strength over the past three seasons, and by a comfortable margin, and at the fourth highest rate with the man advantage. His usage and his linemates are both relatively typical of a top goal scorer and he has not been padding his stats with empty net goals.

The same argument couldn't be made for Ovechkin, whose even-strength scoring rate is not significantly different from the league's other top goal scorers, despite some of the most favourable playing conditions in the group.

This analysis also gave us an idea of where the league's other top goal scorers rank and who might be coming up from the field. When the day finally comes when Stamkos and Ovechkin's goal scoring dominance begins to fall into question, this analytic approach can help find the new leader, whether that's Corey Perry, Max Pacioretty, or someone entirely unexpected, like Michael Grabner. Until then, Stamkos is number one.

Who is the Best at Drawing Penalties?

By Rob Vollman

Before analytics hit baseball, walks were usually treated with ambivalence, and sometimes with even a little contempt. Even though it was an easy way to get a runner on base, and helped the team score runs and win games in much the same fashion as a base hit, advancing to first by keeping your bat on your shoulder didn't garner the hitter much respect.

Hockey's equivalent of the "base on balls" is probably the drawn penalty. Even though it results in a power play, which results in a goal almost one time out of every five, players seldom get credit for making a meaningful contribution to their teams by being on the receiving end of a dirty hit.

In fact, drawing penalties is so poorly regarded that the NHL doesn't even keep the statistic on its website. The totals need to be mined from individual games logs, where its inclusion is also relatively new, or pulled from sites like *Behind the Net* or *Extra Skater* that do that job for you. Those sites also take the extra step of filtering out offsetting and coincidental minors too, incidentally.

Just as there was an opportunity in baseball to improve a team by finding undervalued players that can consistently draw walks, there's an opportunity to improve a hockey team by finding players who can consistently draw power plays. But how?

In this chapter, we are going to do a little more than find the league's best at drawing penalties. The extent to which this is a persistent ability will be established as well as the net impact the league's top penalty drawers can have. And to answer that second question, we're going to make adjustments for a variety of factors that can influence the ability to draw penalties, such as a player's position, the manpower situation, home ice advantage, score effects, the period of play, and even which team was penalized last—conducting and summarizing some fascinating research along the way. Consequently, the leader board won't actually appear until about a half dozen pages in, but it is well worth the wait!

Finally, once the league's best players at drawing penalties and their overall value have been established, we'll briefly explore the extent to which it is truly possible to build a team around this concept, much like some baseball teams have been built on walks. Let's begin!

Penalty Drawing Leaders

The idea of counting drawn penalties first gained widespread attention in the analytic community in 2008, when Gabriel Desjardins made the data readily available on *Behind the Net*. This was two years after pioneering bloggers like Toronto's Chris Young[92], the folks at

---

92 Chris Young, "Leafs Penalties", *The Toronto Star*, Web, November, 2006,
    http://thestar.blogs.com/jabs/2006/11/leafs_penalties.html.

Thrasher's Talons, and Desjardins himself were adding them up by hand, team-by-team[93].

My own experience with drawn penalties began back in the summer 2004, in a Yahoo Group Iain Fyffe had organized called the Hockey Analysis Group (HAG). At the time, it was the only meeting place for what few of us existed, and one of my first questions to the group was to ask for data on drawn penalties. Back then the only known source was the expanded game files on *ESPN*—there was nothing official from the NHL.

Fast forward to today, where the raw numbers are readily available. It comes as no surprise that the captain of the Los Angeles Kings, Dustin Brown, leads the league with 105 drawn penalties over the past three seasons combined. That's 23 more than Philadelphia's Claude Giroux in second place. Jeff Skinner, Evgeni Malkin, Nazem Kadri, T.J. Oshie, and Corey Perry are the only other players over 70.

However, it should be noted that Malkin and Perry have taken a lot of penalties of their own, 57 and 60 respectively, and Brown himself has taken 48. What good is the ability to draw penalties if that same style of play leads to taking more penalties of your own? After all, who is the better penalty drawer, someone who draws 100 penalties but takes 90, or someone who draws only 20 penalties but takes none of his own?

For purposes of this study, let's assume it's the latter, which is why we'll be looking at each player's net penalty differential, which is a player's penalties drawn minus those they've taken themselves. This metric shrinks Brown's lead over the rest of the league considerably. Brown is +57, Skinner +52, and Kadri +50 over the past three years, with Giroux, Matt Duchene, Martin St. Louis, Darren Helm, and John Tavares the only other NHLers who drew at least 40 more penalties than they took themselves.

Where are the Defencemen?

One thing that immediately jumps out is the lack of defencemen among the league leaders. The blueliner with the best penalty differential over the past three seasons is Florida's Brian Campbell, whose modest +17 is tied for 56th overall. Jared Spurgeon, Mike Weaver, Marc-Edouard Vlasic, Dan Hamhuis, Ryan Ellis, Oliver Ekman-Larsson, and Jamie McBain are the only others who are at least +10.

Clearly, defencemen are at a bit of a disadvantage here, much as Bruce McCurdy identified back in 2010[94]. He found that forwards tend to draw 0.12 more penalties than they take for every 60 minutes played, while defencemen take 0.32 more penalties than they draw.

This gap makes perfect sense when you think about it. Given that their job is to get the puck away from forwards and prevent them from scoring any way that they can, it stands to reason

93 Matt (syzerman98), "October: Who drew penalties and who took them", *Thrasher's Talons*, Web, November 3, 2006, http://thrasherstalons.blogspot.com/2006/11/october-who-drew-penalties-and-who.html.
94 Bruce McCurdy, "The Black Art Of Drawing Penalties", *Copper and Blue*, Web, December 6, 2010, http://www.coppernblue.com/2010/12/6/1859996/the-art-of-drawing-penalties.

that defencemen would take a lot more penalties than they draw. This should be especially true for the more defensive-minded options, relative to puck-moving defencemen like Campbell, which is why the list of leaders is a little unusual. Weaver, Vlasic and Hamhuis, for example, are more defensive-minded. Shouldn't we expect to see more puck-movers, such as perhaps Erik Karlsson and P.K. Subban instead? After all, those who are more frequently carrying the puck should be drawing the most penalties, not those primarily tasked with taking it away.

The problem is that there are two sides to the equation here: penalties drawn and penalties taken. Even if they drew the most penalties, puck-moving defencemen who take too many penalties of their own are going to rank behind the more disciplined defensive options. Indeed, P.K. Subban has drawn more penalties than any other defencemen over the past three seasons, with 61, ahead of Ekman-Larsson at 51, with Karlsson, Alexei Emelin, and Kevin Bieksa as the only others over 40, but has also taken a whopping 82 penalties of his own, twice as many as Ekman-Larsson and Karlsson.

Drawn penalties could be an interesting way of determining which defencemen are frequently carrying the puck up the ice but it won't necessarily lead us to a list of those who are most helpful to their teams in terms of net penalties. For defencemen, the key to a good penalty differential is having good discipline of one's own, rather than drawing infractions from others. That's as true for puck-moving defencemen like Campbell and Ekman-Larsson as it is for shutdown options like Hamhuis, Vlasic, and Weaver.

The Effect of Manpower Situation

McCurdy's aforementioned study was in even-strength situations only because the game changes when a team is working a power play or killing penalties. For example, defencemen actually draw more penalties than they take when working with a man advantage, while forwards actually end those power plays (with a penalty of their own) more frequently than they extend them.

I completed a study in *Hockey Prospectus 2013–14*[95] that looked at the effect of manpower situation and position on penalties drawn and taken, per 60 minutes. Here are the results, updated with data from the past three seasons combined.

Penalty Drawing/Taking Rate by Manpower and Position, 2011–12 to 2013–14

Player	Drawn/60	Taken/60	Diff/60
Defencemen 5v4	0.383	0.223	0.160
Forwards 5v5	0.761	0.657	0.104
Forwards 4v5	0.291	0.222	0.068
Forwards 5v4	0.277	0.383	-0.106
Defencemen 4v5	0.066	0.255	-0.189
Defencemen 5v5	0.329	0.617	-0.288

95 Rob Vollman, "Los Angeles Kings", *Hockey Prospectus 2013–14*, August 2014, pg 167–169.
96 Acknowledgement: Raw data on penalty information from *Behind the Net* http://www.behindthenet.ca.

Forwards actually take more penalties per 60 minutes than defencemen at even strength, by a narrow 0.657 to 0.617 margin, but they also draw over twice as many, 0.761 to 0.329 respectively, for reasons we just explored. That means that a forward is expected to create 0.104 extra power plays per 60 minutes of hockey, whereas defencemen give their teams an extra 0.288 penalties to kill over the same length of ice time.

The situation practically reverses itself on the power play, where defencemen draw slightly more penalties than they do at even strength (0.383), but take very few (0.223), thanks to the drastically reduced defensive obligations. The resulting difference of an extra 0.16 power plays per 60 minutes is the largest advantage of any position and manpower situation. And, given that the defenceman is already on the power play, those extra power plays actually result in two-man advantages!

Of course, often a forward will work the point on a power play, so that might skew the numbers somewhat. In general, the rate at which forwards draw and take penalties goes down significantly with the man advantage, but to a far greater extent in the former case. Indeed, the second hardest situation in which to draw a penalty is as a forward working the power play. Why? That's quite a bit harder to determine, but no doubt the defending penalty killers are playing far more carefully.

The most difficult situation in which to draw a penalty is actually as a defencemen while killing a penalty. In fact, it appears to be darn near impossible! Forwards draw penalties at roughly the same rate on the power play as they do shorthanded, but take more of their own on the power play. Defencemen actually take slightly fewer of their own shorthanded, digging their teams into a deeper hole. D-oh!

If the numbers don't add up exactly, remember that not all penalties are drawn by an opposing player, like delay of games penalties for shooting the puck over the glass, for example. That also helps explain why defencemen take more penalties, especially while shorthanded.

What About Score Effects?

Teams protecting big or late leads change their style, which can affect everything from shots to hits, so it makes a lot of sense that it affects penalties, too.

Analytic blogger Tore Purdy, who was known better by his handle JLikens, studied the score effects on minor penalties back in 2010[97]. Looking at all minor penalties that resulted in a power play in the 2008–09 and 2009–10 seasons, he found that teams that were trailing enjoyed a boost in their drawn penalties of about four or five percent, which is comparable to the one we've established in shots and goals (see the chapter on Score Effects).

---

97 JLikens, "Score Effects and Minor Penalties", *Objective NHL*, Web, November 3, 2010,
    http://objectivenhl.blogspot.ca/2010/11/score-effects-and-minor-penalties.html.

Not only did Phil Birnbaum[98] confirm that with a study of his own two years later, but he also discovered that the effect increased with the size of the lead and declined with every passing period. There certainly appear to be many overlapping factors at play.

At first, it appears counter-intuitive that the team in the lead would take (and/or risk) more penalties, but this result actually makes perfect sense when you think about it. Since we already know that a team that's trailing is more likely to have the puck than they would in close game situations (because the other team is hanging back), it stands to reason that they would draw more penalties and/or take fewer of their own.

Therefore, it also stands to reason that really bad teams who are often trailing, should have better penalty differentials as a group, all else being equal. And indeed, the all-time leader in team penalty differential (first recorded in 1964) is the 1976–77 Minnesota North Stars. They enjoyed 128 more power plays than their opponents (in 80 games), but managed just two more power-play goals. That team appears twice more in the top ten, joined by other awful teams from the same era, like the Washington Capitals, the California Golden Seals, and the Kansas City Scouts. That's even more evidence that teams that are frequently trailing tend to get a few more power plays.

This finding means that players on weaker teams should have slightly better net penalty differentials since they're often trailing. While that wouldn't help Dustin Brown of the Los Angeles Kings, it might be helping Toronto's Nazem Kadri or Carolina's Jeff Skinner.

It also means that studying a player's totals exclusively in close game situations will likely results in a more accurate read of his true penalty drawing abilities. In fact, could considering road games only improve this accuracy even further?

How Great is the Home Team Advantage?

It's a commonly held belief that the home team gets a few more power plays than the visiting team, on average. This conviction has a great deal of basis in fact, and I know of at least half a dozen studies that have confirmed it and none that have disproved it. Therefore, the question is not whether the advantage exists, but how significant it is.

It was initially established that the home team enjoyed 11.5% more power plays than their opponents, based on a 2009 study by Vancouver researcher Will Lockwood and the Edmonton Journal[99]. While that number surprised the referees, coaches, and players who were interviewed, it was soon backed up by a careful study completed months later by Jack

98 Phil Birnbaum, "Do NHL referees call make up penalties? Part II", *Sabermetric Research*, January 3, 2012, Web, http://blog.philbirnbaum.com/2012/01/do-nhl-referees-call-make-up-penalties.html.

99 Curtis Stock, "Study reveals referees' home bias", *Edmonton Journal*, March 2, 2009, http://www.edmontonjournal.com/sports/hockey/edmonton-oilers/Study+reveals+referees+home+bias/1343770/story.html.

Brimberg and William J. Hurley[100]. Using 2008–09 data, and accounting for score effects, they found that the home team enjoys 52.5% of a game's power plays, which works out to 10.5% more than the visiting team. And that's not even the highest estimate, a distinction currently owned by the controversial book *Scorecasting*[101], which contended that home teams actually enjoy up to 20% more power plays than the visiting team.

In fact, these studies suggested that not only should score effects and home team bias be controlled for, but potentially for the period too. Why? Because penalties go down as the game progresses, either because teams are taking fewer risks or because officials are more reluctant to call a game-deciding penalty. Either way, drawing penalties gets more difficult as the game goes on.

All of this suggests that we should complete our study by looking only at close game situations in the first period of road games. That wouldn't leave us much data to go on! Besides, I imagine I'm losing the patience of most readers who want to finally get on with it, and find out if Brown really is the best or not. Therefore, I intend to proceed without making these particular adjustments, a complexity-reducing decision for which I hope I'm forgiven, but they should all be kept in mind when reviewing the upcoming results.

Net Penalty Differential

Ok, let's get down to business and figure out who the league's best penalty drawers are. And shame on anyone who just skipped over all the analysis!

It was in *Hockey Prospectus 2013–14*[102] that the following method was first introduced, to measure a player's ability to draw penalties in a way that takes opportunity into account. The Net Penalty Differential (NPD) is calculated in such a way as to remove the advantage given to power-play quarterbacks and also the bias against more defensive-minded defencemen. Here's how it works:

1. Count up a player's penalty differential as normal, penalties drawn minus those taken.
2. Calculate his **expected penalty differential** at even strength by multiplying his even-strength ice time by the appropriate figure in the table three pages above (which will be different for forwards and defencemen).
3. Repeat step two for the power play and the penalty kill, and add all three results together.
4. Subtract the result of step 3 from the total in step 1. That is the player's NPD, the difference between the player's actual penalty differential and what a league average NHLer of the same position would have done with the exact same ice time.

100 Jack Brimberg and William J. Hurley, "Are National Hockey League referees Markov?", *OR Insight* volume 22, December 2009, pg 234–243, available online http://www.palgrave-journals.com/ori/journal/v22/n4/full/ori200912a.html.
101 Tobias J. Moskowitz and L. Jon Wertheim, *Scorecasting: The Hidden Influences Behind How Sports Are Played and Games Are Won,* pg 157.
102 Rob Vollman, "Los Angeles Kings", *Hockey Prospectus 2013–14*, August 2014, pg 167–169.

The table below features the top penalty drawers of the past three seasons, based on their NPD per 82 games (NPD/82). For reference, it also includes their total penalties drawn (PenD) and taken (PenT), and the raw difference (Diff).

Normally, these players would be ranked by their NPD per 60 minutes instead of 82 games, but doing it that way would once again bias it towards forwards, who play fewer minutes than defencemen, an effect that would be even more significant for those assigned bottom-six minutes. Ranking the players by 82 games better represents what each player can achieve over a full season in their current role, with the understanding that this would change if they were moved up or down the depth chart, or if they got more or less time on special teams.

Top 50 Penalty Drawers 2011–12 to 2013–14[103]

Player	Team(s)	GP	PenD	PenT	Diff	NPD	NPD/82
Darren Helm	Det	111	51	10	41	38.5	28.5
Nazem Kadri	Tor	147	76	26	50	47.1	26.3
Jeff Skinner	Car	177	79	27	52	48.5	22.5
Dustin Brown	LA	207	105	48	57	52.7	20.9
Matt Duchene	Col	176	57	12	45	41.2	19.2
Nathan MacKinnon	Col	82	26	7	19	17.3	17.3
Claude Giroux	Phi	207	82	36	46	41.6	16.5
Cory Conacher	3 Teams	126	51	25	26	23.9	15.5
John Tavares	NYI	189	68	28	40	35.7	15.5
Jonathan Huberdeau	Fla	117	39	15	24	21.7	15.2
Martin St. Louis	TB/NYR	206	55	12	43	38.0	15.1
Mark Scheifele	Wpg	74	20	5	15	13.5	15.0
Valeri Nichushkin	Dal	79	19	3	16	14.4	14.9
T.J. Oshie	StL	189	74	36	38	33.8	14.7
Pavel Datsyuk	Det	162	44	12	62	28.5	14.4
Brian Campbell	Fla	212	31	14	17	36.4	14.1
Vladimir Tarasenko	StL	102	30	11	19	17.1	13.8
Jared Spurgeon	Min	176	25	10	15	29.0	13.5
Rick Nash	CBJ/NYR	191	67	32	35	31.1	13.3
Marcus Johansson	Wsh	194	40	5	35	31.2	13.2
Boone Jenner	CBJ	72	28	15	13	11.5	13.1
Patric Hornqvist	Nsh	176	50	19	31	27.8	12.9
Mike Weaver	Fla/Mtl	181	32	19	13	28.4	12.9
Marc-Edouard Vlasic	SJ	211	30	17	13	32.3	12.6
Zach Parise	NJ/Min	197	67	33	34	29.5	12.3
Mats Zuccarello	NYR	102	31	14	17	15.1	12.2
Patrick Kaleta	Buf	102	35	18	17	15.0	12.1
Kris Letang	Pit	123	24	16	8	18.0	12.0
Dmitry Orlov	Wsh	119	15	7	8	17.4	12.0
Richard Panik	TB	75	19	7	12	10.7	11.7
Dan Hamhuis	Van	208	33	22	11	29.5	11.6
Erik Karlsson	Ott	180	42	33	9	25.0	11.4

[103]Acknowledgement: All raw penalty data for my calculations came from *Behind the Net*: http://www.behindthenet.ca.

Ryan Callahan	NYR/TB	186	59	29	30	25.8	11.4
John-Michael Liles	Tor/Car	139	20	11	9	19.2	11.3
Brandon Saad	Chi	126	33	13	20	17.4	11.3
Ryan Ellis	Nsh	144	27	16	11	19.7	11.2
Jason Pominville	Buf/Min	211	49	16	33	28.7	11.2
Ryan O'Reilly	Col	190	34	4	30	25.6	11.0
Jake Gardiner	Tor	167	21	12	9	22.4	11.0
Zemgus Girgensons	Buf	70	17	6	11	9.3	10.9
Teemu Selanne	Ana	192	47	18	29	25.6	10.9
Kevin Klein	Nsh/NYR	190	14	5	9	25.0	10.8
Oliver Ekman-Larsson	Phx	210	51	41	10	27.6	10.8
T.J. Brodie	Cgy	182	26	17	9	23.8	10.7
Patrick Dwyer	Car	194	43	13	30	25.4	10.7
Colin McDonald	NYI	120	30	12	18	15.7	10.7
Chris Tanev	Van	127	14	8	6	16.5	10.6
Gustav Nyquist	Det	97	20	6	14	12.4	10.5
John Carlson	Wsh	212	31	22	9	26.9	10.4
Jamie McBain	Car/Buf	185	19	9	10	23.5	10.4

Minimum 70 Games

Notice how Brown fell from a commanding lead to a narrow one when his own penalties were taken into account, and now he slides all the way down to fourth, when games played and ice time are factored in as well. Still, Brown is worth an extra 20.9 power plays per 82-game season, relative to an average NHL forward assigned the same ice time, or about one extra power play every four games. That's not bad at all!

Is there anyone better than Brown? Darren Helm achieves more on a per-game basis, as do Nazem Kadri and Jeff Skinner, especially when you adjust for all their time with the man advantage. Brown managed to maintain his lead over Claude Giroux, who was passed by Colorado's speedy youngsters Matt Duchene and Nathan MacKinnon. As for defencemen, Brian Campbell edges out Jared Spurgeon for the lead, 14.1 to 13.5, with defensive specialists Mike Weaver and Marc-Edouard Vlasic not far behind.

Anatomy of a Penalty Drawer

How do these players do it? How can we identify a player who is going to be effective at drawing penalties? And is it predictable year to year?

Among forwards, the league's best penalty drawers apparently come in several different shapes and sizes. There are tiny guys that might get knocked over a little easier, like Cory Conacher and Martin St. Louis, big guys that park themselves in front of the net and draw abuse, like Corey Perry, Zach Parise and Rick Nash, speedy players who fight through checks and/or catch opponents out of position, like Matt Duchene and Darren Helm, and of course there are those with unfortunate reputations for diving and embellishing, who I'll try to resist the urge to identify!

DIVING

As for Brown, besides being in the last category (according to former official Kerry Fraser[104]), he's also generally among the league leaders in hits. However, I found only a small correlation between throwing hits and drawing penalties in my aforementioned *Hockey Prospectus 2013–14* study, so that does not appear to be a reliable way to identify them.

Although it would appear that the best place to find great penalty-drawing masters is among those players with the most overall skill, Eric Tulsky[105] surprisingly found very little correlation there either. Estimating a player's overall skill based on his average ice time at even strength, he found virtually no relationship between it and how many penalties a player draws. However, he did find a relationship between that player's skill and how many penalties a player takes himself. Since that constitutes half of the NPD equation, it makes sense that we'd find so many skilled and disciplined players on our leader board.

And how reliably can penalty drawing be predicted? Another piece of good news from Tulsky's study is that even though it can be hard to separate random noise from a consistent ability with so few data points, he did indeed find a strong year-to-year correlation in drawing penalties. That means that we can believe with reasonable confidence that the majority of the players on our three-year leader board will remain there in the coming seasons.

To sum this all up, we know who these players are, we know what they can do, and we know

104 Kerry Fraser, "How to Deal With Players Who Dive to Draw Penalties", *TSN*, May 18, 2012, Web, http://www.tsn.ca/nhl/story/?id=396253.
105 Eric Tulsky, "Hidden value: Penalty differential", *Broad Street Hockey*, July 11, 2013, Web, http://www.broadstreethockey.com/2013/7/11/4504236/hidden-value-penalty-differential.

how many extra power plays they can produce. Furthermore, the value of these players isn't just limited to the additional four or five power play goals the team will score every year. The power plays generated by players like Brown, Helm, Kadri, and Skinner can also kill the clock, change the game's momentum, tire out opposing penalty killers and/or their goalie, can get a key player off the ice, affect the crowds, and so much more. Drawing penalties is a woefully undervalued talent when you consider the full impact these players can have.

Can a Team be Built Around Drawing Penalties?

Increasing the net penalty differential seems like an easy way to improve a team, especially via an increase in a team's scoring. Looking quickly at the 10 teams with the biggest annual increase in power play opportunities recently finds an increase from 2.72 to 2.90 goals per game, or about 15 goals over a whole season. Applying hockey 3-1-1 rule, a team that can significantly improve their net penalty differential can add up to five points in the standings.

However, there could be an artificially imposed upper limit on just how much a team can be improved with the addition of master penalty drawers. Tom Awad made the point way back in 2004 on HAG[106], when he first identified the relationship between drawing and taking penalties. Whether it's due to an individual team's style of play, or whether officials are reluctant to give one side too strong an edge in any given game, a team that draws a lot of penalties take quite a few more too—and vice versa. So, the benefit of adding several players who can draw penalties may decrease as they accumulate.

How significant is this relationship? Awad initially found that "for each extra penalty taken, you draw an extra 0.288 penalties" and that "11% of penalties drawn can be explained by penalties taken."

Of course, this was at the team level using pre-lockout data (albeit 16 seasons worth) and things may have changed recently. However, a team's tendency to take a penalty after drawing one has persisted into the post-lockout era too. The more recent and aforementioned 2009 study by Brimberg and Hurley found what they referred to as an "even-up bias." That is, they found that the team that took the most recent penalty is slightly less likely to take the next one.

Phil Birnbaum[107] confirmed this alleged bias a couple of years later, discovering that only 40.3% of penalties went to whichever team was penalized most recently. He went on to discover that the longer the interval is between penalties, the closer to 50% that number gradually becomes. In other words, the bias fades away over time.

Birnbaum also introduced the concept of the "compassionate referee". He found that the chance of getting the power play increases if one's opponents scored a goal on their last man

106 Tom Awad, "Penalty Drawing", Hockey Analysis Group (msg 477), Web, November 2, 2004, https://groups.yahoo.com/neo/groups/HAG_list/conversations/messages/477.
107 Phil Birnbaum, "Do NHL referees call make up penalties?", *Sabermetric Research*, December 31, 2011, Web, http://blog.philbirnbaum.com/2011/12/do-nhl-referees-call-make-up-penalties.html.

advantage, and decreases if a shorthanded goal was scored instead. These are trends that fans have discovered anecdotally from watching the games, and uncovering the validity of such observations is one of the most compelling aspects of modern hockey analytics.

In my view, the definitive study on this topic is a paper published by Michael J. Lopez and Kevin Snyder in 2013[108], which established these trends beyond any statistical doubt. They also found that the tendency to even up those calls increased with the importance of the game and was slanted more strongly towards the home team.

REFEREE'S CELL PHONE

In an effort to avoid too much controversy, it is possible that all of this can be chalked up to a significant shift in a team's playing style after killing off a penalty, but it's far more likely a result of an official's conscious or subconscious desire to keep things even. Whatever the cause, suffice it to say that there's a mountain of research that demonstrates the diminishing returns of drawing penalties. While adding a few players who can draw penalties can give a team an edge, an entire team of such players would eventually wind up giving the opponents almost as many power plays as were gained.

Closing Thoughts

So who is the league's best at drawing penalties? The safest answer is Dustin Brown, and

---

108Michael J. Lopez and Kevin Snyder, "Biased Impartiality Among National Hockey League Referees", *International Journal of Sport Finance*, 2013, Volume 8, pg 208–223.

there's certainly nothing wrong with that default choice. Using NPD to adjust for a player's opportunities can also build a case for any of Darren Helm, Nazem Kadri, or Jeff Skinner.

To be completely thorough, an analysis would need to account for home team bias, the period of the game, the score, who got the last penalty, and a number of other factors. Such adjustments might wind up jostling the decimal point for a few players, but I doubt it would appreciably change the order of the NPD leader board. While that hardly makes it worth all the added complexity, it is something to keep in mind.

Now that we have demonstrated that this is a significant and repeatable skill, and can easily identify the players to target, can a team be built around this concept? Absolutely, but at a certain point the advantage would start to diminish, for a number of reasons, and the team would start occasionally taking a few more penalties of its own for the additional ones drawn. This makes it wise to have a few such players to push a team in the right direction, but makes it a little more difficult to have a particularly dramatic effect overall.

Who is the Best Penalty Killer?

By Rob Vollman

Can hockey analytics help identify the league's best penalty killer? Given all the factors that go into successfully killing penalties, many of which are outside the control of any one player, it is certainly a very difficult question.

The league's best penalty killer, whomever he may be, has no control over the calibre of power play specialist he faces, for example, nor the quality of his teammates, or what percentage of shots his goalie stops. Furthermore, some teams don't even use their best penalty killers on the top units, especially among forwards, either because his talent is more urgently needed at even strength, or because there are other reasonable penalty-killing options. That makes an already difficult task even harder. Is there an analytic process that can sort this all out?

Although analytics are never intended to provide a truly definitive answer, its use is particularly limited in areas like this. But that's no reason not to try! Although finding the league's best penalty killer may be beyond the reach of analytics at the moment, someday it will not be. That's why it's important to take this first step to move the discussion forward, much as we did last year when using analytics to identify the league's best coaches.

What's the strategy? Well, if we attack this problem from as many different angles as possible, while being clear on the strengths and limitations of each one, we should still be able to build a solid foundation and find some preliminary answers, even with a question as difficult as this. Let's begin!

The Subjective Opinion

Before diving into something new, I like to establish a target. As a colleague of mine once told me, "the best way to get nowhere is to have no idea where you're going before hitting the gas." I couldn't agree more, which is why I want to put together a list of great penalty killers before we even begin.

Whenever a new, objective system is developed, there has to be a way to test the results. Not just statistically, but also for common sense. This is often called the "sniff test." For example, whenever Iain Fyffe developed a new defensive metric, he used to look for Jere Lehtinen among the leader board. If he wasn't among them, then he knew he had some more work to do.

It's amazing how quickly a statistic's acceptance, and even the creator's entire reputation, can be torpedoed by publishing nonsensical results. That's partly why analysts, like Fyffe, use subjectively chosen players as a signal for things that might have been missed.

It's also important for analysts to choose the players who will be used for this sniff test *before* seeing the results of the newly-designed system. Otherwise, they may be biased towards those players that they know scored well and against those who didn't.

There will always be fans who criticize the selected players, obviously. When fans are surprised by the absence of their favourite players and teams in the results, it's natural for them to accuse the analyst of devising a system that will deliberately lead to the designer's desired outcome. For example, one might have accused Fyffe of designing a system in such a way that his favourite defensive player, Lehtinen, will be number one.

In practice, though, this is never the case. To deliberately design a system to favour one team or player over another would take enormous ingenuity and effort on the designer's part. More importantly, however, it would completely fail to achieve the more ambitious goal, which in this case is to find the league's best penalty killer.

With all of that in mind, and please forgive that long preamble, which players should we expect to show up prominently in our results, once this system is designed?

- Last year, the Hockey News[109] named **Jay McClement** as the winner of the Guy Carbonneau Award for the league's top penalty killer, the same player voted first by the NHL Hot Stove back in 2010[110].
- Two separate 2011 fan discussions on Hockey's Future discussion board[111][112] identified the league's best penalty killers as **Mike Richards** and **Henrik Zetterberg** up front, and **Hal Gill** on defence.
- More recently, Thomas Drance of the Score[113] identified **Sean Couturier** as the league's best penalty-killing forward.
- **Zdeno Chara**, **Jordan Staal**, and **Ryan Kesler** all appeared repeatedly in each of these lists as well.

Of course, the mainstream consensus isn't always an accurate reflection of a player's true abilities, but it is often close enough to serve our purposes of highlighting anything that is seriously askew with the results produced by the new system. While it's not exactly the list of players I would have chosen, these eight players appear reasonable enough to me.

One last thing, not only should we expect to see each of these players featured prominently in our results, but it's also reasonable to expect to find the top shorthanded options among the league's better penalty-killing teams. Over the past three seasons, that would include New Jersey (85.7% penally killing percentage), St. Louis (85.4%), Boston (84.8%), Montreal

109 Greg Wyshynski, "THN/Yahoo! NHL Awards: Toughest player, best penalty killer, best fighter", *The Hockey News*, Web, May 17, 2013, http://www.thehockeynews.com/articles/51978-THNYahoo-NHL-Awards-Toughest-player-best-penalty-killer-best-fighter.html.

110 Alexander Monaghan, "Top 10 penalty killing forwards in the league", *NHL Hot Stove*, Web, September 7, 2010, http://nhlhotstove.com/top-10-penalty-killing-forwards-in-the-league/.

111 Discussion Board, "The best penalty killers in the NHL", *Hockey's Future*, Web, November 12, 2011, http://hfboards.hockeysfuture.com/showthread.php?t=1052515.

112 Discussion Board, "Who is the best penalty killer in the NHL?", *Hockey's Future*, Web, February 27, 2011, http://hfboards.hockeysfuture.com/showthread.php?t=883673.

113 Thomas Drance, "The NHL's best penalty-killing forwards this season", *The Score*, Web, January 8, 2014, http://beta.thescore.com/nhl/news/402290.

(84.5%), Los Angeles (84.4%), Vancouver (84.4%), New York Rangers (84.2%), Pittsburgh (84.2%), and Philadelphia (84.2%). Likewise, it should be a surprise to see anyone from Florida (76.5%), New York Islanders (79.6%), Nashville (79.8%), or Carolina (80.0%). It's theoretically possible that several of the league's best penalty killers are on bad teams, but such a result would appear awfully suspicious to me.

Penalty-Killing Defencemen

Let's start with defencemen, the most important two players in a four-man penalty-killing unit. They stand closest to the net and are responsible for clearing out the crease, sweeping away rebounds, removing screens, battling in the corners, preventing cross-ice passes, and keeping the shots to the outside. There are also only six defencemen on the bench from which to choose (five, if the penalized player is a defencemen), as opposed to 12 for the forwards.

Therefore, it stands to reason that the league's best penalty killer is probably a defenceman and is probably leaned on heavily by his team. That's why a good place to start is a hunt for which players spend the most time killing penalties.

Comparing each player's ice time in absolute terms will favour players on highly-penalized teams, so instead they'll be ranked by their share of all of their team's available shorthanded minutes. So, if a player kills four minutes of penalties in a game where they were shorthanded for a total of eight minutes, then that means he had a 50% share of the penalty-killing duties.

This approach isn't foolproof, of course. It's certainly possible that a mediocre penalty killer will get a lot of ice time for any number of reasons, like if he's on a team without any better options (or a bad coach), for instance. It's also possible that the league's best penalty killer will get less ice time than others if he happens to be on a team with other great penalty killers among the remaining five. This is especially true if he's also equally valuable in other manpower situations and being saved for use in those.

With those limitations in mind, the following table lists those top 100 penalty-killing defencemen over the past three seasons by their share of the team's shorthanded minutes (PK%), and also includes a few statistics we'll be looking at momentarily, such as how many goals (GA/60) and attempted shots (AS/60) were taken against them (per 60 minutes), along with how well their teams did in those regards without them.

Top 100 Most Used Penalty-Killing Defencemen, 2011–12 to 2013–14[114]

Player	Team(s)	GP	GA/60	Team	AS/60	Team	PK%
Francois Beauchemin	Ana	200	6.59	5.68	99.6	94.9	64.5
Dan Girardi	NYR	209	5.96	4.50	100.5	80.6	61.4
Bryce Salvador	NJ	161	4.10	4.88	85.9	74.2	61.3
Zbynek Michalek	Pit/Phx	155	4.96	6.10	89.3	93.5	60.0

114Acknowledgement: All raw penalty-killing data for my calculations came from *Behind the Net*: http://www.behindthenet.ca.

Brooks Orpik	Pit	191	5.38	5.88	93.0	85.5	58.7
Jay Bouwmeester	Cgy/StL	211	5.77	4.30	91.8	86.1	58.3
Mike Weaver	Fla/Mtl	181	7.32	7.37	91.2	96.9	58.1
Josh Gorges	Mtl	196	4.93	5.31	89.4	86.8	58.1
Anton Volchenkov	NJ	165	4.75	4.13	86.9	70.9	57.9
Ryan McDonagh	NYR	206	5.92	4.61	97.8	86.5	56.9
Hal Gill	Mtl/Nsh/Phi	114	4.80	4.41	93.6	87.5	56.7
Braydon Coburn	Phi	196	6.21	4.51	89.6	74.9	55.9
Zdeno Chara	Bos	204	5.72	4.51	89.0	83.2	55.3
John Carlson	Wsh	212	7.24	5.56	111.3	102.1	55.1
Alex Pietrangelo	StL	209	4.99	4.85	87.9	84.2	55.0
Travis Hamonic	NYI	190	7.89	6.15	102.6	86.9	53.5
Karl Alzner	Wsh	212	6.57	6.40	112.0	101.8	53.4
Brad Stuart	Det/SJ	190	6.53	5.07	98.1	88.4	53.3
Niklas Hjalmarsson	Chi	196	6.41	5.94	94.7	97.9	53.3
Dion Phaneuf	Tor	210	6.53	6.12	102.9	94.8	52.8
Willie Mitchell	LA	152	5.59	4.49	96.5	87.6	52.4
Jan Hejda	CBJ	205	4.95	6.43	99.8	92.0	52.2
Paul Martin	Pit	146	5.39	4.74	84.9	86.9	52.2
Carl Gunnarsson	Tor	193	6.36	6.15	102.7	95.8	52.1
Kimmo Timonen	Phi	198	5.82	5.04	87.6	79.3	51.9
Mark Stuart	Wpg	191	8.18	5.06	104.0	82.7	51.7
Dan Hamhuis	Nsh/Van	208	5.20	5.19	86.5	83.6	51.5
Filip Kuba	Ott/Fla	117	5.00	8.18	94.8	84.7	51.3
Ron Hainsey	Wpg/Car	185	6.73	6.87	92.2	88.0	50.5
Niklas Kronwall	Det	209	5.73	6.81	92.6	91.7	50.5
Mark Giordano	Cgy	172	5.33	6.88	94.1	97.1	50.4
Andy Greene	NJ	186	5.29	3.77	76.9	84.4	50.3
Fedor Tyutin	CBJ	183	6.22	7.50	93.4	85.4	50.1
Toni Lydman	Ana	109	6.97	5.96	100.0	91.1	50.1
Barret Jackman	StL	206	5.30	4.61	86.8	86.3	49.6
Chris Phillips	Ott	198	6.84	5.17	91.1	85.1	49.4
Jeff Petry	Edm	201	5.95	5.78	98.8	97.9	49.2
Stephane Robidas	Dal/Ana	161	5.53	6.52	102.6	103.4	49.0
Ladislav Smid	Edm/Cgy	199	6.39	5.40	96.1	92.8	49.0
Rob Scuderi	LA/Pit	183	6.12	4.12	96.0	93.1	49.0
Shea Weber	Nsh	205	6.48	7.71	98.5	100.3	49.0
Robyn Regehr	Buf/LA	196	7.17	5.42	101.4	88.7	48.9
Dennis Seidenberg	Bos	160	5.66	3.97	92.3	78.7	48.8
Tim Gleason	Car/Tor	180	7.83	6.83	107.6	93.5	48.5
Andrew MacDonald	NYI/Phi	205	7.99	5.70	102.3	86.8	48.3
Jared Cowen	Ott	157	6.13	6.59	92.5	87.2	48.3
Justin Faulk	Car	180	7.65	6.41	100.4	89.6	48.2
Scott Hannan	Cgy/Nsh/SJ	167	6.37	4.74	92.8	98.5	48.1
Duncan Keith	Chi	200	5.64	5.93	100.3	91.7	48.0
Chris Butler	Cgy	194	5.39	6.03	94.3	94.2	47.8
Eric Brewer	TB	207	7.10	6.28	101.1	101.7	47.7

Marc-Edouard Vlasic	SJ	211	5.63	6.68	95.4	97.5	47.4
Johnny Boychuk	Bos	196	5.32	5.01	90.3	84.8	47.4
Matt Greene	LA	125	6.25	4.90	92.3	93.3	46.9
Jonathan Ericsson	Det	162	5.46	6.48	88.4	90.8	46.8
Rostislav Klesla	Phx	128	5.10	6.20	107.5	98.2	46.8
Ryan Suter	Nsh/Min	209	6.41	6.87	93.9	91.1	46.3
Victor Hedman	TB	180	7.39	6.14	104.8	96.2	46.3
Ryan O'Byrne	Col/Tor	116	5.81	5.79	91.1	93.4	46.0
Douglas Murray	SJ/Pit/Mtl	156	6.45	5.35	100.9	91.7	46.0
Brenden Dillon	Dal	129	6.53	6.62	105.9	101.3	45.5
Brent Seabrook	Chi	207	5.80	6.26	98.4	95.3	45.3
Marc Methot	CBJ/Ott	168	7.04	6.03	87.7	84.7	45.2
Jonas Brodin	Min	124	7.13	7.01	91.6	78.9	44.6
Eric Gryba	Ott	90	4.88	6.32	82.8	90.3	44.2
Trevor Daley	Dal	190	6.88	5.88	106.4	97.8	44.2
Oliver Ekman-Larsson	Phx	210	6.85	6.00	98.3	103.3	44.1
Kevin Klein	Nsh/NYR	190	6.60	5.61	98.2	96.9	43.7
Bryan Allen	Car/Ana	191	6.99	6.28	101.8	99.7	43.6
Jack Johnson	LA/CBJ	208	6.88	5.00	97.5	88.4	43.4
Marc Staal	NYR	139	4.21	5.89	80.8	97.5	43.1
Johnny Oduya	Wpg/Chi	206	5.51	5.97	86.7	102.0	42.8
Zach Bogosian	Wpg	153	6.74	5.26	99.7	92.9	42.7
Andrew Ference	Bos/Edm	191	4.98	4.93	94.1	92.0	42.5
Nicklas Grossman	Dal/Phi	182	5.84	5.49	88.2	82.4	42.0
Nathan Guenin	Ana/Col	83	6.54	6.48	109.5	102.5	41.4
Derek Morris	Phx	161	5.80	6.07	106.7	99.8	41.3
Mark Eaton	NYI/Pit	85	4.99	6.92	93.3	93.5	40.9
Brian Lashoff	Det	106	7.08	4.55	99.2	88.7	40.9
Kevin Bieksa	Van	190	3.85	5.71	87.3	83.8	40.9
Brett Bellemore	Car	72	4.81	8.45	80.0	96.3	40.8
Nick Schultz	Min/Edm/CBJ	199	5.16	6.02	97.6	97.6	40.8
Sheldon Souray	Ana	108	6.47	6.27	99.1	95.2	40.8
Andrej Sekera	Buf/Car	180	6.57	6.32	92.5	94.4	40.7
Tyler Myers	Buf	156	6.51	6.45	107.6	93.5	40.5
Sami Salo	Van/TB	186	6.53	4.83	101.1	91.5	40.5
Drew Doughty	LA	203	5.02	5.52	89.9	93.8	40.1
Kyle Quincey	Col/Det	190	6.69	5.94	87.1	91.6	40.0
Jason Garrison	Fla/Van	205	6.65	5.46	86.2	86.0	39.9
Roman Polak	StL	197	5.26	4.57	86.8	85.8	38.8
Greg Zanon	Min/Bos/Col	100	5.56	6.06	99.7	94.8	38.6
Chris Tanev	Van	127	5.21	5.87	84.0	87.4	38.2
Mike Weber	Buf	161	6.82	5.90	95.0	101.6	38.1
Matthew Carle	Phi/TB	212	4.71	7.30	87.5	98.0	37.9
Marco Scandella	Min	145	5.02	6.98	88.8	91.7	37.9
Brian Strait	Pit/NYI	75	3.93	6.69	86.9	86.7	37.8
Danny DeKeyser	Det	76	6.03	5.25	93.9	91.0	37.7
Justin Braun	SJ	189	7.28	4.87	102.9	90.5	37.6

| Andrei Markov | Mtl | 142 | 6.47 | 5.43 | 102.4 | 86.8 | 37.6 |
| Brett Clark | TB/Min | 90 | 10.92 | 6.14 | 97.2 | 103.8 | 37.5 |

Minimum 70 Games

There's about one defenceman per team, on average, who kills at least 50% percent of his team's penalties, including four who kill over 60%: Francois Beauchemin, Dan Girardi, Bryce Salvador, and Zbynek Michalek. Those are four strong, physical, shot-blocking, veteran defencemen, for sure.

Scanning the list, there are only two defencemen against whom fewer than 4.00 goals are scored per 60 minutes: Kevin Bieksa and Brian Strait. They certainly do not have the same defensive reputation as the other four.

Finally, Andy Greene is the only defencemen against whom fewer than 80.0 shots are attempted per 60 minutes. Is he the man we're looking for?

Before coronating any of these players, there are important reasons to consider why each of these individual measurements are unfair when used by themselves. To find the best penalty killer, they must be used together and not one at a time.

Frequency of Usage

Straight-up usage statistics may be helpful in identifying players who are physical, defensive specialists, like Beauchemin, Girardi, Salvador and Michalek, especially on teams without other strong penaly killing options. But they will miss well-rounded players like Duncan Keith, Ryan Suter, Oliver Ekman-Larsson and Drew Doughty, who are going to be used in a variety of other roles no matter how good they are at killing penalties, especially if their teams have other options. If you're Los Angeles coach Darryl Sutter, for example, are you going to burn Doughty on the penalty kill or leverage Robyn Regehr and Willie Mitchell instead, so that your superstar is free for more action at even strength and on the power play?

We therefore have to ask ourselves to what extent Beauchemin's ice time is due to (1) his own prowess killing penalties, (2) his inability to contribute in other areas, or (3) the weakness of Anaheim's other defencemen in shorthanded situations. Or, in contrast, how much of Doughty's lower ice time is due to (1) his lesser ability to kill penalties, (2) his abilities to contribute in other manpower situations, or (3) the strength of Los Angeles' other defencemen in shorthanded situations. There's no obvious way to quickly pull these concepts apart.

Despite these reasonable concerns, it is interesting to find the two subjectively chosen defencemen from our sniff test near the top of the list, Hal Gill at 11th and Zdeno Chara at 13th. However, they both allow more goals and more attempted shots than their teammates, although by admittedly small margins. Are those measurements fair?

Individual Goals Against Average

A player's personal goals against average has several flaws, some more obvious than others. For instance, the most obvious flaw is its close reliance on a team's goaltending. Consider Andy Greene, for example. Far fewer shots were attempted when he was on the ice, 7.5 per 60 minutes to be precise, but the Devils allowed 1.52 more goals against per 60 minutes. Is it fair that he gets penalized because New Jersey's goalies were apparently less effective behind him than behind his teammates?

Sure, defencemen like Greene could theoretically be allowing fewer shots but of higher quality, by allowing opponents to shoot from inside perhaps, or by failing to remove screens and sweep away rebounds, but there's never been a study that has established that. Instead, most studies have shown the opposite. Over five years ago, Vic Ferrari's[115] study established just how little influence a player has over his own goalie's save percentage. Basically, none at all. Indeed, a cash prize was once offered by Gabriel Desjardins for anyone who could find a player with the persistent ability to reduce the shooting percentage of one's opponents, so you know that analysts have certainly been looking for it!

Indeed, an argument could be made that a low on-ice save percentage could actually be reflective of a *strong* defensive player. The idea is that a player's on-ice save percentage is (obviously) inversely related of the talent of his competition, which is directly related to how much confidence the coach has in the player's defensive abilities. In other words, the fact that opponents score on a higher percentage of their shots when Greene is on the ice could actually mean that he's the best penalty killer, in the eyes of New Jersey's coaches, who deploy him against the league's best shooters.

Take a league average power play like the Minnesota Wild, for the moment. Their top power play unit was roughly Zach Parise, Mikko Koivu and Jason Pominville, while their secondary unit was arguably Dany Heatley, Mikael Granlund, and Charlie Coyle (until Matt Moulson was acquired). The first group scored on 10.9% of their overall shots and the second group just 9.2%. Those players who are perceived to be the best defensively will face those best shooters and consequently will allow more goals per shot when they're on the ice. This one simple argument frustrates most analytic systems designed to measure defensive abilities, whether on the penalty kill or not.

That's one of many reasons why goals aren't always the metric of choice. Not only can they be inversely related to the confidence in a player's defensive abilities but, over the short run, they are subject to the skill (and luck) of the goaltender. In addition, they are so few in number as to be significantly disrupted by random variation.

Not convinced? Consider the following table of NHL goalies and their save percentage (SV%) over the past three seasons while killing penalties. Look at the huge gulf between Cory Schneider and Vancouver's Roberto Luongo (or New Jersey's Martin Brodeur). Or, if you prefer, between Ottawa's Robin Lehner and Craig Anderson.

115Vic Ferrari, "Loaded Dice and NHL Penalty Killers", *Irreverent Oiler Fans*, Web, January 3, 2009, http://vhockey.blogspot.ca/2009/01/loaded-dice-and-nhl-penalty-killers.html.

Top 50 Shorthanded Save Percentages 2011–12 to 2013–14[116]

Goalie	Team(s)	Shots	Goals	SV%
Cory Schneider	Van/NJ	484	35	.928
Anton Khudobin	Bos/Car	191	17	.911
Robin Lehner	Ott	276	25	.909
Frederik Andersen	Ana	118	11	.907
Viktor Fasth	Ana/Edm	146	14	.904
Jeff Zatkoff	Pit	125	12	.904
Jason Labarbera	Phx/Edm	180	18	.900
Brian Elliott	StL	315	32	.898
Antti Raanta	Chi	118	12	.898
Marc-Andre Fleury	Pit	662	68	.897
Ben Scrivens	Tor/LA/Edm	333	36	.892
Chad Johnson	Phx/Bos	129	14	.891
Ben Bishop	Ott/TB	460	50	.891
Michal Neuvirth	Wsh/Buf	373	41	.890
Jonathan Bernier	LA/Tor	404	45	.889
Henrik Lundqvist	NYR	690	77	.888
Josh Harding	Min	277	31	.888
Kari Lehtonen	Dal	823	93	.887
Jonathan Quick	LA	710	82	.885
Ray Emery	Chi/Phi	328	38	.884
Jaroslav Halak	StL/Wsh	509	59	.884
Ryan Miller	Buf/StL	798	94	.882
Johan Hedberg	NJ	177	21	.881
Nikolai Khabibulin	Edm/Chi	261	31	.881
Carey Price	Mtl	728	87	.880
Tuukka Rask	Bos	468	56	.880
Peter Budaj	Mtl	208	25	.880
Justin Peters	Car	208	25	.880
Devan Dubnyk	Edm/Nsh	566	69	.878
Martin Brodeur	NJ	467	57	.878
Sergei Bobrovsky	Phi/CBJ	573	70	.878
Craig Anderson	Ott	736	91	.876
Jean-Sebastien Giguere	Col	291	36	.876
Tim Thomas	Bos/Fla/Dal	472	59	.875
Curtis McElhinney	Phx/CBJ	128	16	.875
Jonas Gustavsson	Tor/Det	287	36	.875
Mike Smith	Phx	785	99	.874
Semyon Varlamov	Col	721	91	.874
Jhonas Enroth	Buf	293	37	.874
Jimmy Howard	Det	679	86	.873
Karri Ramo	Cgy	156	20	.872
Martin Jones	LA	101	13	.871

116Acknowledgement: All raw goaltender shot data for my calculations came from *the NHL*: http://www.nhl.com.

Miikka Kiprusoff	Cgy	365	47	.871
Evgeni Nabokov	NYI	493	64	.870
Pekka Rinne	Nsh	523	68	.870
Roberto Luongo	Van/Fla	562	74	.868
Steve Mason	CBJ/Phi	542	70	.866
Reto Berra	Cgy/Col	112	15	.866
Joey MacDonald	Cgy	171	23	.865
Dan Ellis	4 Teams	222	30	.865

Minimum 100 Shots Faced

Even if you're skeptical of the significance of random variation, and feel that Schneider has a Vezina-worthy talent that only manifests itself when killing penalties, wouldn't that be unfair to those playing in front of Luongo (or Brodeur) instead of him? Wouldn't his extraordinary talent (or luck) skew each player's individual goals against average when trying to compare it across the league?

For all these reasons (and more), a player's individual goals against average just isn't useful in measuring his penalty-killing success. Scoring chances and shots on goal would both be better, but are subject to someone's personal judgment. Therefore, the best available measurement might be attempted shots, which has a lot more events per minute, and is free of both a goaltender's talent/luck and a scorekeeper's personal judgment.

In an ideal world, and one that's hopefully soon upon us, shot-based data can be adjusted for the quality of those shots, including the type, the distance and whether or not they were rebounds and/or screens, but that type of analysis is currently a little bit beyond our reach. Let's proceed with the raw data that's readily available.

Attempted Shots Allowed

At first glance, it may appear that rating our penalty killers by how few attempted shots they permit (per 60 minutes) would be effective, but remember that context is everything. Even if we find a group of players who allow fewer scoring opportunities, we are still left with the puzzle of figuring out whether it was a consequence of their own skill, of those of their linemates, of the weakness of their opponents, or something else entirely.

Notice, for example, that just 29 of these 100 most-used defencemen in that first table allow fewer attempted shots than their teammates, and just 9 of the top 50! That's mostly because the top defencemen are facing the top power play units who are capable of getting more rubber on the net than the second units. A lot more rubber in the case of some teams. But is that the only reason?

The following chart shows the relationship between a defenceman's share of the penalty-killing ice time and the percentage difference in attempted shots allowed when they're on the ice, relative to when they're not. For example, Beauchemin is on the far right side of the chart because he is assigned well over 60% of his team's penalty-killing minutes, and is slightly above the horizontal axis, because Anaheim's opponents attempt about 5% more shots when he's on the ice.

The statistical correlation between these two variables is a mighty 0.52, incidentally, and a gradual upward arc is obvious even to the naked eye. Quite simply, the more you play, the higher volume of shots per minute you're likely to face. That's an interesting finding!

Ice Time and Attempted Shots Allowed, Penalty-Killing Defencemen, 2011–12 to 2013–14

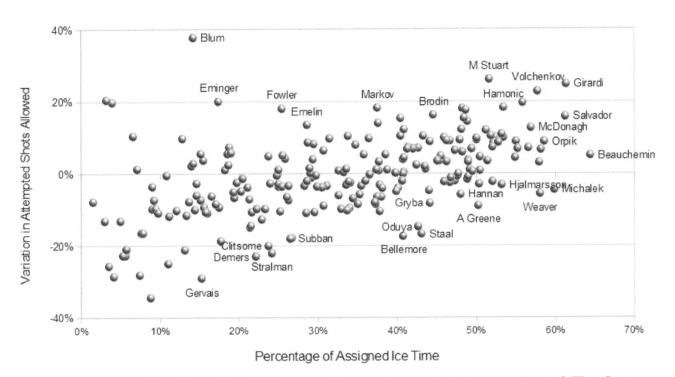

Why do work horses like Beauchemin face a higher volume of shots per minute? The first instinct is that players who get a larger share of ice time, which are those on the right side of the chart, allow a higher number of shots (vertical axis) because they face a higher quality of opponent. While that theory makes sense, and may be true in many cases, it actually isn't the real reason for that increase.

Take Dan Girardi and Ryan McDonagh of the New York Rangers, for example. They are each assigned around 60% of New York's shorthanded minutes, while Marc Staal and Anton Stralman are around 45% and 25%, respectively. The presumably higher level of competition that they face is theoretically why the Rangers' opponents take around 20% more attempted shots while Girardi and McDonagh are on the ice, and about 20% fewer when it's Staal and Stralman.

However, that assumption doesn't hold up under greater scrutiny. Of the three, Stralman has actually faced the highest average quality of competition over the past three seasons. Staal and McDonagh are quite comparable with one another, but Girardi has clearly faced the weakest level of competition of the bunch.

So, if it can't be explained by a tougher set of opponents, why do opponents take more shots against Girardi than against Staal and Stralman? The answer is zone starts. Girardi and McDonagh have started 81.4% and 80.6% of their shifts in the defensive zone over the past three years, while Staal and Stralman have started just 73.5% and 61.9%, respectively. All else being equal, players who start their shifts in the defensive zone are obviously more likely to allow an opposition shot than those starting their shifts in either the neutral or offensive zones.

Defensive Zone Starts

Normally, neutral zone shifts are ignored when calculating a player's offensive zone start percentage, which is meant more as an indication of whether a player is deployed primarily in an offensive or defensive fashion. Since we're interested in how many shifts a defencemen begins with the immediate threat of an attempted shot, we'll calculate our version as the percentage of all shifts that started in the defensive zone.

How important are defensive zone starts? Incredibly important, as it turns out. The correlation between defensive zone start percentage and the variation in attempted shots allowed per 60 minutes is a decent 0.40, among the 170 defencemen who have played at least 120 shorthanded minutes over the past three seasons.

Even to the naked eye, the trend can still be observed. As we move to the right and the percentage of shifts a player starts in the defensive zone goes up, so too does the variation in the number of attempted shots they allow.

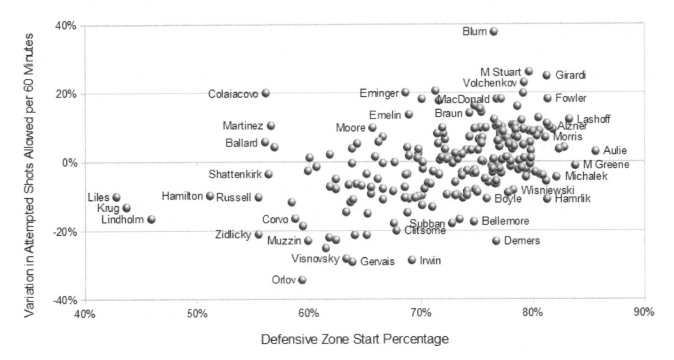

Effect of Zone Starts on Attempted Shots Allowed, Defencemen, 2011–12 to 2013–14

Correlation doesn't necessarily imply causation, of course, but it does make intuitive sense that starting more shifts in the defensive zone will result in a rise in attempted shots against. So, if we can demonstrate a relationship between defensive zone starts and the volume of ice time each player is assigned, then we've got a much stronger theory as to why the league's most frequently used penalty killers allow more shots than everybody else.

So, does this relationship exist? Yes, the correlation between defensive zone starts and each player's share of shorthanded ice time is 0.65, which is the strongest one yet. Again, the trend can be seen with the naked eye (or with reading glasses, if you happen to be farsighted). The players on the right side of the chart, who enjoy a larger share of all shorthanded ice time, also start a higher percentage of those shifts in the defensive zone.

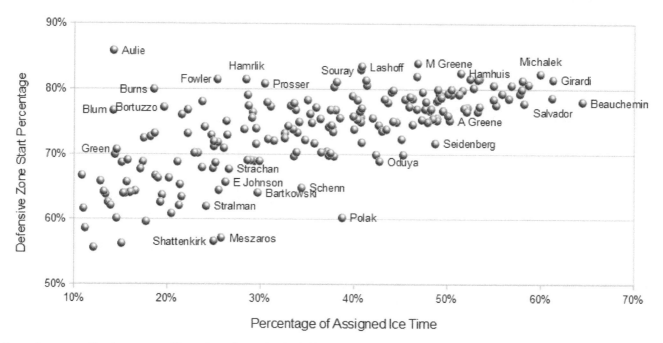

Relationship Between Ice Time and Defensive Zone Starts, Defencemen, 2011–12 to 2013–14

It makes perfect sense. If a shorthanded shift begins in the neutral or offensive zone, then coaches are more prepared to deploy one of their secondary options, like Anton Stralman, for example. But when the shift begins in the defensive zone, they go with their top defensive options, like Dan Girardi.

There you have it. Defencemen who handle a larger share of the shorthanded ice time allow a great volume of shots not because of great competition, but because they're used more frequently in the defensive zone. But that doesn't necessarily mean we should ignore quality of competition.

Quality of Competition

Ice time, attempted shots, and defensive zone starts are a simple matter of record, and one that everyone can understand and agree upon, but that's not the case with quality of competition estimates. Who is to say that one player faces tougher opponents than another? Even with a list of a player's opponents and their ice time, the process of quantifying one list as superior to another is not as straightforward a task as counting shots or adding up ice time.

There are two main approaches to evaluating the average quality of one's opponents, basing it on the attempted shot differential and on average ice time. The results tend to be quite similar, with the former tending to favour more defensive-minded players and the latter tending to favour the league's superstars. Only the first method is readily available in shorthanded situations, however.

Remember our original theory, that the league's most frequently-used defencemen faced more shots because they faced better opponents? If that were true, then there should be a relationship between a player's share of the ice time and his average quality of competition. Let's see those two variables together on the same chart.

Ice Time and Quality of Competition, Penalty-Killing Defencemen, 2011–12 to 2013–14

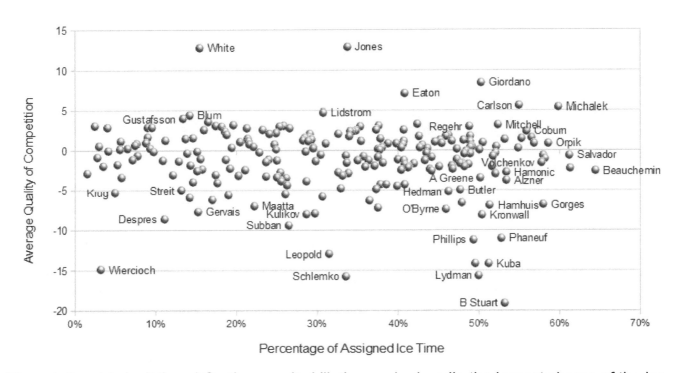

The relationship isn't there! On the penalty kill, those who handle the largest shares of the ice time face roughly the same level of competition as those who don't. While our theory makes perfect sense rationally, the correlation between assigned ice time and average level of competition is practically non-existent.

Unlike what we saw with defensive zone percentages, the chart above has no gradual increase, with defencemen falling on the same flat line no matter how much ice time they're assigned. Defencemen are assigned their shorthanded shifts not so much based on who the opponents are, but in which zone the shift begins.

Even if there was a relationship between those two variables, incidentally, it still wouldn't help us, because there's not much of a relationship between quality of competition and attempted shots either. That's right, the correlation between quality of competition and the percentage difference in attempted shots allowed is an almost-negligible 0.11, far weaker than what we saw with defensive zone percentages.

Don't believe me? Check it out for yourself on the following chart. Assuming the quality of competition metrics are reasonably accurate, there is no obvious relationship between the two variables. Instead of a nice trending line, there is just a blob of players in the middle. Facing tougher opponents doesn't necessarily result in more shots being allowed, most likely because better players face better opponents, as we discovered in the chapter on good players.

Quality of Competition and Shots Allowed, Penalty-Killing Defencemen, 2011–12 to 2013–14

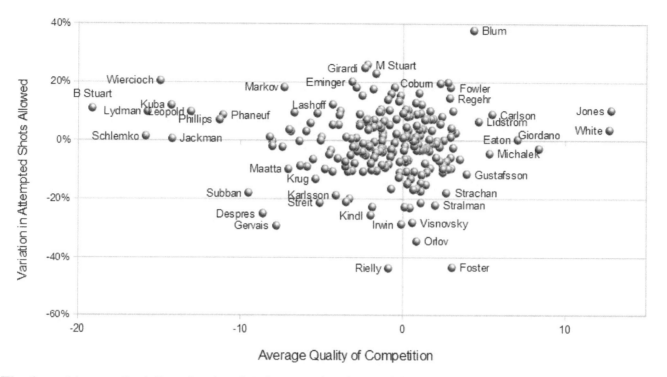

That's not to say that there's absolutely no value in studying each player's quality of competition. Notice, for instance, the collection of defensive-minded veterans who rank poorly by this measurement, like Brad Stuart, Filip Kuba, Tony Lydman, Chris Phillips, Barret Jackman, and so on. Kuba was bought out, Lydman retired, and the others have been pushed down the depth chart. These are players that were likely used more for some combination of their inability to contribute in other situations and the team's lack of other options. Or, in the case of Jackman, the desire to save superior players like Alex Pietrangelo for even strength and/or power play situations.

This chart can also be somewhat helpful in finding the league's better penalty killers, who would be located at the bottom of the graph, where the fewest shots are allowed, and over on the right, where those who face the toughest opponents are found.

For example, Seth Jones and Ian White score well, thanks to their celebrated partners Shea Weber and Nicklas Lidstrom, no doubt. There's also Mark Giordano and Zbynek Michalek, two strong penalty killers, as well as Mark Eaton, for no obvious reason. Let's put both usage-related statistics together into a variant of the player usage chart, which is explained in more detail in the Team Essays chapter.

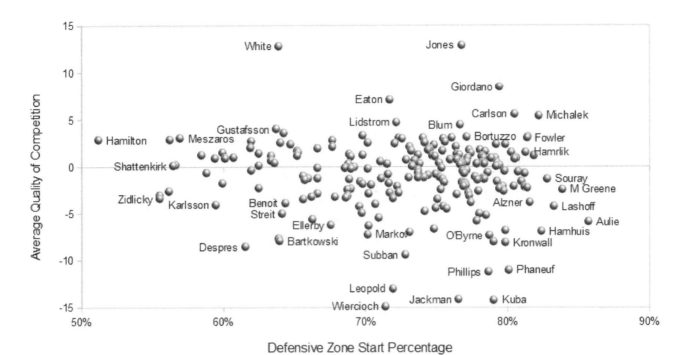

Player Usage Chart, Penalty-Killing Defencemen, 2011–12 to 2013–14

While most of the defencemen we're studying are used in roughly comparable fashion, in that giant mess in the middle the chart, at least we have some idea which ones are used differently, and should therefore hold their results in a different regard.

Those on the left side, for instance, have to play fewer shifts in the defensive zone, and will consequently fare better than their teammates in attempted shot differentials. That's especially true of those below the horizon, who are facing below-average competition. Those on the right side of the graph, on the other hand, are frequently toiling in the defensive zone, and in the case of those above the axis, against top opponents too.

Putting it All Together

While each individual measurement can't help determine who the best penalty killer is, there's great value when they're all used together.

For starters, consider those defencemen whose attempted shot differential percentage is out of place with regards to their usage. That is, anyone who allows fewer shots (relative to his teammates) compared to those around the league who get the same share of shorthanded ice time, start in the defensive zone as frequently, and face the same quality of opponents.

Among those who play at least half of their team's shorthanded minutes, Andy Greene, Mike Weaver, Zbynek Michalek, Niklas Hjalmarsson, Mark Giordano, and Paul Martin are the only six who allowed fewer attempted shots than their teammates.

As we've seen, it's possible that these players allowed fewer shots because they started in their shifts in the defensive zone less frequently than their teammates. That might actually be somewhat the case for Greene, Hjalmarsson and Martin, for instance.

However, of the 100 most frequently-used defencemen, Michalek ranks 5th with a defensive zone start percentage of 82.2%. Weaver is not far behind at 81.3%, who ranks 11th, while Giordano ranks 25th at 79.5%. The only other defencemen in the top 25 who allow fewer attempted shots than their teammates are Matt Greene, Chris Tanev, Marco Scandella and Stephane Robidas, who rank 1st, 13th, 18th, and 22nd in defensive zone start percentage, respectively.

It's also possible that this group's success at preventing shots was a result of the weakness of their respective team's other options and not their own natural talents. After all, the more shots that their teammates allow, the better these six will appear to be in comparison. That could be particularly true in Weaver's case, spending as much time as he did on the league's weakest penalty killers, the Florida Panthers, but far less likely to be true for Greene (Los Angeles) and Tanev (Vancouver).

It's also possible that these defencemen allowed fewer shots because they were playing against lesser opponents. While some excellent questions were raised about the usefulness of the competition estimates, three of these players scored particularly well by that metric. Giordano actually has the highest average quality of competition among the 100 most-used defencemen, Michalek is 4th, and Scandella is 16th.

In addition, although goals against was largely discredited as a viable measurement, everyone but Greene allowed fewer goals than their teammates, too.

And what about the two subjectively-chosen defencemen for our sniff test, Hal Gill and Zdeno Chara? Promisingly, they ranked 11th and 13th in usage, respectively, and 15th and 17th in quality of competition. However, they allowed 7.1% and 6.8% more attempted shots than their teammates, respectively, despite ranking 39th and 50th in defensive zone start percentage.

It's unfortunate that the defencemen with the strongest reputations ranks the lowest in the statistical areas that build the most compelling cases. But taken all in all, this is where the evidence is pointing, so let's stick with Giordano, Michalek, and maybe Scandella as the league's best penalty killers on the blue line.

Penalty-Killing Forwards

Although one of our subjectively chosen penalty killers tops the list (Jay McClement), usage isn't as effective a measurement for forwards as it is for defencemen. Forwards are arguably less important than defencemen at killing penalties, are frequently more important in other manpower situations, and there are twice as many of them from which to choose. But, it's still a good place to start.

Here is the leader board for the top 100 forwards over the past three seasons, ordered once again by the percentage of all shorthanded minutes assigned to them (PK%) including their individual goals against average (GA/60) and attempted shots allowed per 60 minutes (AS/60), complete with a comparison to how the team does in each regard when they're on the bench.

Top 100 Most Used Penalty-Killing Forwards 2011–12 to 2013–14[117]

Player	Team(s)	GP	GA/60	Team	AS/60	Team	PK%
Jay McClement	Col/Tor	209	5.64	6.27	97.7	89.1	59.7
Maxime Talbot	Phi/Col	197	5.45	6.97	93.4	84.9	53.0
Craig Adams	Pit	212	5.21	5.10	92.7	87.0	52.1
Boyd Gordon	Phx/Edm	197	5.98	5.75	110.8	92.7	50.5
Marc-Andre Cliche	Col	76	6.92	5.07	105.7	97.3	50.2
Paul Gaustad	Buf/Nsh	168	9.21	6.44	103.4	87.2	49.2
Sean Couturier	Phi	205	6.17	4.63	81.0	85.2	46.4
Tomas Plekanec	Mtl	209	5.12	5.19	95.8	85.2	46.0
Lauri Korpikoski	Phx	182	7.40	5.07	110.7	95.5	45.9
Daniel Winnik	Col/SJ/Ana	208	4.92	7.50	98.7	91.6	45.5
Drew Miller	Det	206	5.92	6.35	97.1	89.8	45.2
Brooks Laich	Wsh	142	7.25	5.78	113.5	98.2	45.0
Adam Hall	TB/Car/Phi	174	5.48	5.93	91.7	87.6	44.7
Matt Cooke	Pit/Min	212	6.58	5.31	83.9	85.2	44.2
Kyle Brodziak	Min	211	6.60	6.07	89.4	85.7	44.0
Marcel Goc	Fla/Pit	173	8.49	7.86	95.6	95.5	44.0
Frans Nielsen	NYI	210	7.64	6.46	92.8	96.4	43.7
Marcus Kruger	Chi	199	6.46	6.20	106.1	88.0	43.5
Matt Read	Phi	196	5.30	6.01	82.7	83.8	43.4
Brandon Sutter	Car/Pit	211	6.58	5.82	97.0	99.4	43.2
Eric Belanger	Edm	104	5.44	5.83	96.1	84.5	43.1
Sami Pahlsson	CBJ/Van	80	8.61	8.33	87.9	89.0	42.8
Nate Thompson	TB	194	6.89	6.34	104.5	97.6	42.6
Michael Grabner	NYI	187	5.87	8.14	82.6	100.6	41.3
Travis Moen	Mtl	158	6.24	4.39	100.1	85.5	41.3
Patrick Dwyer	Car	194	7.47	6.47	102.5	90.8	41.2
Darren Helm	Det	111	6.43	6.17	88.8	100.6	41.2
Erik Condra	Ott	205	6.78	5.12	92.2	86.1	40.9
Jordan Staal	Pit/Car	192	7.26	5.11	88.9	88.3	40.8
Pascal Dupuis	Pit	169	4.76	5.21	92.6	90.0	40.0
Brian Boyle	NYR	202	5.09	5.10	101.3	86.6	39.8
Tomas Kopecky	Fla	176	8.25	6.85	95.7	87.9	39.6
David Steckel	Tor/Ana	116	7.37	6.07	95.8	96.2	39.4
Manny Malhotra	Van/Car	156	5.88	5.16	95.7	93.6	39.3
Nikolai Kulemin	Tor	188	7.30	6.06	94.9	100.6	39.2

[117]Acknowledgement: All raw penalty-killing data for my calculations came from *Behind the Net*: http://www.behindthenet.ca.

Darroll Powe	Min/NYR	125	6.26	5.38	92.7	90.9	39.2
Nick Spaling	Nsh	195	7.24	6.55	105.5	93.8	39.2
David Moss	Cgy/Phx	156	7.08	6.62	102.0	100.5	39.0
Jerred Smithson	Fla/Edm/Tor	132	6.65	7.96	108.3	95.8	38.7
Joakim Andersson	Det	103	5.25	5.03	96.1	83.7	38.6
Michal Handzus	SJ/Chi	165	5.80	5.61	104.2	90.2	37.9
Patrick Kaleta	Buf	102	5.68	5.95	107.0	92.9	37.6
Ryan Callahan	NYR/TB	186	7.08	4.48	99.1	92.6	37.6
Dainius Zubrus	NJ	186	3.20	4.38	87.2	75.8	37.3
Tim Connolly	Tor	70	6.39	7.85	107.0	98.6	37.1
James Wright	Wpg	97	5.21	6.14	95.0	86.3	37.1
Vernon Fiddler	Dal	204	7.33	5.35	110.6	95.3	37.0
Ryan Kesler	Van	171	5.23	4.24	87.0	83.6	36.7
Jeff Halpern	4 Teams	184	8.21	6.52	94.3	97.6	36.5
Gregory Campbell	Bos	208	5.35	5.13	97.9	81.0	36.4
Jim Slater	Wpg	131	9.63	5.54	109.9	85.0	36.0
Tom Pyatt	TB	144	7.48	6.48	108.6	96.7	35.9
Adam Henrique	NJ	193	5.12	4.13	80.9	78.9	35.7
Joe Pavelski	SJ	212	6.96	5.62	100.1	94.6	35.4
Jesse Winchester	Ott/Fla	84	7.95	7.49	87.4	94.4	35.3
Ryan Smyth	Edm	201	4.41	6.21	91.8	100.0	35.2
Shawn Horcoff	Edm/Dal	189	5.38	6.09	91.3	96.9	35.1
Brian Flynn	Buf	105	5.02	6.19	98.0	99.7	35.0
Patrick Marleau	SJ	212	6.51	5.96	95.6	97.2	34.8
Patrice Bergeron	Bos	203	4.77	4.99	85.5	87.9	34.7
Chris Kelly	Bos	173	5.58	4.19	87.0	86.1	34.7
Jarret Stoll	LA	204	4.90	5.43	101.4	89.0	34.6
Ondrej Palat	TB	95	4.81	7.97	100.0	102.2	34.5
Lance Bouma	Cgy	105	6.37	5.93	106.9	90.6	34.4
Matt Hendricks	Wsh/Nsh/Edm	203	5.93	6.46	106.3	98.2	34.3
Jay Pandolfo	NYI/Bos	80	8.02	5.63	103.3	91.2	34.1
Steve Ott	Dal/Buf/StL	204	6.05	5.95	102.7	93.8	34.1
Antoine Vermette	Phx	212	8.61	7.10	101.9	94.6	34.1
Bryan Little	Wpg	204	6.55	7.13	96.0	94.5	33.6
Derek MacKenzie	CBJ	180	6.41	7.42	89.7	91.7	33.5
Anze Kopitar	LA	211	6.88	4.51	93.6	92.1	33.5
Dominic Moore	TB/SJ/NYR	152	6.89	6.18	98.1	93.7	33.4
Tyler Johnson	TB	96	6.01	7.44	105.0	99.2	33.4
Patrik Elias	NJ	194	4.67	4.46	78.4	80.1	33.1
Travis Zajac	NJ	143	4.97	4.81	83.1	77.6	33.1
Alex Burrows	Van	176	5.86	5.04	89.9	84.0	32.9
Matt Stajan	Cgy	167	6.86	5.20	106.4	87.5	32.9
Vladimir Sobotka	StL	182	6.11	4.18	84.9	87.5	32.8
Stephen Gionta	NJ	114	6.54	4.92	77.6	84.4	32.7
Troy Brouwer	Wsh	211	7.19	6.02	114.5	103.9	32.6
Alexander Burmistrov	Wpg	120	5.06	7.64	78.6	100.7	32.6
Brandon Dubinsky	NYR/CBJ	182	6.38	5.06	93.3	96.3	32.5

Andrew Ladd	Wpg	208	6.64	6.62	89.9	97.7	32.4
Trevor Lewis	LA	193	6.08	5.16	90.6	91.3	32.4
Casey Cizikas	NYI	140	7.62	7.66	101.5	93.6	32.3
Zemgus Girgensons	Buf	70	6.33	6.04	100.8	103.1	32.3
Mark Letestu	Pit/CBJ	190	6.16	6.23	92.6	87.7	32.3
Marian Hossa	Chi	193	7.46	6.13	92.0	99.4	32.2
Jonathan Toews	Chi	182	6.49	5.86	87.5	100.4	32.2
Kaspars Daugavins	Ott/Bos	90	4.00	6.04	92.0	92.4	32.2
Eric Nystrom	Dal/Nsh	201	7.40	6.25	100.9	98.4	32.1
Brandon Prust	NYR/Mtl	172	3.86	5.75	90.5	94.6	32.1
Ruslan Fedotenko	NYR/Phi	120	5.36	4.66	92.3	89.4	32.1
David Backes	StL	204	4.95	5.13	89.5	85.0	32.0
Ryan Jones	Edm	158	5.24	5.98	95.9	95.1	31.3
Alexander Steen	StL	151	4.17	5.38	91.9	84.1	31.3
Cal Clutterbuck	Min/NYI	189	6.53	7.46	92.6	94.3	31.2
Saku Koivu	Ana	186	7.30	5.34	104.9	96.1	31.0
Chris Higgins	Van	190	5.06	5.68	75.5	88.4	30.8
Joey Crabb	Tor/Wsh/Fla	102	8.49	7.02	109.2	101.2	30.8

Minimum 70 Games

The first thing that strikes me about the list of most frequently used penalty-killing forwards is the sheer number of replacement-level players. Many of them don't carry a regular shift at even strength and some of them have one skate in the AHL (or in early retirement). There are very few top-six forwards on this list, and it almost appears as if forwards are selected for the penalty kill based on who is least needed at even strength or on the power play, rather than who might excel defensively.

The second interesting observation is how forwards don't get as large a share of the penalty-killing duties as defencemen do. This makes perfect sense given that there are 12 forwards from which to select two, making it easier to spread out the duties. We should consequently be impressed by the five players who are assigned at least half of their team's shorthanded duties: Jay McClement, Max Talbot, Craig Adams, Boyd Gordon, and Marc-Andre Cliche. It's also interesting that three of them have played for the Colorado Avalanche.

Attempted Shots Allowed

The same kinds of relationships that were established for defencemen between ice time, defensive zone start percentage, and attempted shots apply to forwards too, but to a slightly lesser extent. The statistical correlations are between 0.41 and 0.44 in each case, among those forwards with at least 120 shorthanded minutes over the past three seasons.

Having already explored those relationships with defencemen, let's dive right into the key chart, which is the variation in attempted shots allowed (per 60 minutes), relative to each player's defensive zone start percentage. Essentially, we're looking for players at the bottom of the chart, and to the right, who allow far fewer attempted shots than their usage would normally suggest.

Zone Starts and Attempted Shots, Forwards, 2011–12 to 2013–14

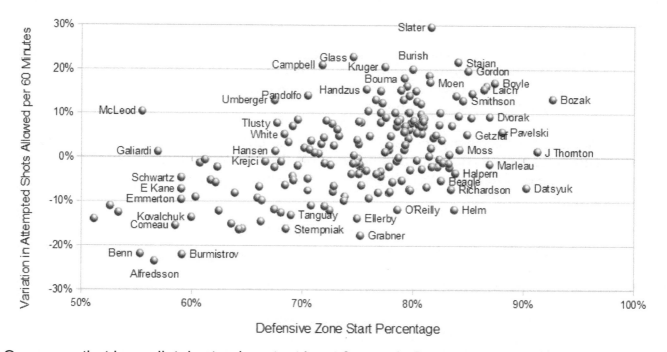

One name that immediately stands out, at least for me, is Darren Helm. When a team has players like Pavel Datsyuk and Henrik Zetterberg at their disposal, and they turn to someone else for 41.2% of the team's shorthanded minutes, then you know he's good.

Helm has the numbers to prove it too, allowing 11.8% fewer attempted shots than his teammates despite starting 83.8% of his shifts in the defensive zone, which is the third highest among those below the horizon. Although such statistics have been deemed less reliable, he also allows fewer goals than his teammates and he ranks sixth in quality of competition among those who play at least a third of their team's shorthanded minutes.

Another strong name is Patrick Marleau, who ranks third with an 87.0% defensive zone start percentage among those who play at least a third of their team's minutes, and yet allows 1.6% fewer shots than his teammates. Datsyuk is the only player who starts a higher percentage of his shifts in the defensive zone while also allowing fewer attempted shots, but he works just 18.5% of Detroit's shorthanded minutes, faces below-average competition, and allows far more goals per minute than his teammates.

Two more interesting names include Michael Grabner of the New York Islanders and Jeff Halpern, who has played for six different teams over the past four seasons. Grabner works 41.3% of shorthanded minutes, while allowing 17.7% fewer attempted shots, and far fewer goals while facing top competition. Of course, he starts only 75.3% of his shifts in the defensive zone.

As for Halpern, he works 36.5% of his various team's shorthanded minutes, starting in the defensive zone 83.9% of the time, and yet allows 3.6% fewer attempted shots than his teammates. However, he does face easier competition and allow far more goals than his teammates.

Brad Richardson and Jay Beagle also stand out, although they're only assigned about a quarter of their team's shorthanded minutes, and against relatively average competition. Still, they start frequently in the defensive zone, allow fewer attempted shots than their teammates, and even fewer goals. They may not be the league's best penalty killers, but they are good value options, much like David Moss perhaps.

And what about our subjectively chosen forwards for the sniff test? Jay McClement leads the way in usage, but allows 9.8% more attempted shots than his teammates, despite a fairly average 80.7% defensive zone start percentage and below-average competition. He does allow fewer goals, though.

Sean Couturier is probably the most encouraging name from our reputation-based collection. He plays a lot of minutes against top competition and still allows 4.9% fewer attempted shots than his teammates. Then again, he has a relatively low 70.5% defensive zone start percentage and allows a lot more goals than his teammates.

Besides Couturier, there are only four other players among the 20 most-used forwards to allow (slightly) fewer shots than their teammates: Matt Cooke, Frans Nielsen, Matt Read, and Brandon Sutter. Of them, only Sutter has an above-average defensive zone start percentage (82.3%), and he also faces top competition. He allows more goals than his teammates, though.

Then there's Jordan Staal and Ryan Kesler, who both have relatively high defensive zone start percentages of 83.4% and 82.6%, respectively. They both face above-average competition, but allow more attempted shots and more goals than their teammates. It certainly appears that our subjectively chosen players do not reinforce the notion of using attempted shot differentials to evaluate the top penalty killers, preferring to line up with the concepts of ice time and defensive zone start percentages, instead.

Finally, there's Henrik Zetterberg and Mike Richards, who fare quite poorly by virtually all of our metrics. Furthermore, Zetterberg is assigned only 16.2% of his team's penalty-killing minutes, and Richards only 28.8%, so why are they so highly regarded by fans? The answer requires the creation of a new metric. Drum roll, please!

Penalty-Killing Extras (PKE)

It's easy to see why fans love Richards, as his lack of ice time didn't stop him from scoring four shorthanded goals over the past three seasons. He also drew four penalties, while taking only a single one, ending three more power plays right there. He also won 125 faceoffs to 102, which could have saved a few scoring chances as well.

Let's create a brand new statistic called the Penalty-Killing Extras (PKE), which is composed of all the little extra things that can be done to kill penalties, like scoring goals (and generating primary assists), drawing penalties (minus those taken), winning faceoffs, and blocking shots.

In each case, we'll give each factor a sensible divisor to translate it all into the common measurement of goals. We'll rather arbitrarily assign half a goal to a primary assist (A1), but the other divisors will be scientific. Drawing a penalty (PenD) will be worth about a fifth of a goal (given league average power play percentages), winning a net faceoff (FOW/L) will be worth 1/40th of a goal, based on the latest study[118], and a blocked shot (BlkS) will be worth 1/20th of a goal, which is roughly the chance of an attempted shot going in.

Top 50 Penalty-Killing Forwards Doing the "Extras" 2011–12 to 2013–14[119]

Player	Team(s)	GP	TOI	G	A1	PenD/T	FOW/L	BlkS	PKE	PKE/60
Adam Henrique	NJ	193	35.7	9	5	4/1	131-148	29	13.1	2.17
Jonathan Toews	Chi	182	32.2	6	4	4/0	131-107	9	9.9	2.06
Eric Staal	Car	209	24.0	6	4	9/2	102-116	8	9.5	2.43
Brad Marchand	Bos	203	27.8	7	2	5/1	2-3	13	9.4	1.95
T.J. Oshie	StL	189	30.1	4	2	11/1	6-8	24	8.2	1.50
Boyd Gordon	Phx/Edm	197	50.5	1	4	5/0	381-346	62	8.0	0.92
Ryan Callahan	NYR/TB	186	37.6	4	3	1/1	5-6	47	7.8	1.42
Antoine Vermette	Phx	212	34.1	4	0	8/2	213-176	29	7.6	1.25
Cal Clutterbuck	Min/NYI	189	31.2	5	2	6/2	2-5	14	7.4	1.47
Logan Couture	SJ	193	24.6	4	3	4/1	44-58	26	7.1	2.03
Daniel Winnik	Col/SJ/Ana	208	45.5	3	2	7/1	17-38	47	7.0	0.84
Erik Condra	Ott	205	40.9	3	3	6/6	6-17	54	6.9	0.84
Matt Read	Phi	196	43.4	5	1	2/0	26-51	32	6.9	0.79
Zach Parise	NJ	197	30.4	3	4	5/1	4-4	20	6.8	1.37
Dainius Zubrus	NJ	186	37.3	3	4	4/0	66-73	23	6.8	1.08
Max Talbot	Phi/Col	197	53.0	4	1	8/2	116-163	44	6.7	0.69
Marian Hossa	Chi	193	32.2	5	3	0/1	4-6	9	6.7	1.35
Andrew Cogliano	Ana	212	29.7	4	1	10/2	27-44	16	6.5	1.15
Joe Pavelski	SJ	212	35.4	2	2	4/2	181-136	38	6.4	1.18
Brandon Sutter	Car/Pit	211	43.2	5	0	6/2	233-268	30	6.4	0.86
Patrice Bergeron	Bos	203	34.7	2	4	2/4	287-219	22	6.4	1.05
Ilya Kovalchuk	NJ	114	25.2	5	2	1/0	0-3	5	6.4	2.53
Mike Richards	LA	204	28.8	4	1	4/1	125-102	9	6.1	1.11
Rick Nash	CBJ/NYR	191	12.1	5	2	1/1	2-2	2	6.1	3.32
Jordan Staal	Pit/Car	192	40.8	4	5	5/3	193-248	11	6.1	0.94
Tyler Johnson	TB	96	33.4	5	1	2/0	85-99	9	6.0	2.12
Lauri Korpikoski	Phx	182	45.9	2	3	5/0	4-15	35	6.0	0.85
Brandon Dubinsky	NYR/CBJ	182	32.5	2	4	8/3	124-134	24	6.0	1.12
Michael Grabner	NYI	187	41.3	4	0	4/2	9-8	29	5.9	0.96

118Michael Schuckers, Tom Pasquali and Jim Curro, "An Analysis of NHL Faceoffs", *Statistical Sports Consulting*, 2012, Web, http://statsportsconsulting.com/main/wp-content/uploads/FaceoffAnalysis12-12.pdf.
119Acknowledgement: All raw penalty-killing data for my calculations came from *Behind the Net*: http://www.behindthenet.ca or *Extra Skater*: http://www.extraskater.com.

Patrik Elias	NJ	197	33.1	4	5	4/2	72-134	10	5.9	1.05
Lars Eller	Mtl	202	26.6	3	2	7/3	96-103	23	5.8	1.12
Daniel Paille	Bos	187	29.6	4	0	4/2	2-6	20	5.3	1.13
Lee Stempniak	Cgy/Pit	181	29.7	2	5	4/0	2-15	6	5.3	1.16
Derek MacKenzie	CBJ	180	33.5	3	2	7/3	89-111	20	5.3	1.02
Loui Eriksson	Dal/Bos	191	29.4	3	2	4/0	2-6	11	5.3	1.01
Matt Cooke	Pit/Min	212	44.2	2	3	4/5	11-16	40	5.2	0.63
Tomas Plekanec	Mtl	209	46.0	4	2	4/4	370-416	26	5.2	0.55
Patrick Dwyer	Car	194	41.2	3	0	4/2	7-9	35	5.1	0.81
Pascal Dupuis	Pit	169	40.0	4	0	2/3	14-21	28	5.0	0.85
Jason Pominville	Buf/Min	211	24.5	3	1	4/0	15-18	15	5.0	1.13
Gabriel Landeskog	Col	199	17.6	3	2	0/0	5-9	21	5.0	1.56
Daniel Alfredsson	Ott/Det	190	16.8	3	1	5/1	12-12	12	4.9	1.60
Claude Giroux	Phi	207	26.2	1	2	8/2	229-198	16	4.8	0.87
Ryan Kesler	Van	171	36.7	2	1	7/2	175-200	37	4.7	0.82
Mikael Backlund	Cgy	149	27.2	4	0	2/1	104-118	16	4.7	1.43
Derek Stepan	NYR	212	29.0	1	6	6/1	101-149	16	4.6	0.93
Chris Kelly	Bos	173	34.7	2	0	7/0	116-121	26	4.6	0.88
Tommy Wingels	SJ	152	21.7	3	1	1/1	1-1	20	4.5	1.93
Bryan Little	Wpg	204	33.6	2	4	3/2	219-241	16	4.5	0.75
Steve Ott	Dal/Buf/StL	204	34.1	0	4	12/7	219-219	29	4.5	0.69

And voila, the top-six forwards who kill penalties!

Richards ranks 23rd by this metric, which is impressive given that he doesn't get nearly as much ice time as a top penalty-killing option. This new statistic doesn't really help Zetterberg though, meaning that his reputation is based on his time as Detroit's top penalty killer far earlier in his career as opposed to anything he's accomplished more recently.

Adam Henrique has a staggering lead over everybody else, thanks to his nine shorthanded goals. In fact, the list is dominated by those with a lot of shorthanded goals, meaning that perhaps too strong an emphasis is being placed on this one aspect.

Given the scarcity of goals over smaller sample sizes, it may be better to base PKE on a fraction of a player's shots instead. And, instead of primary assists, to base that portion on the shorthanded team's attempted shots. That should reduce the effect random variation can have on the results.

Some players made the list despite an absence of scoring, like Boyd Gordon. He ranked sixth, despite having just a single shorthander, because he gets a lot of ice time and contributes in all the other ways. Then again, blocking a lot of shots is a sign that the opposing team frequently has the puck in a position to shoot. And indeed, his team allowed a lot of attempted shots when he was on the ice. So there's definitely plenty of room to improve the design of this new statistic.

Even this rough approach may still have generated a list of players that includes the league's best. It's quite possible that the league's best penalty-killing forward isn't used as frequently as other players on his team because their coaches feel that the advantage they have over the other options is greater at even strength (or the power play), not the penalty kill. That could also be why of the 20 PKE players who weren't among the top 100 in usage, 17 allowed fewer attempted shots per minute than their teammates.

Take Jonathan Toews, for example, who had the highest PKE of the 17 players in question. Could he be the league's best penalty killer? He is so talented that he could likely be the best at whatever aspect of the game he is focused upon. And yet, it is easy to understand why coach Joel Quenneville would use him sparingly for just the key penalty-killing situations, in order to save his strength for his incredible play at even strength and the power play.

There are some forwards who scored well by almost all of these various measurements. That is, players who get at least somewhat of a regular penalty-killing shift, start in the defensive zone against good competition, allow fewer attempted shots than their teammates, and have a decent PKE. Arguably, those who fit that description most closely include Matt Read, Brandon Sutter, Michael Grabner, and Matt Cooke.

PKE for Defencemen

Before we wrap things up, let's look at the PKE leader board for defencemen. It will still be interesting to see if we find Giordano and Michalek among the leaders.

Top 50 Defencemen Doing the "Extras" 2011–12 to 2013–14[120]

Player	Team(s)	GP	TOI	G	A1	PenD/T	BlkS	PKE	PKE/60
Ryan McDonagh	NYR	206	56.9	3	1	7/1	74	8.4	0.89
Josh Gorges	Mtl	196	58.1	0	0	2/1	137	7.1	0.64
John Carlson	Wsh	212	55.1	0	2	7/0	93	7.0	0.68
Mark Giordano	Cgy	172	50.4	1	3	10/3	60	6.9	0.99
Francois Beauchemin	Ana	200	64.5	0	1	3/3	128	6.9	0.60
Alex Pietrangelo	StL	209	55.0	0	2	3/3	106	6.3	0.58
Niklas Kronwall	Det	209	50.5	0	1	6/3	102	6.2	0.65
Victor Hedman	TB	180	46.3	0	6	4/4	52	5.6	0.77
Roman Polak	StL	197	38.8	0	0	7/0	83	5.6	0.77
Niklas Hjalmarsson	Chi	196	53.3	0	1	4/1	86	5.4	0.65
Brent Seabrook	Chi	207	45.3	1	1	7/3	58	5.2	0.70
Zbynek Michalek	Pit/Phx	155	60.0	0	1	3/2	88	5.1	0.65
Mark Stuart	Wpg	191	51.7	1	0	5/9	97	5.1	0.58
Barret Jackman	StL	206	49.6	0	0	8/6	92	5.0	0.52
Shea Weber	Nsh	205	49.0	1	0	8/3	58	4.9	0.63
Dan Hamhuis	Van	208	51.5	0	2	7/3	62	4.9	0.49
Anton Volchenkov	NJ	165	57.9	0	0	4/2	90	4.9	0.57
Dan Girardi	NYR	209	61.4	0	0	5/4	93	4.9	0.47
Bryan Allen	Car/Ana	191	43.6	0	1	2/2	84	4.7	0.67

120Acknowledgement: All raw penalty-killing data for my calculations came from *Behind the Net*: http://www.behindthenet.ca or *Extra Skater*: http://www.extraskater.com.

Willie Mitchell	LA	152	52.4	0	3	3/2	60	4.7	0.60
Ryan Suter	Nsh/Min	209	46.3	1	1	2/2	62	4.6	0.59
Chris Phillips	Ott	198	49.4	0	1	4/1	70	4.6	0.48
Travis Hamonic	NYI	190	53.5	0	1	11/4	54	4.6	0.56
Mike Weaver	Fla/Mtl	181	58.1	0	0	3/0	77	4.5	0.53
Andrew MacDonald	NYI/Phi	205	48.3	0	1	4/1	65	4.4	0.55
Kimmo Timonen	Phi	198	51.9	0	0	6/4	78	4.3	0.41
Robyn Regehr	Buf/LA	196	48.9	0	0	5/1	70	4.3	0.50
Stephane Robidas	Dal/Ana	161	49.0	0	0	8/2	61	4.3	0.59
Jeff Petry	Edm	201	49.2	1	0	5/4	60	4.2	0.45
Marc-Edouard Vlasic	SJ	211	47.4	1	0	5/3	56	4.2	0.58
Chris Butler	Cgy	194	47.8	1	1	3/1	45	4.2	0.56
Carl Gunnarsson	Tor	193	52.1	0	0	4/1	71	4.2	0.49
Jan Hejda	Col	205	52.2	0	0	2/3	87	4.1	0.43
Dion Phaneuf	Tor	210	52.8	0	1	7/5	63	4.1	0.43
Nick Schultz	Min/Edm/CBJ	199	40.8	0	1	1/1	70	4.0	0.53
Karl Alzner	Wsh	212	53.4	0	1	1/5	85	4.0	0.39
Braydon Coburn	Phi	196	55.9	0	1	1/6	89	4.0	0.35
Andy Greene	NJ	186	50.3	1	0	2/2	56	3.8	0.46
Johnny Boychuk	Bos	196	47.4	0	2	3/4	60	3.8	0.48
Bryce Salvador	NJ	161	61.3	0	0	3/4	79	3.8	0.43
Alexander Edler	Van	190	37.3	1	0	4/3	51	3.8	0.56
Kevin Klein	Nsh/NYR	190	43.7	0	0	2/1	70	3.7	0.58
Andrej Sekera	Buf/Car	180	40.7	1	0	4/1	40	3.6	0.59
Justin Faulk	Car	180	48.2	1	1	2/1	38	3.6	0.54
Andrei Markov	Mtl	142	37.6	1	0	4/1	38	3.5	0.69
Christian Ehrhoff	Buf	192	35.4	1	0	4/1	38	3.5	0.57
Nikita Nikitin	CBJ	165	34.0	0	1	3/0	48	3.5	0.68
Mark Fayne	NJ	185	33.6	2	0	0/1	33	3.5	0.63
Alexei Emelin	Mtl	164	28.7	1	1	2/3	43	3.5	0.77
Fedor Tyutin	CBJ	183	50.1	0	1	4/2	51	3.5	0.43

Of the defencemen we previously identified as top penalty-killing options, Giordano ranks 4th, Hjalmarsson 10th, Michalek 12th, Weaver 24th, and Robidas 28th. Our sniff test defencemen, Hal Gill and Zdeno Chara, are still nowhere in sight.

Closing Thoughts

While the various limitations of each single individual statistic make it challenging to identify the league's best penalty killers, putting them all together paints a picture that points in the right direction. This is especially true once we understand the relationship between ice time, defensive zone starts, quality of competition, and attempted shots.

On the blue line, where it's especially critical to get the right players on the ice, Calgary's Mark Giordano and Arizona's Zbynek Michalek bubbled near the top of every list, with Minnesota's

Marco Scandella not far behind. They handle the bulk of their team's shorthanded minutes, in the defensive zone and against top competition, and yet allow fewer attempted shots and goals per minute than their team's other options.

Giordano and Michalek also scored very well in PKE. They may not have been names on our subjectively chosen sniff test, and they don't play for top penalty-killing teams, but they are where all of our evidence is pointing, nevertheless.

As for forwards, where depth-line players who aren't needed elsewhere are sometimes chosen over superior penalty killers, we did manage to create a perspective that shined a light on players like Darren Helm, Michael Grabner, Patrick Marleau, and Jeff Halpern. The analytic evidence didn't paint nearly as clear a picture for forwards, however, and once again the subjectively chosen players didn't finish among our leaders.

In the end, we have a good start and have performed an excellent review of the applications and limitations of the available tools, while establishing some of the key relationships between variables. It will be interesting to see where future developments lead us next.

Who is the Best Power Play Specialist?

By Rob Vollman

At first glance, the question of who is the league's best power play specialist seems like an easy one to solve, with even the simplest of analytics. After all, isn't the best player simply whoever scores the most points on a per-minute basis?

There are a number of problems with that approach, actually. Sample sizes, quality of linemates, defensive liabilities, and the different ways in which players contribute offensively are just some of the ways that a player's scoring rate can be skewed.

That's why a variety of different statistics need to be introduced in order to answer this question. Each of them have their strengths and limitations when used individually, but can start to paint an accurate picture when used together in the right way.

We'll explore each of them momentarily, but first let's dive right in, for a change, with the approach of ranking players by their scoring rate. It does indeed get us most of the way there, after all.

Forwards

The following table includes the combined power play scoring data for all the forwards over the past three seasons, including their playing time with the man advantage (TOI), the percentage that represented of all opportunities (PP%), followed by his games played (GP), goals (G), and assists (A), all ordered by his points per 60 minutes (P/60).

Top 100 Forwards, Power Play Scoring Rate, 2011–12 to 2013–14[121]

Player	Team(s)	TOI	PP%	GP	G	A	P/60
Nicklas Backstrom	Wsh	578.0	64.7	172	11	63	7.68
Claude Giroux	Phi	744.6	60.6	207	16	71	7.01
Carl Soderberg	Bos	144.8	43.2	79	5	11	6.63
Evgeni Malkin	Pit	704.7	80.5	166	21	52	6.22
Sidney Crosby	Pit	555.2	77.7	138	15	41	6.05
Alexander Ovechkin	Wsh	856.2	83.9	203	51	35	6.03
Pavel Datsyuk	Det	494.4	54.7	162	16	31	5.70
John Tavares	NYI	621.1	66.4	189	19	40	5.70
Matt Moulson	NYI/Min	611.7	61.8	204	31	25	5.49
Ryan Nugent-Hopkins	Edm	513.4	53.9	182	9	38	5.49
James Neal	Pit	656.1	69.7	179	30	30	5.49
Logan Couture	SJ	562.6	52.7	193	22	28	5.33
Jason Spezza	Ott	484.4	58.4	160	17	26	5.33

121Acknowledgement: All raw power-play data for my calculations came from *Behind the Net*: http://www.behindthenet.ca.

Taylor Hall	Edm	541.2	55.9	181	21	27	5.32
Paul Stastny	Col	442.5	51.3	190	10	29	5.29
Mike Ribeiro	Dal/Wsh/Phx	612.6	59.5	202	10	42	5.09
Jussi Jokinen	Car/Pit	483.6	43.5	203	12	29	5.09
Ryan O'Reilly	Col	462.6	52.4	190	12	27	5.06
Ryan Getzlaf	Ana	664.3	64.9	203	12	44	5.06
Nathan MacKinnon	Col	181.2	44.8	82	8	7	4.97
Joffrey Lupul	Tor	413.6	52.9	151	17	17	4.93
Phil Kessel	Tor	657.1	60.9	212	20	33	4.84
Reilly Smith	Dal/Bos	173.8	29.3	122	6	8	4.83
Patrick Marleau	SJ	683.2	59.2	212	25	30	4.83
Henrik Zetterberg	Det	563.9	57.0	173	7	38	4.79
Wayne Simmonds	Phi	668.9	53.2	209	30	23	4.75
Anze Kopitar	LA	631.9	54.7	211	13	37	4.75
Joe Pavelski	SJ	663.1	57.6	212	28	24	4.71
Nazem Kadri	Tor	320.5	41.7	147	11	14	4.68
Patrik Elias	NJ	568.4	57.6	194	13	31	4.65
Frans Nielsen	NYI	549.8	53.0	210	12	30	4.58
Craig Smith	Nsh	395.2	41.5	195	15	15	4.55
Johan Franzen	Det	500.6	51.2	172	22	16	4.55
Henrik Sedin	Van	674.0	63.6	200	13	38	4.54
Jamie McGinn	SJ/Col	304.9	29.9	204	14	9	4.53
Ryane Clowe	SJ/NYR/NJ	359.1	41.5	159	8	19	4.51
Joe Thornton	SJ	705.5	61.2	212	6	47	4.51
Mikael Backlund	Cgy	226.6	31.1	149	8	9	4.50
David Krejci	Bos	480.4	51.9	206	5	31	4.50
David Legwand	Nsh/Det	494.2	48.0	209	11	26	4.49
Derick Brassard	CBJ/NYR	549.3	46.9	202	15	26	4.48
T.J. Oshie	StL	469.2	47.6	189	8	27	4.48
David Backes	StL	483.0	45.9	204	18	18	4.47
Andy McDonald	StL	161.8	49.5	62	4	8	4.45
Teemu Selanne	Ana	516.7	53.6	192	16	22	4.41
Jason Arnott	StL	163.4	45.0	72	6	6	4.41
Ondrej Palat	TB	136.5	27.5	95	3	7	4.40
Damien Brunner	Det/NJ	246.1	44.6	104	7	11	4.39
Mats Zuccarello	NYR	260.2	48.0	102	4	15	4.38
Blake Wheeler	Wpg	524.6	50.8	210	14	24	4.35
Martin Erat	Nsh/Wsh/Phx	347.3	37.3	186	5	20	4.32
Patrick Sharp	Chi	584.4	59.2	184	17	25	4.31
Troy Brouwer	Wsh	586.4	55.4	210	22	20	4.30
Chris Kunitz	Pit	712.6	64.8	208	25	26	4.29
Andrei Loktionov	NJ/Car	140.1	19.1	135	4	6	4.28
Scott Hartnell	Phi	589.1	51.6	192	25	17	4.28
Mike Cammalleri	Mtl/Cgy	492.8	54.8	173	12	23	4.26
Tyler Seguin	Bos/Dal	578.4	54.4	209	18	23	4.25
Jordan Eberle	Edm	593.7	55.1	206	18	24	4.24
Jakub Voracek	Phi	693.9	55.2	208	16	33	4.24

Steven Stamkos	TB	594.8	66.8	166	25	17	4.24
Jaden Schwartz	StL	155.9	23.1	132	6	5	4.23
Mark Letestu	Pit/CBJ	312.9	29.0	190	11	11	4.22
Corey Perry	Ana	654.9	62.2	205	24	22	4.21
Ales Hemsky	Edm/Ott	413.1	44.2	182	8	21	4.21
Patrick Kane	Chi	613.5	58.4	198	17	26	4.21
Chris Kreider	NYR	157.1	34.3	89	5	6	4.20
Daniel Sedin	Van	645.2	63.6	192	14	31	4.18
Marcus Johansson	Wsh	474.6	48.3	193	10	23	4.17
Thomas Vanek	Buf/NYI/Mtl	636.1	61.8	194	21	23	4.15
Colin Greening	Ott	217.5	20.5	205	8	7	4.14
Vladimir Tarasenko	StL	174.0	32.8	102	8	4	4.14
Kyle Brodziak	Min	204.2	19.3	211	6	8	4.11
Jaromir Jagr	4 Teams	583.9	53.0	200	15	25	4.11
Jason Pominville	Buf/Min	657.8	61.4	211	16	29	4.10
Mikael Samuelsson	Van/Fla/Det	204.8	45.6	84	7	7	4.10
Ray Whitney	Phx/Dal	600.8	61.1	183	14	27	4.09
Nick Bonino	Ana	294.0	38.1	154	6	14	4.08
Derek Roy	4 Teams	470.5	44.9	197	10	22	4.08
Jeff Carter	CBJ/LA	502.4	51.8	175	23	11	4.06
Matt Duchene	Col	443.3	52.4	176	11	19	4.06
Zach Parise	NJ/Min	624.1	62.3	197	24	18	4.04
Alex Tanguay	Cgy/Col	357.2	56.5	120	3	21	4.03
Radim Vrbata	Phx	551.5	54.6	191	16	21	4.03
Curtis Glencross	Cgy	330.4	44.3	145	13	9	3.99
Mikko Koivu	Min	541.3	62.5	168	3	33	3.99
Cody Hodgson	Van/Buf	496.9	47.1	203	16	17	3.98
Mikhail Grabovski	Tor/Wsh	317.7	34.6	180	8	13	3.97
Max Pacioretty	Mtl	579.5	50.4	196	17	21	3.93
Jarome Iginla	Cgy/Pit/Bos	597.4	59.3	204	15	24	3.92
Lars Eller	Mtl	168.6	14.2	202	5	6	3.92
Jeff Skinner	Car	511.0	51.6	177	15	18	3.87
Colin Wilson	Nsh	341.0	40.3	174	8	14	3.87
Tomas Plekanec	Mtl	527.1	42.6	209	10	24	3.87
Patrice Bergeron	Bos	435.4	46.8	203	13	15	3.86
Tomas Holmstrom	Det	219.0	50.3	74	10	4	3.83
Alexander Steen	StL	422.6	53.1	151	11	16	3.83
Tomas Fleischmann	Fla	564.4	49.6	210	8	28	3.83
P.A. Parenteau	NYI/Col	488.9	55.6	183	13	18	3.80
Brandon Sutter	Car/Pit	174.7	15.5	211	6	5	3.78

Minimum 120 Minutes

While it's quite possible that the league's best power play specialist is among the top five of Nicklas Backstrom, Claude Giroux, Evgeni Malkin, Sidney Crosby and Alexander Ovechkin, each of them are affected by at least a few of the more obvious limitations of this single approach.

Comparing players strictly by their scoring totals simply isn't fair. While no one expects a single statistic, or even a small set of statistics, to answer this kind of question with any level of definitiveness, we need a bit more information before we can crown a winner with any degree of confidence. Fortunately, there are several other pieces of information at our disposal to help complete the picture, which we'll address one at a time.

Problem 1: Even three years can be a small sample size, and one of the reasons Carl Soderberg surprised his way into the top five. With just eight fewer assists, he wouldn't have made the list at all, whereas the same loss wouldn't have budged Giroux by a single position in the table.

Even those with more regular playing time aren't free from the impact of random variation, which is why most players are packed really closely together after the top 15 players or so. Even a single lucky bounce can vault some of these players up to a dozen positions up the rankings.

Of course, we're looking for the league's best player, for whom 600 minutes should be sufficient to rise above the crowd. Still, that's just 10 full NHL games, and probably insufficient for most other purposes.

Proposal: Sometimes looking at more plentiful data, such as shots instead of goals, and passes instead of assists, can provide a more accurate picture of a player's performance.

There are also cases where the problem of small sample sizes can be solved by grouping players together by team, role, or based on some characteristic, for example. That can help determine what style or age grouping is best, but it won't help determine the best player, which is the matter at hand, unfortunately.

Other than that, there's not much we can do to address this because a larger sample size would run the risk of including irrelevant data. That's what could happen if we went back further than three seasons or if we considered even strength data in our analysis.

Problem 2: This scoring rate approach results in the league's top ten playmakers ranking significantly higher than the top ten goal scorers. Top playmakers like Backstrom, Giroux, Malkin, and Crosby are all at the top, while leading goal scorers, like Steven Stamkos and Corey Perry, are much further down than expected. Is it fair to weigh goals and assists equally?

Proposal: The obvious solutions are either to ignore secondary assists or to assign a lesser weight to overall assists, such as 0.64, which will result in equal emphasis between the two. The group of top ten playmakers and top ten snipers will then have the same overall marginal value when that multiplier is used on assists.

But is the underlying premise that snipers and playmakers have equal value correct? That could be an interesting analysis in its own right.

Problem 3: Players don't compete in a vacuum (that would get awfully dusty). Some power plays lack gifted playmakers and/or snipers, or run into hot penalty killers and goalies. Some playmakers, for instance, could be setting up just as many chances as a league leader, but running into hot goalies or struggling alongside inferior shooters. There are doubtlessly some great shooters who are making the most of the limited opportunities their linemates can set up for them.

Those are reasons why players on the same teams are also somewhat bunched together, like Backstrom and Ovechkin, Malkin and Crosby, Tavares and Moulson, Nugent-Hopkins and Hall, Stastny and O'Reilly, Lupul and Kessel, and so many more. This suggests that there's a strong team effect and that some players are getting boosted by great linemates, while others are being dragged down.

Proposal: Just as with the first problem, examining shot-based data instead of goal-based data can sometimes reveal who is generating the most opportunities in a fashion that's a little more independent of the quality of their linemates or opposition goaltending.

There's also individual point percentage, a very old statistic that's making something of a comeback recently. It calculates the percentage of all on-ice goals in which the player either scored or recorded an assist. It helps identify which players are big parts of smaller offences, and who is merely a secondary part of a far more potent force. Unfortunately, this statistic can be skewed by luck over the short term.

Another method is to measure the extent to which a player is being boosted by a particular linemate on a case-by-case basis using WOWY analysis (Without you, With you). That data is conveniently available in 5v5 situations at great statistical sites like David Johnson's *Hockey Analysis*[122], for example, but unfortunately much harder to come by in the 5v4 situations under our current examination.

Problem 4: Context is everything. Further to the previous problem, some of these players are frequently starting their power play shifts already in the opposing zone, and potentially against secondary penalty killers.

Proposal: To an extent, the same statistics that are useful at even strength can be used on the power play, with limited modifications required.

For example, NHL game files provide a count of how many of each player's power play shifts began in the offensive zone and how many didn't. They even reveal which teams won those faceoffs and which teams had to scramble back and start anew from behind their own net.

Quality of competition is a trickier matter, however. We do know who is on the ice at any given time, but how do we determine which players represent tougher competition? We saw in the penalty killing chapter that it's very difficult to rate a collection of players using either their ice time or the number of attempted shots they allow. The former method of estimating quality of competition isn't even readily available, while the latter might not be reliable over such small sample sizes.

122David Johnson, "*Hockey Analysis*", Web, http://www.hockeyanalysis.com.

Problem 5: Some players contribute in ways that don't show up on the scoresheet, like winning faceoffs, causing traffic in front of the net, and screening the goalie. What about them?

Proposal: Consider how many goals were scored while a player was on the ice relative to when he was not. If scoring is up, what difference does it make whose name is on the scoresheet? It's possible that this player was an integral part of that scoring in some fashion or another.

Better yet, consider how many scoring chances or attempted shots occurred, to remove the influence of hot opposing goalies and/or cold shooters.

Even then, however, it can be difficult to establish whether a player is giving his team an advantage or simply lucky enough to be assigned the right linemates. It's also important to account for how frequently they got to begin this shifts in the offensive zone, where attempted shots are just a faceoff win away.

Problem 6: What about those who generate a great deal of scoring but who are prone to taking penalties and/or whose defensive lapses result in shorthanded goals against?

Proposal: Yes, we should take these factors into account, each of which can be translated into the common currency of goals. That being said, the overall difference between even the greatest and the weakest defensive player on the power play is generally not of the greatest significance.

It is also difficult to be certain which players were responsible for such defensive lapses. Nevertheless, the difference in shorthanded scoring (and/or scoring chances, attempted shots) can be considered to get a rough idea whose net benefit to the team might be overstated by looking at scoring alone.

Problem 7: There's also the question of those that work the point on the power play, which is a whole different role and situation, and one that should likely come with a different set of expectations.

There's unfortunately no data source that reveals what percentage of the time players are working the point and/or what their scoring levels are in each situation. The best proxy of which I'm currently aware of is to use a site like Greg Sinclair's *Super Shot Search*[123] to establish what percentage of a player's shots are coming from near the blue line, and use that as an estimate of how much time he is spending back there. This is currently a time-consuming exercise that must be done manually on a case-by-case basis.

Proposal: To get a rough idea of what the impact would be, let's pick the ten players who are best known for working the point on the power play, like Alex Ovechkin, Ryan Getzlaf, Alex Tanguay, Derek Stepan, Jakub Voracek, Jason Pominville, Joe Pavelski, Matt Read, Patrice

---

123Greg Sinclair, "*Super Shot Search*", Web, http://somekindofninja.com/nhl/.

Bergeron, and Pierre-Marc Bouchard. Do these ten have anything in common, statistically?

Ovechkin's work on the point allows him to be assigned 83.9% of power play opportunities, which is second only to Ilya Kovalchuk, who also worked the point. On the other hand, Kovalchuk managed only 3.71 points per 60 minutes, and three of these players (Stepan, Bouchard, and Read) were even lower. Even those who enjoyed more scoring, like Voracek for instance, were actually involved in a lower share of all on-ice scoring.

While this is a pretty rough glance at the topic, it appears that it might be more difficult to get one's name on the scoresheet when working the point. By my estimation, at least 60% of the players on the leader board have worked the point at least occasionally over the past three seasons, potentially yielding a big advantage to those who didn't. This is certainly a topic that warrants more study, but the data is quite limited at the moment.

The Leader Board

Moving on, here's a new table that includes (almost) all of the proposed statistics, including the percentage of all points that the player scored or assisted upon (IPP%), the percentage of all shifts started in the offensive zone (ZS%), attempted shots (Sh/60) and passes (Pa/60) per 60 minutes, the team's goal scoring rate (GFA) and attempted shot rate (AS/60) per 60 minutes, both relative to how the team did without him, and finally the players modified points per 60 minutes (MP/60), with assists worth only 0.64 of a goal.

Top 100 Forwards, Power Play Scoring Rate, 2011–12 to 2013–14[124]

Player	Team(s)	IPP%	ZS%	Sh/60	Pa/60	GFA	Team	AS/60	Team	MP/60
Nicklas Backstrom	Wsh	71.2	80.9	14.0	27.5	10.80	5.14	111.2	81.5	5.33
Alex Ovechkin	Wsh	66.7	79.4	36.6	12.6	9.04	5.12	105.7	72.8	5.14
Carl Soderberg	Bos	72.7	79.0	17.4	41.0	9.12	7.90	95.7	112.1	4.99
Claude Giroux	Phi	79.1	82.7	22.6	34.8	8.86	4.97	115.1	76.1	4.95
Evgeni Malkin	Pit	70.2	80.3	35.2	37.5	8.85	4.21	118.4	83.8	4.62
Matt Moulson	NYI/Min	66.7	80.6	18.3	29.1	8.24	4.92	98.9	78.3	4.61
James Neal	Pit	62.5	80.7	27.6	24.1	8.78	5.46	119.0	86.0	4.50
Sidney Crosby	Pit	70.0	81.0	20.6	28.3	8.65	4.91	114.3	78.9	4.46
Pavel Datsyuk	Det	67.1	78.3	15.0	27.3	8.49	4.25	110.9	93.0	4.35
John Tavares	NYI	71.1	82.0	23.5	24.2	8.02	3.62	103.2	76.9	4.31
Logan Couture	SJ	68.5	78.6	29.0	27.3	7.79	5.70	128.1	108.8	4.26
Taylor Hall	Edm	66.7	75.2	19.4	14.3	7.98	5.48	88.9	76.3	4.24
Jason Spezza	Ott	72.9	78.6	23.8	18.0	7.31	5.38	107.4	85.4	4.17
Nathan MacKinnon	Col	71.4	76.0	21.5	26.5	6.95	5.92	80.1	80.7	4.13
Joffrey Lupul	Tor	63.0	77.2	19.7	23.2	7.83	6.18	93.4	87.5	4.04
Wayne Simmonds	Phi	55.8	84.6	17.9	14.4	8.52	5.40	115.4	80.1	4.01
Joe Pavelski	SJ	59.8	82.5	28.4	30.4	7.87	5.15	127.6	103.2	3.92
Ryan Nugent-Hopkins	Edm	67.1	77.0	16.2	23.4	8.18	5.20	83.7	76.6	3.89
Jamie McGinn	SJ/Col	62.2	78.1	20.9	10.8	7.28	6.03	90.5	96.5	3.89
Patrick Marleau	SJ	59.8	81.7	24.8	21.3	8.08	4.72	125.1	105.6	3.88
Paul Stastny	Col	70.9	78.9	13.0	26.8	7.46	5.58	94.6	80.0	3.87

124Acknowledgement: All raw power play data for my calculations came from *Behind the Net*: http://www.behindthenet.ca except for individual point percentage, shots and passes which came from *Extra Skater*: http://www.extraskater.com.

Johan Franzen	Det	60.3	76.7	21.6	16.5	7.55	5.28	101.5	93.2	3.86
Reilly Smith	Dal/Bos	58.3	74.5	15.5	11.4	8.29	6.72	970	96.8	3.84
Ryan O'Reilly	Col	69.6	80.4	14.3	22.7	7.26	5.28	93.8	80.7	3.80
Jussi Jokinen	Car/Pit	73.2	74.7	16.8	28.0	6.95	7.27	100.9	98.7	3.79
Phil Kessel	Tor	71.6	77.8	24.7	23.8	6.76	6.12	98.1	79.6	3.75
Nazem Kadri	Tor	73.5	71.7	15.5	25.8	6.37	6.15	84.8	96.3	3.74
Craig Smith	Nsh	69.8	74.2	19.1	13.4	6.53	6.67	81.5	81.8	3.73
David Backes	StL	56.3	79.9	16.0	24.8	7.95	5.70	107.3	95.6	3.67
Scott Hartnell	Phi	50.0	83.9	21.5	17.1	8.56	5.97	114.9	83.7	3.65
Mikael Backlund	Cgy	60.7	76.5	13.5	10.3	7.41	6.11	91.1	85.3	3.64
Vladimir Tarasenko	StL	50.0	71.9	19.3	13.8	8.27	7.41	98.6	100.3	3.64
Ryan Getzlaf	Ana	72.7	79.5	23.1	34.5	6.95	4.85	107.0	94.7	3.63
Steven Stamkos	TB	63.6	78.7	27.1	20.1	6.66	4.48	85.9	66.5	3.62
Mike Ribeiro	Dal/Wsh/Phx	62.7	79.1	6.5	23.2	8.13	6.05	97.3	88.3	3.61
Jason Arnott	StL	66.7	79.8	19.8	12.5	6.61	5.72	95.1	108.9	3.61
Jeff Carter	CBJ/LA	63.0	82.4	25.4	14.2	6.45	5.53	101.3	97.3	3.59
Troy Brouwer	Wsh	40.8	79.8	18.6	12.9	10.54	5.47	110.5	86.6	3.56
Jaden Schwartz	StL	55.0	76.0	14.2	11.5	7.70	7.05	98.9	98.0	3.54
Chris Kunitz	Pit	48.6	80.7	15.3	15.0	8.84	6.19	120.0	88.7	3.51
Teemu Selanne	Ana	70.4	81.3	26.5	28.0	6.27	5.77	111.5	93.7	3.49
Corey Perry	Ana	59.7	79.3	20.3	23.9	7.05	4.53	107.4	91.2	3.49
Anze Kopitar	LA	71.4	79.4	15.8	22.1	6.65	4.35	102.3	92.8	3.48
Patrik Elias	NJ	74.6	79.2	12.7	21.9	6.23	5.02	90.3	72.8	3.47
Mark Letestu	Pit/CBJ	66.7	75.2	18.4	22.8	6.33	5.08	104.9	91.6	3.46
Derick Brassard	CBJ/NYR	74.5	78.1	17.7	29.6	6.01	4.93	97.3	99.2	3.46
Colin Greening	Ott	62.5	74.7	18.5	40.0	6.62	6.19	107.0	96.8	3.44
Tomas Holmstrom	Det	56.0	77.0	16.4	12.1	6.85	5.28	108.5	96.9	3.44
Damien Brunner	Det/NJ	58.1	80.5	21.5	29.3	7.56	4.90	89.7	87.8	3.42
Zach Parise	NJ/Min	57.5	78.4	21.0	17.6	7.02	4.91	97.8	72.1	3.41
Curtis Glencross	Cgy	55.0	77.5	11.4	11.8	7.26	5.93	81.7	86.0	3.41
Frans Nielsen	NYI	60.9	80.9	12.8	23.2	7.53	5.66	96.8	92.8	3.40
Tyler Seguin	Bos/Dal	70.7	79.4	27.4	26.2	6.02	5.44	101.6	90.8	3.39
Patrick Sharp	Chi	75.0	84.9	29.5	19.8	5.75	5.06	94.4	83.7	3.39
Andy McDonald	StL	60.0	74.7	14.8	13.7	7.42	7.64	102.8	97.9	3.38
Chris Kreider	NYR	68.8	70.4	13.0	36.7	6.11	5.38	105.8	95.2	3.38
Jordan Eberle	Edm	58.3	78.2	17.7	22.5	7.28	5.82	86.7	75.7	3.37
Thomas Vanek	Buf/NYI/Mtl	62.9	81.5	21.3	26.0	6.60	2.14	99.0	77.0	3.37
Ryane Clowe	SJ/NYR/NJ	69.2	72.7	14.9	32.1	6.52	7.22	101.6	107.2	3.37
Mikael Samuelsson	Van/Fla/Det	70.0	77.7	27.5	26.4	5.86	4.18	101.7	88.9	3.36
Blake Wheeler	Wpg	67.9	76.7	15.9	40.8	6.41	4.84	98.9	84.8	3.36
Andrei Loktionov	NJ/Car	76.9	71.8	14.6	26.6	5.57	4.85	80.5	86.9	3.36
David Legwand	Nsh/Det	61.7	78.6	10.2	19.7	7.28	7.06	87.7	77.7	3.36
Henrik Zetterberg	Det	62.5	81.2	22.1	31.9	7.66	4.24	107.8	93.0	3.33
Henrik Sedin	Van	75.0	83.1	9.3	45.0	6.05	5.60	113.3	86.7	3.32
Patrick Kane	Chi	71.7	83.4	19.4	23.1	5.87	5.36	94.2	94.6	3.29
Ondrej Palat	TB	50.0	69.9	12.7	20.7	8.79	4.84	82.6	74.0	3.29
Kyle Brodziak	Min	63.6	72.1	15.0	33.8	6.46	5.61	94.0	88.7	3.27
Mike Cammalleri	Mtl/Cgy	76.1	82.1	22.2	25.0	5.60	5.91	91.9	86.1	3.25
Cody Hodgson	Van/Buf	60.0	78.6	19.6	30.7	6.64	5.05	93.1	93.7	3.25
T.J. Oshie	StL	56.5	79.4	18.4	30.1	7.93	5.69	109.3	85.3	3.23
Jakub Voracek	Phi	50.0	84.1	28.4	18.7	8.47	5.66	114.4	80.4	3.21
Radim Vrbata	Phx	66.1	79.5	21.9	19.4	6.09	5.37	95.7	84.9	3.20
Dave Bolland	Chi/Tor	71.4	74.7	12.4	28.4	5.22	5.40	76.1	93.6	3.19
Jaromir Jagr	4 Teams	58.8	76.2	18.3	16.3	6.99	4.99	85.4	88.7	3.19
Brandon Sutter	Car/Pit	64.7	59.3	12.4	5.2	5.84	7.81	75.6	104.7	3.16
Jason Pominville	Buf/Min	62.5	81.1	23.5	21.2	6.57	4.21	100.9	76.0	3.15

Max Pacioretty	Mtl	65.5	78.7	21.2	22.7	6.00	4.74	96.4	84.3	3.15
Daniel Sedin	Van	68.2	82.9	19.7	27.7	6.14	5.20	113.7	83.2	3.15
Lars Eller	Mtl	78.6	67.7	19.2	24.2	4.98	5.75	90.0	90.9	3.15
Mats Zuccarello	NYR	63.3	76.2	21.2	19.8	6.92	4.90	109.8	94.8	3.14
Matt Duchene	Col	62.5	80.7	16.9	25.4	6.50	5.65	89.5	84.8	3.13
Marcus Johansson	Wsh	53.2	76.5	9.2	30.3	7.84	8.15	98.7	100.3	3.13
Ray Whitney	Phx/Dal	74.5	78.5	22.5	20.5	5.49	4.07	98.5	82.7	3.12
Patrice Bergeron	Bos	60.9	77.8	19.2	26.7	6.34	7.04	94.3	99.6	3.11
Ales Hemsky	Edm/Ott	64.4	70.7	10.3	11.9	6.54	7.01	78.9	87.4	3.11
Jeff Skinner	Car	62.3	80.9	25.4	29.7	6.22	4.25	98.8	93.1	3.11
David Krejci	Bos	62.1	79.8	13.5	24.7	7.24	5.92	102.5	89.7	3.10
Mikhail Grabovski	Tor/Wsh	61.8	74.2	12.1	24.9	6.42	7.41	86.5	98.3	3.08
Martin Erat	Nsh/Wsh/Phx	67.6	73.6	11.7	30.4	6.39	9.56	87.9	92.7	3.08
Derek Roy	4 Teams	69.6	77.1	19.6	23.2	5.87	6.97	101.8	93.0	3.07
Ryan Callahan	NYR/TB	51.7	82.2	14.5	9.0	6.64	4.52	92.1	89.1	3.07
Joe Thornton	SJ	58.9	82.0	13.9	28.6	7.65	5.23	126.9	102.0	3.07
Nick Bonino	Ana	58.8	72.8	18.2	19.4	6.94	5.77	103.9	98.7	3.05
Jarome Iginla	Cgy/Pit/Bos	51.3	78.2	24.5	22.3	7.63	6.58	95.7	90.0	3.05
Alexander Steen	StL	51.9	78.3	33.9	14.3	7.38	4.99	109.9	87.1	3.02
P.A. Parenteau	NYI/Col	57.4	83.1	16.6	9.0	6.63	5.07	93.0	78.7	3.01
Joel Ward	Wsh	61.9	65.7	13.8	16.6	5.80	8.87	84.7	103.5	2.99
Colin Wilson	Nsh	62.9	76.0	10.9	20.1	6.16	7.23	78.8	83.8	2.98
Brayden Schenn	Phi	61.5	67.6	16.3	20.1	6.12	8.14	84.3	110.8	2.97

Minimum 120 Minutes

That is a lot of data to throw out all at once! Each new statistic will be examined one by one and defined a bit more carefully, in order to help figure out what it's truly telling us about each player and how it can help us identify the league's best.

Individual Point Percentage (IPP%)

This statistic measures what percentage of all on-ice goals a player either scored or assisted upon. It is meant to help determine if he is involved in most of the scoring directly or only indirectly (or not at all). It can help establish if a player's scoring is a generous portion of a small pie or a small piece of a large pie.

The formula is simple, the player's points divided by how many goals his team scored while he was on the ice. In some cases, we go the extra step of calculating it separately for goals and assists.

There's also a shot-based variant where the player's shots and setup passes are divided by all shots instead. Given that setup passes is currently only available through estimates, it's a far less popular approach.

I'm actually uncertain where this statistic came from originally. I first played with it as far back as 2004, including it in my annual super-spreadsheets from day one (the 2006–07 season), but I couldn't tell you where I got it, or if it is just an intuitive idea that occasionally pops up on its own.

Its more recent popularity was definitely triggered by Scott Reynolds[125] during the 2012 lockout, who got the idea from a 2009 article by Tyler Dellow[126]. Since Dellow was one of my few fellow analytics colleagues back in 2004, that's possibly where I could have gotten it too. A new CHL tool from McKeen's[127] has also made it a popular statistic for prospect analysis.

How can this statistic help us here? If the league's best power play specialist plays for a great team with great linemates, then he is likely already on our radar using more traditional statistics. But, if he's on a weaker team and struggling with more mediocre linemates, then he will almost certainly be brought to our attention by ranking well with this measurement.

Essentially, a high IPP% can indicate that a particular player is a critical part of his team's scoring. This could certainly apply in the case of Claude Giroux (79.1%), Mike Cammalleri (76.1%), and Henrik Sedin (75.0%), for example. It's hard to imagine Philadelphia, Calgary, and Vancouver being much of a scoring threat without them.

Consider the same information, but in a more visual format. The following chart includes all the top scorers, with their own scoring on the horizontal axis, and their team's scoring on the vertical axis. In terms of IPP%, those with a really high percentage will be on the bottom/right, while those with low ones will be on the upper/left.

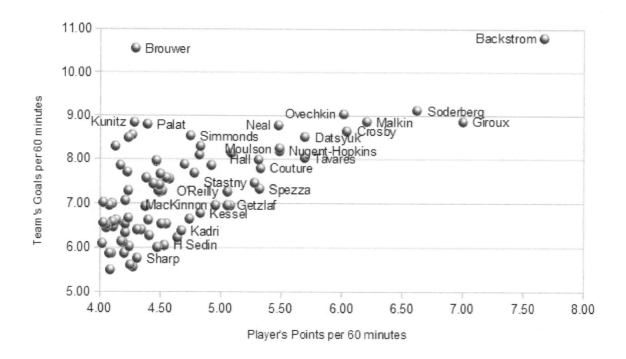

125Scott Reynolds, "Individual Point Percentage on the Power Play (2008–12)", *NHL Numbers*, October 16, 2012, Web, http://nhlnumbers.com/2012/10/16/individual-point-percentage-on-the-power-play-2008-2012.
126Tyler Dellow, "Points v. Scoring", *Battle of Alberta*, November 27, 2009, Web, http://battleofalberta.blogspot.ca/2009/11/points-v-scoring.html.
127McKeen's Hockey, "Minor Hockey Reporting Tool", Web, http://www.mckeenshockey.com/lib/MinorHockeyReportingTool/index.php.

Visualizing a line that runs from the bottom left corner to Backstrom in the top right, Giroux is the only one who truly stands out as being beneath it. His 79.1% IPP% is the highest of those on this second leader board. On the flip side, this perspective is far less kind to Troy Brouwer, Chris Kunitz and Ondrej Palat, who all appear to be small parts of larger offences.

Three of our other top four scoring leaders (Soderberg excluded), Backstrom, Malkin and Crosby, are all nestled between 20th and 26th, with an average IPP% between 70.0% and 71.2%. Ovechkin ranks 39th with 66.7%, but again you have to wonder how much of that more modest result is from working the point so frequently.

How can this perspective help identify other leading candidates? Well, if a great power play specialist has a scoring rate below our five leading candidates, then it is reasonable to expect him to have an IPP% of at least 70%. Why? Because weaker linemates can certainly pull down a player's overall scoring totals, but they shouldn't pull down a player's share of all on-ice scoring. If anything, it should actually be boosted because of how few goals can be scored without him.

That's why we should keep an eye on John Tavares, Jason Spezza, Paul Stastny, Phil Kessel, Nazem Kadri, Ryan Getzlaf, Anze Kopitar, Patrik Elias, Tyler Seguin, Patrick Sharp and Patrick Kane, in addition to the aforementioned Cammalleri and Sedin, as potential candidates for the league's best power play specialists, depending how the rest of their data lines up.

Like all metrics, IPP% also has its limitations. One of the concerns that Dellow expressed right out of the gate was how luck-driven it can be. Particularly high or low results tend to be temporary fluctuations rather than an actual, sustainable view of a player's performance.

In fact, a high IPP% can actually help eliminate some players from consideration, by indicating that a player's scoring levels over the short run were boosted by some good fortune, and may drop off in the long run. It's possible that a player's high IPP% was merely the result of a few extra shots of his bouncing in, or a few extra puck touches of his ultimately resulting in secondary assists, and will gradually fade in the long run. That could explain having players like Lars Eller (78.6%) and Andrei Loktionov (76.9%) on our leader board, for example.

Finally, a high IPP% can also tell us just as much about one's linemates as it does about the player themselves. After all, a marginal player with weak linemates would enjoy an excellent percentage, especially compared with a superior player accompanied by all-stars. Always keep context in mind when using statistic, including this one.

Zone Start Percentage (ZS%)

Typically, neutral zone faceoffs aren't included in a player's offensive zone start percentage, which is meant as more of an indication if a player was used more for his offensive or defensive talents. However, here we intend to use the statistic as an indication of who gets to start most of their shifts in the offensive zone and who has the added responsibility of gaining the zone.

When neutral zone faceoffs are included, the league average for forwards is 75.4%, or a slightly higher 77.8% for those on the top 100 leader board. Patrick Sharp is highest at 84.9%, followed by three Flyers: Wayne Simmonds, Jakub Voracek, and Scott Hartnell. We should consequently expect more from them than, say, Brandon Sutter, who is last on our list at just 59.3%.

How important are these zone starts? Very important, actually. Even to the naked eye, a relationship between offensive zone start percentage and the variation in the number of attempted shots taken is obvious. As the percentage of power play shifts that began in the offensive zone gets higher (i.e., moves to the right), the advantage in attempted shots increases.

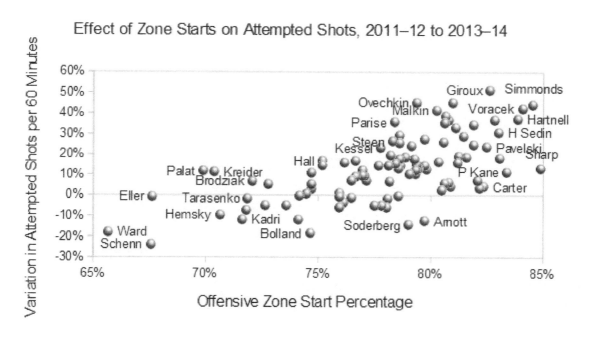

Statistically, the correlation between offensive zone start percentage and the percentage increase in attempted shots is an amazing 0.66, among these top 100 forwards.

Of course, correlation doesn't necessarily imply causation. It makes sense that offensive zone faceoffs would be assigned to the team's top offensive players, like Ovechkin in Washington, and Giroux, Simmonds, Voracek, and Hartnell in Philadelphia. If a power play draw is taken in the defensive zone, why not assign that shift to Joel Ward for Washington or Brayden Schenn in Philadelphia?

So there's a compound effect here. The players who get more offensive zone starts are getting an immediate advantage for attempting shots (and scoring), and also happen to be better players, who generate more shots and goals anyway.

The key is to look for players who give their teams a greater variation in attempted shots than is typical for their share of the offensive zone starts. Those are the players at the top of the chart, including Ovechkin, Giroux, Malkin, and Crosby (the unlabeled point between Malkin and Giroux). Zach Parise is another interesting player who sets himself apart from the crowd.

How do things change when adding quality of competition metrics into the mix and building a rough equivalent of a player usage chart (which is explained in more detail in the Team Essays chapter)? Well, that's actually a bit more of a mess.

Power Play Forwards, Player Usage, 2011–12 to 2013–14

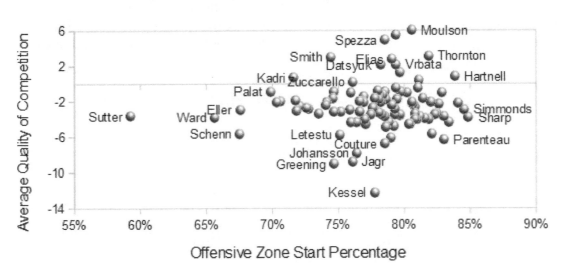

This chart roughly demonstrates which players frequently had to gain the zone first (on the left side of the chart), like Brandon Sutter, Joel Ward, Brayden Schenn and Lars Eller, and the aforementioned players who start their shifts in the offensive zone on the right.

Adding the quality of competition (on the vertical axis) shows which players might be taking on top penalty killers, like Matt Moulson, T.J. Oshie (unlabeled), Jason Spezza, Craig Smith, Patrik Elias and Joe Thornton, for example, and who might be facing secondary units, like perhaps Phil Kessel, Colin Greening, Jaromir Jagr, Marcus Johansson, and Logan Couture. As for the players we've been watching most closely, they're all part of that mess in the middle.

I'm not terribly convinced that quality of competition metrics are useful on special teams, so let's move on.

Goals For Average (GFA)

Players can contribute to scoring in more ways than pulling the trigger or setting up the shot. They can win faceoffs, screen goalies, win battles in the corners, complete outlet passes to the point, and so on. That's why comparing players based on their own individual scoring, or their own share of the team's scoring, isn't entirely fair. This is especially true for those who often work the point. How about giving them more credit for the number of goals that their team scores when they're on the ice?

In absolute terms, a player's GFA is quite team-dependent. That's why three of the top four are Washington Capitals, four of the following six are Pittsburgh Penguins, and four of the remaining seven players in the top 14 are Philadelphia Flyers. For the record, the only four players in the top 14 who aren't from those three teams are Carl Soderberg, Ondrej Palat and Pavel Datsyuk, the former two likely a consequence of a small sample size and the latter because he's awesome.

To address those team effects and get some value out of this statistic, we can instead calculate the boost in team scoring that a player helps provide. For example, scoring is actually tripled when Thomas Vanek is on the ice, and at least doubled with any of Tavares, Malkin, and Backstrom. Datsyuk is a near miss. The other players we've been watching, Giroux, Ovechkin and Crosby, are all together at 9th through 11th by this measure, with boosts in scoring between 76.2% and 78.5%.

How can this help us find overlooked stars? Well, if there's a great player competing on an awful team, then we should see him jump to the top of this list, like Vanek and Tavares. A great player on a great team wouldn't show up on this leader board but, then again, he most certainly would have found other ways on to our radar.

Attempted Shots per 60 Minutes (AS/60)

Rating a team's success when a player is on the ice by the number of goals they score has its limitations, especially over the short run. A team can successfully generate a lot of scoring chances, for example, but run into hot goalies, weak shooters, or plain, old bad luck over a 600 minute stretch of time. In a sample size this small, it only takes a handful of bounces to go the wrong way in order to fall way down the leader board.

That's why it's helpful to confirm goal-based results by looking at shot-based data. Not only can it remove the impact of the opposing goalie, but the additional volume of data can smooth out the wrinkles caused by bad bounces and shooting luck.

In this case, Vanek actually slides down to 17th on our leader board, with a more modest 28.6% increase in attempted shots, while Tavares is 13th with 34.2%. Datsyuk is in 26th with a 19.3% boost, but started only 78.3% of his shifts in the offensive zone, compared to 81.5% and 82.0% for Vanek and Tavares, respectively. That's also why Zach Parise is interesting, having boosted his team's attempted shots by 35.5% despite a similar 78.4% offensive zone start percentage.

Overall, Giroux is still our leader, giving the Flyers a 51.2% boost in attempted shots, with his frequent linemates, Wayne Simmonds, Jakub Voracek (on the point), and Scott Hartnell close behind. Of course, all four of them are above 82.7% and among the league's top 10 in offensive zone start percentage. That makes Ovechkin's 45.2% in second place more impressive, since he started a more modest 79.4% of his shifts in the offensive zone.

Finally, Crosby is in 3rd with 44.9%. The other two players we're watching are right behind: Malkin in 6th with 41.4% and Backstrom 10th at 36.5%. All three of them have offensive zone start percentages between 80.3% and 81.0%.

Shots and Passes per 60 Minutes (Sh/60 and Pa/60)

Just as shot-based data can help confirm team-level results, they can help sort things out at the individual player level too.

While a player's goal-based scoring totals can be influenced by random luck and hot or cold shooters and goalies over the short run, shot-based data is harder to fool. The additional volume of data helps identify which players are consistently taking and/or setting up shots. Over the long run, a player's actual scoring totals tend to gravitate towards those levels.

While we do have a record of which player attempts each shot on the power play, the NHL doesn't record which player set it up. We do have a way of estimating setup passes, which Ryan Stimson[128] discovered was reasonably accurate (within around 5%) only if the player has enough primary assists. That's not likely to be the case for many of these players. Its usage is a somewhat controversial matter within the community, one that's touched on in more detail in the Q&A chapter. If you prefer, think of it as simply a re-presentation of primary assists, one that takes on-ice shooting percentage into account. Or, just disregard it altogether.

When it comes to shot-based data, what we're really looking for is a sober second thought. Not that there's anything inferior about goal-based data, especially with adequate sample sizes, but rather that we'd like to confirm that the players who are most consistently generating goals and assists are also the ones who are consistently taking and setting up shots too. It's also an opportunity to find players who are taking and setting up shots just as consistently, but whose linemates aren't blessed with the same level of luck and/or talent to turn as many of them into goals.

It's great to see the validity of our shot-based perspective confirmed by finding Malkin at the top of our list, a player who takes or generates 72.7 shots per 60 minutes. That's a staggering lead over second place Joe Pavelski, who generates 58.8. Among those with sufficient primary assists to provide a reasonable estimate, Getzlaf (57.6) and Giroux (57.5) are next.

As for the rest of our big five, Ovechkin and Crosby are around 15th with 49.2 and 49.0 respectively. Bear in mind that shot-based data is not always kind to generational talents like these two. Since virtually everything they touch consistently turns to goals, shot-based data doesn't really do their incredible talents any justice.

128Ryan Stimson, "Why Setup Passes and PSR are Unreliable", *In Lou We Trust*, May 7, 2014, Web, http://www.inlouwetrust.com/2014/5/7/5677850/why-estimating-passes-is-unreliable.

The players ahead of them include Blake Wheeler, Logan Couture, Jeff Skinner, Teemu Selanne, Henrik Sedin, Henrik Zetterberg, Tyler Seguin, Mikko Koivu, James Neal, and Patrick Sharp. Whether those are players who are actually generating more scoring opportunities, or just statistical blips caused by estimates or questionable shot quality can hopefully be resolved by using our other metrics, or taking a deeper look on a case-by-case basis.

As for Backstrom, it raises some concern to see him all the way down at 41.5. That means that there's at least some evidence that his high scoring may be particularly reliant on Ovechkin, and that his scoring totals wouldn't otherwise be that dissimilar from the next level of playmakers, like Datsyuk, Spezza and Joe Thornton, without him. Then again, remember that shot-based data isn't always the right perspective for rules-defying talents like Ovechkin.

Modified Points per 60 Minutes (MP/60)

Finally, let's re-visit our first perspective, which was to simply consider everybody's scoring rate, but assigning a weight of just 0.64 for each assist. To be precise, the formula is: assists times 0.64, plus goals, all divided by the player's power play ice time, and then multiplied by 60 minutes.

This modified version of each player's scoring rate will put goals and assists on an equal footing, and puts the top 10 snipers even with the top 10 playmakers. Whether or not that's actually an appropriate thing to do is a little outside the scope of this analysis. Bitter feuds have erupted in the analytic community over far less than deciding how important assists are relative to goals. A safer approach might have been to count primary assists only, instead.

In any event, our big five are relatively close together, with Backstrom (5.33) and Ovechkin (4.99) leading the way, followed by Giroux (4.95), Malkin (4.62), and Crosby (4.46). Their linemate James Neal (4.50) sneaks in between them, as does Matt Moulson (4.61). Right behind this group we find Datsyuk (4.35), Tavares (4.31), and Couture (4.26), each of whom have also been discovered using some of our other perspectives.

Defensive Considerations

Before we put everything together and start making a case for some of these players, let's consider the other things players do to help their team on the power play. Or, at the very least, to avoid hurting them.

Without going into too much detail, I devised a quick metric that converts a player's faceoff record, their penalties drawn and taken, and the number of shorthanded goals the team allowed while he was on the ice to get a rough idea of which player's offensive contributions might be coming at the highest cost. It's an approach quite similar to the PKE statistic introduced in the chapter on penalty killing.

The formula is one fifth of goals against (assuming all five players are equally responsible for those shorthanders), plus 1/40th of faceoff losses minus wins, plus one fifth of the player's penalties taken minus those drawn. That end result is divided by his power play ice time and multiplied by 60, to roughly approximate the number of goals the player cost their team.

It turns out that the results aren't terribly significant. The average player on the power play costs their team just 0.2 goals per 60 minutes, which is barely noticeable in the grand scheme of things.

Some players definitely appear to be worse than others, but none of those currently under consideration as the league's best are any worse that 0.4. In fact, Crosby, Giroux, and Datsyuk don't cost their teams at all! Giroux, for example, drew seven more penalties than he took, while dominating the faceoff circle 480 to 367. That's yet one more reason to build our first case for him.

The Top Candidates

Analytics aren't about providing definitive answers but in gathering information that points in persuasive directions. After all of this analysis, it appears that we can make a strong analytic case for about four or five players in particular, and can identify about another 10 potential candidates from the field. Let's examine each one in more detail.

The Case for Claude Giroux

I think the strongest case for best power play specialist can be made for Philadelphia's Claude Giroux. Over the past three seasons, he has been one of only two players to average at least 7.0 points per 60 minutes on the power play, and only Alexander Ovechkin has logged more minutes. Even once his scoring is adjusted to balance goal scorers with playmakers, Giroux is still top three.

What's more, the Flyers go from 4.97 goals and 76.1 attempted shots per 60 minutes to an amazing 8.86 goals and 115.1 attempted shots when Giroux is on the ice, a massive jump that puts him in the top 10. Sure, he started 82.7% of his shifts in the offensive zone, which ranks 9th among the top players, but his numbers are disproportionally dominant.

Those who see things differently might partially credit his linemates Wayne Simmonds, Scott Hartnell, or Jakub Voracek for that jump, but I don't see it that way. After all, Giroux is in on an amazing 79.1% of the scoring when he's on the ice, and no one else even comes close. His own linemates are only between 50% and 58.8%, and should probably be the ones thanking him, since he sets up 34.8 shots per 60 minutes, second to Evgeni Malkin. Add in his own attempted shots, and his total offence is 4th in the NHL.

Finally, we saw that Giroux's scoring doesn't come at much of a defensive price. In fact, he drew seven more penalties than he took, and dominated the faceoff battle 480 to 367.

While today's analytics can't offer any foolproof guarantees about who really is the league's best power play specialist, the strongest case can certainly be built for Claude Giroux.

The Case for Sidney Crosby or Evgeni Malkin

One of the safest picks for the league's best power play specialist is Sidney Crosby, who is very likely the league's best player, especially on the offensive side of the spectrum. Very few people would argue too strongly against such a selection, or his more offensive-minded teammate Evgeni Malkin.

There's a reasonable analytic basis to each selection as well. Only two players have a higher scoring rate over the past two seasons than Malkin and Crosby (Backstrom and Giroux), and that's despite handling a whopping 80.5% and 77.7% of power play minutes, respectively. Only Ovechkin is higher and the next highest is their linemate James Neal, all the way down at 66.4%.

They're in on 70.2% and 70.0% of the team's scoring, respectively, which is essentially the standard of excellence that only a dozen players can consistently exceed. Neal is in on 62.5%, and Chris Kunitz just 48.6%, so it's obvious which duo is driving the bus on this great power play.

Malkin takes 35.2 shots per 60 minutes, second only to Ovechkin's 36.6, and his estimated 37.5 setup passes per 60 minutes is top five. Add it up, and no one can match the 72.7 shots per 60 minutes that he's personally involved in, the nearest being Joe Pavelski at 58.8.

The Penguins score 8.85 goals per 60 minutes when Malkin's on the ice, and 8.65 with Crosby, compared with 4.21 and 4.91, respectively, when they're not. That's a huge leap! Malkin is one of only four players with whom scoring doubles and Crosby's boost is also in the top 10. The end scoring result is bested only by Washington's Backstrom and Ovechkin, Giroux, and their linemate Neal.

The same pattern holds up when looking only at the attempted shots they generate, which jumps from 83.8 to 118.4 with Malkin, and 78.9 to 114.3 with Crosby, the 6th and 3rd biggest boosts in the league, respectively. The end result is actually higher than Giroux and the Capitals' star duo and, other than their linemates, behind only San Jose's Joe Thornton (126.9), Logan Couture (128.1), Joe Pavelski (127.6), and Patrick Marleau (125.1).

And what of defensive considerations? Malkin's offence comes at a bit more of a price. Pittsburgh's goals-against average is 1.28 with him on the ice, versus 0.97 with Crosby. He's also 147-136 in the faceoff circle versus 372-260 for Crosby, and ended 13 power plays with penalties of his own (while drawing five), while Crosby hasn't taken a 5v4 penalty in at least three seasons (while drawing two). The end result is a swing of about half a goal per 60 minutes.

So who is driving the bus? Normally we would do a WOWY (Without you, With You) analysis, looking at how the team does when one of them is one the ice without the other. Unfortunately, that data is unavailable in 5v4 situations. I privately asked David Johnson, who manages the *Hockey Analysis* website[129] that typically hosts such information, and he felt that while the data he had simply wasn't definitive either way, it was hard to go wrong with either one.

Johnson suggested I look at their 5v5 data, despite the limited data (they have played only 201.3 minutes together over the past three seasons combined). Together, Crosby and Malkin scored 4.47 and 4.17 points per 60 minutes, respectively, and when apart, Crosby drops to 3.11, and Malkin about the same distance to 2.69. Nothing conclusive there!

He also suggested looking at the 2011–12 season, when injuries kept Crosby to just 22 games. That year Malkin scored 5.83 points per 60 minutes on the power play and he has scored 6.52 points per 60 minutes in the two seasons since then. Not exactly overwhelming evidence, but Crosby might have a slight edge for the driver's seat.

Either way, when you add it all up, a strong case can be made for either of Pittsburgh's superstars. The only real point against them is the compound effect that is at play. If they were split up, would their numbers remain superior to other power play specialists toiling by themselves (or with more mortal linemates), like John Tavares or Thomas Vanek? It's possible, but these remain two dominant power play specialists who can each reasonably be considered the best.

The Case for Alexander Ovechkin or Nicklas Backstrom

Throughout the argument for Malkin, I repeatedly typed the phrase "second only to Ovechkin", so wouldn't that make him the more logical choice for the league's best power play specialist?

After all, Ovechkin is one of only five players who has averaged at least 6.0 points per 60 minutes over the past three seasons, and his 51 goals trump second place Matt Moulson by a whopping 20. Given his league-leading 36.6 shots per 60 minutes, we know that's no fluke. Malkin (35.2) and Alexander Steen (33.9) are the only other two players to hit the net at least 30 times per 60 minutes.

Our modified scoring rate, which places equal weight on goals and assists, ranks Ovechkin second to his centre Nicklas Backstrom. That's especially impressive when we consider how frequently "the Great Eight" works the point with the man advantage, and the fact that he's assigned 83.9% of all power play minutes, far more than Backstrom (64.7%), and virtually anyone in the NHL except Malkin (80.5%) and Crosby (77.7%).

Speaking of Backstrom, can a case be made for him? On the surface, it certainly appears that the talented setup man is indispensable to Ovechkin, helping boost the team's attempted shot

129David Johnson, *Hockey Analysis*, Web, http://www.hockeyanalysis.com.

rate from a lowly 72.8 to 105.7 per 60 minutes, and goals scored from 5.12 to 9.04 per 60 minutes. Those are the 2nd and 10th biggest boosts in the league.

While there are certainly compelling points in Backstrom's favour, the total of his shots and estimated setup passes per 60 minutes is just 41.5. This suggests that he would be among strong upper-tier playmakers like Jason Spezza and Joe Thornton without the game's top sniper playing alongside him. This interpretation is not going to sit right with those who place more value on secondary assists, which Backstrom provides in spades.

We could perhaps offer something more definitive if WOWY data were available in 5v4 situations, but it's not. For what it's worth, Backstrom has actually done better *without* Ovechkin in 5v5 situations over the past three seasons, scoring 1.77 points per 60 minutes with him and 1.98 points without him. The opposite is true of Ovechkin, whose scoring drops from 1.92 points per 60 minutes when they're together, down to 1.59 without Backstrom. If the same is true on the power play, then a case can most certainly be made for the Swedish playmaker.

As for Ovechkin, his tremendous scoring may come at a slight cost, as the Capitals have given up 19 shorthanders when he's been on the ice over the past three seasons, or 1.33 per 60 minutes. This is quite inconsequential relative to all the additional offence he provides, however.

The strongest argument for Ovechkin being the league's best power play specialist is based on a strong emphasis on goal scoring, downplaying Backstrom's contributions, and making an allowance for the greater volume of minutes Ovechkin handles, especially while working the point. If those three arguments can be established, then Ovechkin's selection as the league's best power play specialist would follow.

The Case for Someone Else

It is entirely possible that the league's best power play specialist is not one of the four more obvious candidates, but someone who toils on a team with lesser secondary talents. Assuming that's the case, who might it be? In my view there are about six to ten players from the field for whom a case can also be built, especially Pavel Datsyuk and John Tavares.

It probably wouldn't surprise anyone if a player of Datsyuk's enormous talent was the game's best power play specialist, and perhaps not long ago he truly was. Over the last three years, he's been top ten in power play scoring rate at 5.70, even with the modified version, at 4.35.

Detroit scored 8.49 goals per 60 minutes when he's on the ice, the highest of anyone who doesn't play for the big three (Washington, Philadelphia, and Pittsburgh), and up from 4.25 when he's not on the ice. Only four other players have provided that much of a boost, which is also apparent when looking at attempted shots.

His all-around play has also resulted in just seven goals against (or 0.85 per 60 minutes), a record of 257–190 in the faceoff circle, and taking only one penalty while drawing two. On the flip side, Datsyuk has worked only 54.7% of power play opportunities, which seems a little low. He has also enjoyed the tremendous advantage of having Henrik Zetterberg on his wing.

Detroit does have a good power play, and it does make sense that someone from perhaps San Jose, Chicago, or Anaheim could also have the league's best specialist. In this case, we would look at someone like Logan Couture, Patrick Sharp, or Ryan Getzlaf, each of whom are in a fair deal of the team's scoring, and generate a lot of shots or passes.

The most likely option among those who don't play for a team with a strong power play is John Tavares of the New York Islanders. He isn't as fortunate as everyone else to have superstar linemates, managing instead with the likes of Matt Moulson, Frans Nielsen, and P.A. Parenteau. Tavares nevertheless has a top 10 scoring rate, even once modified. He understandably works a hefty 66.4% of power plays, and is still in on 71.1% of the scoring, right in line with Crosby and Ovechkin.

Most impressively, the Islanders' scoring is boosted to an excellent 8.02 goals (and 103.2 attempted shots) per 60 minutes with him on the ice, up from a paltry 3.62 goals (and 76.9 shots) without him. He is one of only four players with whom scoring has doubled when he was on the ice, and is 13th in shot-based boost. The Isles have also allowed just 0.48 goals against per 60 minutes, when he's been out there.

There is the possibility of another Tavares somewhere in the field, someone playing an equally big part of a weaker offence. Thomas Vanek, the Sedins, and Mike Cammalleri all come to mind, but without analytic support anywhere near what can be put together for Tavares.

In the end, we may never truly know how well someone like Tavares or Datsyuk would do if they enjoyed the same conditions as Giroux, Crosby, Malkin, or Ovechkin but it's not outside the realm of possibility that they would do just as well, or possibly even better.

Defencemen

Subjectively speaking, 2012 and 2013 Norris Trophy winners Erik Karlsson and P.K. Subban are the two obvious candidates for the league's best power play specialist, with Shea Weber, the runner up in 2011 and 2012, close behind. Do the analytics line up? Essentially, yes.

There are a few key differences on the power play between forwards and defencemen to bear in mind. First of all, a power play quarterback can work up to 70% of the team's minutes with the man advantage, which is noticeably more than all but a few forwards.

Secondly, defencemen are a much smaller part of the scoring than forwards. With tips and bounces and rebounds, they don't often get as much opportunity to record their names on the scoresheet from way back on the blue line. And when they do, it's typically as an assist instead of a goal, in a ratio that's well over three to one.

Finally, everything is confused by the fact that some forwards work the point and that some defencemen, like Dustin Byfuglien or Brent Burns, move up front on the power play.

With all of that in mind, let's examine the compressed leader board for defencemen, including each player's ice time (TOI), the percentage that represents of all power play opportunities (PP%), their goals (G) and assists (A), their scoring rate (P/60), what percentage that represents of all the team's scoring (IPP%), the team's goal scoring rate when they're on the ice (GFA), and when they're not (Team).

And yes, that's a lot of numbers to be thrown out all at once, but we're using the exact same statistics as we did with forwards and should therefore be looking for the same things while being aware of the same limitations. We will also interpret the data right away. And notice that we don't have enough data for reliable pass estimates, nor enough goals to mess around with the modified scoring rate.

Do remember to keep an eye on sample size. Since there are only six defencemen from which to choose, sometimes a depth option can get decent exposure on the power play. A few good bounces can make those players (and certain rookies) almost indistinguishable from a legitimate power play threat (analytically, at least). That may be the case for the first four players on the list, in fact.

Top 100 Defencemen, Power Play Scoring Rate, 2011–12 to 2013–14[130]

Player	Team(s)	TOI	PP%	G	A	IPP%	GFA	ZS%	Team	P/60
Eric Gelinas	NJ	143.6	47.1	3	12	78.9	7.94	66.4	6.32	6.27
Torey Krug	Bos	199.7	54.6	6	14	80.0	7.51	83.2	8.67	6.04
Patrick Wiercioch	Ott	238.3	49.6	6	16	75.9	7.30	73.3	6.69	5.54
Morgan Rielly	Tor	140.2	38.1	1	11	63.2	8.13	69.7	6.06	5.14
Shea Weber	Nsh	675.9	69.1	22	32	58.7	8.17	81.2	4.76	4.79
Cody Franson	Tor	431.7	47.1	5	29	69.4	6.81	76.4	5.70	4.73
Ryan Whitney	Edm/Fla	209.0	46.0	2	14	69.6	6.60	72.9	7.10	4.59
Alex Pietrangelo	StL	570.8	52.8	9	34	63.2	7.15	75.2	6.12	4.52
Dustin Byfuglien	Wpg	617.4	66.5	15	31	74.2	6.02	80.4	4.82	4.47
Kevin Shattenkirk	StL	609.2	56.0	11	34	61.6	7.19	80.0	6.02	4.43
Erik Karlsson	Ott	697.2	73.7	9	42	68.9	6.37	78.3	6.02	4.39
Niklas Kronwall	Det	622.8	52.5	11	34	55.6	7.80	78.4	4.47	4.34
Zdeno Chara	Bos	488.9	53.2	20	15	62.5	6.87	76.8	6.68	4.30
Marc-Andre Bergeron	TB/Car	182.7	50.1	1	12	72.2	5.91	70.1	3.96	4.27
Kris Letang	Pit	478.4	72.4	10	24	49.3	8.65	79.6	6.90	4.26
Kimmo Timonen	Phi	691.6	56.9	8	41	52.1	8.16	82.8	5.96	4.25
John Carlson	Wsh	470.4	44.2	9	24	51.6	8.16	73.1	8.27	4.21
Mark Streit	NYI/Phi	665.2	61.7	8	38	56.1	7.40	78.8	6.84	4.15
Mike Green	Wsh	393.8	57.9	8	19	45.8	8.99	75.9	9.85	4.11
Alexander Edler	Van	608.0	59.7	14	27	65.1	6.22	82.7	5.41	4.05
James Wisniewski	CBJ	536.4	60.9	6	30	73.5	5.48	79.8	5.92	4.03

130Acknowledgement: All raw power-play data for my calculations came from *Behind the Net*: http://www.behindthenet.ca.

Brent Burns	SJ	422.3	44.3	7	21	66.7	5.97	75.1	7.46	3.98
Corey Potter	Edm/Bos	197.7	33.1	1	12	56.5	6.98	74.9	8.55	3.95
Filip Kuba	Ott/Fla	214.2	37.9	3	11	50.0	7.84	70.9	6.16	3.92
Duncan Keith	Chi	586.7	55.7	6	31	62.7	6.13	81.2	5.02	3.78
Brian Campbell	Fla	812.3	70.3	7	44	63.0	5.98	79.5	2.79	3.77
Nick Leddy	Chi	466.2	41.8	6	23	64.4	5.79	73.0	5.27	3.73
Jay Bouwmeester	Cgy/StL	434.9	39.1	4	23	56.3	6.62	67.9	6.65	3.73
Keith Yandle	Phx	790.9	71.3	8	41	61.3	6.07	78.8	5.08	3.72
Sergei Gonchar	Ott/Dal	566.7	54.5	4	31	62.5	5.93	73.7	5.97	3.71
Ryan Suter	Nsh/Min	745.6	71.6	7	39	50.0	7.40	79.1	5.07	3.70
Alec Martinez	LA	244.8	33.1	5	10	68.2	5.39	68.9	5.59	3.68
Nicklas Lidstrom	Det	245.0	62.1	4	11	50.0	7.35	77.7	5.21	3.67
Dion Phaneuf	Tor	683.6	63.9	9	32	52.6	6.85	79.2	6.06	3.60
Dennis Wideman	Wsh/Cgy	551.3	63.9	10	23	60.0	5.99	79.6	5.58	3.59
Michael Stone	Phx	134.4	20.5	3	5	66.7	5.36	69.7	6.67	3.57
Slava Voynov	LA	459.9	45.8	5	22	58.7	6.00	73.9	5.51	3.52
Mark Giordano	Cgy	511.5	59.3	12	18	50.0	7.04	79.3	5.14	3.52
Victor Hedman	TB	324.1	34.5	2	17	52.8	6.66	73.8	5.47	3.52
Jay Harrison	Car	187.9	18.8	3	8	55.0	6.39	70.6	5.09	3.51
Andrei Markov	Mtl	603.4	71.0	6	29	52.2	6.66	80.4	4.13	3.48
Matt Irwin	SJ	190.5	35.9	5	6	44.0	7.87	60.1	7.25	3.46
T.J. Brodie	Cgy	330.8	37.2	2	17	76.0	4.53	71.4	7.51	3.45
Carlo Colaiacovo	StL/Det	175.3	37.1	0	10	58.8	5.82	71.7	6.88	3.42
P.K. Subban	Mtl	833.4	69.1	11	36	56.6	5.98	79.4	4.18	3.38
Erik Johnson	Col	426.6	50.1	3	21	54.5	6.19	77.7	5.64	3.38
Raphael Diaz	Mtl/Van/NYR	268.1	31.3	0	15	78.9	4.25	74.1	5.61	3.36
Chris Phillips	Ott	214.5	20.6	6	6	54.5	6.15	65.5	6.31	3.36
Kevin Bieksa	Van	357.6	35.4	4	16	54.1	6.21	68.6	5.98	3.36
Paul Martin	Pit	358.0	46.7	3	17	42.6	7.88	72.1	7.65	3.35
Andy Greene	NJ	304.4	31.7	4	13	60.7	5.52	64.6	5.85	3.35
Kurtis Foster	4 Teams	180.8	47.6	1	9	45.5	7.30	80.5	6.63	3.32
Justin Schultz	Edm	384.1	58.3	4	17	56.8	5.78	77.3	6.57	3.28
Sami Vatanen	Ana	128.6	41.6	2	5	63.6	5.13	76.1	7.32	3.26
Travis Hamonic	NYI	223.8	24.3	4	8	52.2	6.17	63.2	7.31	3.22
Tobias Enstrom	Wpg	522.4	64.1	6	22	50.0	6.43	79.1	4.50	3.22
Dan Boyle	SJ	717.2	65.5	7	31	45.8	6.94	81.2	6.35	3.18
Jonas Brodin	Min	171.1	27.3	4	5	56.3	5.61	60.2	6.45	3.16
Matthew Carle	Phi/TB	457.4	37.3	6	18	57.1	5.51	70.8	6.88	3.15
Marek Zidlicky	NJ	592.9	59.8	10	21	53.4	5.87	78.0	4.67	3.14
Yannick Weber	Mtl/Van	250.2	37.6	6	7	65.0	4.80	74.8	4.18	3.12
Jared Spurgeon	Min	443.7	49.7	8	15	56.1	5.54	73.7	6.54	3.11
Matt Niskanen	Pit	485.5	47.0	6	19	46.3	6.67	73.5	8.87	3.09
Ryan Murray	CBJ	136.0	38.6	3	4	58.3	5.30	75.0	8.06	3.09
Joni Pitkanen	Car	175.0	53.1	2	7	50.0	6.17	78.9	4.66	3.09
Alex Goligoski	Pit/Dal	606.4	55.5	4	27	53.4	5.74	76.1	5.30	3.07
Cam Fowler	Ana	608.8	62.4	7	24	50.8	6.01	77.4	5.56	3.06
Carl Gunnarsson	Tor	137.7	14.2	0	7	50.0	6.10	60.4	6.85	3.05

Michael Del Zotto	NYR/Nsh	532.9	53.3	2	25	57.4	5.29	79.7	5.92	3.04
Joe Corvo	Bos/Car/Ott	319.0	43.6	3	13	50.0	6.02	76.9	5.39	3.01
Dan Hamhuis	Van	399.9	36.4	1	19	60.6	4.95	72.1	6.11	3.00
Dougie Hamilton	Bos	200.8	44.3	4	6	43.5	6.87	78.2	6.65	2.99
Lubomir Visnovsky	Ana/NYI	422.9	65.1	3	18	55.3	5.39	80.8	6.34	2.98
Jason Demers	SJ	284.2	34.1	3	11	53.8	5.49	72.7	6.22	2.96
Roman Josi	Nsh	426.4	52.4	3	18	47.7	6.19	77.2	7.76	2.96
Oliver Ekman-Larsson	Phx	650.8	59.3	10	22	43.8	6.73	77.4	4.44	2.95
Sheldon Souray	Dal/Ana	185.3	36.7	4	5	40.9	7.12	72.4	6.00	2.91
Fedor Tyutin	CBJ	453.1	43.2	1	21	52.4	5.56	75.4	5.45	2.91
Dmitry Kulikov	Fla	434.4	44.6	6	15	53.8	5.39	72.6	4.12	2.90
Andrej Sekera	Buf/Car	290.1	31.1	5	9	58.3	4.96	74.0	5.32	2.90
Sami Salo	Van/TB	471.0	42.5	4	16	44.4	6.47	80.4	5.95	2.88
Jason Garrison	Fla/Van	500.9	44.8	12	12	54.5	5.27	77.8	5.73	2.88
Ryan Ellis	Nsh	252.2	35.8	4	8	54.5	5.23	69.3	7.58	2.86
Seth Jones	Nsh	147.8	38.4	2	5	41.2	6.90	81.7	6.58	2.84
Tyson Barrie	Col	258.8	51.9	3	9	48.0	5.80	80.9	6.26	2.78
John-Michael Liles	Tor/Car	367.4	50.5	5	12	53.1	5.23	78.7	6.33	2.78
Marco Scandella	Min	131.5	18.2	1	5	46.2	5.93	62.6	5.68	2.74
Kris Russell	CBJ/StL/Cgy	311.4	39.8	5	9	56.0	4.82	74.3	6.37	2.70
Francois Beauchemin	Ana	338.7	33.1	5	10	39.5	6.73	69.8	5.35	2.66
Tyler Myers	Buf	365.3	44.9	5	11	57.1	4.60	74.2	4.95	2.63
Grant Clitsome	CBJ/Wpg	205.8	26.5	3	6	69.2	3.79	70.5	5.67	2.62
Stephane Robidas	Dal/Ana	320.9	38.4	3	11	50.0	5.24	73.4	5.37	2.62
Christian Ehrhoff	Buf	596.4	59.4	3	23	38.8	6.74	79.8	3.09	2.62
Justin Faulk	Car	440.4	46.9	6	13	44.2	5.86	78.4	5.05	2.59
Philip Larsen	Dal/Edm	163.3	27.4	3	4	50.0	5.15	68.6	5.12	2.57
Brent Seabrook	Chi	443.3	41.0	8	11	55.9	4.60	72.3	5.93	2.57
Tomas Kaberle	Car/Mtl	280.1	58.4	1	11	48.0	5.35	80.9	6.92	2.57
Jake Muzzin	LA	282.9	43.1	4	8	50.0	5.09	72.9	6.75	2.55
Jake Gardiner	Tor	354.2	41.5	3	12	44.1	5.76	68.9	7.22	2.54
Jack Johnson	LA/CBJ	713.4	60.6	7	23	51.7	4.88	77.8	5.31	2.52

Minimum 120 Minutes

Using this rather impressive collection of data, let's see how strong a case can be built for our likeliest candidates: Erik Karlsson, P.K. Subban, and Shea Weber or possibly somebody else.

The Case for Erik Karlsson

At first glance, the case for Karlsson doesn't appear to be very strong. Just compare his numbers to the nearly identical statistics of St. Louis' top pairing, Alex Pietrangelo and Kevin Shattenkirk, for example. Each of those Blues score at a slightly higher rate than Karlsson and, while their respective teams score at roughly the same rate without them, the Blues do a lot better with Pietrangelo and Shattenkirk than the Senators do with Karlsson.

266

Then again, there's a compound effect at play. Shattenkirk and Pietrangelo are out there with each other, Karlsson's out there with guys like Filip Kuba, an aging Sergei Gonchar, Joe Corvo, or even Chris Phillips. There's a big difference there!

Karlsson is consequently leaned on more heavily and gets more of the ice time, 73.7% of it compared to 56.0% and 52.8% for Shattenkirk and Pietrangelo. There are only five other defencemen behind Karlsson who play at least 70% of their team's power play minutes: Kris Letang, Ryan Suter, Keith Yandle, Andrei Markov, and Brian Campbell. Shea Weber and P.K. Subban just missed.

Karlsson is also in on more of the on-ice scoring, 68.9% of it, relative to 61.6% and 63.2% for Shattenkirk and Pietrangelo, respectively. Dustin Byfuglien and James Wisniewski are the only regulars who have been in on more of their team's scoring than Karlsson. In the former case, it's likely because he frequently plays forward, and in the latter case it's because his team's power play is potentially even weaker than Ottawa's.

Is Karlsson the league's best playmaker on the point? When you consider both his ice time and his talent, it's easy to see why the speedy Swede is one of only four defencemen to record 40 assists over the past three seasons, behind Brian Campbell, and in front of Kimmo Timonen and Keith Yandle (with Ryan Suter and Mark Streit close behind).

These assists aren't a result of lucky bounces but of consistently creating chances. While the lack of primary assists makes it hard to estimate the number of setup passes for all but a few of the top defencemen, Karlsson and Campbell are clearly on top here. They're the only players with at least 300 setup passes over this time range, although Yandle is just one short.

Even on a per-60-minutes basis, where a few bounces can send anyone up the chart, Karlsson is still fourth with 28.2 setup passes. His total offence of 55.1 shots and passes per 60 minutes is the highest among power play regulars, tucked in between oft-forwards Dustin Byfuglien and Brent Burns.

The only real knock against Karlsson is having allowed 15 goals while he's been on the ice, which is tied with Dion Phaneuf for the lead. In the end, that could be a relatively miniscule price to pay for potentially the league's strongest scoring threat.

The Case for P.K. Subban

The most common counter-argument to Karlsson's candidacy for the league's top power play specialist from the point would obviously be for P.K. Subban. Unfortunately, comparing the two is a little like comparing apples to oranges, since one is more of a speedy playmaker and the other is more of a cannon.

As far as cannons go, is Subban the best? He has fired 212 shots over the past three seasons, 52 more than second place Dan Boyle. When including the shots that are blocked or miss the net, his lead more than doubles, 455 to 348. On a per-60-minutes basis, only six defencemen top Subban in attempted shots, including most notably Jason Garrison.

Unfortunately, only 11 of those shots have gone in for Subban, and his 3.38 points per 60 minutes ranks 45th, tied with Erik Johnson of Colorado. That doesn't sound like the results one would expect from the league's best power play specialist!

Subban is a work horse, playing 69.1% of the team's power play minutes, but is actually in on just 56.6% of the team's on-ice scoring. He has also had Andrei Markov assisting him, which no doubt boosted his numbers in a fashion similar to Pietrangelo and Shattenkirk.

The Habs enjoy a huge advantage whenever Markov is on the ice. The veteran Russian is one of only six defencemen who have helped boost team scoring by at least 50%, and leads the way from a shot-based perspective, lifting the Habs by 30.4% in attempted shots. It's therefore hard to be convinced that Subban really is the best in the game (yet), when he might not even be the best on his team.

And just like Karlsson, there's a non-trivial price to pay for Subban's scoring. A total of 13 goals have been scored against the Habs when he's been on the ice and he's negated a lot of those power plays by taking 16 penalties of his own. That's six more penalties than second place Mark Giordano. Of course, Calgary's captain has a worse differential overall because he hasn't drawn any of his own, while Subban leads all defencemen with eight.

Add it all up, and the case for Subban isn't as strong as we might have thought, even when shooting is valued more than playmaking.

The Case for Shea Weber

If you want a cannon from the point, the best option is probably Shea Weber. He and Zdeno Chara are the only defencemen with at least 20 goals on the power play over the past three years and, in fact, the only three with more than 15.

Among those defencemen who have worked the power play at least semi-regularly over the past three years, no one has a higher total scoring rate than Weber (4.79), though former Predator Cody Franson is close.

Despite their lack of big-name forwards, Nashville's power play is actually quite potent whenever Weber's on the ice. The only two defencemen on the ice for more goals per 60 minutes is Washington's Mike Green (8.99) and Pittsburgh's Kris Letang (8.65), and those teams have considerably more firepower than the Predators. In fact, Washington actually scored at an even greater rate of 9.85 goals per 60 minutes *without* Green.

As for Nashville, its scoring was boosted from 4.76 goals per 60 minutes without Weber to 8.17 with him on the blue line, that 71.5% boost being the league's fourth best. Only Christian Ehrhoff, Brian Campbell, and Niklas Kronwall are higher, and in at least the first two cases it speaks as much to the weakness of the team's other options as it does to their own talent.

Andrei Markov and Oliver Ekman-Larsson are the only other two defencemen over 50%.

However, the same boost doesn't exist when considering attempted shots instead of goals. Despite an offensive zone start percentage of 81.2%, Weber boosted Nashville's attempted shots by only 7.0%. That's why he appears on the bottom-right side of the following chart, while those who give their teams the greatest shot-based advantage are on top.

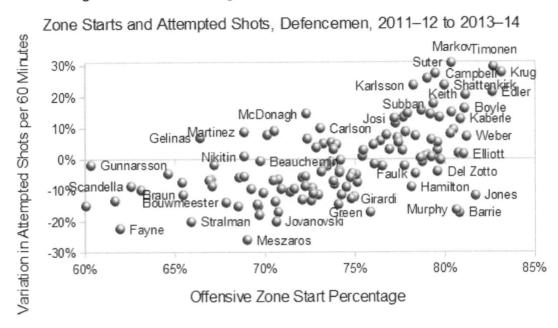

Zone Starts and Attempted Shots, Defencemen, 2011–12 to 2013–14

To argue against Karlsson is generally to argue in favour of having a cannon to blast from the point instead of a speedy playmaker, and to argue against the importance of attempted shots. If so, the most logical alternative candidate to propose as the league's best power play specialist is Shea Weber.

The Case for Someone Else

It's naturally quite possible that someone from the field could actually be a superior power play specialist to both Karlsson and Weber, but merely hasn't had the right linemates, opportunities, or playing conditions to post the same kind of numbers. If that were true, who would it be?

Based on this data, one possibility is Brian Campbell. In his prime, he was simply fantastic with the man advantage in Buffalo, San Jose and Chicago, but we can only speculate as to how effective he'd be today if he was still competing on a team with a first-class power play.

Even on a team like Florida, he has still managed 44 assists over the past three seasons, which is more than anyone else, and with only three others over 40. Of course, being on a weaker team has helped him enjoy more power play ice time than anyone except Subban, and his 70.1% share of all opportunities with the man advantage is exceeded by only five players.

Campbell is the key to an otherwise terrible power play. His 3.77 points per 60 minutes may seem low compared to giants like Karlsson and Weber, but it's actually 63.0% of all his team's scoring. That's higher than all but a handful of regulars.

Florida's scoring actually doubles when he's on the ice, from 2.79 to 5.98, a claim that only be matched by Christian Ehrhoff. In terms of attempted shots, the Panthers are 27.1% better off when Campbell's on the ice, the fourth biggest boost in the NHL. That's why he's in the privileged company of Karlsson, Suter, and Markov on the attempted shot chart.

Looking at boosts in scoring is a great way to find less heralded power play gems. In third place, for example, is Niklas Kronwall, who boosted Detroit's scoring from 4.47 goals per 60 minutes to 7.80. However, his jump in attempted shots per 60 minutes is only 7.3%, from 94.8 to 101.7. Still, Kronwall's nifty scoring rate of 4.34 points per 60 minutes is within 0.03 of Karlsson's.

Another big boost is the one Kimmo Timonen gives the Flyers, which goes up from 5.96 to 8.16 goals per 60 minutes when he's on the ice, and from 85.2 to 110.3 attempted shots per 60 minutes. Of course, there could be a team effect at play here from working the point behind the incredible Claude Giroux. Pittsburgh's Kris Letang and Washington's John Carlson and Mike Green could be enjoying the same kind of favourable team effect.

And how about Toronto's Cody Franson? His power play scoring rate of 4.73 points per 60 minutes is quite eye opening, thanks to being in on 69.4% of the team's scoring. However, he only gives the Leafs a 5.8% boost in attempted shots.

A few other cases were already mentioned previously, such as a strong case for Andrei Markov, which was briefly mentioned in the case for Subban, and reasonable ones for Zdeno Chara (in the case for Weber), or Alex Pietrangelo and Kevin Shattenkirk (in the case for Karlsson). Each of those arguments could potentially be flushed out into something reasonably persuasive, if necessary.

Finally, the two types of players that are harder to evaluate are those that have spent a lot of time up front, like Dustin Byfuglien and Brent Burns, and those for whom we simply don't have enough data, like Morgan Rielly, Eric Gelinas, Torey Krug, and Patrick Wiercioch. Sample sizes this small combined with all the contextual variables make it possible that any of a dozen players could plausibly be the league's best power play specialist.

Despite the surprisingly compelling evidence for about a half-dozen defencemen, nobody really leaps out enough to dethrone our two candidates, Erik Karlsson and Shea Weber.

Closing Thoughts

As usual, there's no one single analytic that can provide anything definitive. Each individual statistic has their own applications and limitations but, when used together with the proper context kept in mind, they can start to paint some convincing pictures.

Among forwards, the strongest case can be built for Philadelphia's Claude Giroux. He plays a lot of minutes, has a very high scoring rate, and is directly involved in a great deal of his team's scoring. He takes a lot of shots, sets up a lot more, and the team does far better when he's on the ice than when he's not. His all-around play results in more faceoff wins and a greater number of 5v3s (when he draws penalties on the power play), leaving us without a single analytic where he doesn't shine.

That being said, strong arguments can also be made for superstars like Sidney Crosby, Evgeni Malkin, Nicklas Backstrom, and Alexander Ovechkin. A case can even be constructed for players like Pavel Datsyuk and John Tavares. In the end, however, my interpretation of the data is leaning firmly towards Giroux.

As for defencemen, the speedy playmaker Erik Karlsson is probably the best player from the point, in my view. Working largely alone in the Canada's national capital, no one else has logged his minutes, generated and/or set up as many shots, is as big a part of their team's scoring, and has boosted their team's fortunes to the same extent. There may be a few that can best him in one department or another, but not in all four.

What Value do Enforcers Have in Today's NHL?

By Iain Fyffe

Enforcers reduce dirty play, prevent injuries, generate momentum, and create more space for the star players whom they protect. At least, that's what "they" say, but is it true?

Hockey analytics can be a useful weapon in answering this question by examining controversial topics with the cold, objective lens of statistical data. First, I'll introduce a new statistic to help identify the dirty players from whom the enforcers are tasked with protecting their star players, then measure to what extent, if at all, the enforcers curb those players, and that behaviour. Finally, I'll attempt to identify and measure their other contributions. At the risk of drawing an instigator minor, let's drop the gloves and jump right in.

Who Are the Most Dangerous Players in the NHL?

There is a certain subset of NHL players who are generally held in low regard by fans and even other players (at least, when they're on other teams). They're known by a variety of names: cheap-shot artists, rats, dirty players, or Brad Marchand. Certain acts in hockey are illegal specifically because they are dangerous to other players: high-sticking, boarding, slashing, elbowing, and many others. And the players who habitually break these rules are the ones called rats. They're dangerous because they engage in these dangerous plays far more than other players.

It is often difficult to determine which players should be considered dirty and which should not. If he plays for your favourite team, usually he's just hard-nosed, gritty, and an energy player. If he plays for a hated team, on the other hand, he's a cheap, dirty player who should be thrown out of the league. In an effort to quantify the dangerous play of NHL players, Paul Busch[131] (of the blog *It's Not Part of the Game*) developed a statistic he calls *Rat PIM*, which is simply the penalty minutes a player accumulates from major penalties (other than fighting) and from roughing, slashing, cross-checking, boarding, and unsportsmanlike conduct fouls.

Although unsportsmanlike conduct is not necessarily dangerous in itself, the type of player who takes this penalty the most is certainly the dangerous type in general, as we'll see. Besides, there is little that is less sportsmanlike than playing in a dangerous manner.

Here, I'm going to adapt this idea, and modify Busch's formulation a bit, and the result will be called Dirty Rat Penalty Minutes (DRPM). Busch's Rat PIM includes roughing, which is excluded here because so many roughing penalties are coincidental, meaning they are mutual rather than one player attacking another. Also, roughing is closely tied to fighting, so if we exclude fighting, we should probably exclude roughing as well. Busch's formulation also excludes a wide variety of dangerous penalties, which, while less common than slashing and

---

131 Paul Busch, "The Rats are Taking Over the Game", *It's Not Part of the Game*, February 3, 2013, Web, http://itsnotpartofthegame.blogspot.ca/2013/02/the-rats-are-taking-over-game_3.html.

cross-checking, should still be considered. These include charging, elbowing, high-sticking and kneeing, among others. As such, DRPM is defined as follows:

Dirty Rat PM = *Penalty minutes from all penalties other than goaltender interference, holding, holding the stick, hooking, instigating, interference, roughing and tripping minors, fighting majors, misconduct, game misconduct, and match penalties.*

DRPM are defined in a negative manner for two reasons: (1) there are many more penalties that we want to include in the definition than exclude and (2) because of how our data source presents penalty data. ESPN.com lists penalties by type for NHL players, but does not list every type of penalty, only some of the most common penalties. So using their data, we can exclude instigating, hooking, tripping, roughing, holding, interference, holding the stick, and goaltender interference. Unfortunately, we cannot exclude delay of game since this data is not provided by ESPN.com, so that requires a review of game summaries for the year.

This process captures all kinds of rattish penalties that Busch does not consider, including but not necessarily limited to: butt-ending, charging, checking from behind, clipping, closing hand on the puck, diving, elbowing, head-butting, illegal check to the head, kicking, kneeing, slew-footing, spearing, and throwing equipment. These are dangerous or otherwise problematic penalties that characterize cheap-shot artists.

— TWO MINUTES FOR 'SLASH'-ING —

SLASH HAS PLAYED THE US NATIONAL ANTHEM TWICE AT LA KINGS GAMES

Let's take a look at the 2013–14 NHL leaders in DRPM:

Top 30 Dirty Rats, 2013–14[132]

Rank	Player	Team	GP	DRPM
1	Brad Marchand	Bos	82	44
2	Ryan Garbutt	Dal	75	40
3	Chris Neil	Ott	76	32
4	Zack Smith	Ott	82	32
5	Scott Hartnell	Phi	78	31
6	Antoine Roussel	Dal	81	31
7	Dion Phaneuf	Tor	80	30
8	Erik Gudbranson	Fla	65	29
9	Brenden Morrow	StL	71	29
10	Brandon Dubinsky	CBJ	76	29
11	Kyle Quincey	Det	82	29
12	James Neal	Pit	59	28
13	Mark Stuart	Wpg	69	28
14	Radko Gudas	TB	73	28
15	Eric Gryba	Ott	57	26
16	Martin Hanzal	Phx	65	26
17	Zac Rinaldo	Phi	67	26
18	David Backes	StL	74	26
19	Chris Kunitz	Pit	78	26
	David Perron	Edm	78	26
21	P.K. Subban	Mtl	82	26
	Blake Wheeler	Wpg	82	26
23	Tom Wilson	Wsh	82	25
24	Evgeni Malkin	Pit	60	24
25	Steve Downie	Col/Phi	62	24
26	Taylor Hall	Edm	75	24
27	Scottie Upshall	Fla	76	24
28	Eric Staal	Car	79	24
29	Brenden Dillon	Dal	80	24
30	Corey Perry	Ana	81	24

The response "Brad Marchand" to the question "who is the dirtiest player in the league?" may be the least surprising answer suggested in this book, to any question. If we look at how these penalties break down, we get a little more insight into just how these dirty players ply their dirty trade. The categories are defined as follows:

- *Checking fouls*: boarding, charging, clipping, elbowing, illegal check to the head, kneeing
- *Stick fouls*: broken stick, butt-ending, cross-checking, high-sticking, slashing, spearing
- *Unsportsmanlike fouls*: diving, throwing equipment, unsportsmanlike conduct
- *Delaying fouls*: concealing puck, closing hand on puck, delay of game (all kinds)
- *Interference fouls*: holding, hooking, interference, interference on goaltender,

132Acknowledgement: Raw penalty data from *NHL*, http://www.nhl.com and *ESPN*, http://www.espn.com.

tripping
- *Fighting/roughing*: fighting, instigating, roughing
- *Misconducts*: game misconduct, match penalty, misconduct

Penalties by Type, DRPM Leaders, 2013–14[133]

	Marchand	Garbutt	Neil	Z. Smith	Hartnell	Roussel
Checking fouls	8	12	2	8	8	9
Stick fouls	34	18	24	18	23	16
Unsportsmanlike fouls	2	10	6	6	0	6
Total DRPM	*44*	*40*	*32*	*32*	*31*	*31*
Delaying fouls	0	6	2	4	2	4
Interference fouls	12	28	32	16	20	14
Fighting/roughing	8	12	95	39	30	80
Misconducts	0	20	50	20	20	80
Total non-DRPM	*20*	*66*	*179*	*79*	*72*	*178*
Total PIM	*64*	*106*	*211*	*111*	*103*	*209*

So Marchand earned his rattish crown through the dangerous use of his stick. In 2013–14, he took two cross-checking penalties, five slashing, and 10 high-sticking. Marchand has serious problems controlling his stick. He also took two boarding and two elbowing fouls to round out his DRPM.

Now, to be fair to Marchand, this is only one possible answer to the question of who's the biggest rat, even when specifically using DRPM to find the answer. Marchand may be the most frequent offender on an absolute basis, but he is not the worst in relative terms. He took a regular shift at forward all season long, giving him much more opportunity for dangerous play than many other cheap-shotters had. If instead we look at the leaders in DRPM per 60 minutes of ice time (minimum 100 minutes), we have the following:

Top 30 Dirty Rats, per 60 minutes, 2013–14[134]

Rank	Player	Team	DRPM	TOI	DRPM/60
1	George Parros	Mtl	6	100	3.60
2	Tim Jackman	Cgy/Ana	15	256	3.52
3	Frazer MacLaren	Tor	6	108	3.33
4	Mattias Tedenby	NJ	8	150	3.20
5	Zac Rinaldo	Phi	26	515	3.03
6	John Scott	Buf	18	378	2.86
7	Tom Sestito	Van	22	497	2.66
8	Mark Borowiecki	Ott	7	164	2.56
9	Daniel Carcillo	LA/NYR	22	528	2.50
10	Eric Boulton	NYI	6	147	2.45
11	Ryan Garbutt	Dal	40	979	2.45
12	Phil Varone	Buf	4	103	2.33
13	Tom Wilson	Wsh	25	651	2.30

133Acknowledgement: Raw penalty data from *NHL*, http://www.nhl.com and *ESPN*, http://www.espn.com.
134Acknowledgement: Raw penalty data from *NHL*, http://www.nhl.com and *ESPN*, http://www.espn.com.

14	Jordan Caron	Bos	14	382	2.20
15	Richard Clune	Nsh	18	490	2.20
16	Chris Neil	Ott	32	897	2.14
17	Brenden Morrow	StL	29	845	2.06
18	Ryan Whitney	Fla	4	117	2.05
19	Brad Marchand	Bos	44	1307	2.02
20	Paul Bissonnette	Phx	6	185	1.95
21	Kevin Westgarth	Car/Cgy	10	311	1.93
22	Derek Dorsett	NYR	18	562	1.92
23	Jeremy Welsh	Van	4	130	1.85
24	Mark Fistric	Ana	16	524	1.83
25	Harry Zolnierczyk	Pit	4	132	1.82
26	Ryan Reaves	StL	16	537	1.79
27	Tanner Glass	Wpg	23	789	1.75
28	Antoine Roussel	Dal	35	1079	1.95
29	Drew Shore	Fla	8	288	1.67
30	Steve Downie	Col/Phi	24	874	1.65

These are the players who, when they're on the ice, you really need to watch out for. They engage in dangerous, illegal acts (other than fighting) far more than other players. The average 2013–14 DRPM per 60 minutes for all skaters was 0.36, meaning that #2 George Parros took a dangerous penalty at TEN TIMES the league-average rate. He's clearly a very dangerous player.

Here, Brad Marchand demonstrates that his #1 ranking in total DRPM is not simply due to playing regular minutes; he's among the top 20 on a per-minute basis as well, meaning that his reputation as a dirty player is richly deserved according to this measure as well.

It is noteworthy that so many players with a high per-minute rate of DRPM played relatively few minutes in 2013–14. Many of them played only part of the season in the NHL, and the great majority of them played only a few minutes per game when they were in the lineup. So you might suggest that the minimum amount of 100 minutes is too low, that it might produce misleading results. However, it seems clear that, given the number of high-DRPM rate players played so few minutes, that setting the minimum any higher would in fact produce the misleading results since it would arbitrarily exclude so many dangerous players from our analysis of dangerous players.

This fact is also noteworthy because it does suggest that NHL coaches recognize that dangerous players hurt their team's chances of winning, in general. If such play was beneficial to a team, one would expect to see the players who engage in it the most have more ice time than they do. On the other hand, of course, many of these players are long-term NHLers, suggesting that their coaches still value their contributions even if they do play dangerously. But make no mistake: the players listed above are hazardous to the health of other players. If their coaches won't keep them in line, who will?

Who Can Save Us From Those Dirty Rats?

Like bringing in a cat to solve a mouse problem, conventional NHL wisdom holds that in order to keep the rats in check, you need enforcers. Without enforcers to keep order on the ice (by inflicting physical punishment through the illegal act of fighting), the rats would run rampant. At least, more rampant than they do anyway, since even with enforcers in today's NHL there are still many rats. Of course, if NHL teams would just stop putting the rats on the ice in the first place, then teams would also not have to employ enforcers, so this justification seems extremely weak even on its surface. If NHL coaches did not want rats in the league, they would stop playing them. So the reality appears to be that NHL coaches do not want rats *on other teams*, while having no compunction about playing rats themselves. It's not "part of the game", it's a purely selfish motivation.

Enforcers have been in the NHL for quite some time, though there was no such thing as an enforcer in the NHL's earliest years. There were certainly violent players, who were considered dangerous and detrimental to the game. However, these players tended to be among the better players of the day; they wouldn't have lasted otherwise. Newsy Lalonde, for example, was a very violent player, but one of the very best of his generation, which allowed him to have a long career despite his habit of playing dangerously.

Before there were enforcers in today's mould (that is, players whose primary role was physical violence, playing few minutes, and scoring essentially not at all), there were policemen. These were quality hockey players who were also specifically tasked with physical violence. The most well-known example of a policeman is probably Montreal's John Ferguson. Even if Ferguson was not called upon to engage in illegal physical violence, he would still have a place in an NHL lineup. This is not true of today's enforcers, who play only a few minutes per game, suggesting that if punching other players in the face were not valued, they would not be in the league. This type of player is a relatively recent innovation.

So now the question becomes, if there have been policemen and enforcers in the NHL to keep the rats under control for decades, why are there any rats left at all? The justification doesn't even pass the sniff test. If enforcers prevent rats, then there should not be any rats, because we know there are plenty of enforcers. And yet there are also plenty of rats. We can't blame the instigator rule; that rule seems to do a very poor job at preventing fights since there are still so many fights in the NHL. Indeed, there still numerous players paid to fight, and only to fight.

Moreover, enforcers are supposed to keep rats in line with the threat of physical violence. If a rat makes a dirty play, he's supposed to face retribution in the form of getting punched in the face. But an enforcer cannot force a rat to fight. Brad Marchand took part in exactly zero fights in the 2013–14 NHL season. How is the threat of violence supposed to work if the rat can simply refuse to fight? Most fights are in fact between two enforcers. Is engaging a rat's teammate in the very thing the teammate has been hired to do supposed to be some kind of deterrent? The enforcer's job is to fight. If an enforcer has to fight because he has a rat as a teammate, then he's just doing his job. There is no deterrent there.

But there is a larger issue here. When we looked at the list of biggest rats per minute played, you may have noticed that a good number of the players on that list were themselves enforcers. Ken Campbell once tweeted[135],"You need goons like Colton Orr to protect skill players like Tomas Plekanec from guys like Colton Orr." This is more than just a pithy comment, there is a great deal of truth to it. Let's look at the 2013–14 NHL leaders in fighting majors per 60 minutes of playing time (FM/60), and at the same time examine their rank in DRPM per 60 minutes. The relationship just screams out to be seen:

Top 30 Most Frequent Fighters, per 60 minutes, and DRPM, 2013–14[136]

Player	Team	TOI	FM/60	Rank	DRPM/60	Rank
George Parros	Mtl	100	5.40	1	3.60	1
Frazer McLaren	Tor	108	4.44	2	3.33	3
Matt Kassian	Ott	146	3.70	3	0.82	159
Jay Rosehill	Phi	168	3.57	4	0.71	196
Eric Boulton	NYI	147	3.27	5	2.45	10
Krys Barch	Fla	328	2.38	6	1.10	71
Tim Jackman	Cgy/Ana	256	2.34	7	3.52	2
Luke Gazdic	Edm	389	2.31	8	1.23	53
Tom Sestito	Van	497	2.29	9	2.66	7
Jared Boll	CBJ	211	2.25	10	1.13	67
Richard Clune	Nsh	490	1.96	11	2.20	15
Mike Brown	Edm/SJ	400	1.80	12	0.60	245
Anthony Peluso	Wpg	306	1.57	13	0.98	103
Zenon Konopka	Min/Buf	466	1.55	14	1.03	87
Brian McGrattan	Cgy	510	1.29	15	1.06	79
Tom Wilson	Wsh	651	1.29	16	2.30	13
Cody McCormick	Buf/Min	383	1.25	17	0.63	234
Colton Orr	Tor	290	1.24	18	1.24	52
B.J. Crombeen	TB	559	1.18	19	1.07	77
Kevin Westgarth	Car/Cgy	311	1.16	20	1.93	21
Ryan Reaves	StL	537	1.12	21	1.79	26
Mark Borowiecki	Ott	164	1.10	22	2.56	8
Derek Dorsett	NYR	562	1.07	23	1.92	22
Shawn Thornton	Bos	562	1.07	24	0.64	226
Cam Janssen	NJ	118	1.02	25	0.00	646
Patrick Maroon	Ana	763	1.02	26	0.47	318
Aaron Volpatti	Wsh	301	1.00	27	1.20	56
Chris Neil	Ott	897	1.00	28	2.14	16
Brandon Prust	Mtl	666	0.99	29	0.90	130
Cody McLeod	Col	732	0.98	30	1.15	66

Frazer McLaren and George Parros were the two most frequent fighters in the NHL in 2013–14, and they were also the two of the three biggest rats on a per-minute basis. This is not the result of them being rats and therefore being engaged in fights by enforcers; they are most certainly viewed as being enforcers themselves. And it's not just these two. There were 755

135Ken Campbell, Tweet, February 9, 2013, @THNKenCampbell.
136Acknowledgement: Raw penalty data from *NHL*, http://www.nhl.com and *ESPN*, http://www.espn.com.

NHL skaters who played at least 100 minutes in 2013–14, so each decile (tenth) is made up of 75.5 players. If there were no relationship between fighting and taking Dirty Rat penalties, we would expect three of the most frequent fighters to be among the top 30 most frequent rats. As we can see in the table above, there are in fact 18 of the top 30 fighters in the top 10% of Dirty Rats, and 23 are in the top 20%.

The pattern is persistent. Just outside of the top 30 frequent fighters, we find yet more rats. Paul Bissonnette was 31st in fighting majors, and 20th in DRPM. Matt Carkner was 37th and 68th respectively, Zac Rinaldo 38th and 5th, John Scott 39th and 6th, and Daniel Carcillo 44th and 9th.

At a minimum, it's absolutely clear that even if enforcers could be an effective way to keep the rats in line, the specific enforcers that NHL teams employ actually make the problem much worse because they engage in dangerous play at rates even higher than those players they are intended to keep in line. The fact that many of these players have been enforcers in the NHL for a substantial amount of time indicates that coaches and general managers are either ignorant of the fact that these players take dangerous penalties themselves, or simply do not care. The latter case would suggest that the "keep the rats in line" explanation, when used by them, is either a smokescreen or a rationalization, intended to justify a practice that really only continues due to tradition.

Even if you want to argue that the enforcers only engage in dirty play against rats who refuse to fight, this would not held because it simply escalates the problem rather than solving it. If you hit a rat from behind to avenge something that rat did, you become a rat from the perspective of the other team's enforcer, who then does something dirty to get back at you, which then makes him a rat in your eyes, and so on and so on.

We can check to see if the players that an enforcers fouls with DRPM are indeed rats themselves. Game summaries from NHL.com list not only the player who took each penalty, but the player who was the victim of each penalty. As such, we can use the targets' DRPM rating to determine how rattish the targets of a particular player's dirty rat penalties are.

First we need a baseline. Let's take a look at the forwards who compiled the most DRPM in 2013–14 but engaged in three or fewer fights. These are the players who have no trouble with committing dangerous fouls but, when challenged to a fight, will tend to back down. Such a player could be called a turtle, but kappa might be a better name. Not the tenth letter of the Greek alphabet, mind you, but the creature from Japanese myth. Kappas are malevolent humanoid turtle-things, and their heads looks a bit rattish as well, so that helps the analogy work. At any rate, our five kappas are Brad Marchand (44 DRPM, no fights), Ryan Garbutt (40 DRPM, two fights), Zack Smith (32 DRPM, three fights), Scott Hartnell (31 DRPM, two fights), and Brenden Morrow and Brandon Dubinsky (both with 29 DRPM and one fight).

We'll give Brad Marchand a bit of a break here, and instead look at Ryan Garbutt.

Ryan Garbutt's Victims and their DRPM, 2013–14[137]

Target	DRPM rank	Penalty
Andre Benoit	322	High-sticking
Andre Benoit	322	High-sticking
Jordan Eberle	610	Slashing
Ryan Getzlaf	445	Slashing
Nicklas Grossmann	126	Boarding
Dan Hamhuis	531	Cross-checking
Travis Hamonic	507	High-sticking
Barrett Jackman	142	Boarding
Jay McClement	488	Slashing
Johnny Oduya	42	Illegal check to the head
Mathieu Perreault	86	Kneeing
Peter Regin	461	Slashing
Colby Robak	719	Boarding
Wayne Simmonds	106	Elbowing
Jordan Staal	485	Slashing
Jiri Tlusty	240	Unsportsmanlike
Average	*352*	

Performing the same analysis for the other five kappas provides the following results:

Kappa's Victims and their DRPM, 2013–14

Kappa	Team	DR Penalties	Target DRPM Rank
Ryan Garbutt	Dal	16	352
Brad Marchand	Bos	22	363
Zack Smith	Ott	14	281
Scott Hartnell	Phi	14	342
Brenden Morrow	StL	12	390
Brandon Dubinsky	CBJ	13	519
Average			*374*
Weighted Average			*371*

Given that there are 755 players who had a DRPM rank for 2013–14, this suggests that the kappas are basically indiscriminate with respect to who they foul. If the targets were randomly distributed among these 755 players, we would expect the average DRPM rank to be 378. Now we can compare them to the enforcer-rats, those who both fight a lot (top 30 in fights per 60 minutes) and foul a lot (top 100 in DRPM rank), a requirement that 21 of the top 30 most frequent fighters meet.

Top Enforcer-Rat Victims and their DRPM, 2013–14

Enforcer-Rat	Team	DR Penalties	Target DRPM Rank
George Parros	Mtl	3	43
Frazer McLaren	Tor	3	138
Eric Boulton	NYI	2	225

137Acknowledgement: Raw penalty data from *NHL*, http://www.nhl.com and *ESPN*, http://www.espn.com.

Krys Barch	Fla	3	328
Tim Jackman	Cgy/Ana	6	594
Luke Gazdic	Edm	4	87
Tom Sestito	Van	11	327
Jared Boll	CBJ	2	310
Richard Clune	Nsh	8	158
Zenon Konopka	Buf/Min	4	305
Brian McGrattan	Cgy	2	194
Tom Wilson	Wsh	11	341
Colton Orr	Tor	3	212
B.J. Crombeen	TB	5	271
Kevin Westgarth	Car/Cgy	2	22
Ryan Reaves	StL	8	276
Mark Borowiecki	Ott	2	201
Derek Dorsett	NYR	9	392
Aaron Volpatti	Wsh	3	135
Chris Neil	Ott	16	266
Cody McLeod	Col	4	618
Average		*111*	*259*
Weighted Average			*289*

As such, it does seem that there is a slight tendency for the enforcer-rats to target somewhat more rattish players than the kappas do, by about 22%. But at the very least, the majority of the enforcer-rats are as bad as the worst rats (kappas), and the great majority of enforcers are in fact enforcer-rats. Indeed, the gap shrinks considerably when you exclude unsportsmanlike conduct penalties from DRPM, which have a strong tendency to be drawn against rats but is not really a dangerous foul, and is somewhat questionable about whether it should be included. Without unsportsmanlike conduct, the kappas have an average target DRPM ranking of 381, while the enforcer-rats have a figure of 335, only 12% better.

Paul Busch[138] has noted that teams with more fighting majors tend to have more Rat PIM and concludes that fighting therefore does not reduce Rat PIM, but in fact increases it. However, he does not demonstrate causation. You could just as easily say that teams that get involved in chippier games (resulting in Rat PIM) have to resort to fighting to make sure those games do not get out of hand. Mere correlation is not enough to reach such a conclusion. Busch[139] also studied all NHL games of November 2013 and compared the Rat PIM (according to his formulation) before and after a fight occurred in the game, finding that there were three times as many Rat PIM after a fight than before it. However, he did not control for the timing of the fight, so a fight early in the game would obviously be expected to have more Rat PIM after it than before.

To address both causation and timing, I designed the following study. In order to make sure that an equal period of time was considered both before and after a fight, I examined only

138Paul Busch, "Rat PIM Update – Leafs Enforcers Policing the Game", *It's Not Part of the Game*, May 10, 2013, Web, http://itsnotpartofthegame.blogspot.ca/2013/05/rat-pim-update-leafs-enforcers-policing.html.
139Paul Busch, "Rat PIM Update – A Month of Fighting", *It's Not Part of the Game*, December 29, 2013, Web, http://itsnotpartofthegame.blogspot.ca/2013/12/rat-pim-update-month-of-fighting.html.

fights in the second period of 2013–14 NHL games. I compiled the number of DRPM in the two ten-minute increments before each fight occurred, and in the two ten-minute increments after each fights occurred. There were 150 fights in the second period, and the results are as follows:

DRPM Before and After a Fight, 2013–14[140]

Time Frame	DRPM Pre	DRPM Post	Change%
+/- 10:01 to 20:00	119	115	-3.4
+/- 0:01 to 10:00	125	153	22.4

When interpreting these results, it is important to note that the null hypothesis in this case would not be that the DRPM change is zero. Since some fights result directly from a dirty rat penalty, fights and DRPM are not entirely independent. In fact 13 fights in the study resulted from the same play that involved a dirty rat penalty. So this means that if fighting is completely neutral in its effect on DRPM, we would expect a small negative DRPM change post-fight.

This is not what we find, however. We do see a small negative DRPM change when comparing 10:01 to 20:00 minutes before and after the fight, but for fights that result from a dirty rat penalty, that penalty is not included because of the more distant timing. A change this small is not significant, representing only two minor penalties over the entire 2013–14 season.

The results for the time period closer to the fight are significant, however. Comparing 0:01 to 10:00 minutes before and after a fight, there is a huge jump in DRPM after the fight. The increase of 22.4% is even larger than it first appears, since again the null hypothesis would be a small reduction. This evidence strongly suggests that not only are DRPM and fighting correlated, fighting actually causes more DRPM.

Taking all of this together, it is clear that enforcers do not control rats in the NHL. The presence of enforcers has not eliminated rats from the game, and indeed the means enforcers would use to keep them in line cannot actually do so, since the rat can simply refuse to fight. But most importantly, the main reason that enforcers do not control rats is that, by and large, ***the enforcers are the rats***.

If Enforcers Don't Control the Rats, What Good Do They Do?

All right, so let's say that enforcers don't do anything to prevent cheap shots and dirty hits. Heck, let's say that the presence of enforcers even increases the likelihood of such things because the enforcers generally partake in dangerous play at high rates. Indeed, we probably should say all of this, since this is where the evidence leads us. Okay, fine, enforcers do not prevent cheap shots. But we all know there is more than one rationalization—sorry, "reason"—that enforcers help hockey teams. So let's have a look at the other effects enforcers might have on the game.

140Acknowledgement: Penalty data from *NHL*, http://www.nhl.com.

For ideas, we can turn to Travis Hughes[141], who described the traditional arguments in support of enforcers like so, "Fighting holds players accountable for their actions, it protects star players, it gets your team excited and can give them a momentum boost, and it intimidates the other team and allows more room for skilled players to work their magic." He also concluded that the accountability idea was "bullshit", which agrees with our analysis thus far. There has been a good deal of analytical research done in the past few years with respect to the effect that fighting has on the game. Let's review some of it here.

In January 2014, Rob Vollman[142] examined how dedicated enforcers were used by NHL teams up to that point in the 2013–14 season. He found that, unsurprisingly, enforcers play almost exclusively against third and fourth-liners. However, even though they faced relatively easy competition, almost without exception their teams are dominated by their opponents in terms of playing hockey, specifically measured by Corsi. This means that any value an enforcer might have in some sort of intangible way has to overcome the fact that they cost their teams goals while they're on the ice. Thankfully, they're not on the ice all that often, which limits the damage. And even this sort of thinking is flawed, since if the enforcers have intangible effects that do not actually result in tangible (as in measurable) effects on the ice, then said intangibles are not useful in winning hockey games. But let's press on anyway.

The enforcers will also have to overcome the injuries their task produces in order to produce positive value to their teams and to the game. In 2011[143], I analyzed data released by the NHL for the 2010–11 season related to man-games lost to concussion and concluded that a fight is **43 times more likely** to result in a man-game lost to concussion than a legal hit is. This illustrates how dangerous repeated blows to the head are (not that we didn't already know that), and it also rebuts the slippery-slope argument often made about keeping fighting in the game. That is, if we get rid of fighting because it's dangerous, then we'll have to get rid of body-checking as well, and then we'll have Ice Capades! This is ridiculous; a fight is far, far more dangerous than a body check, and so far we have no reason to believe that a fight provides any positive value at all, while a legal hit has some value to a team. The two things are not comparable.

In 2013, Adam Gretz[144] studied the incidences of injury for team with and without enforcers in the lineup, finding that the presence of an enforcer in the lineup does nothing to protect a team from a violent act that results in a match penalty, a fine or a suspension. With an enforcer it was once every 36.9 games, and without an enforcer it was once every 36.1. So enforcers do not seem to protect their teams against injuries or from the most violent plays.

---

141 Travis Hughes, "Why Do Hockey Players Fight?", *Morning Skate*, October 14, 2011, Web, http://www.sbnation.com/nhl/2011/10/14/2489931/hockey-fight-arron-asham-jay-beagle.

142 Rob Vollman, "Are Enforcers Still Valuable to NHL Teams?", *Bleacher Report*, January 25, 2014, Web, http://bleacherreport.com/articles/1935940-are-enforcers-still-valuable-to-nhl-teams.

143 Iain Fyffe, "Headshots: Should Fighting be a Target?", *Hockey Prospectus*, October 17, 2011, Web, http://www.hockeyprospectus.com/puck/article.php?articleid=1131

144 Adam Gretz, "The Enforcer Fallacy: Hockey's Fighting Specialists Don't Protect Anyone", *Regressing*, October 11, 2013, Web, http://regressing.deadspin.com/the-enforcer-fallacy-hockeys-fighting-specialists-don-1442618145.

Gabriel Desjardins[145] studied the idea that fighting affects the "momentum" in the game in 2009. Using data from hockeyfights.com, where fans vote on who won each NHL fight, Desjardins determined that winning a fight does, in fact, have a positive effect on a team's chance of winning. Of course, it was a tiny, tiny effect, requiring approximately 80 fights won in order to result in a single win for one's team. Let's have a look how this would translate for an enforcer.

Again according to hockeyfights.com[146], Brian McGrattan was easily the most successful fighter in the NHL in 2013–14, winning all 11 of his fights; Luke Gazdic won 11 and drew two in 15 fights to finish second. For McGrattan's career, he has a record of 47-17-9 according to that site, for an impressive winning percentage of .705. But this means he is only +30 in fights for his career, in 309 games played. Based on Desjardins' findings, McGrattan's fighting has therefore been worth about 3/8ths of a win over his career, or about two goals (since a win takes about six marginal goals, according to hockey's 3-1-1 rule). That's an average of about half a goal for a full season. Moreover, these two goals that McGrattan may have gained by winning fights still don't overcome the Goals Versus Threshold (GVT) he has compiled when forced to play hockey, a career mark of -2.8[147]. And this is the NHL's most successful fighter. Many enforcers have losing records in fights according to nhlfights.com, and would therefore be costing their teams points in the standings through punching.

Even worse for McGrattan is the fact that other studies have since concluded that winning a fight does not have a positive effect on scoring goals or winning games. Xavier Weisenreider[148] studied all fights in the 2012–13 NHL season and concluded that "there was no tangible evidence that winning fights affected the outcome of hockey games, and the idea that losing sends more goons onto the ice in order to claim momentum needs to be questioned. There is a slight correlation between winning fights and scoring more goals than the opponent, but any possible causation would require further examination."

Research released by Terry Appleby[149] in 2012 made a brief splash in the media, since it concluded that fighting does increase the momentum in a hockey game, with momentum being defined as the number of shots taken per minute. This research is no longer available online, however Jonathan Willis[150] analyzed it at the time, noting its flaws. In particular, the increase in momentum was equally likely to apply to either or both teams, meaning that net effect would be a wash. In the same vein, Phil Birnbaum[151] made an extensive study of fights from 1967 to 1985, testing all kinds of scenarios trying to find some effect, and concluded that

145 Gabriel Desjardins, "Fighters Prosper, but Just Barely", *Hockey Prospectus*, July 16, 2009, Web, http://www.hockeyprospectus.com/puck/article.php?articleid=222.
146 Acknowledgement: Fight data from *Hockey Fights*, http://www.hockeyfights.com.
147 Acknowledgement: Career GVT data from Tom Awad.
148 Xavier Weisenreider, "The True Impact of a Hockey Fight", *Georgetown Sports Analysis, Business, and Research Group*, October 13, 2013, Web, http://georgetownsportsanalysis.wordpress.com/2013/10/13/the-true-impact-of-a-hockey-fight/.
149 This reference is not available online.
150 Jonathan Willis, "Does the Momentum Boost from Fighting Help Teams Win Games?", *Oilers Nation*, January 11, 2012, Web, http://oilersnation.com/2012/1/11/does-the-momentum-boost-from-fighting-help-teams-win-games.
151 Phil Birnbaum, "Do Hockey Fights Lift a Team's Performance?", *Sabermetric Research*, January 10, 2012, Web, http://blog.philbirnbaum.com/2012/01/do-hockey-fights-lift-teams-performance.html.

"[a]t best, there might be a small effect in certain specific circumstances ... but much, much less than sportscasters make it out to be." Those circumstances were when a goon player on a goon team fights when his team is losing, and the result was about 1/8th of a goal. However, Birnbaum also notes that this result was not statistically significant, meaning that it might simply be an illusion. Indeed, his method comes awfully close to data mining, where positive correlations are sought out, rather than first formulating a plausible hypothesis and then testing it. In any amount of data, there are bound to be some positive correlations to be found by chance, thus it isn't surprising that Birnbaum found something.

All right, so existing research is at best inconclusive and at worst strongly indicates that fighting has no value in an NHL game. But one of Hughes' suggested traditional arguments hasn't been addressed here: that enforcers give skilled players room to play. Sure, this seems a very suspect idea to begin with, since the best skill players play 20-plus minutes per game, with plenty of power play time, whereas enforcers generally play a few minutes per game on the third or fourth line, and don't get a sniff at man-advantage situations. Be that as it may, perhaps just the fact that there is an enforcer in your lineup will keep the opposing team from focusing on your star player too much, not only with dirty plays but with legal hits as well.

There are no rigorous studies on this idea that I am aware of, so here's a quick-and-dirty one. I looked at all players in the top 20 in NHL scoring in 2013–14 (69 or more points) and identified any enforcers on their teams. I did not use a rigorous definition of enforcer, exercising a bit of judgement, excluding players who fought some but also took a regular shift. Then I compared the scoring totals for these players in games where at least one enforcer was in the lineup to their totals in games when there was not an enforcer playing for their side. Totals (in a GP-G-A-PTS format, and Power Play Goals, PPG) for those players who played at least 10 games without an enforcer are as follows:

Scoring Leaders With and Without Enforcers, 2013–14

Player	Enforcer(s)	With	PPG With	Without	PPG Without
Sidney Crosby	Glass	65-28-52-80	1.23	15-8-16-24	1.60
Ryan Getzlaf	Jackman, Maroon	66-22-48-70	1.06	11-9-8-17	1.55
Corey Perry	Jackman, Maroon	70-38-33-71	1.01	11-5-6-11	1.00
Phil Kessel	McLaren, Orr	68-33-36-69	1.01	14-4-7-11	0.79
Taylor Hall	Brown, Gazdic	61-24-38-62	1.02	14-3-15-18	1.29
Joe Pavelski	Brown, Pelech	53-28-22-50	0.94	29-13-16-29	1.00
Joe Thornton	Brown, Pelech	53-8-47-55	1.04	29-3-18-21	0.72
Patrick Marleau	Brown, Pelech	53-23-20-43	0.81	29-10-17-27	0.93
Anze Kopitar	Carcillo	26-9-16-25	0.96	56-20-25-45	0.80
David Krejci	Thornton	62-15-37-52	0.84	18-4-13-17	0.94
Kyle Okposo	Boulton, Carkner, Gallant, Halmo, Johnson	57-20-38-58	1.02	14-7-4-11	0.79
Blake Wheeler	Peluso	53-22-32-54	1.02	29-6-9-15	0.52
Average			*0.99*		*0.99*

The null hypothesis in this case would be that enforcers have no effect, on the whole, on high-scoring players' ability to score. We would expect that their points-per-game would be the same with or without an enforcer. Since that's exactly what we find, we cannot reject this hypothesis, meaning that this study suggests that enforcers have no effect on the ability of star players to ply their trade.

Noteworthy is the fact that, despite not being good hockey players and therefore reducing the average quality of a star player's teammates, enforcers do not actually appear to decrease their scoring either. This is not surprising, however, because again enforcers almost never have ice time with these star players. They are fourth-liners, time-fillers.

Closing Thoughts

Based on the analytical work done to date on the question of whether fighting provides any positive value to NHL hockey teams, the answer is no, there is no reason to think so. Indeed, there is reason to believe that it does harm, at the very least in the sense of pernicious, life-destroying injury in the form of repeated concussions. Arguments in support of fighting are all anecdotal, and anecdotes are not evidence. Vollman showed that despite playing almost exclusively against opponents' worst players, enforcers were still dominated on the ice in terms of playing hockey. NHL coaches know that enforcers are the weakest hockey players they have, but continue to play them. Presumably they must believe that there is positive value, but this has yet to be supported by any sort of even semi-rigorous analysis.

Even those researchers who found a positive effect noted how small it was. Gabriel Desjardins[152], one of the few to find a positive effect, said that "the direct benefit is probably on the order of having the equipment guys make sure nobody's playing with an illegal stick." Jonathan Willis[153] summarized it well in 2013 when he said "No team in the NHL fights less often than the Detroit Red Wings. Not coincidentally, no team benefits from the presence of fighting in hockey more than the Detroit Red Wings." That is, putting an enforcer out on the ice hurts your hockey team's chances of winning. And isn't winning hockey games what the NHL is supposed to be about?

152Gabriel Desjardins, "Fighters Prosper, but Just Barely", *Hockey Prospectus*, July 16, 2009, Web, http://www.hockeyprospectus.com/puck/article.php?articleid=222.
153Jonathan Willis, "Why the Detroit Red Wings Benefits Most from Fighting in the NHL", *Bleacher Report*, November 14, 2013, http://bleacherreport.com/articles/1850711-why-the-detroit-red-wings-benefit-most-from-fighting-in-the-nhl.

Questions and Answers

By Rob Vollman

There were a few interesting topics that didn't warrant an entire, dedicated chapter of their own and have been summarized here.

How Important are Controlled Zone Exits and Entries?

Excellent question.

When I was a child, I invented a game that I could play with my hockey cards. It was a very simple game, divided into three zones, where the object was to win faceoffs, advance the puck through the zones, and attempt shots. A dice and the scoring stats on the backs of the cards would determine the success of each venture. In certain cases, where a successful advance appeared unlikely, a team had the option of shooting the puck into the next zone, surrendering it to the opponent, rather than risk losing it in the current zone with a failed advance.

A real game of hockey can be considered in similar terms. Regardless of the precise tactics, getting control of the puck, advancing through the zones in a controlled fashion, and then attempting a shot is the ultimate objective of the sport. That's why it's no surprise that the next steps in hockey analytics include the study of the controlled exit of the defensive zone and the controlled entry of the opposing zone.

When Taylor Hall[154] asked how he could improve his Corsi, the analytics community was already ready and waiting with his answer: controlled zone entries. Entering the opposing zone in possession of the puck, and denying that same privilege to your opponents, is an obvious way of improving a player's or team's shot differential.

Of course, I couldn't accurately simulate each player's ability at gaining zones and/or preventing zone entries with the simple statistics on the backs of hockey cards. Even with what's available today, I couldn't tell you which players or teams are better than others, or even if offensive zone entries are harder than defensive zone exits.

I would absolutely love to break down a game into these six sub-games (zone exits, zone entries, converting possession into shots, and the prevention of all three), and study each team's turnover and takeaway rates. It would be fascinating to break down each player's skills in each situation since, obviously, some players are intended for some of these tasks more than others. That could help explain the line and zone matching that we see on player usage charts, for example.

---

154 Taylor Hall, personal interview with Ryan Rishaug, *TSN*, March 11, 2014, Web, http://www.tsn.ca/VideoHub/?collection=72&show=305424.

Unfortunately, the NHL does not track this information. The only source of data is informally collected by a variety of analysts and bloggers. Zone entry data, for example, was first counted in the 2011–12 season by Eric Tulsky[155] and Geoff Detweiler of *Broad Street Hockey* for Philadelphia, who also recruited Bob Spencer[156] to track the data for the Minnesota Wild. Tulsky recruited others to gather data over the past two seasons and, this summer, Corey Sznajder is personally and manually collecting the data for the entire 2013–14 season. As a bit of a teaser, here's what he had at the time this book went to press, when he had completed roughly half the games.

The first column (% of All) is the percentage of all of a game's zone entries that were attempted by that team, and is obviously a decent proxy for puck possession. Next is the percentage of a team's zone entries that were successfully carried in (rather than dump and chase), followed by the same information, but for the opposing team. The final column is the edge the team enjoyed in that regard.

Zone Entries, 2013–14[157]

Team	% of All	Carried In	Opp Carry	Edge
Dallas	51.0	54.2	45.1	9.1
Chicago	54.1	54.7	46.0	8.7
Tampa Bay	52.1	54.3	47.4	6.9
Anaheim	49.3	48.1	43.3	4.8
Edmonton	48.3	48.5	43.8	4.7
Colorado	48.8	50.9	46.8	4.1
Pittsburgh	50.5	46.0	42.0	4.0
New Jersey	49.9	44.7	41.2	3.5
Detroit	52.6	46.6	43.4	3.2
Ottawa	50.8	49.9	46.8	3.1
Los Angeles	52.1	42.5	40.0	2.5
Boston	51.9	46.8	45.6	1.2
Montreal	48.7	47.1	47.6	0.5
St. Louis	52.0	45.3	45.2	0.1
Minnesota	50.9	43.4	43.4	0.0
Philadelphia	49.7	43.8	44.1	-0.3
Columbus	49.7	42.6	43.7	-1.1
NY Islanders	48.8	47.3	49.5	-2.2
Carolina	50.1	47.1	49.5	-2.4
Winnipeg	49.0	43.0	45.7	-2.7
NY Rangers	49.6	43.2	46.5	-3.3
Calgary	48.3	46.8	50.5	-3.7
Arizona	51.1	42.4	46.3	-3.9
San Jose	49.5	42.6	46.5	-3.9
Toronto	46.7	46.3	50.4	-4.1

155 Eric Tulsky, "Zone Entries: Introduction to a Unique Tracking Project", *NHL Numbers*, June 20, 2012, Web, http://nhlnumbers.com/2013/8/14/zone-exits-an-introduction.

156 Bob Spencer, "Minnesota Wild Zone Entries 2011-12: First Sixty Games", *Hashtag Hockey*, September 17, 2012, Web, http://hashtaghockey.com/2012/09/17/minnesota-wild-zone-entries-2011-12-first-sixty-games/.

157 Acknowledgement: Data received in personal correspondence with Corey Sznajder.

Florida	50.4	44.5	49.0	-4.5
Vancouver	49.3	43.8	48.8	-5.0
Buffalo	47.3	43.2	49.3	-6.1
Washington	50.1	45.3	51.5	-6.2
Nashville	48.7	40.9	48.3	-7.4

Chicago, Tampa Bay, and Dallas are the teams most notable for carrying the puck into the offensive zone in a controlled fashion, with Colorado being the only other team to do so at least half the time. Despite being known as the league's strongest possession team, Los Angeles is one of the team's most likely to dump it in, along with San Jose and Arizona.

Defensively, Washington, Calgary and Toronto are the teams that allow opponents to enter their zone with possession most frequently, something that Los Angeles, New Jersey, and Pittsburgh are least likely to permit. While the better teams appear to be on top overall, the strategy of attempting controlled zone entries didn't appear to work well for Edmonton, and San Jose seems to have done just fine without it.

As for zone exits, I believe they were first collected by Jonathan Willis[158] later in 2011–12, and ultimately by Corey Sznajder[159] in the 2012 Stanley Cup. Just as Tulsky organized the gathering of zone entry data two summers ago, Pierce Cuneen[160] did the same for zone exits last summer.

Here's what Sznajder has so far for the 2013–14 season. The first column (Exit%) is the percentage of the time that the team successfully left the defensive zone in possession of the puck. Since occasionally a team can retain possession after shooting or chipping it out of the zone, the second column (Poss%) refers only to those cases where it was carried or passed out of the zone in a controlled fashion. Sznajder also tracked the percentage of the time a zone exit resulted in a turnover (Turnover%) or an icing (Icing%).

Zone Exits, 2013–14[161]

Team	Exit%	Poss%	Turnover%	Icing%
St. Louis	33.2	29.8	6.1	2.2
Ottawa	32.1	29.2	7.5	1.9
Chicago	31.9	29.0	5.9	2.1
NY Islanders	32.0	28.6	7.2	2.2
Dallas	31.3	28.6	6.7	1.9
Arizona	30.8	28.4	6.0	2.2
Washington	29.1	28.0	6.6	1.9
Columbus	30.1	27.7	6.5	2.1
Calgary	30.7	27.6	5.6	2.6

158Jonathan Willis, "Magnus Paajarvi, Packhorse?", *Edmonton Journal*, October 10, 2011, Web, http://www.coppernblue.com/2011/11/11/2554850/jeff-petry-theo-peckham-zone-exits.

159Corey Sznajder, "Defense Pairings and Zone Exits", *Shutdown Line*, December 18, 2011, Web, http://shutdownline.com/hurricanes/statistical-analysis/defense-pairings-and-zone-exits.html.

160Pierce Cuneen, "Zone Exits: an Introduction", NHL Numbers, August 14, 2013, Web, http://nhlnumbers.com/2013/8/14/zone-exits-an-introduction.

161Acknowledgement: Data received in personal correspondence with Corey Sznajder.

Nashville	30.8	27.3	6.9	2.3
Detroit	29.7	27.3	6.4	1.9
Pittsburgh	30.6	27.1	6.4	1.7
Carolina	30.3	27.1	7.7	2.3
Anaheim	30.0	26.9	6.5	2.6
Boston	29.2	26.8	6.3	2.1
Minnesota	29.3	26.7	6.4	2.0
Colorado	29.0	26.7	7.5	2.4
Florida	29.1	26.6	6.7	2.1
Toronto	28.2	26.5	7.5	2.5
New Jersey	29.7	26.3	6.1	2.3
Edmonton	28.9	26.3	7.5	2.0
Tampa Bay	28.8	26.2	6.8	1.8
NY Rangers	29.6	26.2	6.6	2.1
Los Angeles	28.7	26.2	7.0	1.6
Montreal	29.2	26.1	6.8	2.8
Winnipeg	28.1	26.0	6.9	1.5
Philadelphia	28.7	26.0	6.2	2.3
Buffalo	28.4	25.4	7.4	2.5
Vancouver	28.2	25.3	6.8	2.5
San Jose	28.5	25.1	6.7	2.4

Defencemen like Alex Pietrangelo, Erik Karlsson, and Duncan Keith might be responsible for the success St. Louis, Ottawa, and Chicago have had in controlling the play out of their own zone, although the Senators were second to the Carolina Hurricanes in turning the puck over as they did so. Once again, San Jose is surprisingly at the bottom of the league, followed by Vancouver and Buffalo.

With the data finally starting to trickle in, we're starting to see some interesting results. For example, Tulsky has used this data to help define the importance of neutral zone play[162], and has calculated that an attempt to gain the zone in a controlled fashion will generate twice as many shots as the dump and chase. That helps explain why those old Russian teams of the 1970s, who were known to track zone entries[163], preferred regrouping in order to gain the zone in a controlled fashion rather than dumping it in.

Amazingly, Tulsky[164] also found that the depth lines generated the same number of shots as the top lines in controlled entries (0.56) and in dump-ins (0.25), even when he controlled for odd-man rushes. The difference is that the top lines attempt more controlled zone entries overall, capitalize on a higher share of them, and score on more of their shots.

---

[162] Eric Tulsky, "How Important is Neutral Zone Play", *NHL Numbers*, July 9, 2012, Web, http://nhlnumbers.com/2012/7/9/how-important-is-neutral-zone-play.

[163] David Staples, "The Soviet breakthrough in hockey stats", *Edmonton Journal*, March 6, 2012, Web, http://blogs.edmontonjournal.com/2012/03/06/the-soviet-breakthrough-in-hockey-stats-why-brian-burke-has-it-wrong-part-2/.

[164] Eric Tulsky, "More on the Advantages of Puck Possession over Dump and Chase", *NHL Numbers*, July 11, 2012, Web, http://nhlnumbers.com/2012/7/11/more-on-the-advantages-of-puck-possession-over-dump-and-chase.

Zone exits haven't been studied to quite the same extent as zone entries, but preliminary results are already starting to reveal how invaluable puck-moving defencemen can be. This is because they can get the puck out of the defensive zone far more reliably than the shutdown, stay-at-home variety, who are more focused on preventing the opponents from converting possession into scoring chances.

It would be interesting to see how significantly zone entries and exits are influenced by score effects, which are obviously at play here. After all, I imagine that teams that are protecting late leads will tend to dump it in more frequently, and will be more likely to allow opponents to exit their own zone.

Going forward, we will have to be particularly careful with the analysis of this data. In conversations with real NHL players, I've had it confirmed that there are real reasons for the dump and chase, namely that the opposing team doesn't frequently leave players with any other options. In fact, Justin Bourne[165] explained that the correct play is often dictated by the defender and that it's hard for the average player to gain a properly defended zone more than 2% of the time. He feels that this type of work can be fantastic on the defensive side, evaluating which teams aren't forcing enough dump-ins, and also to help evaluate each player's style. Beyond that, his best advice is to be very cautious when evaluating and applying zone entry and exit data.

What's next? I'm eagerly waiting for the completed and detailed results of Sznajder's "All Three Zones Project", which has already raised about $4,000 on GoFundMe.com. Trust me, that's a tremendous show of support in the world of hockey analytics. That data will be invaluable at answering some of the questions I've had since childhood about hockey's six main sub-games.

In the conclusion of last year's book, when I wrote how I hoped that *Hockey Abstract* would be "one of many such books that help guide hockey further in to the world of sports analytics", Sznajder's is definitely the kind that I had in mind. It might be time to go dig out my hockey cards and dice again!

How Accurate are the Passing Estimates?

The short answer is that I don't know. The long answer is that they are believed to be accurate within about 5% or so, but only over multiple-season sample sizes.

Normally, when a new statistic is introduced, it is compared against real data, and has its predictive value statistically established. Until that work is complete, most analysts will ignore these new developments. After all, what good is any number without at least some sense of its accuracy?

165Justin Bourne, "The player perspective on the current value of zone entries as a hockey stat", *The Score*, October 29, 2013, Web, http://hashtaghockey.com/2012/09/17/minnesota-wild-zone-entries-2011-12-first-sixty-games/.

Unfortunately, there is no real data when it comes to setup passes. There's great value in knowing who is setting up the shots, just as there's great value in knowing who is taking them. It's a reasonable way of figuring out who is making their plays in a fashion that's independent of their linemate's shooting abilities, or the luck and/or talent of opposing goaltenders. Given everything that's currently recorded in NHL game files, it's absolutely crazy that passes aren't counted. We know who was on the ice for every giveaway and icing, but we have no idea who is making the passes that result in shots. It's nuts!

In the past, bloggers and analysts have organized efforts to manually count everything from scoring chances to zone entries and exits, but curiously not for passes. Perhaps because it was believed that the NHL would soon start recording it themselves?

All we are left with is an estimate, one which is based on the premise that a player's share of all on-ice primary assists is probably equal to his share of all setup passes, too. The formula is simply each player's primary assists divided by the team's on-ice shooting percentage (minus the player's own shots and goals), and calculated separately for each manpower situation.

Despite its simplicity, this estimate isn't without controversy, as I warned Darryl Metcalf when he first added the statistic to his site, *Extra Skater*. While most analysts love the idea of counting passes, and agree that the estimate appears to make sense, some still see the whole concept as being "silly".

"What does setup passes tell you that primary assists and on-ice shooting percentage do not?", they ask. Good question. And you could just as easily ask what Corsi tells you that shots for, shots against, and ice time do not. Even at its worst, it's a simple and useful representation of existing statistics into a more useful form.

And how else can a player's playmaking abilities be measured? For years we've relied on assists, which can be skewed by everything from the skill (and luck) of their linemates and opposing goalies, to how many opportunities they get with the man advantage. Even the use of primary assists is of negligibly better value, in my opinion.

This past year did see the introduction of a new playmaking metric by Brian MacDonald called PLAY[166] that was based off a paper he and his colleagues wrote about quantifying playmaking in hockey[167]. PLAY is not unlike the passing estimate, especially in its results. The primary difference is that it's based on the difference between the number of shots a player's teammates take when he's on the ice and when he's not (also known as a WOWY analysis).

It's always encouraging when two different approaches of measuring the same thing arrive at similar results, much as we've seen with league translations, the dollar value of a goal, the scoring rate of a top-six forward, and so on. This is also why it's a real strength to have so

166Brian MacDonald, "PLAY – A Playmaking Metric, Part 1 – Intro", Greater Than Plus Minus, July 28, 2013, Web, http://www.greaterthanplusminus.com/2013/07/play-playmaking-metric-part-1-intro.html.
167Brian MacDonald, Christopher Weld, David C. Arney, "Quantifying playmaking ability in hockey", Department of Mathematical Sciences and Network Science Center, United States Military Academy, July 25, 2013, Web, http://www.academia.edu/4104016/Quantifying_playmaking_ability_in_hockey.

many different perspectives in our community, attacking each topic from so many different angles. We gain confidence in the results when they match up, and can dig deeper to find the truth when they don't.

MacDonald measured its accuracy by using PLAY in the first half of one season to predict assists in the second half. First-half assists had correlations with second-half assists of 0.19 for defencemen and 0.30 for forwards, while his new metric scored correlations of 0.41 and 0.46, respectively. Over a full season, the year-to-year correlation is 0.54 for both positions.

The only real problem with PLAY is that it isn't readily available anywhere, nor is the exact formula published to calculate it ourselves. In fact, the most recently published data is from the 2010–11 season. While that's not terribly convenient for those of us writing books, some people do need to make a living on their work and can't just give everything away for free.

So, we are once again left with our passing estimate. Fortunately, we are not completely without actual data with which to measure its accuracy, as Ryan Stimson[168] manually counted passes for the New Jersey Devils last season. His work was at even strength only, however.

Here's how the estimates (Est.) compare with the actual results, once adjusted for the his calculation that only 79.2% of New Jersey's shots were the result of a pass.

Setup Passes, New Jersey Devils, Estimated vs Actual, 2013–14[169]

Player	GP	A1	Est.	Actual	Diff%
Jaromir Jagr	82	15	258	281	-8.2
Travis Zajac	80	11	213	253	-15.8
Marek Zidlicky	81	10	181	188	-3.7
Patrik Elias	65	10	190	189	0.5
Ryane Clowe	43	8	147	115	27.8
Damien Brunner	60	6	131	71	84.5
Anton Volchenkov	56	5	83	33	151.5
Michael Ryder	82	5	139	150	-7.3
Adam Henrique	77	5	128	210	39.0
Eric Gelinas	60	5	72	50	44.0
Dainius Zubrus	82	5	103	189	-45.5

Minimum 5 primary assists

Whoa! While the estimates for the Devils with the most primary assists (A1) appear to be at least within the realm of reason, it falls apart quite dramatically as the sample size drops below 10. In such small sample sizes, perhaps a formula that includes all assists, instead of just primary assists, would be far more helpful.

This particular estimate, however, appears to be completely unreliable in single-season sample sizes for all but a few players per team (at most). While it might be useful over larger spreads of time, it's quite understandable how these results would lead Stimson to conclude

168Ryan Stimson, "Why Setup Passes and PSR are Unreliable", *In Lou We Trust*, May 7, 2014, Web, http://www.inlouwetrust.com/2014/5/7/5677850/why-estimating-passes-is-unreliable.
169Acknowledgement: Setup passing data from *Extra Skater,* http://www.extraskater.com.

that the estimate is "unreliable", "a terrible stat", and "flawed", when served in single-season portions (analytics folks can be harsh critics).

Hopefully, more dedicated analysts like Stimson will record passing data this season and we can see how well the numbers coalesce over larger samples. Personally, I imagine most fans will simply wait for the NHL to record the real data, rather than trying to improve an estimate that will inevitably be tossed away some day.

Here is the updated leader board for the top 100 forwards, for the past three seasons combined. Remember to be skeptical of the estimates for any player with relatively few primary assists (A1), like Riley Sheahan, Peter Mueller, and Aleksander Barkov.

Forwards Top 100 Passes per Game (P/GP), 2011–12 to 2013–14[170]

Forward	Team(s)	GP	A1	SP	SP/GP
Evgeni Malkin	Pit	166	95	1571	9.46
Henrik Sedin	Van	200	81	1692	8.46
Sidney Crosby	Pit	138	78	1124	8.14
Joe Thornton	SJ	212	85	1698	8.01
Eric Staal	Car	208	83	1644	7.90
Ryan Getzlaf	Ana	203	87	1522	7.50
John Tavares	NYI	189	72	1369	7.24
Blake Wheeler	Wpg	210	75	1511	7.20
Claude Giroux	Phi	207	85	1479	7.14
Mikko Koivu	Min	168	64	1186	7.06
Patrick Kane	Chi	198	77	1378	6.96
Jordan Staal	Pit/Car	192	50	1318	6.86
Daniel Sedin	Van	192	58	1316	6.85
Phil Kessel	Tor	212	79	1441	6.80
Ray Whitney	Phx/Dal	183	59	1222	6.68
Joe Pavelski	SJ	212	59	1406	6.63
Anze Kopitar	LA	211	66	1391	6.59
Jason Spezza	Ott	160	56	1038	6.49
Logan Couture	SJ	193	53	1250	6.48
Henrik Zetterberg	Det	173	70	1101	6.36
Matt Duchene	Col	176	57	1106	6.28
Pavel Datsyuk	Det	162	58	1014	6.26
Patrik Elias	NJ	194	65	1212	6.25
Mats Zuccarello	NYR	102	31	631	6.19
Valtteri Filppula	Det/TB	197	56	1212	6.15
Mike Ribeiro	Dal/Wsh/Phx	202	62	1227	6.07
Corey Perry	Ana	205	59	1235	6.02
David Krejci	Bos	206	63	1239	6.01
T.J. Oshie	StL	189	57	1132	5.99
Martin Havlat	SJ	127	31	759	5.98
P.A. Parenteau	NYI/Col	183	55	1087	5.94

170Acknowledgement: Setup passing data from *Extra Skater,* http://www.extraskater.com.

Riley Sheahan	Det	44	13	257	5.84
Derek Stepan	NYR	212	63	1236	5.83
Patrice Bergeron	Bos	203	61	1183	5.83
Jordan Eberle	Edm	206	66	1200	5.83
Taylor Hall	Edm	181	65	1048	5.79
Kyle Turris	Phx/Ott	185	46	1071	5.79
Zach Parise	NJ/Min	197	57	1140	5.79
Steven Stamkos	TB	166	52	958	5.77
Tyler Seguin	Bos/Dal	209	62	1199	5.74
Bryan Little	Wpg	204	55	1169	5.73
Brad Richards	NYR	210	57	1194	5.69
Jonathan Toews	Chi	182	55	1034	5.68
Alex Tanguay	Cgy/Col	120	36	675	5.63
Thomas Vanek	Buf/NYI/Mtl	194	62	1076	5.55
Matt Moulson	NYI/Buf/Min	204	58	1124	5.51
Ilya Kovalchuk	NJ	114	37	628	5.51
Martin St. Louis	TB/NYR	205	69	1124	5.48
Marian Hossa	Chi	193	58	1058	5.48
Alexander Semin	Wsh/Car	185	55	1014	5.48
Nicklas Backstrom	Wsh	172	58	939	5.46
Marcus Johansson	Wsh	193	57	1044	5.41
Milan Lucic	Bos	207	55	1118	5.40
David Desharnais	Mtl	207	57	1113	5.38
Mike Cammalleri	Mtl/Cgy	172	37	923	5.37
Peter Mueller	Col/Fla	75	15	402	5.36
Mike Richards	LA	204	47	1091	5.35
Aleksander Barkov	Fla	54	12	288	5.33
Jeff Skinner	Car	176	40	937	5.32
Paul Stastny	Col	190	49	1007	5.30
Nazem Kadri	Tor	147	42	774	5.27
Carl Soderberg	Bos	79	23	411	5.20
Teddy Purcell	TB	209	68	1087	5.20
Brad Marchand	Bos	203	43	1052	5.18
Steve Ott	Dal/Buf/StL	204	37	1052	5.16
Jason Pominville	Buf/Min	211	55	1086	5.15
Jarome Iginla	Cgy/Pit/Bos	204	57	1043	5.11
Mikhail Grabovski	Tor/Wsh	180	41	920	5.11
Ryan O'Reilly	Col	190	43	970	5.11
Kyle Okposo	NYI	198	49	1008	5.09
Marian Gaborik	NYR/CBJ/LA	170	42	865	5.09
Johan Franzen	Det	172	49	874	5.08
Alex Galchenyuk	Mtl	113	27	573	5.07
Patrick Sharp	Chi	184	55	931	5.06
Jamie Benn	Dal	193	53	976	5.06
Joffrey Lupul	Tor	151	45	763	5.05
Rick Nash	CBJ/NYR	191	44	965	5.05
Cody Hodgson	Van/Buf	203	46	1025	5.05

Ryane Clowe	SJ/NYR/NJ	159	37	802	5.04
Daniel Alfredsson	Ott/Det	190	46	957	5.04
Teemu Selanne	Ana	192	44	962	5.01
Max Pacioretty	Mtl	195	48	975	5.00
Drew Stafford	Buf	196	44	963	4.91
Loui Eriksson	Dal/Bos	191	48	936	4.90
Vladimir Tarasenko	StL	102	24	499	4.89
Vinny Prospal	CBJ	130	30	634	4.88
Bobby Ryan	Ana/Ott	198	46	965	4.87
David Legwand	Nsh/Det	209	52	1006	4.81
Olli Jokinen	Cgy/Wpg	209	47	1006	4.81
James Neal	Dal/Pit	179	50	860	4.80
Derick Brassard	CBJ/NYR	202	45	969	4.80
Andrew Ladd	Wpg	208	45	995	4.78
Matt Cullen	Min/Nsh	192	49	914	4.76
Martin Hanzal	Phx	168	38	796	4.74
Jakub Voracek	Phi	208	55	984	4.73
David Backes	StL	204	46	963	4.72
Vincent Lecavalier	TB/Phi	172	41	806	4.69
Evander Kane	Wpg	185	47	863	4.66
Tomas Fleischmann	Fla	210	50	978	4.66
Radim Vrbata	Phx	191	40	889	4.65

Minimum 20 games

When watching a game and counting the passes by hand, it appears that five is a good game, six is excellent, while seven is exceptional.

That's one reason why Evgeni Malkin's 9.46 passes per game is quite surprising. He is estimated to set up a full shot per game more than any other player, and three more per game than all but 18 NHL players. There's obviously a reason James Neal has scored 88 goals in 179 games as a Penguin, and also reason to doubt whether he can maintain that 40-goal pace playing in Nashville, whose top player (Matt Cullen) sets up linemates only half as frequently.

The only other surprises at the top of the leader board, to me at least, include Blake Wheeler (8th) and Jordan Staal (12th). It's also surprising to see Martin St. Louis way down in 48th. It's possible that he has sniper Steven Stamkos to thank for his 2013 Art Ross, and that his 7 assists in 19 games for the New York Rangers is more indicative of his true playmaking pace these days.

While this pass statistic is primarily meant for forwards, it can also be used for defencemen. They don't set up nearly as many shots, and quite a few of their relatively rare primary assists are a result of either a break-out pass to someone who goes on to score by himself or a hard shot from the point that was deflected in.

That's not to say that there's no value in a quick look at the leader board for defencemen. As impressive as Malkin is among forwards, Erik Karlsson dominates the blue line with almost two more setup passes per game than Keith Yandle has in second place. Wow.

Defencemen Top 50 Passes per Game (P/GP), 2011–12 to 2013–14[171]

Defenceman	Team(s)	GP	A1	SP	SP/GP
Erik Karlsson	Ott	180	68	1237	6.87
Keith Yandle	Phx	212	55	1037	4.89
Ryan Murphy	Car	52	8	242	4.65
Andrei Markov	Mtl	142	35	648	4.56
Brian Campbell	Fla	212	46	967	4.56
Alex Pietrangelo	StL	209	55	948	4.54
Slava Voynov	LA	184	37	825	4.48
Mark Streit	NYI/Phi	212	49	940	4.43
Drew Doughty	LA	203	42	889	4.38
Patrick Wiercioch	Ott	95	20	413	4.35
Kris Letang	Pit	123	37	510	4.15
James Wisniewski	CBJ	153	35	632	4.13
Joni Pitkanen	Car	52	10	211	4.06
Kimmo Timonen	Phi	198	48	783	3.95
Mike Green	Wsh	136	30	526	3.87
Zdeno Chara	Bos	204	43	783	3.84
Alex Goligoski	Pit/Dal	199	43	762	3.83
Vitor Hedman	TB	179	43	669	3.74
Sergei Gonchar	Ott/Dal	195	35	723	3.71
Brent Burns*	SJ	180	31	663	3.68
P.K. Subban	Mtl	204	47	748	3.67
Michael Del Zotto	NYR/Nsh	190	35	649	3.42
Jaroslav Spacek	Mtl/Car	46	7	157	3.41
Duncan Keith	Chi	200	47	669	3.35
Marek Zidlicky	Min/NJ	192	34	640	3.33
Dan Boyle	SJ	202	31	673	3.33
Jared Spurgeon	Min	176	29	561	3.19
Kevin Shattenkirk	Col/StL	210	36	669	3.19
Jay Bouwmeester	Cgy/StL	211	38	671	3.18
Ryan McDonough	NYR	206	33	650	3.16
Carlo Colaiacovo	StL/Det	95	12	299	3.15
Dan Hamhuis	Nsh/Van	208	37	647	3.11
Jake Muzzin	LA	121	16	373	3.08
Andrej Meszaros	Phi/Bos	125	20	382	3.06
Roman Josi	Nsh	172	29	525	3.05
Jason Garrison	Fla/Van	205	31	625	3.05
Calvin de Haan	NYI	52	7	158	3.04
Ryan Suter	Nsh/Min	209	41	634	3.03
Eric Gelinas	NJ	61	13	184	3.02
Dougie Hamilton	Bos	106	14	315	2.97
Sami Vatanen	Ana	56	9	166	2.96

171Acknowledgement: Setup passing data from *Extra Skater,* http://www.extraskater.com.

Erik Johnson	Col	184	30	544	2.96
Dennis Wideman	Wsh/Cgy	174	30	510	2.93
Olli Maatta	Pit	78	12	226	2.90
Jake Gardiner	Tor	167	25	481	2.88
Christian Ehrhoff	SJ/Buf	192	33	550	2.86
Tyler Myers	Buf	156	20	446	2.86
Alexander Edler	Van	190	25	541	2.85
Paul Martin	Pit	146	25	409	2.80
Oliver Ekman-Larsson	Phx	210	31	588	2.80

Minimum 20 Games

Remember to be highly skeptical of anyone with fewer than 20 primary assists, including 10 of these 50 defencemen. While Karlsson, Yandle, Markov, Campbell, and Pietrangelo can safely be considered the real deal, let's take some time before making any judgments about Ryan Murphy or Patrick Wiercioch.

I'll leave the final words to Stimson, who concluded his own piece with the hope that "over time, hopefully more people track passes and shot-generation in the way that I do. Only then will we have real data to work off of and not have to settle for estimates." Amen.

What is Delta?

By Tom Awad

In the chapters on "What Makes Good Players Good", I made reference to a statistic called Delta. What is Delta, and why am I using it rather than the more familiar Corsi or Fenwick statistics?

Expressed in its simplest form, Delta is simply Fenwick adjusted for Shot Quality, leading to an "Expected Goal" value. I first introduced Delta way back in 2010[172], before the concept of Expected Goals had become more common. Delta is a way of expressing Fenwick numbers while keeping them in units of goals, which is the fundamental currency that hockey is expressed in.

As has been covered in the chapter about Shot Quality as well as "What Makes Good Players Good", while Shot Quality is not a significant contributor to team success or failure in the NHL, it does exist, and it can be expressed at the individual level as well as the team level: certain players have a play style that leads to them having fewer, high-quality chances, while others prefer outside shots, leading to high shot differential. Both styles have their benefits and may be suited to different types of players, but Fenwick cannot differentiate between them.

Corsi and Fenwick also have other limitations, they are highly influenced by zone starts as well as the score of the game. As explained in the Score Effects chapter, when the score isn't tied in the third period, the trailing team will typically have a huge advantage in shots that

---

172 Tom Awad, "Plus-Minus and Corsi have a Baby", *Hockey Prospectus*, January 21, 2010, Web,
http://www.hockeyprospectus.com/puck/article.php?articleid=436.

doesn't translate into goals, they are taking lower-quality shots and allowing high-quality ones. As a result, "Fenwick Close", defined as Fenwick when the score is tied or within 1 goal in the first two periods, has become the default Fenwick measure. This works well in that it avoids bias, but ends up throwing away almost 35% of the data in the NHL, which is unfortunate. Delta can naturally correct for that by weighing each shot by the game score, achieving the same thing as score-adjusted Fenwick[173].

Like Fenwick and Corsi, Delta can also be adjusted for Quality of Competition and Quality of Teammates. However, Delta is also easier to compare to other measures. When a player has an Adjusted Delta of +5.0 over the entire season, you know that it means that he contributed +5 goals through his possession play. It's harder to perform that equivalency when we say a player has a Fenwick of +3.0 per 60 minutes.

Lastly, comparing Delta with Fenwick acts as a proxy for Shot Quality. This can be useful when trying to understand why a player or team has the results that they do; for example, Phil Kessel last season had a Corsi For of 1230 and an Corsi Against of 1557, giving him very bad possession numbers (a Corsi % of only 44.4%). However, when weighted by Shot Quality, we can see that he was on the ice for an equivalent of 59 Expected Goals For and 64 Expected Goals against, a more reasonable 48%. This goes part of the way in explaining why, despite the terrible Corsi numbers, his team still managed to outscore its opponents by 8 goals at 5-on-5 while he was on the ice.

Update: In 2013, Michael Parkatti developed a very similar metric, labeling it with the more intuitive name of "Expected Goals"[174], and he has been reporting them on a game-by-game basis for Edmonton Oilers games.

Why Didn't Ottawa Finish First in 2013–14?

Last year, I published my life's work, slapped my name right there on the cover, and then proudly proclaimed within that the Ottawa Senators were the favourites for the President's Trophy.

"Are you sure that's wise?", asked my friend Timo Seppa. After all, that's not exactly as safe a prediction as Chicago or Boston, and while I might look like a genius if I'm right, I'm going to look like a fool if I'm wrong.

"That's just one chapter", I explained to Timo, "plus, it's more about the methodology than the results. People know what it is, and what it isn't, and it'll be ok."

The methodology to predict the standings, to briefly recap last year's book, is to start with a

173 Eric Tulsky, "Adjusted for Score Effects to Improve Our Predictions", *Broad Street Hockey*, January 23, 2012, Web, http://www.broadstreethockey.com/2012/1/23/2722089/score-adjusted-fenwick.

174 Michael Parkatti, "Testing the Predictive Value of Expected Goals vs Other Metrics", *Boys on the Bus*, November 26, 2013, Web, http://www.boysonthebus.com/2013/11/26/testing-the-predictive-value-of-expected-goals-vs-other-metrics/.

luck-neutral version of the last year's standings, which includes adjustments for injuries, post-regulation win-loss records, and shooting and save percentages. Then, adjust for the impact of all roster changes, which are calculated using GVT, a popular high-level, catch-all statistic. That's basically all there is to it. Since no personal opinions are involved, teams like Ottawa can finish on top.

In any event, Timo knew that I was taking a bigger risk than I thought, because years of publishing the annual *Hockey Prospectus* guide has shown him how seriously some fans can take statistical projections. He was worried that a blown prediction could skew the reader's perception of that model, and possibly of the rest of my work, too.

Fortunately, that did not happen. Well, that second part, at least. Virtually everything my model projected for Ottawa was wrong, and they finished nowhere near first place. In fact, the Senators actually missed the playoffs by five points. The good news is that readers took the projection in the proper context, and had no trouble keeping their composure. In fact, some of the kinder readers felt that it was the Senators who blew it, and not my model.

But, let's be truthful. It was *way* off. So what went wrong?

First of all, the model held an optimistic view of how good the Senators really were in 2012–13. Despite being on pace for 198 goals for and 178 goals against in reality, they would have scored 254 goals with more shooting luck, and a healthy Jason Spezza and Erik Karlsson, according to my calculations. And, even with more mortal goaltending (Ottawa posted a .935 save percentage that year), they would still have allowed only 202 goals. Remember, this is a team that outshot their opponents by 2.15 shots (or 6.48 attempted shots) per game at even strength, even without Karlsson and Spezza.

In retrospect, I feel that there were two potential blind spots in my model that may have caused this optimism.

1. Overstating the extent to which teams can bounce back from injuries, by failing to take into account how well their replacements had performed. With Spezza and Karlsson back on the ice, for example, all those young stars wouldn't have had the same opportunities to contribute.

2. Expecting every team's shooting and save percentages to regress to the same point (league average) might be overselling those teams with particularly poor shooters, goaltending, or team defence.

I've put some thought into that second point this summer and how the model regresses every team's shooting and save percentages back to the league average, no matter who they are. While that approach is justified by a mountain of independent studies, I couldn't help but wonder if it truly makes intuitive sense that teams all have the same resting point. Isn't it more reasonable to believe that certain teams have better goaltending and/or have defensive systems that allow lower quality shots? Or that all of their snipers might give teams like Chicago a higher natural shooting percentage than a team like Florida?

It was a time-consuming process, but I went all the way back to the 2005 lockout, and calculated each team's **expected shooting percentage**[175] as the team's shots multiplied by the previous career (and era-adjusted) shooting percentage of those that took them. As you can see from the chart below, there's an obvious relationship between a team's expected shooting percentage and their actual shooting percentage.

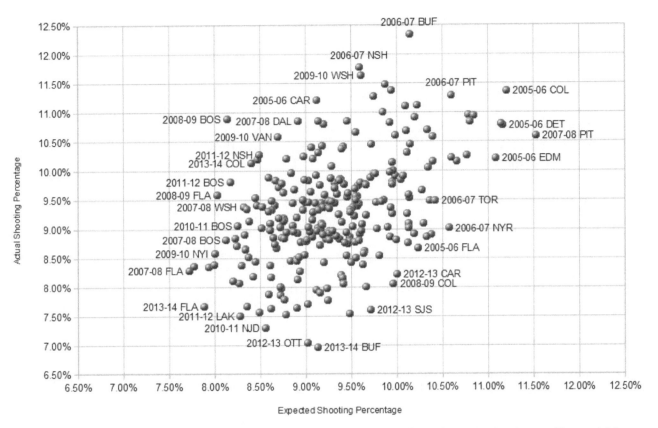

Given each player's shot totals and their previous career shooting percentage, it would have been reasonable for Ottawa to have scored on about 9.0% of their shots in 2012–13, instead of 7.0%, for example.

Crunching the numbers, I was thrilled to find out that expected shooting percentage has a closer correlation with a team's actual shooting percentage than the league average, and was hoping that I could use this in its place in my model. Unfortunately, I found that its predictive power was very limited. A team's shooting percentage in the following season had very little relationship with a team's expected shooting percentage from the year before. So, we're stuck with using the league average.

I suppose this is just a very drawn-out way of saying that the model isn't very good at predicting a team's shooting and save percentages, and isn't likely to get any better. Finding a

175Rob Vollman, "Calculated expected shooting percentage", *Habs Eyes on the Prize*, June 30, 2014, Web, http://www.habseyesontheprize.com/2014/6/30/5844400/nhl-expected-shooting-percentage-regress-prediction.

way to predict these percentages could be the next big breakthrough in analytics. Until then, the model will remain limited in this regard.

Furthermore, not only did the model overestimate how good Ottawa was in 2012–13, but it also held an optimistic view of what the impact of the off-season changes would be. I calculated that the arrival of Bobby Ryan, Clarke MacArthur, Cory Conacher, and Joe Corvo, minus the departure of Sergei Gonchar, Jakub Silfverberg, Daniel Alfredsson, and Ben Bishop, would have a positive net impact of about 28 goals (scored and prevented).

And what happened? Bobby Ryan played most of the season with a sports hernia, while departed players like Ben Bishop competed for the Vezina trophy, and Daniel Alfredsson led the Detroit Red Wings in scoring. D-oh!

In the end, the model had the Senators pegged for 269 goals for, 208 against, and a league-leading 105 points. But their goaltending unexpectedly tumbled all the way down to .912, their shot differential worsened by almost four shots a game, and they wound up with 236 goals for and 265 against. The only bright light was their 102-point pace in the second half, but by then it was too late.

So, the model pretty much blew it in every way possible. And, in the interests of transparency, that's not the only team it got wrong. I collected the pre-season projections of 26 other analysts and, in terms of division rankings, only a single one fared worse than my model. Refunds, anyone?

In fairness, projecting the standings is an enormously difficult task. With injuries, goaltending, luck, in-season transactions, rookie development, veteran decline, coaching decisions, hot and cold streaks and so on, it's practically a fool's errand. If a projection turns out to be wrong, how can you tell if it's because circumstances change or because it wasn't an accurate perspective of the team in the first place?

After all, 15 of those 26 analysts actually reached a similar conclusion about Ottawa as my model did, whether they used analytics or not. Maybe that's partly why I got a free pass on the Senators, but was strongly questioned about its pessimistic view of Edmonton and Buffalo, two teams that it actually wound up getting right.

Who knows? Maybe we all had the Senators pegged right, but things changed. Projections can be a great point-in-time perspective, but you really need to keep it up to date with the changing situations in order for it to continue being useful over time. That's the only way to tell if expectations should be changed or whether a team is merely on a hot or cold streak.

As a group, we "experts" haven't figured out how to project the standings. At various points in the season, not a single set of projections was more accurate than simply using last year's standings. In the end, half of the analysts beat last year's standings, but negligibly in all but three cases (*The Hockey News*, Chris Morgan, and *NBC*'s James Neveau).

The following leader board is ranked by the total difference in divisional rankings for each team. For example, projecting a team for 1st when they actually finish 4th (or vice versa) would result in a score of 3 for that team.

Accuracy of Expert Projections, 2013–14

Analyst	Diff
James Neveau, NBC	40
Chris Morgan, the Examiner	40
The Hockey News	40
Sean Hartnett, CBS	42
Chris Peters, CBS	42
Kevin Allen, USA Today	44
Neil Greenberg, Washington Post	44
Mitchell Tierney, the Last Word	44
Chris Stubits, CBS	46
Matt Brigidi, SB Nation	48
Jason Lewis, Hockey Buzz	48
Sports Pickin	48
VUKOTA, Hockey Prospectus	48
Ted Starkey, SB Nation	50
Eric Tulsky, SB Nation	50
Last Year's Standings	*50*
Tyler Bleszinski, SB Nation	52
Steve Lepore, SB Nation	52
Adam Gretz, SB Nation	52
Brian Cazeneuve, Sports Illustrated	52
Travis Hughes, SB Nation	54
Bruce Ciski, SB Nation	54
Mike Zeisberger, QMI	54
Chris Blanchard, XN Sports	54
Dave Lozo, the Score	54
Rob Vollman's Hockey Abstract	*56*
James Mirtle	60

Even with a group this size, there were quite a few teams that everybody got wrong. For instance, nobody had Colorado or Anaheim as high as 1st, Tampa Bay 2nd, or even Calgary 6th. Similarly, nobody predicted Chicago or Los Angeles as low as 3rd, nor the Oilers 7th and the Islanders 8th. That's 8 of 30 teams finishing outside the range defined by 26 experts.

That's why pre-season projections, like the ones I'm actually going to have the audacity to present once again ("if only to find out what will definitely *not* happen", according to one "fan" of my work), need to be taken with a grain of salt. Consider the source, and its perspective, and be aware that things can change quickly.

Before diving in, let's summarize all the major roster changes that occurred late in the season, through the summer, and right up until the end of July, when this book went to print. Be sure to make adjustments for any transactions that occurred since then.

— NHL G.M.S —

PROM NIGHT, 1971   FREE AGENCY DAY, 2014

The net impact for each team's goals for (GF) and against (GA) is calculated in terms of GVT. While all players were considered in my calculations, only those whose impact will exceed at least a goal were explicitly listed.

Major 2014 Roster Changes and Net Impact

Team	Notable Removed	Notable Added	GF	GA
ANA	Bonino, Perreault, Penner, Koivu, Winnik, Selanne, Hiller	Kesler, Heatley, Thompson, Stoner, LaBarbera, Leblanc	-29.8	5.0
ARI	Vrbata, Greiss, Ribeiro, Morris, Bissonnette	Erat, Gagner, Dubnyk, Reese, Crombeen, Vitale	-8.3	11.7
BOS	Iginla, Johnson		-12.3	15.5
BUF	Miller, Ehrhoff, McBain	Gorges, Gionta, Meszaros, Stewart, Benoit, Neuvirth	16.7	3.9
CAR	Peters, Malhotra	McClement	0.1	8.5
CBJ	Umberger, MacKenzie, Comeau, Skille	Hartnell, Gibbons	1.6	5.0
CGY	Cammalleri, Stempniak, Butler	Hiller, Raymond, Engelland	-2.5	-0.2
CHI	Handzus, Brookbank	Richards	4.3	-2.5
COL	Stastny, Parenteau, Benoit, Sarich, Giguere	Iginla, Stuart, Briere, Winchester, Redmond, Gervais	-1.1	-3.3
DAL	Whitney, Robidas	Spezza, Hemsky	11.4	9.7
DET	Alfredsson		-4.7	0.4
EDM	Hemsky, Gagner	Pouliot, Purcell, Fayne, Nikitin	12.4	-29.6
FLA	Gibert, Winchester, Goc, Weaver	Luongo, Jokinen, Mitchell, Bolland, MacKenzie	7.5	-18.5

LA	Mitchell	Cracknell	2.5	7.1
MIN	Prosser	Vanek, Bickel	14.0	4.1
MTL	Gionta, Gorges, Briere, Diaz	Parenteau, Gilbert, Weaver, Malhotra	5.9	10.1
NJ	Volchenkov, Fayne, Loktionov, Carter	Cammalleri, Havlat, Ruutu	13.1	15.0
NSH	Hornqvist, Spaling, Legwand, Klein	Neal, Ribeiro, Volchenkov, Roy, Jokinen	17.0	-5.3
NYI	Vanek, MacDonald, Martinek	Halak, Johnson, Grabovski, Conacher, Kulemin, Brennan, Skille	0.7	-29.9
NYR	Pouliot, Richards, Callahan, Boyle, Stralman, Del Zotto, Dorsett	St. Louis, Boyle, Stempniak, Klein, Kostka, Hunwick	-0.2	5.2
OTT	Spezza, Conacher	Legwand, Chiasson, Johnson	-5.5	-5.4
PHI	Hartnell, Meszaros	Umberger, MacDonald	-11.0	1.6
PIT	Niskanen, Neal, Jokinen, Gibbons, Orpik, Engelland, Vitale, Glass	Hornqvist, Greiss, Goc, Ehrhoff, Spaling, Downie, Comeau	-18.8	8.2
SJ	Boyle, Havlat, Stuart	Tennyson	-11.4	6.5
STL	Halak, Roy, Polak, Morrow, Stewart	Stastny, Gunnarsson, Butler, Ott, Ferriero, Lehtera, Lindstrom	-0.9	13.4
TB	St. Louis, Kostka, Purcell, Salo, Thompson, Crombeen	Garrison, Callahan, Stralman, Morrow, Nabokov, Boyle	0.4	-14.8
TOR	Raymond, Gunnarsson, Ranger, Bolland, Kulemin	Winnik, Polak, Robidas, Komarov, Sontorelli, Booth, Frattin, Kontiola	-5.4	-11.8
VAN	Luongo, Garrison, Santorelli, Kesler, Booth	Miller, Vrbata, Bonino, Sbisa, Dorsett	6.0	-10.3
WPG	Montoya, Jokinen, Setoguchi, Halischuk	Perreault	-0.3	11.2
WSH	Grabovski, Erat, Neuvirth	Niskanen, Orpik	-1.7	-10.3

With that information, we can reproduce last year's study and determine where teams will finish this season based on a luck-neutral version of last year's standings, which are listed first, and the team after the summer's roster changes, which is listed second.

Expected Standings, 2014–15

Team	GF	GA	PTS	GF	GA	PTS
Chicago	241	211	100	246	208	102
Los Angeles	236	198	103	239	205	101
Vancouver	233	217	96	239	207	101
San Jose	265	213	105	254	219	101
Detroit	234	200	102	229	201	100
NY Islanders	232	236	91	232	206	99
Tampa Bay	219	217	92	220	203	97
Carolina	243	217	99	244	226	97
Florida	218	230	89	226	211	96
Columbus	228	211	97	230	216	96
NY Rangers	234	215	97	234	220	96
Minnesota	202	202	92	216	206	95
Boston	238	201	102	225	217	94
Dallas	242	235	94	254	245	94
New Jersey	194	190	93	207	205	93
St. Louis	227	210	97	226	224	93
Nashville	208	229	86	225	224	92
Pittsburgh	236	212	99	217	220	91
Anaheim	250	221	99	220	226	90

Ottawa	239	250	89	233	245	89
Winnipeg	235	236	92	234	247	89
Edmonton	200	261	76	212	231	87
Philadelphia	228	236	90	217	238	86
Washington	221	253	84	219	242	86
Colorado	213	238	85	212	234	86
Arizona	224	229	91	216	241	85
Calgary	209	231	86	207	231	85
Montreal	218	241	86	224	251	85
Toronto	208	265	77	203	253	79
Buffalo	182	253	72	199	257	77

Why couldn't Chicago and Los Angeles have finished on top of my list last year?

Some teams are higher than expected because they had really bad luck last season, like perhaps Carolina, and others because they have improved their teams in the summer, like the Islanders, the Panthers, and the Oilers. Likewise, some teams are lower than expected because they might have had a few good bounces last year, like Toronto, Montreal and Colorado, or because their rosters might have taken a step in the wrong direction since then, like Anaheim.

I don't necessarily agree with these results, as you probably know from reading the brief team essays. As covered in the discussion on expected shooting percentages, the model appears to overrate teams with poor shooting and/or goaltending, and underrates those with the opposite. Specifically, and based on my own personal judgment, I take greatest issue with:

- Boston and Pittsburgh as bubble teams, when I believe they'll be fighting for the Eastern crown. The impact of losing their backup goalie seems to be overstated, much like the loss of Iginla. Likewise, GVT overvalues the loss of players like Neal and Niskanen.
- Vancouver in the hunt for the division crown, when they should finish outside the playoff picture.
- Anaheim outside the playoffs, when they're practically a guarantee.
- Washington so far out of the playoff picture. They may have overpaid to fix their blue line, but they definitely improved it.
- Florida and Carolina as legitimate playoff teams. I'll admit that they're underrated and could catch some teams by surprise, but they'll be fighting for a wild card spot.
- The Islanders fighting for a division crown instead of a playoff spot. I really like their moves this summer, and they have some great youth, but climbing that high will be at least a two-step process.

On the other hand, I'm surprisingly comfortable with:

- Toronto and Philadelphia outside the playoff picture. Given their poor possession numbers, there's a potential disaster in both cities, especially if they have some bad luck in nets.

- Colorado missing the playoffs, but not by that much. Even those who aren't into analytics caught a glimpse of their weaknesses in their opening round series with the Minnesota Wild.
- Detroit being a playoff home seed. Imagine how good they would have been last year without all those injuries, and then consider all their great young prospects.
- Montreal outside the playoffs. They may have overachieved in the postseason, but they certainly earned their way in, and should do so again.

I'll concede that it was probably unnecessary to go on for about six pages, but it helps to demonstrate why mistakes are as exciting in analytics as successes. In this case, the impact of Spezza's and Karlsson's injuries were exaggerated, the net effect of the roster changes was way off, the goaltending crashed, and, quite frankly, the team performed far worse than they should have.

Most importantly, this reminds us of the limitations of projections, whether they use analytics or not. So many things that have an enormous impact on the standings can change throughout the course of a season, many of which are unpredictable. Pre-season projections, whatever they are based on, should be taken in the proper perspective, and kept up to date as circumstances change.

Conclusion

Once again, this is the only conclusion you'll find in a *Hockey Abstract* book. Analytics can certainly shed light on an issue, but the great debates never reach a final conclusion.

Thanks to our editor Tina Dubois, illustrator Joshua Smith, and to everyone who has enjoyed our work, supported us, and helped spread the word.

Remember that all the raw data for the charts and tables can be found on the *Hockey Abstract* website. Our twitter handles and emails can be found in the author biographies. Please don't be shy about reaching out to us!

Let the discussions continue!

Glossary of Terms

This is only a quick and dirty reference of analytic terms used in this book. Use the alphabetical index to find more complete explanations.

3-1-1 Rule
Three goals gets a team about one point in the standings and costs about one million dollars.

Advanced Statistics
All statistics beyond those recorded in newspaper box scores. Also, non-traditional statistics.

Behind the Net
A hockey statistics data website hosted by Gabriel Desjardins.

Bill James
Author of the *Baseball Abstract* and pioneer of the baseball analytics revolution.

Checking Line
Secondary players, normally quite gritty, who primarily focus on defensive hockey.

Close Game
A game within a single goal in the first two periods or tied in the third period or overtime.

Compassionate Referee
The concept that an official is less likely to call another infraction on a recently penalized team.

Correlation
A statistical term calculating the effect to which two variables are related.

Corsi
A differential based on all attempted shots, including those blocked or that missed the net.

Defence-Independent Goalie Rating (DIGR)
Save percentage adjusted based on the average quality of shots faced.

Defensive Shell
While protecting a lead, allowing a higher volume of shots against, over lower quality.

Delta
A shot-based, situation-neutral statistic developed by Tom Awad in 2010.

Dirty Rat Penalty Minutes (DRPM)
Penalty minutes from infractions most likely to result in injury.

Elite Players
Defined here as players in the top 25% of the league.

Expected Shooting Percentage
A team's expected shooting percentage based on the individual shots taken and previous career shooting percentages of its players.

Extra Skater
A hockey statistics data website hosted by Darryl Metcalf.

Fenwick
A differential based on all attempted shots, including those that missed the net but (unlike Corsi) not including blocked shots.

Goalie Usage Chart
Graphical visualization of how a goalie performs relatively to quality of opposing shooters and average distance of shots.

Goals Versus Threshold (GVT)
The value of a player's contributions in terms of goals relative to a replacement-level player. Developed by Tom Awad in 2003.

High Leverage Situation
A situation where plays can have a disproportionally significant impact on the game.

Hockey Abstract Checklist
A high-level checklist to establish a team's approximate level of competitiveness.

Hockey Prospectus
A website hosted by Timo Seppa that features statistical hockey analysis.

Home Plate Save Percentage
A goalie's save percentage in shots taken in a dangerous zone in front of the net.

Individual Points Percentage (IPP%)
The percentage of all a team's on-ice points on which a player recorded a goal or an assist.

Inductinator
A system that determines the intrinsic standards to be voted into the Hall of Fame.

Kappa
Players who commit dangerous fouls, but who refuse to fight.

Luck-Neutral Standings
A version of the standings with the transient components of injuries, post-regulation records, and save and shooting percentages removed.

Net Penalty Differential (NPD)
Penalties drawn minus those taken, adjusted for manpower situations and position.

NHL Translation
An estimate of what a player's non-NHL scoring totals would be in the NHL. Also, NHL Equivalency (NHLe).

Null Hypothesis
One which asserts that the two variables being examined have no relationship upon each other.

One Stat Argument
The belief that goaltenders should be evaluated using even-strength save percentage only.

PDO
Shooting percentage plus save percentage, also see Shooting Percentage Differential.

Penalty-Killing Extras (PKE)
The measurable things penalty killers can do.

Persistence
A statistical term that measures the extent to which a variable is consistent over time.

Player Usage Chart (PUC)
A graphical portrayal of how a player is being used.

Possession-based
A hockey system aimed at keeping possession of the puck and denying such possession to the opponents.

Post-Expansion Era
The 1967–68 season to the current day, when the league expanded beyond 6 teams.

Pre-War Era
From 1929–30's adoption of forward passing rules until 1944–45, when the players had yet to return from fighting World War II.

Projectinator
A system devised to predict the NHL success of pre-draft prospects.

Quality of Competition (QoC)
A high-level and Corsi-based measure of the average level of competition a player faces developed by Gabriel Desjardins.

Quality Start (QS)
A measurement of whether a goalie played well enough for his team to win.

Recording Bias
The bias introduced by the different way scorekeepers judge game events, most notably shots. Also, scorekeeper bias.

Relative
Expressing a statistic relative to a player's team and their results without the given player.

Replacement Level
A general term for a player whose contributions are similar to that of an AHL call-up.

Sample Size
A statistical term referring to the amount of data on which an analysis is based.

Score Effects
The skewing effect teams either sitting on or chasing leads can have on statistics, most notably shots.

Scoring Line
The top-line players whose primary purpose is to generate scoring (rather than prevent it).

Selection Bias
The bias introduced when the manner in which players are selected for an analysis affect the outcome.

Setup Passes
A pass that results in a shot.

Shooting Percentage Differential
Shooting percentage minus opponent's shooting percentage, also see PDO.

Shot Quality
The combined impact of the timing, type, circumstances and location of a shot, sometimes together with the shooter's skill.

Shutdown
A player (or line) tasked with preventing top opponents from scoring.

Sniff Test
Looking for major flaws in a statistic by comparing the results to established subjective opinion.

Tier 1 Player
Defined as a player who is in the top 25% of the NHL.

Top-Four Defenceman
A defenceman who is in one of the top four positions of his team's depth chart.

Top-Six Forward
A forward who is in one of the top six positions (or top two lines) of his team's depth chart.

Tough Minutes
A player usage assignment that usually begins in the defensive zone, against top-line competition, and/or alongside replacement-level linemates (or some reasonably tough combination thereof).

Transient
A statistical term referring to any property which is temporary (or inconsistent) in nature.

Two-Way Player
A player whose focus is both on defensive play and on scoring.

Win Threshold
The save percentage a goalie requires for his team to finish even.

WOWY (Without You, With You)
An analysis comparing how a given player performs with and without a particular linemate.

Zone Starts (ZS)
The percentage of all non-neutral shifts a player started in the offensive zone (not counting on-the-fly line changes).

About the Authors

Rob Vollman

Twitter: @robvollmanNHL
Email: vollman@hockeyabstract.com
Website: http://www.hockeyabstract.com

Best known for Player Usage Charts and his record-breaking *ESPN Insider* contributions, Rob Vollman was first published in the Fall 2001 issue of the *Hockey Research Journal*, and has since co-authored six books in the *Hockey Abstrac*t and *Hockey Prospectus* series.

While modern advanced statistical hockey analysis stands on a mountain of complexity, Rob's work is best known for being expressed in clear, focused and applicable terms, and often presented in a humourous and entertaining way. Whether you're arguing about the worst trades in history or which team improved most in the off-season, Rob's objective approach will add clear, cold facts to the discussion in a style that is undeniably engaging—and convincing!

Rob's most popular innovations include Player Usage Charts, Quality Starts for goaltenders, Goals Versus Salary (GVS) to measure a player's cap value, his history-based projection systems, his new Setup Passes statistic, and advances in the field of NHL Translations and League Equivalencies (NHLe), to understand how well players coming from other leagues will perform.

Rob Vollman's analysis can be found regularly at *Hockey Prospectus*, *ESPN Insider* and *Bleacher Report*, and is featured in the *Hockey News*, the *Globe and Mail*, the *Washington Post*, *McKeen's magazine*, *Hockey Night in Canada*, and radio programs in over a dozen cities.

Iain Fyffe

Twitter: @IainFyffe
Email: hockeyhistorysis@gmail.com
Website: http://hockeyhistorysis.blogspot.com

Iain Fyffe has been doing hockey analytics since before there was really such a thing as hockey analytics. He started the *Puckerings* website in 2001 to publish his work. Later known as *Hockeythink*, it was the first dedicated hockey analytics site (as far as he knows, anyway). There he pioneered the idea of using a player's plus-minus components to estimate player ice time, and developed widgets such as the Disciplined Aggression Proxy to make use of the NHL's then-new RTSS stats. He has also written for the *Hockey Zone Plus*, *Fantasy Hockey* and *Hockey Prospectus* sites, and at the last-named site developed the Projectinator, a tool designed to predict the future value of draft-eligible players based on their junior and college statistics.

Iain considers himself at least as much a historian as an analyst of hockey (he was the first person to research and publish Hall-of-Famer Dan Bain's career statistics), and now focuses on applying analytic methods to historical data, seeking to excavate meaning from the misshapen heaps of archaic information. A member of the *Society for International Hockey Research* (SIHR) since 2000, he has served on the editorial committee of the *Hockey Research Journal* since 2006 (including four years as editor), and has had eight articles published in its pages. One such article was reprinted in *Pucklore, the Hockey Research Anthology*. Iain also contributed to two editions of the *Hockey Prospectus* annual, for 2010–11 and 2011–12.

"The convergence of hockey history and analysis" is the tagline of Iain's blog *Hockey Historysis*, where he now focuses his research efforts. In early 2014 he published *On His Own Side of the Puck*, a book discussing the origins and development of early ice hockey rules, which was previously a subject characterized by a great deal of unknowns and uncorroborated assertions. In late 2014, he will publish *A Nor'west Blizzard*, a book on the history of hockey in Manitoba from 1890 to 1925.

Tom Awad

Email: tom.awad@gmail.com

There is likely no single person on Earth who likes numbers more than Tom Awad. He started tabulating hockey statistics by hand at age 11 while watching the Montreal Canadiens games in his parents' basement. Even back then, he found the numbers to be as fascinating as the games. His Eureka moment came when he came across a friend's copy of *Total Baseball* and discovered Pete Palmer's Linear Weights. He immediately designed something similar for hockey and tested it by transcribing the full statistics of the 1995–96 season by hand. Goals Versus Threshold (GVT) was born.

Tom may be best known for GVT but, over the years, he has performed statistical analysis of the draft, shot quality, player usage, goaltending, and much more. He developed the projection system known as VUKOTA which was found by David Staples of the Edmonton Journal to be the most accurate of seven systems for two consecutive seasons. He is a founding member of *Hockey Prospectus* and his analysis has also been published in *ESPN*

Insider, *Arctic Ice Hockey*, and Montreal's *Journal Metro*.

When not analyzing hockey numbers, Tom can often be found analyzing other numbers in his job as an Electrical Engineer in Montreal, or discussing mathematics, physics or the relative merits of Sauron and Unicron with his children David, 8, and Karina, 6. His wife Marisa (age redacted) sadly does not share his love of numbers, but nobody's perfect.

Josh Smith, Illustrator

Twitter: @joshsmith29

Josh is a freelance writer, illustrator, photographer, former radio host, and one-time (literally, just once) stand-up comedian from Long Beach Island, New Jersey.

His work has been featured on Yahoo! Sports, the Hockey Writers, the Whistle, and other sites. He also runs Scouting the Refs, a site dedicated to hockey officiating.

Alphabetical Index

3-1-1 Rule..98, 106, 213, 284, 309
All Three Zones Project...291
Backstrom, Nicklas...................184, 188, 195, 197, 243, 249, 261, 271, 295
Barrasso, Tom..11
Behind the Net.....................................99, 116, 196, 204, 309
Beirnes, Shane..103
Birnbaum, Phil...208, 213, 284, 285
Bishop, Ben...................85, 89, 94, 96, 106, 118, 119, 178, 179, 223, 302
Bourne, Justin..291
Brodeur, Martin...............29, 31, 85, 86, 89, 94, 97, 99, 103, 162, 163, 222-224
Brown, Dustin...............................155, 205, 208, 210, 214
Busch, Paul...272, 273, 281
Cammalleri, Mike........136, 162, 163, 191, 193, 194, 197, 201, 244, 250, 252, 253, 263, 295, 304, 305
Campbell, Brian...............................152, 205, 210, 211, 265, 267-269, 297
Chabot, Lorne...14
Chara, Zdeno...................30, 74, 132, 133, 217, 219, 221, 232, 241, 264, 268, 270, 297
Compassionate Referee...213
Cooper, Stephan...110
Corsi...............5, 6, 50, 51, 53, 55, 58, 69, 103, 114, 117, 283, 287, 292, 298, 299, 309-311
Couturier, Sean...............................171, 197, 217, 233, 237
Crawshaw, Thomas...125
Crosby, Sidney..........30, 36, 114, 172, 173, 188, 190, 194-197, 201, 243, 245-247, 249, 253, 255-261, 263, 271, 285, 294
Datsyuk, Pavel.................30, 148, 149, 210, 236, 243, 249, 256, 258, 259, 262, 263, 271, 294
Defence-Independent Goalie Rating (DIGR)..................87, 198, 199, 309
Defensive Shell...47, 309
Dellow, Tyler...45, 101, 252, 253
Delta...58, 63, 68, 69, 298, 299, 309
Desjardins, Gabriel..................45, 47, 80, 86, 106, 107, 109, 204, 222, 284, 286, 309, 311
Dirty Rat Penalty Minutes (DRPM).................................272-276, 278-282, 309
Drance, Thomas...217
Dubnyk, Devan.....................86, 88, 90, 94, 97, 118, 131, 151, 223, 304
Elliott, Brian...................85, 86, 88, 90, 94, 95, 97, 109, 177, 223
Emptage, Nick..84, 125
Empty Net Goals...104, 142, 200, 203
Even-up Bias...213
Expected Goals...54, 57, 67, 298, 299
Expected Shooting Percentage...301, 306, 310
Extra Skater.................................99, 116, 196, 204, 292, 310
Fenwick...50, 51, 53, 298, 299, 310
Ferrari, Vic...92, 222
Garik of Hockey Graphs...108
Getzlaf, Ryan...................65, 128, 129, 195-197, 244, 248, 250, 253, 257, 263, 280, 285, 294

Giacomin, Ed...9-11

Giordano, Mark.............................136, 137, 219, 230-232, 240-242, 265, 268

Giroux, Claude...... 144, 170, 171, 196, 205, 210, 211, 239, 243, 245, 246, 249, 252-260, 263, 270, 271, 294

Goalie Usage Chart..92, 310

Grabner, Michael..............165, 190, 193-195, 197, 201, 203, 233, 236, 238, 240, 242

Gretz, Adam...283, 303

GVT..4, 53, 284, 300, 304, 306, 310, 315

Harding, Josh...85, 86, 89, 93, 95, 96, 119, 157, 223

Helm, Darren...........................123, 149, 205, 210, 211, 213, 215, 233, 236, 242, 261

High Leverage Situations...64, 65, 100, 310

Hockey Abstract Checklist....................112, 116, 117, 121, 126, 127, 310

Hockey Analysis Group (HAG)....................................4, 62, 167, 205, 213

Hockey Prospectus...................66, 84, 107, 109, 116, 206, 209, 212, 300, 303, 310, 314, 315

Hollett, Flash...20

Home Plate Save Percentage...88, 310

Howell, Harry...17

Hughes, Travis...283, 303

Individual Point Percentage (IPP%)..................247, 249, 251-253, 264, 310

Inductinator....................4, 8-17, 19, 21-23, 25, 26, 28, 29, 31, 310

James, Bill...2, 5, 6, 9, 112, 309

Johnson, David..47, 90, 197, 247, 261

Kadri, Nazem.....................180, 205, 208, 210, 211, 213, 215, 244, 250, 253, 295

Kappa...279-281

Karlsson, Erik............168, 169, 206, 210, 263, 264, 266-271, 290, 296-298, 300, 307

Keith, Duncan.....................................30, 74, 140, 219, 221, 265, 290, 297

Kessel, Phil......65, 180, 181, 190, 193, 195-197, 201, 244, 247, 250, 253, 255, 285, 294, 299

Kopitar, Anze.....................65, 154, 155, 234, 244, 250, 253, 285, 294

Laprade, Edgar...24, 25

Lopez, Michael...97, 214

Luck-Neutral Standings...300, 305, 310

Lundqvist, Henrik...........29, 85-88, 90, 93-97, 99, 105, 106, 108, 118, 133, 145, 167, 177, 223

Luongo, Roberto........29, 85, 89, 91, 95, 97, 101, 106, 119, 152, 153, 183, 222, 224, 304, 305

MacDonald, Brian...107, 292

Malkin, Evgeni..... 30, 65, 161, 172, 173, 188-190, 193, 195-197, 201, 205, 243, 245-247, 249, 253, 255-261, 263, 271, 274, 294, 296

Marcel Model..108

Marchand, Brad........43, 132, 133, 190, 192, 194, 196, 200, 238, 272, 274-277, 279, 280, 295

McClement, Jay...........................65, 139, 181, 217, 232, 233, 235, 237, 280, 304

McCurdy, Bruce...99, 110, 205, 206

McGrattan, Brian...278, 281, 284

Metcalf, Darryl...292, 310

Michalek, Zbynek.............................130, 218, 221, 230, 231, 240, 241

Myrland, Phil...45, 91, 92, 99-101, 104, 107

Neal, James...........147, 161, 172, 173, 188-190, 192, 193, 195-197, 199, 201, 243, 249, 258, 260, 274, 296, 305, 306

Net Penalty Differential (NPD)...................60, 61, 205, 208, 209, 213, 311

NHL Translations..109, 125, 177, 292, 311, 314
Nicholls, Bernie..23, 24
One-Stat Argument..83, 86, 311
Ovechkin, Alexander.....30, 43, 65, 184, 185, 188-190, 192, 193, 195, 197, 200-203, 243, 245, 247-249, 253-263, 271
Pacioretty, Max.............................158, 189, 190, 192, 195, 197, 200, 201, 203, 245, 251, 296
Parise, Zach.........................36, 58, 156, 157, 210, 211, 222, 238, 245, 250, 255, 256, 295
Parkatti, Michael..124, 299
PDO...41, 311
Penalty-Killing Extras (PKE)..237-240, 242, 258, 311
Perry, Corey...............60, 128, 190, 193-196, 201-203, 205, 211, 245, 246, 250, 274, 285, 294
Peter, Bruce..107
Pettapiece, Rob..110
Phaneuf, Dion...74, 181, 219, 241, 265, 267, 274
Pietrangelo, Alex.........................70, 177, 219, 230, 240, 264, 266-268, 270, 290, 297, 298
PLAY (Playmaking Metric)...292, 293
Player Usage Chart..........5, 112-116, 126, 129, 136, 140, 155, 159, 160, 166, 170, 172, 192, 230, 255, 287, 311, 314
Pollock, Richard...106
Provost, Claude..26
Pulling the Goalie...104
Purdy, Tore (JLikens)..50, 92, 207
Quality of Competition.....53, 58, 68, 69, 74, 108, 113, 114, 134, 136, 194, 225, 228-232, 236, 241, 247, 255, 299, 311
Quality of Teammates...58, 66, 68, 69, 299
Quality Starts (QS)...5, 83-86, 99, 111, 118, 311, 314
Rask, Tuukka................43, 85-88, 90, 92, 93, 95, 96, 106, 108, 109, 118, 132, 133, 145, 223
Really Bad Start...85, 105
Rebounds...33, 35, 36, 38, 40, 44, 91, 218, 222, 224, 263
Recording Bias..88, 93, 102, 108, 312
Reynolds, Scott...106, 252
Richards, Brad..41, 58, 140, 183, 237, 295
Richards, Mike...155, 197, 217, 237, 238, 295
Roy, Patrick...9, 104, 124
Schneider, Cory............................85, 86, 88, 90, 94, 97, 98, 103, 108, 119, 162, 163, 222-224
Score Effects............5, 39, 45, 47, 49-52, 77, 102, 204, 207, 209, 291, 298, 312
Scorecasting...209
Sedin, Henrik..36, 244, 250, 252, 258, 294
Selection Bias..84, 102, 312
Seppa, Timo...299, 310
Setup Passes.....................5, 196, 251, 257, 260, 262, 267, 292, 293, 297, 312, 314
Shooting Percentage Differential..41-43, 55-57, 312
Shot Distance.....................12, 34-38, 40, 86-88, 90-93, 200-202, 224, 261, 310
Simmonds, Wayne.........................40, 170, 171, 244, 249, 254, 256, 259, 280
Sinclair, Greg..116, 248
Sniff Test............................216, 221, 232, 237, 241, 242, 277, 312
Society for International Hockey Research (SIHR)..4, 315

319